MERCHANTS OF CULTURE

JOHN B. THOMPSON is a professor of sociology at the University of Cambridge and Fellow of Jesus College, Cambridge. His previous publications include *Books in the Digital Age*.

Praise for *Merchants of Culture*

"*Merchants of Culture* is an eye-opening tour of both American and British trade publishing. Veterans in the publishing world will learn a lot, and novices will feel welcome, in this behind-the-scenes examination of how book publishing works in an age of mass marketing and digitization. Thompson knows more about contemporary publishing than any other scholar and he asks just the right questions of his sources. Theoretically sophisticated but not burdened by academic apparatus, this is a landmark work."
—Michael Schudson, Columbia University

"Thompson's groundbreaking research into the world of consumer book publishing provides a fascinating insight into the high-risk culture on both sides of the Atlantic. Revealed is the world of agents and scouts, of auctions and deals, often with large sums of money paid out to authors, as publishers gamble in the hope of signing the next Harry Potter or Dan Brown. Thompson's work is of the highest quality and should be read by all those concerned about our literary culture and its future."
—Angus Phillips, director of Oxford International Centre for Publishing Studies

"For the uninitiated, *Merchants of Culture* provides a very perceptive, thorough, and in-depth view of how trade publishing really works in the English-speaking world today. For those of us in the business or for writers who are mystified by their publisher's behavior, it offers a penetrating account of our business by a very shrewd, analytical observer. This book is the only thing I've ever read about our industry that has really got it."
—William Shinker, president and publisher of Gotham Books and Avery Books, Penguin Group (USA) Inc.

"Thompson's analysis of UK and U.S. trade publishing is extraordinarily acute and insightful. It should be required reading for new entrants to the industry—but it will also illuminate many things for old publishing hands."
—Helen Fraser, former managing director of Penguin Books Ltd.

"This uncommonly perceptive and thorough study tells you all you need to know about the publishing industry at a time of momentous change."
—Drake McFeely, chairman and president of W. W. Norton & Company

"Just completed a first-class degree course in trade publishing and the 'making of a bestseller'—at least I feel like I have after reading *Merchants of Culture* by John B. Thompson . . . From now on whenever anyone asks me how they can get published or get a job in publishing I'm going to tell them to buy this book because it is simply perfect at summing up how the whole messy business works and explaining why it very frequently doesn't work."
—Andrew Crofts, author of *The Freelance Writer's Handbook*

"A must-read for anyone interested in books and the publishing industry, this is an easy-to-understand, fascinating account of the history of the publishing industry in the UK and U.S., and a coherent explanation for the current pressures facing the main players . . . A fascinating book and one that I would heartily recommend."
—Caroline Hooton, writer and blogger for *Quippe's Journal*

"Thompson's book really needs to be required reading for any author who's attempting to pitch their first book. . . . He takes you inside the Sausage Being Made process of moving from proposal to book and, most harrowingly, to marketing and promotion. I think prospective writers would have a much shrewder idea of what to do, and get a sense of how little this process has to do with simply being a 'good writer' who 'writes pretty,' and how much of it has to do with an editor's instinctive feel for where a book goes, acquired through what Thompson calls a 'web of collective belief' among a knot of publishing professionals, largely based in New York, how it sits with their list, and how many it must sell for the book even to be worth bidding on."
—PamelaHaag.com

"By an order of magnitude, this is the best book on the economics of contemporary publishing."
—Tyler Cowen, professor of economics at George Mason University and blogger for *The Marginal Revolution*

"Fascinating . . . a tremendous primer into the political economy of the publishing industry. Highly recommended."   —*Displacement Activity*

"A must-read for any writer trying to get a handle on what the future portends."   —Erik Olsen, WeWantedToBeWriters.com

"Professor Thompson's great achievement, at this time of tumult in the publishing industry, is to offer a comprehensive and dispassionate view of the forces that have shaped and continue to shape these organizations. Anyone who is interested in our shared cultural well-being ignores the implications of his work at their peril."   —Ben Bennetts, *Things Unrespected*

MERCHANTS OF CULTURE

The Publishing Business in the Twenty-First Century

SECOND EDITION

JOHN B. THOMPSON

A PLUME BOOK

PLUME
Published by the Penguin Group
Penguin Group (USA) Inc., 375 Hudson Street, New York, New York 10014, U.S.A. • Penguin Group (Canada), 90 Eglinton Avenue East, Suite 700, Toronto, Ontario, Canada M4P 2Y3 (a division of Pearson Penguin Canada Inc.) • Penguin Books Ltd., 80 Strand, London WC2R 0RL, England • Penguin Ireland, 25 St. Stephen's Green, Dublin 2, Ireland (a division of Penguin Books Ltd.) • Penguin Group (Australia), 250 Camberwell Road, Camberwell, Victoria 3124, Australia (a division of Pearson Australia Group Pty. Ltd.) • Penguin Books India Pvt. Ltd., 11 Community Centre, Panchsheel Park, New Delhi – 110 017, India • Penguin Group (NZ), 67 Apollo Drive, Rosedale, Auckland 0632, New Zealand (a division of Pearson New Zealand Ltd.) • Penguin Books (South Africa) (Pty.) Ltd., 24 Sturdee Avenue, Rosebank, Johannesburg 2196, South Africa

Penguin Books Ltd., Registered Offices: 80 Strand, London WC2R 0RL, England

Published by Plume, a member of Penguin Group (USA) Inc. Originally published in the United Kingdom in 2010 by Polity Press; a second edition was published in 2012.

First American Printing, April 2012
10   9   8   7   6   5   4   3   2   1

CIP data is available.

ISBN 978-0-452-29772-2

Printed in the United States of America

CONTENTS

Preface to the Second Edition   xi

Preface to the First Edition   xiii

Introduction   1

1   The Growth of the Retail Chains   26

2   The Rise of Literary Agents   59

3   The Emergence of Publishing Corporations   101

4   The Polarization of the Field   147

5   Big Books   188

6   Extreme Publishing   223

7   Shrinking Windows   238

8   The Wild West   292

9   The Digital Revolution   313

10   Trouble in the Trade   377

Conclusion: Facing an Uncertain Future   403

Appendix 1   Selected Imprints of the Main Publishing Corporations   410

Appendix 2   Note on Research Methods   415

Bibliography   425

Index   430

PREFACE TO THE SECOND EDITION

Writing about a present-day industry is always going to be like shooting at a moving target: no sooner have you finished the text than your subject matter has changed – things happen, events move on and the industry you had captured at a particular point in time now looks slightly different. Immediate obsolescence is the fate that awaits every chronicler of the present. There is no remedy apart from revising and updating the text if and when the opportunity presents itself, though even then you will always remain a step behind the flow of events, freezing a world at the very moment that it slips away from you.

Thirty or forty years ago, the risks of obsolescence would not have seemed so great to someone writing about the book publishing industry: sure, the industry was changing in important ways, but the basic principles and practices that characterized the industry were not being called into question. Publishing houses were being bought up by large corporations, retail chains and literary agents were becoming more powerful and the traditional world of trade publishing was being transformed into a big business. But the book itself as a cultural object – that unique combination of print and paper, the fusing together of the written word and the material artefact – was being produced in much the same way as it had been for centuries. Today that is no longer so. As we enter the second decade of the twenty-first century the oldest of the media industries finds itself in the throes of tumultuous change, struggling to cope with the impact of a technological revolution that is stripping away some of the old certainties, undermining traditional models and opening up new possibilities in ways that are at once exciting and disorientating. What once seemed like a quiet backwater of the media industries has suddenly become news.

In preparing the text for the paperback edition I have concentrated on ensuring that the book takes account of significant new developments and that empirical data are updated where it is important to do so. There are many contexts where data from 2008 or 2009 continue to provide a good picture of how the industry looks today, and I have therefore left the figures as they were. But there are other contexts, especially in the chapter on the digital revolution, where a more thorough updating was necessary – when you're in the midst of a revolution, two years can seem like an eternity. I returned to around 20 of my sources in London and New York and spoke with them about the changes that have taken place, partly in order to make sure that I was fully apprised of the most important developments but also in order to see how their views have altered over time as they have struggled to cope with the changes swirling around them. Once again, I am enormously grateful to these individuals – who will, as before, remain anonymous – for their time, generosity and openness. However, I have resisted the temptation to rewrite the text and revisit every actor and organization: while much has happened, the basic structures and dynamics of the world of Anglo-American trade publishing remain pretty much as I described them. Of course, we cannot rule out the possibility that these structures and dynamics will be transformed over time by the changes currently taking place: no one should ever underestimate the disruptive potential of new technologies. But at the same time we must see that the development and implementation of new technologies are always part and parcel of a broader set of social relations in which agents and organizations are bound together in relations of cooperation, competition and sometimes conflict with one another, and where outcomes are shaped as much by structures of power as they are by the intrinsic properties of technologies as such. This book describes those structures, shows how they arose, how they shape the practices of actors in the field and how they are changing today, and it intentionally leaves open the question of how far these structures will be altered in a future that remains – and is likely to remain for some while to come – uncertain.

J.B.T., Cambridge

PREFACE TO THE FIRST EDITION

It is a matter of some puzzlement that the one sector of the creative industries about which we know very little is the sector that has been with us for the longest time – the book publishing industry. First established in the fifteenth century thanks to the celebrated inventions of a goldsmith in Mainz, the printing and publishing of books is a business that has been around for more than half a millennium, and yet we know very little about how this industry is organized today and how it is changing. Books continue to command a good deal of attention in newspapers, radio and other media; they remain a staple source of inspiration and raw material for films and other forms of popular entertainment; and writers – especially novelists, historians and scientists – are still endowed with a stature in our societies, an aura even, that is accorded to few other professions. But on the rare occasions when the publishing industry itself comes under public scrutiny, more often than not it is because another journalist is eager to announce that, with the coming of the digital age, the publishing industry as we know it is doomed. Few industries have had their death foretold more frequently than the book publishing industry, and yet somehow, miraculously, it seems to have survived them all – at least till now.

It was partly with the aim of filling this lacuna in our understanding that I set out, nearly a decade ago, to study systematically the contemporary book publishing industry. I began by working on a sector of the industry that was close to my own world as an academic – namely, the field of academic publishing, which included the university presses, the commercial academic publishers (like Taylor & Francis, Palgrave Macmillan and SAGE Publications) and the college textbook publishers (like Pearson and McGraw-Hill). The results of that research were published in 2005 in *Books in the Digital Age*. Since then I have immersed myself in a very different world – that of general interest trade publishing, the world of bestsellers like Dan Brown's *The Da Vinci Code* and Rhonda Byrne's *The Secret*, of brand-name authors like Stephen King and John Grisham, of the many styles and genres of fiction and non-fiction, from commercial to literary, from misery memoir to serious history, politics and current affairs. I have studied this world in the way that an anthropologist would study the practices of a tribe inhabiting some remote island in the South Pacific, only in this case the tribe lives and works, for the most part, in a small section of an island squeezed between the Hudson and East rivers in New York and on the banks of the Thames in London. Their practices may initially strike the outside observer as strange, even at times bizarre. But the assumption underlying my work is that once we understand the structure of this world and how it has evolved over time, even the most surprising things do not seem so strange after all.

The research for this book was carried out over a period of four years, from 2005 to 2009; I am grateful to the Economic and Social Research Council (ESRC) in the UK for a generous grant (RES-000-22-1292) which supported this research and enabled me to spend extended periods of time in New York and London. During this time I carried out around 280 interviews with senior executives, publishers, editors, sales directors, marketing directors, publicists and other managers and employees in many publishing firms, from the large corporations to the small indie presses; I also interviewed many agents, authors and booksellers, including some of the central buyers from the large retail chains. I am grateful to all of these individuals for being so generous with their time – and in some cases allowing me to interview them more than once. In a world where time is calibrated as carefully as money, I am very conscious of the fact that I was showered with temporal gifts. Their willingness to participate, their patient explanations of what they do and how they do it and their frank assessments of the challenges they face were the indispensable bases on which I have built my account of their world. For the most part, my interviewees remain anonymous; there are a few cases where I've allowed them, with their permission, to speak in their own name when I felt it would be helpful for the reader (or easy for a reader with any knowledge of the field to recognize who they were). But the fact that most of my sources remain anonymous, and that they and their companies are usually given pseudonyms, should not be allowed to obscure the magnitude of my debt.

I could not have completed this book without the generous assistance of Alanna Ivin and her assistants, who transcribed many hours of interviews with unstinting determination and professionalism. I am very grateful to Michael Schudson, Angus Phillips, William Shinker, Helen Fraser, Drake McFeely, Andrea Drugan, four anonymous readers for the ESRC and several of my interviewees – who shall also remain anonymous – who set aside the time to read an earlier draft of this text and provided me with many helpful comments. I am also grateful to Ann Bone for her skilful and meticulous copy-editing, to David Drummond for his inspired cover design and to the many people at Polity – including Gill Motley, Sue Pope, Sarah Lambert, Neil de Cort, Clare Ansell, Sarah Dodgson, Breffni O'Connor, Marianne Rutter and Colin Robinson – who steered this book through the publication process. My thanks, finally, to Mirca and Alex, who helped to create the space for this book to be written and who, in the case of Alex, never ceased to remind me of the primordial joy of reading books.

MERCHANTS OF CULTURE

INTRODUCTION

Imagine for a moment that you are in the office of a scout in New York. It's a sunny afternoon in November 2007; the sky is a brilliant blue and the air has the chill of late autumn. The office block is an old building, dating from the late nineteenth century; the offices have been tastefully redeveloped, with bright walls and polished wooden floors. Out of the window you can see several water tanks standing on the roofs of buildings, a common sight from upper-floor offices in this part of midtown Manhattan. A scout is a talent-spotter. She (usually they are female) generally works on a retainer for publishers in Italy, Spain, Germany, France, Scandinavia and elsewhere, looking for books that would be suitable for their clients to translate and publish in their own countries and languages. Scouts are the eyes and ears of foreign publishers in the heartlands of Anglo-American publishing. They are most commonly based in New York or London, working for publishers based in Rome, Frankfurt, Berlin, Paris, Madrid, Lisbon, Copenhagen, Stockholm, Rio, São Paulo, Tokyo and elsewhere; rarely does the direction of reporting go the other way. The scout you are talking to today – let's call her Hanne – is telling you about how she finds out about the new book projects that are out on submission to the New York houses and are likely to be published in the next year or so, and in the course of her account she mentions a proposal for a book called *The Last Lecture* by Randy Pausch. 'Who is Randy Pausch?' you ask. 'You don't know who Randy Pausch is?' she replies, a tone of mild astonishment in her voice. 'No, never heard of him. Who is he and what is the book?' And so she begins to tell you the story of Randy Pausch and *The Last Lecture*.

1

Randy Pausch was a professor of computer science at Carnegie Mellon University in Pittsburgh (now the story must be told in the past tense, though in 2007 Hanne used the present tense). He was a specialist on computer–human interfaces and had published numerous technical papers on aspects of programming, virtual reality and software design. But in September 2007 Pausch's career suddenly took an unusual turn. He had been invited to give a lecture at Carnegie Mellon in a series called 'The Last Lecture' – a series in which professors are asked to think about what matters most to them and sum up the wisdom they would like to pass on to their students in a single lecture, as if it were their last. By a tragic twist of fate, this was, in all likelihood, one of the last lectures that Randy Pausch would be giving: this 46-year-old father of three was dying from a terminal form of pancreatic cancer. The lecture, on the subject of 'really achieving your childhood dreams', was delivered to an audience of some 400 students and staff on 18 September 2007; the hour-long lecture was videoed so that his children could watch it when they were older. In the audience was a columnist from the *Wall Street Journal*, Jeff Zaslow, who had heard about the lecture on the grapevine and driven down from Detroit to attend. Like many who were there, Zaslow was deeply moved by the occasion, and he wrote a short article about it for his column in the *Wall Street Journal*. The article appeared on 20 September with a link to a short five-minute clip of highlights from the lecture. ABC's *Good Morning America* TV show saw the article in the *Journal* and invited Pausch on to the show the following morning. Media interest grew and Pausch was invited to appear on the *Oprah Winfrey Show* in October. In the meantime, the lecture video was posted on YouTube and millions of people watched either the short clip or the full-length version.

Shortly after the article appeared in the *Wall Street Journal*, publishers in New York began emailing Pausch to see if he would be interested in writing a book based on it. 'I found this laughable,' explained Pausch, 'since at the time the palliative chemo was not yet working, and I thought I was down to about six weeks of good health.' But after some reflection he agreed to do it, on the understanding that he would co-author the book with Jeff Zaslow and that Jeff would actually write it. Jeff contacted his agent in New York and the agency took charge of preparing a proposal and submitting it to publishers. The agency turned down a pre-emptive bid and sent out a short, 15-page proposal to numerous New York publishing houses in October. Within two weeks they had done a deal. 'So how much did it go for?' you ask Hanne. '$6.75 million,' she replies. '$6.75

million?! You must be joking!' 'No, seriously, it was bought by Hyperion for $6.75 million,' she explains. 'They closed the deal a couple of weeks ago. It will be a short book, about 180 pages, and they're planning to publish it next April.' You can't quite believe what you've just heard. Why would anyone pay $6.75 million for a book called *The Last Lecture* by a professor of computer science with no track record as a successful author? Maybe $40,000 or $50,000, you think, or perhaps even a modest six-figure sum if you were feeling particularly bullish. But $6.75 million? How could a publishing company talk itself into laying down this kind of money on what would seem like a wild bet? To an outside observer this seems amazing, surprising, utterly bizarre. Even Pausch himself confessed to being astonished by the size of the advance ('the book getting a large advance-on-royalties took us both by surprise'). How can we make sense of this seemingly bizarre behaviour? To many it will seem like another example of the 'irrational exuberance' of markets, but is it really as irrational as it seems?

To answer these questions properly we will need to step back from the details of our story and make a detour. We will need to understand something about how the world of trade publishing has changed over the last 40–50 years and how it is organized today – who the key players are, what pressures they face and what resources they have at their disposal. We will also need to introduce some concepts that will help us make sense of this world, and help us to see how the actions of each key player are conditioned by the actions of others. For these players are not acting on their own: they are always acting in a particular context or what I shall call a 'field', in which the actions of any agent are conditioned by, and in turn condition, the actions of others.

Publishing fields

What is a field? I borrow this term from the French sociologist Pierre Bourdieu and freely adapt it for my own purposes.[1] A field is a structured space of social positions which can be occupied by agents and

---

[1] See Pierre Bourdieu, *The Field of Cultural Production: Essays on Art and Literature*, ed. Randal Johnson (Cambridge: Polity, 1993); Pierre Bourdieu, 'Some Properties of Fields', in his *Sociology in Question*, tr. Richard Nice (London: Sage, 1993), pp. 72–7; Pierre Bourdieu, *The Rules of Art: Genesis and Structure of the Literary Field*, tr. Susan Emanuel (Cambridge: Polity, 1996).

organizations, and in which the position of any agent or organization depends on the type and quantity of resources or 'capital' they have at their disposal. Any social arena – a business sector, a sphere of education, a domain of sport – can be treated as a field in which agents and organizations are linked together in relations of cooperation, competition and interdependency. Markets are an important part of some fields, but fields are always more than markets. They are made up of agents and organizations, of different kinds and quantities of power and resources, of a variety of practices and of specific forms of competition, collaboration and reward.

There are four reasons why the concept of field helps us to understand the world of publishing. First, it enables us to see straightaway that the world of publishing is not one world but rather a plurality of worlds – or, as I shall say, a *plurality of fields*, each of which has its own distinctive characteristics. So there's the field of trade publishing, the field of scholarly monograph publishing, the field of higher education publishing, the field of professional publishing, the field of illustrated art book publishing and so on. Each of these fields has its own peculiar traits – you cannot generalize across them. It's like different kinds of games: there is chess, checkers, Monopoly, Risk, Cluedo and so on. To the outside observer they may all look similar – they're all board games with little pieces that move around the board. But each game has its own rules, and you can know how to play one without knowing how to play another. And publishing is often like that: people who work in the business tend to work in one particular field. They become experts in that field and may rise to senior positions of power and authority within it, but they may know nothing at all about what goes on in other fields.

The second reason why the notion of field helps is that it forces us to look beyond specific firms and organizations and makes us think, instead, in *relational* terms. The notion of field is part of a theory that is fundamentally relational in character, in the sense that it assumes that the actions of agents, firms and other organizations are oriented towards other agents and organizations and predicated on calculations about how others may or may not act in the field. Agents, firms and other organizations never exist in isolation: they are always situated in complex relations of power, competition and cooperation with other firms and organizations, and the theory of fields forces us to focus our attention on this complex space of power and interdependency. The theory constantly reminds us that the actions of any particular agent or organization are always part of larger whole, a

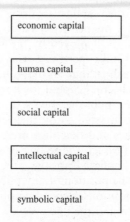

Figure 1   Key resources of publishing firms

system if you like, of which they are part but over which they do not have any overall control.

The third reason why the notion of field helps is that it calls our attention to the fact that the power of any agent or organization in the field is dependent on the kinds and quantities of resources or *capital* that it possesses. Power is not a magical property that some individual or organization possesses: it is a capacity to act and get things done that is always rooted in and dependent on the kinds and quantities of resources that the agent or organization has at its disposal.

So what kinds of resources or capital are important in publishing fields? We can see, I think, that five types of resources are particularly important in publishing fields: what I shall call 'economic capital', 'human capital', 'social capital', 'intellectual capital' and 'symbolic capital' (figure 1).[2] Economic capital is the accumulated financial resources, including stock and plant as well as capital reserves, to which publishers have access, either directly (in their own accounts)

---

[2] This account is based on John B. Thompson, *Books in the Digital Age: The Transformation of Academic and Higher Education Publishing in Britain and the United States* (Cambridge: Polity, 2005), pp. 30–6. However, I've added social capital to the original scheme, since it became clear that this form of capital, important in all publishing fields, is particularly important in trade publishing, where networking is vital.

or indirectly (through their ability to draw on the resources of a parent company or raise finance from banks or other institutions). Human capital is the staff employed by the firm and their accumulated knowledge, skills and expertise. Social capital is the networks of contacts and relationships that an individual or organization has built up over time. Intellectual capital (or intellectual property) consists in the rights that a publisher owns or controls in intellectual content, rights that are attested to by their stock of contracts with authors and other bodies and that they are able to exploit through their publications and through the selling of subsidiary rights. Symbolic capital is the accumulated prestige and status associated with the publishing house. The position of any publishing house will vary in the social space of positions, depending on the relative quantities of these five forms of capital they possess.

It is easy to see why publishers need economic capital: as the principal risk-taker in the publishing chain, publishers must be able to draw on their financial resources (or those of financial agents and institutions to which they are linked, such as banks or parent companies) at various stages in order to finance the production and publication of books and in order to build and expand the business. Early in the publishing cycle they must be prepared to pay an advance on royalties to an author or an author's agent. At later stages publishers must invest in the production of the book, paying the bills of copy-editors, typesetters, designers, printers, etc., and tying up resources in stock which may or may not be sold, and they must invest in marketing and promoting the book. The larger the capital reserves of the publisher, the larger the advances they are able to offer in the highly competitive game of acquiring content, the more they are able to invest in marketing and promotion and the more they are able to spread the risks of publishing by investing in a larger number of projects in the hope that some will bear fruit.

It is also easy to see why publishers need human capital: like other organizations, publishing firms are only as good as their staff. A highly trained and highly motivated workforce is a vital resource for a publishing firm and in many ways the key to its success. This is true at all levels, but particularly true at the level of editorial staff, since this is the creative core of the publishing firm. The success of the firm depends crucially on the ability to attract and retain highly motivated editors who are able to identify and acquire the new projects that are likely to be successful and are able to work effectively with authors to maximize the potential of these projects. In the highly competitive field of trade publishing, an editor is as good, and only as good, as the track record of the books that he or she has acquired and published over the years: this record *is* his or her CV. Editors who have the right combination of judgement, taste, social flair and financial nous are highly valued assets, and their ability to spot successful books becomes vital to the overall success of the firm. But the other side of this equation is that an editor who greatly over-pays for a book that flops, or who buys a string of books that perform below expectations, may come to be seen as more of a liability than an asset and may find that their judgement is called into question, their job is in danger and their career is at risk.

However, even the best editors do not work on their own: they need good contacts. Much of their time is spent cultivating relationships with agents on whom they are largely and increasingly dependent for the supply of new book projects: the famous publisher's lunch is not just a pleasant perk of the job but a necessary condition of doing the job effectively, precisely because this is a field in which networks and relationships – i.e. social capital – is crucial. The importance of relationships applies to other sides of the business too. Publishing houses invest a great deal of time and effort in developing close relationships with suppliers and retailers and they work hard to manage and protect these relationships because they are vital to their success. And the larger the publisher is, the more they may be able to call on their business partners to do favours for them – for example, ask a printer to prioritize an important reprint and deliver it within three or four days, or call up the product manager at a major retailer and ask them to pay special attention to a book that the publisher regards as a key title.

Publishers possess another kind of resource that is vital to their success: intellectual capital (or what is often called intellectual property). The distinctive feature of the publishing firm is that it possesses the right to use and exploit intellectual content, to 'publish' or make available this content in forms that will generate a financial return. This right is regulated by the contracts it signs with authors or agents and other content-controlling sources, such as foreign publishers. Hence a publisher's stock of contracts is potentially an extremely valuable resource, since it establishes legal entitlements to the content (or potential content) which the publisher is able to exploit. But the precise value of this resource depends on many things. The value of a contract for a particular book depends, for instance, on whether the book will actually be written and delivered in a suitable time period, how profitable the book will be (that is, what kind of revenue stream less costs, including advances, it is likely to generate) and what territorial and subsidiary rights it includes (whether it includes world rights in all languages or merely North American rights, for instance). A publisher's stock of contracts represents the sum total of rights it possesses over the intellectual content that it seeks to develop and exploit. A contract can be a valuable resource but it can also be a liability, in the sense that it can commit the publisher to producing a book which, given the level of advance paid out and other costs incurred in producing and marketing the book, may turn out to be a loss-maker rather than a profitable proposition.

It is easy to see why publishers need economic, human, social and intellectual capital, but why do they need symbolic capital? Symbolic capital is best understood as the accumulated prestige, recognition and respect accorded to certain individuals or institutions.[3] It is one of those intangible assets that is enormously important for publishing firms. For publishers are not just employers and financial risk-takers: they are also cultural mediators and arbitrators of quality and taste. Their imprint is a 'brand', a marker of distinction in a highly competitive field. Publishers seek to accumulate symbolic capital just as they seek to accumulate economic capital. It is important to them partly because it is important to their image, to the way they see themselves and want to be seen by others: most publishers see themselves and want to be seen by others as organizations that publish works of 'quality', however that might be defined (and there are many ways that it can be). No major publisher would willingly embrace the idea that their sole purpose in life is to publish schlock (even if they accept, as some do, that they need to publish some schlock in order to do other things). But it is also important to them for good organizational and financial reasons. It strengthens their hand in the struggle to acquire new content because it makes their organization more attractive in the eyes of authors and agents: many authors want to be published by houses that have established a high reputation in their particular genre of writing, whether it is literary fiction or crime novels or biography or history. It strengthens their position in the networks of cultural intermediaries – including booksellers, reviewers and media gatekeepers – whose decisions and actions can have a big impact on the success or otherwise of particular books. A publisher who has established a reputation for quality and reliability is a publisher that agents, retailers and even readers will be more inclined to

---

[3] See Pierre Bourdieu, *Language and Symbolic Power*, ed. John B. Thompson (Cambridge: Polity, 1991); John B. Thompson, *The Media and Modernity: A Social Theory of the Media* (Cambridge: Polity, 1995), p. 16.

trust. And it can also translate directly into financial success: a book that wins a major literary prize will very commonly experience a sharp upturn in sales, and may even lift the sales of other books by the same author.

While symbolic capital is of considerable importance to publishing firms, it is also important to see that other players in the field, including agents and authors, can and do accumulate symbolic capital of their own. Authors can become brands in their own right – most well-known writers, like Stephen King, John Grisham, James Patterson, Patricia Cornwell, etc., are brand-name authors in this sense. They have acquired large stocks of symbolic capital and are able to use this to their advantage. In the early stages of their writing career, a publishing firm may have invested in the building of their brand, but as they become better known and develop a fan base of regular readers, the author's brand separates off from the publisher's brand and becomes less and less dependent on it. This puts them or their agents in an increasingly strong position when it comes to negotiating contractual terms with publishers and tends to ensure that their new books, regardless of who publishes them, are well positioned in the circuits of distribution and reception.

All five forms of capital are vital to the success of a publishing firm, but the structure of the publishing field is shaped above all by the differential distribution of economic and symbolic capital, for it is these forms of capital that are particularly important in determining the competitive position of the firm. Publishers with substantial stocks of economic and symbolic capital will tend to find themselves in a strong position in the field, able to compete effectively against others and to see off challenges from rivals, whereas firms with very small stocks of economic and symbolic capital are in a more vulnerable position. This does not mean that firms which are less well endowed will necessarily find it difficult to survive – on the contrary, the publishing field is an enormously complex domain and there are many ways in which smaller firms can compete effectively, outmanoeuvring larger players or finding specialist niches in which they can flourish. Moreover, it is important to see that economic capital and symbolic capital do not necessarily go hand in hand: a firm with small stocks of economic capital can succeed in building up substantial stocks of symbolic capital in the domains where it is active, gaining a reputation for itself that far exceeds its strength in sheer economic terms – in other words, it can punch above its weight. The accumulation of symbolic capital is dependent on processes that are very different in nature from those that lead to the accumulation of economic capital, and the possession of large quantities of one does not necessarily imply the possession of large quantities of the other.

The importance of economic and symbolic capital in the field of trade publishing can be seen in another way. For most trade publishers, the 'value' of a particular book or book project is understood in one of two ways: its sales or sales potential, that is, its capacity to generate economic capital; and its quality, which can be understood in various ways but includes its potential for winning various forms of recognition such as prizes and glowing reviews, or in other words, its capacity to generate symbolic capital. These are the only two criteria – there simply are no other. Sometimes the criteria go together, as in those cases when a work valued for its quality also turns out to sell well, but all too often the criteria diverge. Yet an editor or publisher may still value a work because they believe it to be good, even though they know or strongly suspect that sales will be modest at best. Both criteria are important for all publishers in the field, but the relative importance assigned to one criterion or the other varies from one editor to another, from one imprint or house to another and from one sector of the field to another. In large publishing corporations, it is not uncommon for certain imprints to be thought of as 'commercial' in character, that is, oriented primarily towards sales and the accumulation of economic capital, while other imprints are thought of as 'literary' in character, where sales are not unimportant but where the winning of literary prizes and the accumulation of symbolic value are legitimate goals in themselves.

As with other fields of activity, the publishing field is an intensely competitive domain characterized by a high degree of inter-organizational rivalry. Firms draw on their accumulated resources in an attempt to give themselves a competitive advantage over their rivals – to sign up bestselling authors and books, to gain the most media attention, etc. The staff of every publishing house are constantly looking over their shoulders to see what their competitors are doing. They constantly scrutinize the bestseller lists and study their competitors' more successful books to see whether they can pick up clues about how they might develop their own publishing programmes. This kind of inter-organizational rivalry tends to produce a degree of homogeneity or 'me-too' publishing among the firms who publish in the same areas – one successful chick-lit book will spawn a dozen look-alikes. But it also produces an intense desire to find the next big thing, as firms are constantly seeking to prevail over their competitors by being the first to spot a new trend.

While many fields of activity are intensely competitive, the publishing field has a competitive structure that is distinctive in some respects. In terms of their competitive position, most publishers are janus-faced organizations: they must compete both in the *market for content* and in the *market for customers*. They must compete in the market for content because most publishing organizations do not create or own their own content. They must acquire content by entering into contractual relations with authors or their agents, and this puts them in a competitive position vis-à-vis other publishers who may wish to acquire the same or similar content. A huge amount of effort is invested by editors and publishers in cultivating relations with the agents and others who control access to content. But just as publishers have to compete for content, so too they have to compete for the time, attention and money of retailers and customers once a book has been produced. The marketplace of books is enormously crowded – and becomes ever more crowded as the number of titles published increases every year. Marketing and sales staff devote a great deal of time and effort trying to ensure that their titles stand out from others and are not simply lost in the flood of new books appearing every season. The financial resources of the firm, the social skills and networks of their staff and the accumulated symbolic capital of the imprint and the author are all important factors in shaping the extent to which they can achieve visibility for their titles in the highly competitive and increasingly crowded marketplace for books.

I've given three reasons why the notion of field is helpful for understanding the world of publishing but there is a fourth – in my view, the most important. I'm going to argue that each field of publishing has a distinctive dynamic – what I call 'the logic of the field'. The logic of a publishing field is a set of factors that determine the conditions under which individual agents and organizations can participate in the field – that is, the conditions under which they can play the game (and play it successfully). Individuals who are active in the field have some degree of practical knowledge of this logic: they know how to play the game, and they may have views about how the rules of the game are changing. They may not be able to explain the logic of the field in a neat and concise way, they cannot give you a simple formula that sums it all up, but they can tell you in great detail what it was like when they first entered the field, what it's like now and how it has changed over time. To use a different metaphor, the logic of the field is like the grammar of a language: individuals know how to speak correctly, and in this sense they have a practical knowledge of the rules of grammar, but they may not be able to formulate these rules in an explicit fashion – they can't tell you, for example, what the rule is for the use of the subjunctive in English. As Wittgenstein would say, their knowledge of the language is that they know how to use it, they know how to go on. And part of my job as an analyst of the world of publishing is to listen to and reflect on the practical accounts of the agents who are active in the field, to situate these accounts in relation to the agents' positions in the field and to seek thereby to work out the logic of the field – that is, to formulate it in a way that is more explicit and systematic than one is likely to find in the practical accounts of the agents themselves.

My focus here is on the field of English-language trade publishing – that is, the sector of the publishing industry that is concerned with publishing books, both fiction and non-fiction, that are intended for general readers and sold primarily through bookstores and other retail outlets. I won't be looking at other fields of publishing – at academic or professional publishing, for example; these fields are organized in very different ways and we cannot assume that the factors that shape the activities of trade publishers will be the same as those that shape the activities of publishers in other fields.[4] My focus is also restricted to the English language, and in practice this means the United States and Britain,[5] simply because publishing fields, like all cultural fields, have linguistic and spatial boundaries and we cannot assume that the dynamics of trade publishing in the English language will be the same as they are in Spanish, French, German, Chinese, Korean or any other language – indeed, the dynamics of trade publishing in other languages are quite different in certain respects. There are even important differences between the United States and Britain, and yet there is also a deep structural similarity in the way that trade publishing works in Britain and the United States, so much so that it makes good sense to see British and American trade publishers as belonging to the same Anglo-American field.

---

[4] The very different logics of the fields of scholarly book publishing and higher education publishing are analysed in Thompson, *Books in the Digital Age*.
[5] There are of course countries other than the United States and Britain within the international field of English-language publishing, including Australia, New Zealand, Canada and South Africa, and the dynamics of trade publishing in each of these countries have their own distinctive characteristics. However, the volume of output in the United States and Britain and the scale and geographical reach of their publishing industries mean that these two countries have long had a dominant role in the international field of English-language trade publishing.

The fact that the Anglo-American publishing industry is the dominant industry in the international arena of trade publishing today is not accidental: it is rooted in a long historical process, stretching back to the nineteenth century and before, which established the English language as the de facto global language and gave Anglo-American publishers an enormous competitive advantage vis-à-vis their counterparts in other languages, who found themselves operating in much smaller and more restricted fields.[6] Today the United States and Britain publish many more new books than other countries and their book exports, measured in terms of volume of sales, are much higher.[7] Moreover, books and authors originally published in English tend to dominate the translation market. Translations from English often feature prominently on the bestseller lists in Europe, Latin America and elsewhere, whereas translations from other languages seldom appear on the bestseller lists in Britain and the US. In the international marketplace of books, the flow of translations and bestsellers is skewed heavily in favour of books and authors originating in the English-speaking world.[8]

---

[6] On the rise of English as a global language, see David Crystal, *English as a Global Language* (Cambridge: Cambridge University Press, 1997). For further discussion of the global dominance of English and its implications for the shaping of publishing fields, see Thompson, *Books in the Digital Age,* pp. 41–3.

[7] In 2002, around 215,000 new titles were published in the US and around 125,000 in the UK, compared to around 79,000 in Germany, around 70,000 in Spain and around 59,000 in France. (See tables 9 and 10 below for details on title output in the US and the UK. For details on title output in European countries, see *Publishing Market Watch: Final Report,* submitted to the European Commission (27 Jan. 2005), at http://ec.europa.eu/information_society/media_taskforce/doc/pmw_20050127.pdf) According to United Nations data, exports of printed books (excluding dictionaries and encyclopaedias) from the US in 2008 totalled $2.36 billion, and book exports (excluding dictionaries and encyclopaedias) from the UK totalled $2.15 billion; these figures were well ahead of Germany (total book exports of $1.5 billion), France ($791 million) and Spain ($755 million). Data available from http://data.un.org.

[8] Analysing UNESCO data, Wischenbart found that more than half of all books translated globally are from English language originals, whereas only 6 per cent of translations go from all other languages into English; see Rüdiger Wischenbart, 'The Many, Many Books – For Whom?' (11 Sep. 2005), at www.wischenbart.com/de/essays__interviews_rw/wischenbart_publishing-diversity_oxford-2005.pdf. For a more detailed analysis of translations in Europe, see Rüdiger Wischenbart, *Diversity Report 2008: An Overview and Analysis of Translation Statistics across Europe* (21 Nov. 2008), at www.wischenbart.com/diversity/report/Diversity%20Report_prel-final_02.pdf. Further discussion of translations and bestseller lists in Europe and the Anglo-American world can be found in Miha Kovač, *Never Mind the Web: Here Comes the Book* (Oxford: Chandos, 2008), pp. 121–7.

So does the field of Anglo-American trade publishing have a logic, and if so what is it? That is the question to which this book seeks to provide an answer. Some may doubt whether the world of trade publishing has a logic at all – what we have, they will say, is a complex sphere of activity in which many different agents and organizations are doing many different things, and any attempt to reduce this complexity to an underlying logic of the field is bound to be misleading. Well, let us see; maybe they are right, maybe they are wrong. The social world is a messy place but it is not completely without order, and the task I have set myself is to see if we can discern some order in the plethora of details that make up the diverse practices of everyday life. Of course, I shall not seek to recount all the details – nothing would be more tedious for the reader – nor shall I claim to be able to account for everything that happens in the field. There will always be exceptional events, exceptional actors and exceptional circumstances, but the exceptions should not blind us to the rules. Some actors and some details will feature more prominently in our story than others, and for this I make no apologies. Finding order is about prioritizing detail, attributing more significance to some actors and events than to others, precisely because they tell us more than others do about the underlying structure and dynamics of the field.[9]

The publishing chain

In addition to the concept of field, there is one other concept, or set of concepts, that we need in order to understand the world of trade publishing – the publishing chain. The publisher is one player in a field, and the way that publishers relate to other players is shaped by a chain of activities in which different agents or organizations perform different roles which are all oriented towards a common goal – namely, the production, sale and distribution of this particular cultural commodity, the book.

The publishing chain is both a *supply chain* and a *value chain*. It is a supply chain in the sense that it provides a series of organizational links by means of which a specific product – the book – is gradually produced and transmitted via distributors and retailers to an end user

---

[9] The notion of the logic of the field is discussed in more detail in ch. 8.

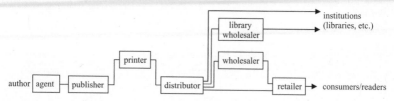

Figure 2   Book supply chain

who purchases it. Figure 2 offers a simple visual representation of the book supply chain. The basic steps in the book supply chain are as follows. The author creates the content and supplies it to the publisher; in trade publishing this process is typically mediated by the agent, who acts as a filter selecting material and directing it to appropriate publishers. The publisher buys a bundle of rights from the agent and then carries out a range of functions – reading, editing, etc. – before delivering the final text or file to the printer, who prints and binds the books and delivers them to the distributor, which may be owned by the publisher or may be a third party. The distributor warehouses the stock and fulfils orders from both retailers and wholesalers, who in turn sell books to or fulfil orders from others – individual consumers in the case of retailers, and retailers and other institutions (such as libraries) in the case of wholesalers. The publisher's customers are not individual consumers or libraries but rather intermediary institutions in the supply chain – namely, the wholesalers and retailers. For most readers, the only point of contact they have with the book supply chain is when they walk into a bookstore to browse or buy a book, or when they browse the details of a book online, or when they check out a book from a library. For the most part they have no direct contact with publishers and know very little about them; their primary interest is in the book and the author, not in the publisher.

The publishing chain is also a *value chain* in the sense that each of the links purportedly adds some 'value' in the process. This notion is more complicated than it might at first seem, but the general idea is clear enough: each of the links performs a task or function which contributes something substantial to the overall task of producing the book and delivering it to the end user, and this contribution is something for which the publisher (or some other agent or organization

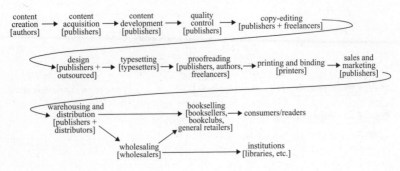

Figure 3   Publishing value chain

in the chain) is willing to pay. In other words, each of the links 'adds value'. If the task or function is not contributing anything substantial, or if the publisher (or other agent) feels that it does not add enough value to justify the expense, then the publisher (or other agent) may decide to cut the link out of the chain – that is, to 'disintermediate' it. Technological change may also alter the functions performed by particular links in the chain. The functions of the typesetter, for example, have been radically transformed by the advent of computerization, and some typesetters have sought to take on new functions, such as marking up texts in specialized languages like XML, in order to protect their position (or to reposition themselves) in the value chain.

Figure 3 summarizes the principal tasks or functions in the publishing chain. This diagram is more elaborate than figure 2 because each organization in the supply chain may carry out several functions (the agents or organizations that typically perform the various tasks or functions are indicated in brackets).

The starting point of the value chain is the creation, selection and acquisition of content – this is the domain where authors, agents and publishers interact. The interaction is much more complex than it might at first seem. Sometimes it is a simple linear process: the author writes a text, submits it to an agent who takes it on and then sells it to a publisher. But often it is much more complicated than this simple linear process would suggest: an agent, knowing what publishers are looking for, often works closely with his or her clients to help shape their book projects, especially in the area of non-fiction, and proposals may go through multiple drafts before the agent is willing to send them out, or a publisher may have an idea for a book and seek to commission an author to write it, and so on. It is not altogether unhelpful to think of agents and publishers as 'gatekeepers' of ideas, selecting those book projects they believe to be worthwhile from the large number of proposals and manuscripts that are submitted to them 'over the transom' by aspiring authors and rejecting those that don't come up to scratch.[10] But even in the world of trade publishing, which probably concurs with this model more closely than other sectors of the publishing industry, the notion of the gatekeeper greatly oversimplifies the complex forms of interaction and negotiation between authors, agents and publishers that shape the creative process.

In trade publishing, both agents and publishers are involved in selecting content, working with authors to develop it and exercising some degree of quality control. The essential difference between the agent and the publisher is that they sit on opposite sides of the table in the market for content: the agent represents the interests of the author and is selecting and developing content with a view to selling it (or, more specifically, selling a bundle of rights to exploit it), whereas the publisher is selecting content with a view to buying it (or buying the bundle of rights) and then developing it for publication. The development of the content will commonly involve reading draft material and editing it (sometimes several times); it may also involve picture research, copyright clearance and various kinds of quality control. Many of the other functions in the publishing chain, such as copy-editing, text and jacket design, proofreading and indexing, will either be handled by specialized staff in-house or will be outsourced, depending on the publisher. Virtually all publishers today outsource typesetting, printing and binding to specialized typesetting firms and printers. Most publishers retain responsibility for sales and marketing, although some smaller publishers may buy in sales and distribution services from specialized firms or from other publishers who take on third-party clients. The sales reps sell to the booksellers, retailers and wholesalers (many smaller booksellers are supplied by wholesalers), and the booksellers and retailers stock the books, display them and seek to sell them to individual consumers/readers. Books are supplied to booksellers, retailers and wholesalers on a sale-or-return basis, so that unsold stock can be returned to the publisher

---

[10] The notion of publishers as gatekeepers of ideas is developed by Lewis A. Coser, Charles Kadushin and Walter W. Powell in *Books: The Culture and Commerce of Publishing* (New York: Basic Books, 1982), discussed further below.

for full credit.[11] The publisher employs a range of marketing and publicity strategies, from advertising and authors' tours to attempts to get authors on radio and television programmes and to get books reviewed in the national press, in an effort to bring books to the attention of readers and drive sales (or 'sell-through') in the bookstores, which is the only way of ensuring that books which have been notionally 'sold' into the retail network are not returned to the publisher.

Each task or function in the publishing chain exists largely by virtue of the fact that it makes some contribution, of varying degrees of significance, to the overall objective of producing and selling books. Some of these tasks (design, copy-editing, typesetting, etc.) are within the range of activities that could be done by a single publishing organization, although a publisher may decide to disaggregate the functions and contract them out in order to reduce costs and improve efficiency. Other tasks are rooted in activities that are quite distinct and that have, in historical terms, a more settled institutional differentiation. This differentiation may be characterized by harmonious relations between the agents and organizations involved, since all have something to gain from cooperation; but they can also be characterized by tension and conflict, since their interests do not always coincide. Moreover, particular positions within the chain are not necessarily fixed or permanent. Changes in working practices, economic developments and technological advances can all have a major impact on the publishing chain, as tasks that were previously commonplace or essential are bypassed or eclipsed.

Given that the publishing chain is not rigid and that particular tasks or functions can be eclipsed by economic and technological change, what reason is there to believe that the role of the publisher itself might not be rendered redundant? What are the core activities

---

[11] The practice of allowing booksellers to return stock for full credit has a long history in Europe but was used rarely and half-heartedly by American publishers until the Great Depression of the 1930s, when publishers began experimenting seriously with returns policies as a way of stimulating sales and encouraging booksellers to increase stockholdings. In spring 1930, Putnam, Norton and Knopf all introduced schemes to allow booksellers to return stock for credit or exchange under certain conditions, and in 1932 Viking Press announced that orders for new books would be returnable for a credit of 90 per cent of the billed cost (see John Tebbel, *A History of Book Publishing in the United States*, vol. 3: *The Golden Age between the Two Wars, 1920–1940* (New York: R. R. Bowker, 1978), pp. 429–30, 441). The practice of returns subsequently became a settled feature of the book trade and marks it out as somewhat unusual among retail sectors.

How publishers add value

Figure 4   Key functions of the publisher

or functions of the publisher? Are these activities that could be phased out by new technologies, or that could be done by others? Could publishers themselves be disintermediated from the publishing chain? These questions have been raised often enough in recent years: in an age when anyone can post a text on the internet, who needs a publisher anymore? But the issues are more complicated than they might seem at first sight, and to address them properly we need to examine more carefully the key functions traditionally performed by the publisher and distinguish them from other activities that can be outsourced to freelancers or specialized firms. Figure 4 highlights six key functions of the publisher – it is by carrying out these tasks or functions that the publisher has traditionally made a distinctive contribution to the value creation process.

The first function is content acquisition and list-building. This is in many ways the key function of the publisher: to acquire and, indeed, help to create the content that will be turned into the books that comprise the publisher's list. The publisher acts not just as a filter or gatekeeper but in many cases plays an active role in creating or conceiving a project, or in seeing the potential of something and helping the author bring it to fruition. Some of the best publishers are those who are able to come up with good ideas for books and find the right authors to write them, or who are able to turn what might be a rather inchoate idea in the mind of an author into something special, or who are simply able to see potential where others see only dross. There is a real skill here that involves a blending together of intellectual creativity and marketing nous, and that distinguishes outstanding editors and publishers from those who are run of the mill.

The second function is financial investment and risk-taking. The publisher acts as the banker who makes resources available up front, both to pay advances to authors and agents and to cover the costs of acquisition, development and production. In the entire publishing chain it is only the publisher, in the last analysis, who takes the real financial risks – everyone else gets paid (assuming that the author has received an advance on royalties and that the publisher has paid the bills). If the book fails to sell, it is the publisher who writes down any unsold stock and writes off any unearned advance. In the book publishing chain, the publisher is the creditor of last resort.

The third and fourth functions are content development and quality control. In some cases the content provided by an author is in excellent condition and needs very little input from the publisher, but in many areas of publishing this is the exception rather than the rule. Draft manuscripts are commonly revised and developed in the light of comments from editors and others. It is also the responsibility of the publisher to assess the quality of the text and to ensure that it meets certain standards. These standards will of course vary from one publisher to another and a variety of assessment procedures may be used, ranging from the judgement of in-house editors to evaluations by one or more external readers who are specialists in the field (although in trade publishing it is rare to go out of house). Quality control is important for the publisher because it is one of the key means by which they are able to build a distinctive profile and brand in the publishing field and thereby distinguish themselves from other houses.

The fifth function is what could be loosely described as management and coordination. This label describes a range of management activities that are an integral part of the publishing process, from the management of specific projects which may be exceptionally complex to the management of specific activities or phases in the life cycle of the book. For example, even if copy-editing is outsourced to freelancers, the freelancers must be given work and instructions, their terms of work must be agreed and they must be paid, and all of this requires management time and expertise; this is often handled by a dedicated in-house manuscript editor or desk editor. Similarly, even though typesetting, design and printing may be outsourced to specialized firms, the whole production process, from copy-edited manuscript to bound books, must be managed; this is usually done in-house by a production manager or controller. Decisions must be taken about prices and print runs, and stock must then be managed throughout the life cycle of the book. The copyright must also be managed through the sale of subsidiary rights (translations, reprints, serialization, etc.). All of these activities require a great deal of management time and expertise, and in most cases they are handled by in-house managers who have responsibility for specific sectors of the production and publishing process.

The sixth and final function is sales and marketing. I have bundled these activities together although they are in fact quite distinct. Marketing comprises a range of activities concerned with informing potential customers of the availability of a book and encouraging them to buy it. These activities include catalogue preparation and mailing, advertising, direct mail, sending out review copies and, more recently, various kinds of e-marketing. Most trade publishers also have a separate publicity manager and/or department whose task is to cultivate relations with the media and secure media coverage for a book – coverage that ranges from reviews, extracts and interviews in the printed press to radio and television appearances, book signings and author tours. Marketing and publicity have the same aim – namely, to make consumers/readers aware of books and persuade them to buy them; the only real difference is that the publisher pays for marketing, whereas publicity, if you can get it, is free. The task of the sales manager and the sales team is to call on the key accounts – which include the bookselling chains, independent booksellers, online booksellers, wholesalers and a variety of general retailers from supermarkets to warehouse stores – to inform them of the forthcoming books, solicit orders and manage the publisher's relations with their key customers, with the aim of ensuring that books are stocked and available in bookstores for consumers to browse and buy.

These various sales and marketing activities are concerned not simply to bring a product to the marketplace and let retailers and consumers know that it is available: they seek, more fundamentally, to *build a market* for the book. To publish in the sense of making a book *available to the public* is easy – and never easier than it is today, when texts posted online could be said to be 'published' in some sense. But to publish in the sense of making a book *known to the public*, visible to them and attracting a sufficient quantum of their attention to encourage them to buy the book and perhaps even to read it, is extremely difficult – and never more difficult than it is today, when the sheer volume of content available to consumers and readers is enough to drown out even the most determined and well-resourced marketing effort. Good publishers – as one former publisher aptly put it – are market-makers in a world where it is attention, not content, that is scarce.

These six key functions of the publisher define the principal respects in which publishing firms 'add value'. Whether these are functions that will always be performed by traditional publishing firms, or whether, in the changing information environment brought about by digitization and the internet, at least some of these functions will be eclipsed, marginalized, transformed or taken over by others, are questions to which there are, at this point in time, no clear answers. But before speculating about the imminent disintermediation of publishing firms, one would be well advised to reflect carefully on the functions actually performed by publishers in the cultural economy of the book, on which functions will continue to require fulfilment in the future and, if they do, on who will perform them and how.

What follows

There are three key developments that are crucial for understanding the logic of the field of trade publishing, and these will occupy our attention in the first three chapters: the growth of the retail chains and the broader and ongoing transformation of the retail environment of bookselling (chapter 1); the rise of the literary agent as a key power broker in the field of English-language trade publishing (chapter 2); and the emergence of transnational publishing corporations stemming from successive waves of mergers and acquisitions, beginning in the 1960s and continuing through to the present day (chapter 3). I will seek to show how these three key developments have created a field that is structured in certain ways, a field that shapes the ways in which agents and organizations can act and that has certain consequences; chapters 4–8 examine these consequences. Taken together, this analysis of the key developments and their consequences will lay bare what I'm calling the logic of the field of English-language trade publishing. Chapter 9 will examine the digital revolution and its implications for the book publishing industry, while chapter 10 will offer a more normative reflection on the world of trade publishing and its costs. The concluding remarks will briefly consider some of the challenges the publishing industry faces as it enters the second decade of the twenty-first century.

In developing this account of the contemporary world of trade publishing in Britain and the United States, I rely largely on the insights gained through my interviews with practitioners in the field (a more detailed discussion of my research methods can be found in appendix 2). I also draw on data gathered by Nielsen BookScan, the

Book Industry Study Group (BISG), Subtext and other sources. I make use of other studies and books on the book business when it is helpful to do so but I have generally found these to be of limited use for various reasons. The study carried out by Louis Coser, Charles Kadushin and Walter Powell, alluded to earlier, remains the best of these studies and an indispensable reference point for anyone interested in the modern book publishing industry.[12] But the research on which this study was based was carried out more than 30 years ago, in the late 1970s, and the world of publishing has changed quite profoundly since then. Moreover, this study was focused solely on the United States, and hence it lacks the more comparative and international perspective to which any study of the creative industries today, in our increasingly globalized world, must aspire. It is not without significance that, of the five largest publishing houses that are key players in the field of American trade publishing today, four are owned by large international media corporations which have substantial stakes in the UK, Europe and elsewhere.

At around the same time as the study by Coser and his colleagues appeared, Thomas Whiteside published a series of articles in the *New Yorker,* subsequently incorporated into a book, which cast a more critical eye on the world of New York trade publishing.[13] This was a time – around 1980 – when the takeover of many publishing houses by large corporations with diverse media interests was eliciting growing concern in many quarters about the possibility that the literary values associated with these houses were being eclipsed by the search for a new kind of lightweight, downmarket content that would be as suitable for TV talk shows and movie tie-ins as traditional books. Whiteside's insightful analysis lends support to these concerns and highlights some of the key trends that have continued to shape the industry in the years since. But as with the work of Coser and his associates, the value of Whiteside's study today is limited both by its age and by its exclusive focus on the United States. Moreover, the central theme of his critique – the idea that trade publishing was becoming part of a movie tie-in business in which the big Hollywood studios were increasingly calling the shots – now looks, with the benefit of hindsight, to be an exaggeration. It is undoubtedly true that movie tie-ins can be big business for trade publishers and can

---

[12] Coser et al., *Books.*
[13] Thomas Whiteside, *The Blockbuster Complex: Conglomerates, Show Business, and Book Publishing* (Middletown, Conn.: Wesleyan University Press, 1980).

generate welcome spikes in sales, but movie tie-ins and the sale of
movie rights have turned out to be less important for trade publishers
than Whiteside thought. Other aspects of our contemporary media
culture, such as the celebrity status and 'well-knownness' which stems
from being seen and heard in the media, are more important for
understanding the world of trade publishing than the links with the
Hollywood movie business, or than the idea that books were becoming the 'software' of multimedia packages in an increasingly integrated communications–entertainment complex.

Apart from the studies by Coser et al. and Whiteside, many of the
other books on the modern publishing industry that have appeared
in the last decade or two have been books written by publishers
themselves. The books by André Schiffrin and Jason Epstein, *The
Business of Books* and *Book Business* respectively, are probably the
most interesting recent examples of this genre.[14] Both Schiffrin and
Epstein were distinguished publishers and editors in the world of
American trade publishing – Schiffrin was the director of Pantheon
for many years until he fell out with its corporate owners and resigned
in 1989 to set up his own not-for-profit house called The New Press,
while Epstein was editorial director at Random House for many years
and enjoyed a long and distinguished career as one of America's most
successful editors. Their books are thoughtful reflections on the state
of trade publishing in America at the turn of the millennium; they
lived through and experienced personally the huge changes that have
swept through the industry since the 1960s and 1970s, and their
books bear witness to the scale and the costs – both in cultural and
in personal terms – of these changes. But their accounts are inextricably entangled with their own personal experiences and career tra-
jectories. These are not even-handed accounts of an industry
undergoing dramatic change, nor do they purport to be: they are
memoirs with a critical edge. They are personal and sometimes opin-
ionated accounts – gracefully written, rich in anecdote, tinged with
a shade of nostalgia – of an industry as seen from the particular
perspectives of two protagonists who have charted their own courses
through the complex and turbulent world of publishing. That the
protagonists have charted their courses so successfully and recounted
them so eloquently is a tribute to their remarkable talents as publish-

---

[14] André Schiffrin, *The Business of Books: How International Conglomerates Took
Over Publishing and Changed the Way We Read* (London: Verso, 2000); Jason
Epstein, *Book Business: Publishing Past Present and Future* (New York: W. W.
Norton, 2001).

ers and authors, but this does not alter the fact that their accounts are, by their very nature, partial. These books are symptoms and reflections of a world in change as much as they are analyses of it.

While I have learned much from these and other accounts of the modern publishing industry, I have tried to do something which no one else has attempted. While the existing literature tends to be focused on the publishing industry in one country and most commonly the United States, I have sought to be international and comparative in my analysis, focusing on the field of English-language trade publishing which, by its very nature, is something more than American trade publishing and something less than book publishing, even trade book publishing, per se. I have sought to ground my analysis in a careful consideration of the facts and empirical trends but I have not restricted myself to a mere recitation of facts and figures. The account I offer is both analytical and normative: an attempt to lay bare the fundamental dynamic that has shaped the evolution of this field over the last few decades and, on the basis of this analysis, to offer a critical reflection on the consequences of these developments for our literary and intellectual culture. And I shall try to show that, when we grasp the logic of this field, we shall be able to make sense of those actions of agents and organizations within the field that might otherwise seem bizarre, including the actions of the organization that undertook to publish a small book by a hitherto largely unknown professor of computer science who happened to deliver an inspiring last lecture on realizing your childhood dreams.

— 1 —

THE GROWTH OF THE RETAIL CHAINS

The dramatic transformation of the retail landscape has been one of the key factors shaping the evolution of the field of English-language trade publishing since the 1960s. Throughout the first half of the twentieth century, bookselling in the United States and Britain was handled primarily by a plethora of small independent bookstores that were spread across the country, on the one hand, and a variety of non-book retailers like drugstores, department stores, newsagents and news-stands, on the other.[1] The bookstores tended to cater for an educated and cultivated clientele – the so-called 'carriage trade' – while the non-book retailers, who carried books along with many other commodities, tended to sell books to a wider range of the public. Department stores in the US began carrying books in the late nineteenth century. Macy's of New York began selling books in 1869 and quickly became one of the largest booksellers in the country.[2] By 1951 it was estimated that department stores accounted for between 40 and 60 per cent of all retail trade book sales in the US.[3] Books were attractive for department stores to carry because they were regarded as prestigious, aspirational goods. They appealed to the cultivated tastes of well-to-do customers, adding an aura of seriousness and respectability to the store and attracting the kind of customer who had money to spend.

---

[1] See Laura J. Miller, *Reluctant Capitalists: Bookselling and the Culture of Consumption* (Chicago: University of Chicago Press, 2006), ch. 2.
[2] Ibid., p. 35.
[3] Ibid.

From mall stores to superstores

The traditional patterns of the retail book trade – small independent booksellers on the one hand, department stores and other non-book retailers on the other – began to change in the US with the rise of the mall stores in the early 1960s. This development was linked to a major demographic shift that was taking place in the United States at this time, as the middle classes moved out of city centres and into the suburbs that formed the expanding satellites of American cities.[4] With the migration of the middle classes to the suburbs and the rise of the automobile as the primary means of transport, the suburban shopping mall became the new locus of the American retail trade. In 1962 the Walden Book Company, which for many years had operated a network of rental libraries on the East Coast, opened its first retail outlet in a shopping mall in Pittsburgh. Four years later the Dayton Hudson Corporation – a company formed by the merger of two department stores in the American Midwest – opened the first B. Dalton bookstore in a suburban shopping mall in Minneapolis. In 1969 the Corporation bought the Pickwick Bookshop in Hollywood, together with other Pickwick outlets, and in 1972 the two operations were merged to form B. Dalton Booksellers. By 1980 there were more than 450 B. Dalton stores located in shopping malls across the United States. Waldenbooks also expanded rapidly during the 1960s and 1970s; by 1981 Waldenbooks had 750 sites and claimed to be the first bookseller to operate bookstores in all 50 states.

As it turned out, the 1970s were the heyday of the mall-based bookstores; in the course of the 1980s they were gradually eclipsed by the rise of the so-called superstores, especially the chains of Barnes & Noble and Borders. Barnes & Noble was an old bookselling company whose origins dated back to the establishment of a second-hand book business by Charles Montgomery Barnes in Wheaton, Illinois, a suburb of Chicago, in 1873. Barnes's son, William, moved to New York in 1917 and set up a wholesale book business with G. Clifford Noble, supplying textbooks to schools, colleges and libraries in New York. At the outset, Barnes & Noble was primarily a wholesale operation, selling to educational institutions rather than individual customers, but it gradually became increasingly involved in retail sales, leading to the opening of a large bookstore on Fifth Avenue and 18th Street in Manhattan, which was to become the

---

[4] Epstein, *Book Business*, pp. 103ff.

company's flagship. By the 1970s, however, Barnes & Noble had fallen on hard times. John Barnes, grandson of the founder, had died in 1969 and the business had been bought by Amtel, a conglomerate that manufactured toys, tools and other products; business declined and Amtel soon decided to divest themselves of their new acquisition. In 1971 Barnes & Noble was bought by Leonard Riggio, who had founded a successful student bookstore while he was a student at New York University in the 1960s and had set his sights on building up a bookselling business. Under Riggio's management, Barnes & Noble expanded its operations in New York and Boston, opening more stores and acquiring a couple of local chains. In 1986 Barnes & Noble bought the B. Dalton bookstore chain from Dayton Hudson, and in 1989 they acquired Scribner's Bookstores and Bookstop/Bookstar, a regional chain in southern and western United States. These acquisitions turned Barnes & Noble into a national retailer and one of the largest booksellers in America.

At the same time as Barnes & Noble was expanding its bookstore chain from its original base on the East Coast, Borders was building a national chain of bookstores from its base in the Midwest. In 1971 Tom and Louis Borders opened a small used bookstore in Ann Arbor, Michigan; they moved to larger premises in 1975, expanded the business and ran it successfully for many years. In 1985 they opened a second bookstore in Detroit to see whether they could replicate their success in a less academic setting. The success of the Detroit store encouraged them to expand into other locations in the Midwest and Northeast. In 1992 Borders was bought by the retail giant Kmart, which had acquired the mall-based bookstore chain Waldenbooks in 1984. Kmart merged Borders with Waldenbooks to form the Borders Group, which went public in 1995. By this stage, the Borders Group and Barnes & Noble had become the dominant book retail chains in the United States and their sales were five to ten times those of the other national chains, such as Crown and Books-A-Million.

In the course of the 1990s both Borders and Barnes & Noble expanded rapidly, seeking to extend their presence across the United States and to consolidate their positions as dominant players in the retail book trade. In both cases their expansion was based on the concept of the 'book superstore', which differed in certain key respects from both the mall stores and the independents. Often located in prime city locations, the book superstores were designed as attractive retail spaces that drew customers in and encouraged them to browse – they were clean, spacious, well-lit stores with sofas and coffee shops and areas to relax and read. The stores were open for up to a hundred hours a week, seven days a week; they emphasized customer service and attractive, eye-catching displays. The chains competed with one another and with other chains and independents by giving deep discounts (30–40 per cent) on frontlist[5] bestsellers and modest discounts (10–20 per cent) on other hardcovers and by the range and depth of their stock. They centralized stock purchasing and inventory control, which gave them a great deal of leverage in their negotiations with suppliers and enabled them to realize substantial economies of scale. In many cases they stocked merchandise other than books, such as magazines, music CDs, computer games and videos. They sought to make the experience of buying books easy, unthreatening and enjoyable for individuals who were not accustomed to going into a traditional bookstore.

As the rivalry between Barnes & Noble and Borders intensified in the early 1990s, both companies closed many of the mall stores in their B. Dalton and Walden chains and opened more superstores instead. In the year from 1993 to 1994, for example, Barnes & Noble closed around 52 B. Dalton stores, the total number of which fell from about 750 in 1993 to 698 in 1994; at the same time, it increased the number of superstores from 200 to 268. During the same time period, Borders closed 57 Walden stores, the total number of which fell from 1,159 to 1,102, and it nearly doubled the number of superstores, from 44 to 85 (see table 1).[6] The old mall-based bookstores were gradually giving way to the rise of the book superstores.

By 2006, Barnes & Noble was operating 723 bookstores across the United States, which included 695 superstores and 98 mall stores; its total sales were around $4.8 billion.[7] The company had diversified into the video games and computer software retail business and was operating a large number of video game and entertainment software stores under various trade names including Babbage's, Funco and Software Etc. It had also become involved in publishing, acquiring Sterling Publishing in 2003 – a non-fiction trade publisher with some 5,000 books in print – and publishing an extensive line of classics under the Barnes & Noble imprint. In 2009 Barnes & Noble

---

[5] 'Frontlist' refers to new and recently published books. A title is commonly treated as frontlist for up to 12 months, after which it becomes a backlist title.
[6] See Stephen Horvath, 'The Rise of the Book Chain Superstore', *Logos*, vol. 7, no. 1 (1996), p. 43.
[7] Stephanie Oda and Glenn Sanislo, *The Subtext 2007–2008 Perspective on Book Publishing: Numbers, Issues and Trends* (Darien, Conn.: Open Book, 2007), p. 67.

Table 1 The expansion of Borders and Barnes & Noble, 1993–1994

	Sales ($ million)		Number of stores	
	1993	1994	1993	1994
Borders				
Borders superstores	225	425	44	85
Waldenbooks	1,146	1,086	1,159	1,102
Total	**1,371**	**1,511**		
Barnes & Noble				
B & N superstores	600*	958	200*	268
B. Dalton	737*	665	750*	698
Total	**1,337**	**1,623**		

* estimate.
Source: *Logos* (1996).

entered the ebook market by launching its own ebook reader, the Nook, and selling ebooks from its own website.

The Borders Group, with total sales of around $4.1 billion in 2006, was the second largest book retail chain in the US at this time, operating around1,063 bookstores in the US, including 499 superstores under the Borders trade name and around 564 mall-based Waldenbooks stores. Borders had also expanded internationally, opening a number of Borders stores outside the US (mainly in the UK and the Pacific Rim) and acquiring Books Etc. in the UK in 1997. But in the early 2000s the Borders overseas operation began to run into difficulties. In 2007 the UK business – which by then comprised 42 superstores in the UK and Ireland and 28 branches of Books Etc. – was sold to a private equity group, Risk Capital Partners, for a modest initial sum of £10 million. It was bought out by the management in July 2009 and went into administration in November 2009. All 45 Borders stores in the UK were closed on 22 December 2009. Borders' US business also went into decline; its last recorded profit was in 2006 and from then on its annual sales fell and its losses grew. In February 2011 Borders announced that it had filed for Chapter 11 bankruptcy protection and by September all remaining Borders stores had been closed down.

The bankruptcy of Borders marked the end of an era, in the sense that the long-running rivalry between Barnes & Noble and Borders, which saw the two book retail giants rolling out their superstores across America, was now over. But the profound changes currently taking place in the retail marketplace will pose major challenges for Barnes & Noble and the smaller retail chains that remain. Bricks-and-mortar bookstores have long faced serious competition from online retailers like Amazon and from mass merchandisers (more below); now they face the real threat that a growing proportion of book sales will be realized as ebooks that bypass the physical book-stores altogether. Total revenues from the Barnes & Noble bookstores have been declining since 2007. Barnes & Noble is a significant player in the ebook marketplace but well behind Amazon in terms of market share, and it's not clear whether the growth of its ebook revenues will be sufficient to offset the decline of bookstore sales. While Barnes & Noble will pick up some of the sales that would previously have been credited to Borders, it is likely that the overall proportion of retail sales accounted for by the superstore and mall bookstore chains – which was probably about 45 per cent in 2006[8] – will decline significantly in the coming years.

There is no doubt that the rolling out of the nationwide book chains in the 1990s and the intense competition that developed between them greatly increased the availability of books to millions of ordinary Americans. People living in parts of the country that had, until then, been poorly served by bookstores suddenly found that there were now two or more large bookstores within driving distance, carrying a range of stock that had simply not been available before in a bricks-and-mortar store. But this dramatic transformation of the retail landscape had its costs and consequences too.

The most visible consequence – one that has been much commented upon and much lamented – was the precipitous decline of the independent booksellers. While this decline predates the rise of the superstores, it was undoubtedly hastened by it. In 1958, one-store independent booksellers were selling 72 per cent of trade books in the US; by 1980 this had fallen to less than 40 per cent of trade sales.[9] As the chains opened new superstores in the metropolitan areas across America in the 1990s, more and more independents closed down, forced out of business by the two-pronged pressure of rising overheads (and especially the rising costs of real estate) and declining revenues. The American Booksellers Association, which represents many independent booksellers, lost more than half its members in

---

[8] Ibid., p. 64.
[9] Whiteside, *The Blockbuster Complex*, p. 41.

the 1990s and early 2000s: its membership fell from 5,100 in 1991 to 1,900 in 2004. Whether ABA membership figures are an accurate reflection of the actual number of independent booksellers in the US is debatable,[10] but no one disputes the fact that the number of independent booksellers has fallen significantly and that their market share has declined. In 1993, the chains accounted for around 23 per cent of retail sales in the US; by the end of the decade, this had risen to over 50 per cent. During the same period, the market share of independent booksellers fell from 24 per cent to around 16 per cent. This decline continued into the 2000s, so that by 2006 independent bookstores probably accounted for only about 13 per cent of retail sales in the US.[11]

There can be no doubt that the decline of the independents was partly the outcome of predatory expansionist activity by the chains – this was not the only factor, to be sure, but it would be ingenuous to suppose that it played no role. The chains explicitly targeted those metropolitan districts or zip codes where the demographics were favourable to the sale of books, and these tended to be the same districts where independent booksellers were already located. Once the superstore opened, with its extensive stock range and aggressive discounting, it was very difficult for the small independent down the street to compete. On the other hand, many of the independents that closed down were poorly run businesses that didn't serve their customers well. Their stores were disorganized, their stock-holding erratic, their accounts non-existent and they did little to make book-buying a pleasurable and rewarding experience for the consumer. 'Did the independents go out of business because Barnes & Noble and Borders expanded and were predatory? Absolutely,' said one former employee of a chain who was responsible for identifying sites for new superstores in the early 1990s. 'The other side of the story is that they went out of business because you can't be an amateur in this business anymore. Because bookselling was a noble profession, there seemed to be a fence between us and the rest of the economy; suddenly people woke up to the fact that you have to know what you're doing.' The independents that survived tended to be those that

---

[10] See Ted Striphas, *The Late Age of Print: Everyday Book Culture from Consumerism to Control* (New York: Columbia University Press, 2009), p. 56. Striphas points out that in 1997 the ABA estimated that there were around 12,000 independent retail bookstores in business in the US; ABA members would have accounted for less than a third of these.

[11] Oda and Sanislo, *The Subtext 2007–2008 Perspective*, p. 64.

were well run and that built strong links with their local communities by hosting events of various kinds; it also helped if they owned their own real estate, or if they were protected by zoning regulations that restricted the activities of the chains. By 2007 there were probably only 400 independent booksellers left that were of real importance for trade publishers in the US. But by this time the decline of the independents appeared to have levelled off, as those that remained had succeeded in finding a strategy that would enable them to survive in the face of intense competition from the chains and other outlets. And for certain kinds of books, their role was and remains greater than their number and size – judged purely in terms of their revenue and their share of retail sales – would suggest.

The long decade of struggle between the chains and the independents ended unquestionably in victory for the chains, but there were skirmishes along the way that resulted in important gains for independent booksellers. The most important of these was undoubtedly the series of legal challenges brought against the chains and the large publishing houses by independent booksellers associations which alleged that the publishers were giving preferential terms and discounts to the chains in contravention of federal antitrust law. In mounting their case against the publishers and the chains, the independent booksellers appealed to a piece of federal legislation called the Robinson-Patman Act, which was passed in 1936 to curb what were seen as anticompetitive practices by producers who allowed chain stores to purchase goods at lower prices than other retailers. The Act prohibits price discrimination on the sale of goods to equally situated retailers when the effect is to reduce competition. Following a legal challenge brought by the Northern California Booksellers Association against the paperback publishers Avon and Bantam in 1982 and the launch of a Federal Trade Commission investigation in 1988, the American Booksellers Association announced a lawsuit in 1994 against five publishers for discriminatory practices that favoured the chains.[12] By the autumn of 1996 all of the publishers had settled out of court, admitting no wrongdoing but agreeing to abide by rules ensuring non-discrimination in pricing, credit and returns.[13] In March 1998 the ABA filed another lawsuit, this time against the two major chains, Barnes & Noble and Borders, alleging

---

[12] For a full account of the legal challenges, see the excellent discussion in Miller, *Reluctant Capitalists,* ch. 7.
[13] Ibid., pp. 179–80.

that they had violated the Robinson-Patman Act and California unfair trade practices laws (the suit was filed in the US District Court for Northern California). Again, the case was settled out of court; neither Barnes & Noble nor Borders admitted any wrongdoing, and they agreed only to pay the ABA a sum less the cost of its legal fees. This was something of a defeat for the independents, who agreed to destroy all documents obtained during the case and to refrain from any further litigation for three years.[14] But the upshot of this prolonged legal battle was the emergence of a much clearer and more transparent system for discounting and co-op advertising,[15] as well as an acute sensitivity to the risks involved in tampering with this system. The publishing houses make their discount schedules and co-op arrangements explicit so that all retailers know what they are when they are buying books and formulating promotion plans. In principle this creates a level playing field, as the large chains should not be able to use their size to force publishers to offer higher discounts, although in practice the issues are not always so clear-cut, as we shall see.

A second consequence of the rise of the retail chains was a gradual shift in the ways that books were stocked and sold. This shift began with the mall stores in the late 1960s and early 1970s, and it went hand in hand with the application to bookselling of the methods of selling and stock management that were being used in other retail sectors. Situated in the high-traffic retail space of the shopping mall, B. Dalton and Waldenbooks had to organize their stores in ways that would maximize stock turnover. Table displays and dump bins were used to stimulate impulse buying and multiple purchases. Computerized systems of stock management were introduced to monitor stock levels and stock turn, so that fast-selling titles could be promptly reordered and stock that was not selling could be returned. These retail practices were incorporated into the operating principles of the new superstores that were opened in the 1990s. The sheer size of the superstores gave Barnes & Noble and Borders more leeway in terms of the range and depth of stock. They could stock more specialized books and more slow-moving backlist titles than the mall stores, with their much smaller floor area, could afford to keep on the shelves, and this became an important part of their value proposition. Nev-

---

[14] Ibid., p. 180.
[15] Co-op advertising is a cost-sharing arrangement between the publisher and the retailer in which the publisher pays for part of the retailer's promotion costs. This is discussed in more detail in ch. 7.

ertheless, the superstores continued to place a great deal of emphasis on maximizing stock turnover in the highly visible space at the front of the store, where new books and bestsellers were stacked on tables and in dump bins and where publishers were charged for display space. As the national roll-out of the superstores began to grind to a halt around 2000 and the superstore chains began to look more carefully at the relations between investment in stock, overheads and revenues and became more concerned about cash flow, their book-buying decisions became more cautious and they became more proactive about returning slow-moving stock. The chains had succeeded in bringing bookstores into the shopping malls and city centres where Americans did the rest of their shopping, had made books more available than ever before and had turned book-buying into a consumer experience like any other. But the more books were treated like any other commodity and subjected to the same principles of retailing, the more the chains would be forced to focus on fast-selling titles by brand-name authors at the expense of those titles that would add depth and range to the store but that would have much slower stock turns.

This inevitable shift was largely the consequence of the cost of real estate. Maintaining large bookstores in the shopping malls and city centres where there is high consumer traffic, and therefore competition for retail space, is a very costly business, and it is difficult to cover these costs and generate profits in a low-margin activity like bookselling. The pressure to reduce your investment in slow-moving stock, to focus more attention on fast-moving bestsellers and to look for other ways of improving margin – such as charging publishers more for display space and stocking non-book goods like chocolate and stationery where margins are higher – is difficult to resist. Epstein puts the point well: 'In bookselling as in any retail business, inventory and rent are a trade-off. The more you pay for one, the less you can spend on the other.'[16] Hence the growing dominance of the retail book chains, from the mall stores to the superstore chains, tended over time to accentuate the importance within the industry of fast-selling frontlist titles by authors with a good track record and a degree of name recognition. The chains were more likely to stock these books in substantial quantities and more likely to display them in prominent front-of-store positions, thereby increasing their chances of selling well. Books by less well-known authors were not ignored

---

[16] Epstein, *Book Business*, p. 103.

– on the contrary, the central buyers in the chains were always eager to find new authors and new titles that might appeal to their customers. But decisions about which books to buy, in what quantities, how to promote and display them and how long to keep stock on the shelves were being taken in contexts that were shaped by the increasingly stringent financial demands of running large retail businesses in expensive real estate. These were contexts that tended, over time, to reduce the levels of tolerance for slow-moving stock.

The rise of the retail chains had a third consequence which has been less appreciated but which was enormously important for the evolution of the publishing industry: it created a new market for what could be described as the 'mass-market hardback'. Much has been written about the paperback revolution started by Allen Lane in Britain, with his launch of the Penguin imprint in the 1930s, and by the rise of Pocket Books, Bantam, Dell, Fawcett, the New American Library and other paperback houses in the US in the period after the Second World War. From the 1940s on, the sales of mass-market paperbacks grew enormously; paperbacks were being sold in newsagents, drugstores, supermarkets, airports, bus terminals and railway stations as well as in more conventional bookstores. Mass-market paperback sales became the financial driving force of the industry, and the sale of paperback rights became a principal source of revenue for the hardcover houses. By the 1960s the industry itself had bifurcated into two separate businesses – hardcover publishing, on the one hand, and paperback publishing, on the other. 'The perception was that the only similarity between the two is that we both published books,' explained one senior executive who had entered the paperback side of the business in the late 1960s. 'The hardcover side was snobby, literary, prestigious, tweedy – all the things you would expect in that era. And the paperback business was sort of second class – we got the books a year later, we got no credit for the words, we were all about marketing, packaging, distributing and selling books. So you had these two universes coexisting, neither respecting the other very much but one totally dependent on the other for product.' While the paperback business depended on the hardcover business for product, the hardcover houses depended heavily on royalty income from paperback sales to run their businesses.

The rise of the mall-store chains in the late 1960s and 1970s stimulated the sales of paperbacks and strengthened further the position of the paperback houses, as the mall stores embraced the paperback and made it available in a bookstore environment that was much more inviting and less intimidating for consumers than the traditional bookstore. By the mid-1970s, some of those working in the paperback houses began to realize that their business model – which made them dependent on the hardcover houses even though they, the paperback houses, were generating the real volume sales – was not a terribly good one. There were even cases where the publisher at a paperback house who had came up with the idea for a book was obliged to find a hardcover house to publish the initial hardcover edition, so that they could then license the paperback edition from them. 'It would be like me coming to you and saying "look, I don't have any editors here, edit this book for me, publish it in hardcover, I'll give you the book to do that and then I will pay you some portion of the success I have after you do that,"' explained a publisher who had started his career as an editor at a paperback house. Some of the employees at the paperback houses – usually the younger ones who were less wedded to the traditional model and less worried about offending the hardcover houses who were their traditional source of product – saw the need to start publishing books on their own. So in the 1970s the paperback houses began to originate their own titles, initially publishing them as paperback originals and then, by the late 1970s, publishing their own hardcover books. Crucially, they applied to hardcover publishing some of the techniques they had developed in the world of mass-market paperback publishing, such as using more attractive packaging and extending distribution to non-traditional outlets, and they were able in this way to achieve hardcover sales that were unprecedented in volume. This was the origin of the 'hardcover revolution'.

The hardcover revolution

As the mall-store chains evolved into the chains of superstores that were being rolled out across the country, the hardcover revolution gained momentum. The application of mass-market publishing strategies to hardcover books dovetailed nicely with the non-traditional merchandising methods of the chains, including the use of discounting and dump bins; and the fact that the chains were opening large superstores across the country and developing more efficient systems for supplying their stores meant that the volume of books that could be put out into the marketplace on publication was much greater than it had ever been. In the 1970s, a book that sold 500,000 copies in hardcover would have been a huge success, practically unheard of in the industry. Thirty years later, an equivalent success would be in the region of 8–10 million copies – that is, around 20 times greater. In the early 2000s, hardcover sales in excess of a million copies were not unusual, and new books by brand-name authors often sold more than this. Dan Brown's *The Da Vinci Code*, first published in 2003, had sold more than 18 million copies in hardcover in the US alone by 2006 – albeit exceptional, hardcover sales figures of this magnitude were simply unimaginable in earlier decades. As the sales of hardcovers increased, the old relationship between hardcover and paperback publishing was gradually inverted: whereas in the 1950s and 1960s, paperback publishing was the financial driving force of the trade publishing business, in the 1980s and 1990s hardcover publishing was increasingly becoming the financial foundation of the industry.

There were three other aspects of this hardcover revolution that were particularly important. First, as paperback publishers realized the value of publishing their own books, they began to use their growing financial strength to acquire hardback houses. This enabled them not only to expand their publishing programmes but also to secure their supply chains, so that they became less dependent on buying books from hardcover houses which were commanding higher and higher advances for paperback rights. This was a principal driver of the so-called 'vertical integration' of the publishing business, which became an integral part of the conglomeratization of publishing houses that characterized the period from the 1960s to the 1990s.

A second aspect of the hardcover revolution is that it diffused the principles of the mass marketing of books throughout the industry as a whole. Prior to this revolution, mass-marketing techniques were restricted largely to the province of mass-market paperback publishers, who were commonly looked down upon by many who worked on the hardcover side of the business. But as the hardcover revolution gained momentum in the 1980s, practices that had originally been developed for the mass marketing of paperbacks became increasingly commonplace throughout the industry. Partly this was because, with the growing vertical integration of the industry, the bifurcation into hardback and paperback publishing, which had been such a pervasive feature of the industry in the 1970s and before, was beginning to break down. Partly it was also because many of the managers who rose to positions of power in the new publishing corporations that were taking shape in the 1980s were people who had honed their skills in the world of mass-market paperback publishing and were now able to introduce – even impose if necessary – more market-oriented values and practices into those sectors of the industry that had hitherto remained rather aloof.

Cover design is a good example that illustrates how, in the day-to-day activities of a large publishing corporation in the late 1980s, the market-oriented values of mass-market paperback publishing began to prevail over the values and practices of the traditional hardcover business. A senior executive who had come out of mass-market paperback publishing and joined one of the large corporations in the 1980s recounted how, at the time, those who worked in the hardcover division were very resistant to changing the covers on their books in response to what sales reps might say:

> I remember going into a planning meeting one day in the hardcover division and I brought the sales reps in. They'd been to these meetings before but never with a voice. Most of the books had no jackets but one book did – it was a major title and the sales reps were whispering to me that the cover was terrible. One put his hand up and said 'I think I'm going to have trouble selling that book with that cover.' Well, I can't remember who attacked him first – it was either the art director, the publisher, the editor or all three. It was like 'Who the hell are you to be telling us whether or not we've got it right?' And I shook my head – it was a pivotal moment for us because I went back in afterwards and said, 'You know what, stick with that approach and you're absolutely going to fail. These sales guys have to go in and sell your book to the person who's going to sell your book, and if you can't sell to them they can't sell your book – you've got to wake up to it.' Some got it faster than others but I would say that over the course of the next couple of years we turned over almost all of those people. Some just never got it.

For many editors and publishers who had learned their trade in the world of traditional hardcover publishing, this confrontation with the values and practices of mass-market paperback publishing was a rude awakening. For many it was a question of either adapting to the new way of doing things or getting out. Some adapted and even thrived, going on to forge very successful careers as hardcover publishers who embraced the principles derived from mass-market paperback publishing and put them into practice in developing their hardcover lists, becoming legendary figures in their own right. But many of the old-school hardcover publishers of this time – the late 1980s – simply disappeared, forced out by the cultural revolution taking place at the heart of the firm.

A third consequence of this transformation is that it led, slowly but ineluctably, to the withering of the market from which the revolution had originally sprung – that of the mass-market paperback. This was due partly to the very success of the hardback revolution of the 1980s and early 1990s, and to the capacity of the new systems of distribution created by the book retailing chains to get large numbers of hardcover books into the marketplace very quickly. It was also due in part to the increased use of discounting by the chains and by other retailers who were selling books, a practice that greatly reduced the price differential between hardcover and paperback books. In the 1970s and before, the price differential was commonly around 10:1 – a mass-market paperback might cost a tenth of the price of the original hardcover edition. By the 1990s and early 2000s, when some retailers were selling new hardcovers at 40 per cent off the retail price, the price differential could be as little as 3:1. Moreover, as the baby-boomer generation which had driven the paperback revolution of the 1960s and 1970s began to age, they became more affluent and their needs began to change. The difference between $5 and $15 for a new book mattered less to them than the ability to get it quickly – why wait for another year until the paperback edition was available? – and to read it in a format that was kinder to ageing eyesight than the small typeface of the mass-market paperback. Hence, as the sales of hardcovers increased in the course of the 1990s and early 2000s, the market for mass-market paperbacks began to shrink. Publishers responded to this trend by making more use of the trade paperback format, which had been pioneered by Jason Epstein in the early 1950s when, as a young trainee editor at Doubleday, he came up with the idea of reprinting quality books in a sturdy paperback format, larger than the mass-market paperback, more expensive and on better-quality paper – the idea that underpinned Doubleday's Anchor Books and the many imprints at other houses that were soon modelled on it.[17] The shrinking of the market for mass-market paperbacks in the 1990s and early 2000s went hand in hand with the expansion of the market for trade paperbacks, as more and more hardcover books were put into trade paperback format rather than being repackaged as mass-market paperbacks. But the expansion of the market for trade paperbacks should not obscure the fact that the real revolution which transformed the industry in the 1980s and early 1990s was the massive growth in hardcover sales, stemming from the highly

---

[17] See Epstein, *Book Business*, ch. 2.

successful application to hardcover publishing of a set of values and practices that had been first developed in the world of the mass-market paperback.

The rise of Amazon

As Barnes & Noble and Borders were rolling out their national chains of superstores, a new mode of bookselling was beginning to emerge that would add another dimension to the reshaping of the retail landscape that was taking place in the 1990s: online bookselling. The key player here was, of course, Amazon. The brainchild of Jeff Bezos, a Princeton computer science graduate, Amazon.com opened for business from a suburban garage in Seattle in July 1995; by the end of 1998 it had become the third largest bookseller in the US.[18] Amazon's sales grew at a phenomenal rate throughout the late 1990s, increasing from $15.75 million in 1996 to $610 million in 1998, but so too did its losses: by 1998, Amazon was reporting losses of $124.5 million, which was more than 20 per cent of its turnover. By 2000, Amazon's cumulative losses were a staggering $1.2 billion. Achieving profitability became an increasingly urgent corporate goal. In 2003 Amazon reported its first net annual profit of $35 million on net sales of $5.2 billion. By 2007 it was reporting net income of $476 million on net sales of $14.8 billion.

Spurred on by the astonishing growth of Amazon in the late 1990s, others began to enter the online bookselling market. Barnes & Noble had watched the rise of Amazon with growing concern, and in March 1997 it opened its own online bookstore, b&n.com. In 1998 Bertelsmann, which had already been planning to launch its own internet business, BooksOnline, acquired a 50 per cent stake in b&n.com for $200 million and rolled its proposed US operation into it. By 1999, b&n.com was posting sales of $202 million, making it the fifth largest bookselling establishment in the US. Barnes & Noble bought out Bertelsmann's stake in b&n.com in 2003, and the following year it took full control of the online business. Although b&n.com is separate from Barnes & Noble and has a different corporate structure, the two companies work closely together and collaborate on the purchasing and managing of inventory, among other things. This

---

[18] Robert Spector, *Amazon.com: Get Big Fast* (London: Random House, 2000), p. 216.

gives b&n.com a certain competitive advantage vis-à-vis Amazon, its main rival, since it enables b&n.com to draw on a more extensive range of in-house inventory. The Borders group also launched its own online operation in 1997, but Borders.com trailed far behind Amazon and b&n.com, achieving sales of only $27 million in 2000. In 2001 Borders announced that it was handing its loss-making online operation over to Amazon, which became responsible for running the operation, fulfilling orders and providing customer service.

The great advantage of the online retailers is that they are able to offer a huge range of titles, many times more than the bricks-and-mortar bookstore. When Amazon.com started business, it claimed to offer over a million titles – 'Earth's Biggest Bookstore' was the tagline – compared with about 175,000 titles in the largest terrestrial bookstore in the US. But of course, the comparison was not entirely fair, since Amazon's listings were derived from the database of *Books in Print* and the books were not actually held as inventory. Amazon relied heavily on the major wholesalers, Ingram and Baker & Taylor, to supply the inventory: when Amazon received an order from a customer, it ordered the book from one of the wholesalers, unpacked it when it arrived in its Seattle distribution centre, repacked it and mailed it to the customer. This model had the huge advantage of being inventory-free, but the disadvantage was that it was relatively slow since books had to be ordered and mailed twice. So in 1996 Amazon began to expand its warehouse capacity and to build regional distribution centres, enabling it to fulfil orders more quickly and reduce the costs involved in double-handling the books. But the more Amazon moved in the direction of warehousing its own inventory, the more capital it tied up in physical stock and real estate, and the more it began to resemble a traditional retailer and to experience the financial pressures and problems associated with conventional bricks-and-mortar operations.

The online retailers competed with one another and with terrestrial bookstores not only in terms of the range of titles offered and those held in stock, but also by deep discounting. Amazon was preoccupied with 'the customer experience', and its research had led it to conclude that the three things that mattered most to book-buying customers were selection, convenience and price. By offering over a million titles it could excel on selection; by being open 24/7 and aiming to ship books directly to the customer as quickly as possible, it could score high on convenience; and by discounting a substantial proportion of its titles it could compete against the superstores on price. Amazon offered a discount of 10 per cent on 300,000 titles, a discount of 30 per cent on the top 20 hardback and top 20 paperback titles, and a discount of 40 per cent on a select number of titles. When b&n.com went live in 1997, it offered discounts on 400,000 titles, including discounts of up to 50 per cent on some bestsellers. To some extent, the online retailers could offer deep discounts of this kind because their overheads were lower than those of bricks-and-mortar book-stores, but they continued to offer substantial discounts despite the fact that they were running losses year on year because they regarded this as crucial to their ability to compete with the superstores. Both Amazon and b&n.com also introduced free shipping on orders over a certain amount to ensure that the total price of purchases remained low.

From its original base in the US book market, Amazon expanded its operations overseas and diversified its product range. A significant proportion of Amazon's client base had always been overseas, but in 1998 Amazon moved directly into the European market by acquir-ing the British online bookseller Bookpages and the German online bookseller Telebuch and using them to launch Amazon.co.uk and Amazon.de. Other international branches were subsequently opened in Japan, France and Canada. By 2007, 45 per cent of Amazon's revenue was being generated outside of North America. Amazon also diversified beyond its core business of books, in part by acquiring other online retailers and adding them to what was rapidly becoming a vast online shopping centre. In 1998 it added music CDs and videos, in early 1999 it moved into toys and electronics, and in September 1999 it launched zShops, an online shopping zone offering a wide range of goods from clothes and household appliances to pet supplies.

By 2006, online bookselling accounted for about 11 per cent of the book retail market in the US.[19] This included all online booksell-ers, but Amazon had become by far the largest player with around 70 per cent of the online book market. In just ten years Amazon had risen from nothing to become one of the most important retail outlets for publishers – indeed, for many university presses and smaller pub-lishers, Amazon had become their single most important customer. Even the large trade houses soon found that Amazon was among their top two or three accounts – one large house said that Amazon represented about 8 per cent of its business overall in 2006 and was growing by around 20 per cent a year. For some kinds of books, like

---

[19] Oda and Sanislo, *The Subtext 2007–2008 Perspective*, p. 64.

hardcover non-fiction, Amazon's market share was already as high as 20 per cent.

For publishers, the meteoric rise of Amazon and other online retailers was a welcome addition to the existing channels to market. At a time when terrestrial retailing was being consolidated increasingly in the hands of the large retail chains and many independents were falling by the wayside, the emergence of online retailing represented a major reconfiguration of the bookselling business. It proved to be particularly good for selling backlist titles and books of a more specialized kind, or books by authors who were not already well known, which the bricks-and-mortar bookstores were becoming less inclined to stock. One of the appealing features of Amazon as a retail channel – for publishers as well as authors – is that it responds quickly and visibly to demand: the more frequently a book is ordered on Amazon, the higher it is ranked in Amazon's sales rankings. So even if a book is not strongly supported by the central buyers at the retail chains, it can find an effective market through Amazon; and if it does particularly well on Amazon, the central buyers at the chains may, on occasion, reconsider their initial decision and place a more substantial order after all. 'Every retailer looks at Amazon all the time,' explained one bookseller who used to manage a team of central buyers for a major chain. 'Because it's live, it's an honest chart, it changes frequently on real sales and you can see that in action. So you can fix something in a day if needs be. You can order stock and it can be there the next day. And that's something you have to really get engrained into the culture of the buyers – if you make a mistake don't panic; you can fix it very easily.'

At the same time, the rise of Amazon, and of online bookselling more generally, created new dangers for publishers and exacerbated some old ones. For one thing, the online environment proved to be particularly well suited to the selling of used books, as online retailers like Biblio, AbeBooks and Alibris could operate as clearing houses for hundreds of small used-book merchants who were spread across the country and, indeed, the world. When Amazon and b&n.com entered the used-book market, acting as clearing houses for used-book merchants and listing used books alongside new books in the search results, this brought much larger customer bases into the used-book market – not just individuals who were specifically looking for used books and were familiar with the specialist online booksellers who supplied them, but anyone who was buying books online. While college textbook publishers in the US had been accustomed to dealing with the used-book market for many years, used-book sales were now becoming a matter of growing concern for trade publishers as well. And there was some evidence to suggest that their concern was not without foundation: a survey carried out in 2005 suggested that sales of general trade used books reached $589 million in 2004, up 30 per cent from 2003.[20] Total used-book revenue in 2004 exceeded $2.2 billion and while textbooks and other course materials represented the largest share (73 per cent), most of them sold through college bookstores, the most dramatic growth was in the area of general trade-book sales and in sales through online channels. At a time when overall sales growth in the industry was very modest, a growth of 30 per cent in used-book sales was very worrying indeed, since used-book sales, while very profitable for booksellers, contributed nothing to the revenues of publishers or the royalties of authors.

A second concern for publishers was that, as Amazon grew in size and became an increasingly important channel to market, so too it became more powerful and more able to use its size as a bargaining tool to try to extract better terms and conditions from publishers – higher discount, more co-op advertising money, better payment terms and so on. Publishers were accustomed to facing pressure from the large retail chains for better terms and conditions, but now they were faced with similar pressure from a new player that was rapidly becoming one of their most important customers. 'Whether it's payment terms or co-op or freight, there are lots of ways that 800-pound gorillas can force you into things,' reflected one seasoned sales director. 'Do I worry about that? Sure I do. The bigger they are, the more power they can wield.' His worry was reflected in his behaviour: he hesitated to talk about these issues, my questions were followed by pregnant pauses while he carefully weighed up his words, and he asked me more than once for reassurance that his comments would not be attributed. No sales director would wish to fall out with what has become one of his most important customers. And there is always the fear – not entirely groundless, as we shall see – that Amazon might use its ability to remove books from its site or disable the 'buy' button as a weapon in the struggle to improve its terms of trade. The fact that Amazon is a large and growing customer for most publishers, that it is much bigger than any other online retailer and that it is also a very *visible* site, in the sense that many readers will look for books on Amazon and many authors will go to Amazon to check the

---

[20] *Used-Book Sales: A Study of the Behavior, Structure, Size, and Growth of the US Used-Book Market* (New York: Book Industry Study Group, 2006), p. 9.

availability of their own books, has put Amazon in a strong negotiating position. It could be very damaging for a publisher if its books were no longer listed on Amazon, or if they were listed but not available for purchase: being available on Amazon has increasingly become the litmus test of availability per se.

The growing role of mass merchandisers

Bookstores, whether independents or chains, were never the only outlets for books: as noted earlier, they were also commonly sold in non-specialist retail outlets like drugstores and department stores. In the 1980s and 1990s, publishers found new outlets for books in the expanding chains of large discount stores, like Wal-Mart, Kmart and Target, and in the emergence of the warehouse stores – the so-called Price Clubs. Sam Walton opened his first Wal-Mart Discount Store in Arkansas in 1962; within five years it had become a chain with 24 discount stores across the state. From the 1970s on, Wal-Mart expanded its chain, first by opening stores in neighbouring states and then by expanding across the US and overseas. By 2005 Wal-Mart had 3,800 stores in the US and 2,800 elsewhere. Wal-Mart had become the largest retailer in the United States, Canada and Mexico; it had also become the second largest grocer in Britain, thanks to its acquisition of Asda in 1999 for $10 billion.[21]

Wal-Mart opened its first warehouse club, called Sam's Club (after Sam Walton), in Midwest City, Oklahoma, in 1983, but the origin of the warehouse store is usually attributed to Sol Price, an attorney from San Diego. Having inherited a vacant warehouse in the early 1950s, Price encouraged a number of wholesalers to fill it with an assortment of goods ranging from jewellery and furniture to alcohol, which was sold at wholesale prices to a membership which consisted of government employees. The business, which he launched in 1954 under the name of FedMart, was a success, and when Price sold it in 1975 it had grown into a chain of 45 stores. Building on the success of FedMart, Sol Price and his son Robert founded the first Price Club store on the outskirts of San Diego in 1976. The retail concept was simple: sell a broad range of goods in high volume and at low prices, usually at around 10 per cent mark-up from the wholesale price. In

---

[21] Charles Fishman, *The Wal-Mart Effect: How an Out-of-Town Superstore Became a Superpower* (London: Penguin, 2006), p. 6.

order to maintain low prices, overhead costs were kept to a minimum: products were stocked on pallets or high shelves on the warehouse floor, the warehouses themselves were located on cheap industrial land on the outskirts of cities and staffing was minimal. Restricting the membership reduced the risk of bad cheques and shoplifting, and modest membership fees helped cover the overhead costs. After an initial disappointing year, the Prices broadened the membership to include employees of hospitals, financial institutions and utilities, and this proved sufficient to enable the business to grow. By the mid-1980s, the Prices had opened 20 warehouses, most of which were in California, and the company was generating profits of $45 million on sales of $1.9 billion.

The success of Price Club spawned many imitators, including Costco Wholesale Club, Sam's and BJ's. Costco was co-founded by James Sinegal, who had worked with Sol Price at FedMart and the Price Company before leaving to form Costco with Jeffrey Brotman in 1983. Costco was based on principles very similar to the Price Club, and from its original base in Seattle it quickly became a major competitor. Sam's Wholesale Club was established by Wal-Mart in 1983 and grew rapidly; by 1993 Sam's had pulled ahead of Price Club and become the largest wholesale club in the US, with 434 stores and nearly half the market. Partly as a response to the threat from Sam's, the Prices decided to merge with Costco, which then ranked third among the wholesale clubs in terms of overall revenue. The new company, PriceCostco, proved to be an unstable union; Robert Price left the company in 1994, and in 1997 it changed its name to Costco Wholesale. Costco and Sam's are now the leading wholesale clubs and are of roughly similar size; with a turnover of $64.4 billion in 2007, Costco has the highest sales volume, though Sam's, with 713 stores, has more retail outlets.

The rise of the mass merchandisers, including Wal-Mart, Kmart, Target and the wholesale clubs like Price Club, Sam's, BJ's and Costco, created a wide range of new retail outlets where books could be sold. These were retail venues that reached deep into the community and had a high level of throughput in terms of shopping traffic: it is estimated that 90 per cent of Americans live within 15 minutes of a Wal-Mart store, and each year 93 per cent of American households shop at least once at Wal-Mart.[22] From roughly the mid-1990s on, these mass-merchandising chains became increasingly important

---

[22] Ibid., pp. 5–6.

Table 2   Market share of major accounts for two commercial bestsellers

	Market share (%)	
	2005 novel	2008 novel
Barnes & Noble	13	15
Borders	8	11
Costco	21	18.7
Wal-Mart	15.8	18.2
Sam's	17	11
Target	7.5	5.9
Amazon	2.9	5.4

Hardcover sales for the first three weeks after publication.

retail outlets for certain kinds of books – for bestsellers above all, and especially for bestselling commercial fiction by brand-name authors, selling initially in hardcover and subsequently in mass-market paperback. 'They carry very few books,' explained one sales analyst at a large publishing firm, 'but on the books they carry, they sell a lot.'

Table 2 shows the market share of the major US retailers for the sales of two bestselling novels by a leading commercial fiction writer. One book was published in 2005 and the other in 2008; the figures are based on sales of the hardcover edition during the first three weeks after publication. While the market shares for each account vary somewhat from one book to the next, the overall pattern is clear: Costco is the single largest account, with a 21 per cent market share for the 2005 book and 18.7 per cent for the 2008 book; Wal-Mart and Sam's (which is owned by Wal-Mart) are among the next most important accounts, with market shares of 15.8 and 18.2 per cent in the case of Wal-Mart and 17 and 11 per cent in the case of Sam's. Taken together, the mass merchandisers (including Target) account for over half of the sales of these books during the first three weeks of sale – 61.3 per cent in 2005 and 53.8 per cent in 2008. Barnes & Noble's market share was 13 per cent in 2005 and 15 per cent in 2008, while Borders had 8 and 11 per cent. Taken together, the book superstore chains accounted for roughly a quarter of the sales (21 per cent in 2005 and 26 per cent in 2008). Amazon's share grew from 2.9 per cent in 2005 to 5.4 per cent in 2008. These seven accounts – four of the key mass merchandisers, the two book superstore chains and Amazon – accounted for 85 per cent of the sales of these bestselling hardcover books during the first three weeks after publication. All remaining outlets – including the remaining chains such as Books-A-Million and all the independent bookstores taken together – accounted for only 15 per cent of sales.

The sales pattern illustrated by these two books is particular to this type of book – that is, a commercial bestselling novel by a brand-name author, released initially in hardcover. For other types of book – for a work of literary fiction, for instance, or a biography or serious work of non-fiction – the distribution of sales by channel would be very different: Barnes & Noble, Borders, Amazon and the independents would account for a larger share, while the mass merchandisers would have a much smaller share (and, for most books, no share at all). The sales pattern by channel varies greatly from one category of book to another, one format to another, one author to another and, indeed, one book to another. The sales distribution also varies by type and format of book from one mass merchandiser to another, reflecting in part the different demographic profiles of their customers. For example, Wal-Mart tends to do better with commercial fiction in hardcover and mass-market paperback, whereas Target, with its more affluent customer base, tends to do better with trade paperbacks. The mass merchandisers offer a very limited range of bestselling books, carefully selected for their customers. They discount heavily, sometimes by as much as 43 per cent – charging, say, $15.95 for a hardcover with a list price of $27.95. Other retailers, including the book superstore chains, find it difficult to match these prices. 'The clubs, and Wal-Mart and Target, stole the bestseller business from the superstore chains, just as the chains had stolen the bestseller business from the independents before that,' explained the sales analyst. 'And they did it because of discounting, which is exactly how the chains stole it from the independents.' Margins are wafer-thin, but the mass merchandisers are able to make books profitable by keeping their overheads to a minimum and by achieving high sales volume. The books are often stacked on pallets or tables and are kept in stock only as long as they are selling at a certain rate – typically, for one major wholesale club, at least 1,800 copies a week for new hardcovers. Books that are selling more slowly than this are returned to clear the space for other titles. Hence the return rates from the mass merchandisers tend to be high – generally around 50 per cent, but returns can be as high as 80 per cent for some books. This is a high-volume, low-margin business where the sales opportunities are great – the mass merchandisers can shift large numbers of books – but the risks

Table 3   Estimated shares of US book retail market, 2006

	Percentage	Estimated dollars in millions
Superstores/chains	45	5,571
Libraries, schools	16	1,980
Independents	13	1,609
Internet	11	1,362
Bookclubs/mail order	10	1,238
Other (mass merchandisers, wholesale clubs, drugstores, etc.)	5	619
Total		$12,380

Sales data from Book Industry Study Group; book sales only (excluding music, magazines, gifts, stationery, cafés, etc.).
Source: Stephanie Oda and Glenn Sanislo, *The Subtext 2007–2008 Perspective on Book Publishing* (Darien, Conn.: Open Book, 2007), p. 64.

in terms of returns are also much higher than they are in other retail channels.

The dramatic changes in the marketplace over the last 40–50 years have produced a retail landscape that is a far cry from the array of independent bookstores, department stores and other outlets where books were sold in the 1950s and before. Table 3 provides an estimate of the retail book market in the US in 2006, broken down by channel. The superstores and book chains accounted for about 45 per cent of the $12.4 billion retail book market, while the independents accounted for around 13 per cent.[23] Online retailers accounted for around 11 per cent of the market, with book clubs and mail order accounting for another 10 per cent. Other outlets, including the mass merchandisers and warehouse clubs, probably accounted for around 5 per cent overall, although on certain bestselling titles their market share would have been much higher, as we have seen. This is a marketplace in which, over a period of some 40 years, there has been a dramatic shift of market share from a plethora of independent booksellers and stores (whether drugstores or department stores) to large retail chains

---

[23] The retail book market represents only part of total book sales. US sales for all books, including tests for the educational market, were $38.08 billion in 2006, an increase of 3.1 per cent from 2005. Unit sales for all books (excluding tests) were flat in 2006 – 3.1 billion units, an increase of 0.5 per cent from 2005. See Oda and Sanislo, *The Subtext 2007–2008 Perspective*, p. 1.

– first the mall store chains, then the superstore chains and now the mass merchandisers and wholesale club chains – and to online retailers (especially Amazon). It is a shift in which a handful of major retailers – Barnes & Noble, Borders, Amazon and, for certain kinds of bestsellers, Costco, Wal-Mart, Target and Sam's – emerged as the key customers for publishers and as key players in the struggle to gain visibility for books and bring them to the attention of consumers in an increasingly crowded marketplace. This small set of key retailers has come to wield enormous power in the field of trade publishing, since publishers do not sell directly to consumers but depend increasingly on these retail giants to make their books available to consumers and encourage them to buy.

The peculiarities of the British

The transformation of the retail landscape in the United States was mirrored by similar changes in the UK; most of the players were different, some of the customary practices were peculiarly British and the consequences were in some respects more radical, but the overall pattern was the same. For most of the twentieth century, the British book trade had been regulated by the Net Book Agreement – an informal arrangement between publishers and booksellers that had been proposed by Macmillan in the 1890s following a period of turmoil and intensive price competition in the publishing industry.[24] The Agreement was based on the idea that publishers would set a fixed or 'net' retail price for each book they published; booksellers would agree to sell the books at the net price in return for a discount that would enable them to make a reasonable margin. Any bookseller who broke the rules would not be supplied on trade terms by the publishers. The Agreement came into force on 1 January 1900 and remained in place for nearly the whole of the twentieth century, creating a relatively stable commercial environment for publishers and booksellers.

The NBA was not without its critics, however, and it was challenged on numerous occasions. In 1959 it was referred to the Restrictive Practices Court, a special tribunal that had been established by the Restrictive Trade Practices Act of 1956, and the case was heard

---

[24] See John Feather, *A History of British Publishing*, 2nd edn (London: Routledge, 2006), pp. 100–2.

in 1962.[25] The Registrar of Restrictive Trading Agreements argued that the NBA was an illegal price-fixing cartel which acted against the public interest, whereas the publishers and booksellers associations argued that, given the cultural and educational value of books, it was in the public interest to have a wide network of stock-holding bookstores and that this would be destroyed if underselling were allowed, leading to a decline in the quality and quantity of books published. The Chairman of the Court ruled in favour of the publishers and booksellers and the NBA survived.

The reprieve, however, was only temporary. The NBA faced renewed pressure in the early 1990s from a number of retailers and consumer publishers who wanted to experiment with discounting in the hope that lower prices would drive a higher volume of sales. Terry Maher, head of the Pentos retail group which had acquired Dillons – an academic bookseller with its main store in Gower Street, London and a couple of small campus bookshops – in 1977 and begun to roll out a national chain of bookstores in the late 1980s, had always opposed the NBA. 'I just thought the Net Book Agreement was stupid – it was an irritant,' he recalled. 'When we had a few shops, it didn't matter that much, but once we had a national chain and we were branding Dillons nationally, it became more of an irritant.'[26] Dillons began experimenting with price promotions in 1989, including an attempt – cut short by an injunction secured by the Publishers Association – to discount the titles shortlisted for the 1990 Booker Prize. In 1991 Reed Consumer Books withdrew from the Agreement – the first of the major publishers to do so – and in August 1994 the Director General of the Office of Fair Trading decided that the NBA should be reviewed again by the Restrictive Practices Court. A period of confusion and uncertainty followed. In September the Publishers Association announced that it would defend the NBA and the following day Tim Hely Hutchinson – then CEO (chief executive officer) of Hodder Headline – announced that he was going to de-net their books on the day after Christmas. In September 1995 Random House and HarperCollins both announced that they would no longer be bound by the Agreement, and shortly after the retailer WH Smith –

---

[25] Ibid., p. 202.
[26] Terry Maher, in Sue Bradley (ed.), *The British Book Trade: An Oral History* (London: British Library, 2008), p. 228. For a full account of Maher's campaign against the Net Book Agreement, see Terry Maher, *Against My Better Judgement: Adventures in the City and in the Book Trade* (London: Sinclair-Stevenson, 1994), ch. 4.

previously one of the staunchest defenders of the NBA – announced a major de-netted promotion with them. The NBA was effectively dead. In March 1997 the Restrictive Practices Court sealed the coffin by ruling that the NBA was illegal. From this point on, retailers were free to discount books and to sell them at any price they chose.

Prior to the dissolution of the NBA, Britain had experienced the growth of book retailing chains in a way that was somewhat similar to the US. In the 1970s and before, WH Smith, the general high-street bookseller, newsagent and stationer, was the most important player in the retail book market in Britain. Originally established as a wholesale newsagent and stationer in London's East End at the end of the eighteenth century, WH Smith had expanded rapidly in the nineteenth century thanks to a series of exclusive deals with the major railway companies to operate bookstalls in railway stations.[27] By the 1970s WH Smith probably controlled as much as 40 per cent of the retail book market in the UK. The rest of the market was accounted for by some well-established, traditional independent booksellers, like Hatchards of Piccadilly, a few small chains like Blackwell and Hammicks and a plethora of small independent bookstores. Unlike the United States, Britain had not experienced the rise of mall bookstore chains in the 1960s and 1970s, as this phenomenon was linked to the social geography of the American city, with the migration of the middle classes to the suburbs and the growth of the suburban shopping malls based on high levels of car ownership.

The bookselling environment in Britain began to change significantly in the 1980s, thanks in large part to the rapid rise of Waterstone's and Dillons. Tim Waterstone joined WH Smith in the late 1970s but was sacked in 1982. At the time he had been working on a paper on bookselling in Britain and had come up with a plan for a new kind of bookstore – 'a store which would have an extraordinarily well-informed inventory, extraordinarily well-informed staff and a sort of messianic desire to sell books, independent bookselling at its best, but to have them as a chain,' as he put it. He managed to raise £6,000 to open his first bookstore in the Old Brompton Road in London, and then raised further finance to roll out a chain of stores across the country. These were large bookstores in central, high-street locations, filled with huge amounts of stock including many backlist titles and designed in ways that were attractive to customers and conducive to browsing. The stores were similar in conception and

---

[27] Feather, *A History of British Publishing*, p. 94.

design to the superstores that were being opened by Barnes & Noble and Borders in the US in the 1980s but the idea appears to have been developed independently.[28] While Waterstone's was actively expanding its national network, the Pentos Group began, from 1986 on, to roll out a national chain of bookstores under the Dillons brand; by 1989 it was operating 61 bookstores across the country. A third chain was started up in 1987 by James Heanage, an entrepreneur with a background in advertising who had spotted an opportunity to develop a network of attractive, well-run bookstores in small and medium-sized towns in southern England; the first two Ottakar's bookstores were opened in Brighton and Banbury in 1988 and the chain continued to expand over the next decade. By the end of the 1980s, there were two major bookselling chains rolling out stores nationwide and a third chain opening bookstores in the smaller towns and cities of southern England. The volume of retail space for books was expanding rapidly and dramatically. All three chains were competing against one another and taking market share away from WH Smith. They were also forcing many independents out of business, partly through predatory activities and partly because many of the independents were poorly run businesses which simply could not compete with much larger and more professionally run bookstores, just as in the US.

The rivalry between Waterstone's and Dillons was brought to an end in the course of the 1990s, when the UK book retail sector underwent a process of consolidation. In 1993 Tim Waterstone sold the company to his former employer, WH Smith, for £49 million and the business was integrated with 48 Sherratt & Hughes stores, which were converted into the Waterstone's brand. As an autonomous business within the WH Smith Group, Waterstone's expanded rapidly and became the leading specialist bookseller in the UK. In 1998 Waterstone's was sold to the HMV Media Group, which had been set up, under the chairmanship of Tim Waterstone, by the music corporation EMI and an American venture capital group called Advent, in order to acquire Waterstone's and merge it with Dillons. HMV had bought Dillons in 1995 when the Pentos Group, which owned Dillons at the

---

[28] Tim Waterstone had spent some time in New York when he was working for WH Smith in the late 1970s and was familiar with Barnes & Noble, but at that time Barnes & Noble was known primarily for its large discount store on Fifth Avenue and had not begun to roll out its book superstores. 'I wasn't looking at Barnes & Noble and Borders in the 1980s, not at all,' he recalled. 'I was just obsessed with what I was doing here, frankly.'

time, was declared bankrupt. The HMV Media Group paid £300 million for 115 Waterstone's stores and £500 million for EMI's two chains – 78 Dillons stores and 271 HMV music stores. For a year the two rival bookselling brands were maintained, but in 1999 the Dillons name was dropped and the stores were rebranded as Waterstone's. In 2002, the HMV Group operated 197 Waterstone's stores, mostly in the UK and Ireland, as well as 328 HMV stores selling music, videos and games. WH Smith also expanded its holdings in the 1990s, using the proceeds from its sale of Waterstone's to acquire the 232 stores of the Scottish-based John Menzies chain in 1998, bringing the total number of branches in WH Smith's high-street and travel chains to 741.

By the end of the 1990s, the absorption of Dillons into Waterstone's had put the newly expanded Waterstone's in a dominant position in the UK book retail market, but it also marked the beginning of a period of change for the retail giant. HMV's music stores were very successful at the time, and the management at HMV decided to apply to Waterstone's some of the retailing principles that had worked so well for the music stores – including a greater emphasis on campaigns and front-of-store promotions, higher stock turn and reducing the range of inventory. It was a model that went against the grain of Tim Waterstone's conception of bookselling: 'HMV wanted to go into the mid-market, to reproduce in the book market what they had so brilliantly done in the music market. But it just did not work in books, and I didn't even want to try it in books,' he explained. 'Waterstone's depends on heavy inventory, it depends on heavy investment in stock, it depends on the quality of its backlist. If you start dragging the inventory out, what you're doing is dragging out the backlist. And once you start dragging out the backlist, the whole character of the bookselling changes. You're left with a frontlist, and if you're left with a frontlist then you're led into a discount war.' In 2001 Tim Waterstone resigned as chairman.

In the late 1990s and early 2000s, Waterstone's also faced threats from new players who entered the market. In 1997 the US-based Borders Group expanded into the UK by acquiring Books Etc.; within five years Borders was operating 37 Books Etc. stores and 21 superstores in the UK and had become one of Waterstone's major competitors. But the overseas expansion of Borders didn't last; Borders sold the UK business in 2007, as noted earlier, and allits stores in the UK were closed down in 2009.

The other US-based book retailer who entered the UK market proved to be more resilient. Having acquired the British online bookseller Bookpages in 1998, Amazon quickly expanded its presence in the UK and took a growing share of the market. By 2006 internet booksellers had captured around 11 per cent of the retail book market in the UK – the same share as in the US – and Amazon was overwhelmingly the largest player. While Amazon sells across the whole range of books, it is particularly well suited to selling the more specialized books and older backlist titles, thus eroding the revenue that Waterstone's and other bricks-and-mortar bookstores were able to generate from backlist sales.

The other set of key players that entered the British retail book market in the late 1990s were the supermarkets – Tesco, Asda and Sainsbury's. It was the collapse of the Net Book Agreement in the mid-1990s that cleared the way for the entry of the supermarkets into the retail book market. Prior to that, the supermarkets had been largely uninterested in bookselling; the only books they sold were bargain books. The reason was simple. For supermarkets, the ability to compete on price is crucial – it is one of the key ways they are able to secure competitive advantage vis-à-vis other retailers. So long as the Net Book Agreement was in place, the ability to use price as a competitive tool for the sale of books was simply not available to them. However, once the NBA had gone, books became an attractive addition to the non-food mix of the large supermarkets. Part of the strategic aim of large supermarkets like Tesco was to grow non-food to be as strong as food, and non-food 'can be funerals, it can be garden centres or whatever we're going into now,' explained one former buyer for Tesco. 'Books were seen to be part of entertainment and part of consumer's disposable income.' But the supermarkets had to be able to sell the books at prices that were sufficiently low that 'it's not considered a purchase any more – it's, you know, stick it in the basket.' Once the NBA had collapsed, the supermarkets could negotiate terms with publishers that would enable them to discount heavily and achieve the kinds of prices they felt they needed to make books a 'stick it in the basket' good. And books had some additional advantages for the supermarkets. They were one of the few goods that could be returned to the supplier if they didn't sell, thus protecting the retailer from the risk of being left with lots of unsold stock on the shelves. And they were one of the few products in a supermarket sold with a recommended retail price printed on it, so shoppers could see how much cheaper they were able to buy it at the supermarket.

The supermarkets started with paperbacks, and then three or four years later began to move into frontlist hardcovers and children's books. So in the course of the late 1990s, a diversified book offering evolved within the supermarkets. The major supermarket chains brought in specialized book buyers who worked at the head offices and were visited regularly by sales reps from the major publishing houses. The buyer's priority was 'chart' – that is, books that were either on, or were likely to make it on to, the paperback or hardcover bestseller lists. The supermarkets watched the bestseller lists produced by newspapers like the *Sunday Times* but they also produced their own bestseller lists, based on their own sales records. Even the largest supermarket stores had a limited amount of shelf space devoted to books, so the buyer had a small number of slots – maybe six or twelve slots, depending on the store – which could be filled with new titles every two weeks. Titles move up and down the chart and they stay on the shelves so long as they're selling. If the book continues to sell well it will be kept on the shelves – 'Something like Martina Cole could be there for eight months.' But if the sales fall off or are simply too low, the title is pulled out of the stores and returned to the publisher.

The impact of these changes in the retail landscape in Britain in the late 1990s and early 2000s was dramatic. For trade publishers, the changes meant that a declining proportion of their sales was coming through traditional book retail outlets and a growing proportion was coming through non-traditional outlets, especially the supermarkets. This can be seen from table 4, which gives the breakdown of sales by channel for a major UK trade house in 2000 and 2006. In 2000, Waterstone's and Ottakar's together accounted for 28 per cent of sales; by 2006, their joint share had fallen to 23 per cent. (In 2006 Waterstone's bought Ottakar's; they are grouped together here for both 2000 and 2006 in order to establish a common point of comparison.) WH Smith's share fell slightly from 13 per cent in 2000 to 12 per cent in 2006. Other chains, including Borders, Books Etc., Blackwell and others, accounted for 11 per cent in both years. Independents' share fell significantly, from 8 per cent in 2000 to a mere 3 per cent in 2006. Wholesalers fell from 14 per cent to 9 per cent. By contrast, internet sales – and these are overwhelmingly Amazon – rose from 2 per cent in 2000 to 7 per cent in 2006; even these figures probably underestimate the real volume and increase in online retail sales, since Amazon and other online retailers acquire some of their stock from wholesalers. However, the most striking percentages in this table are those indicating sales through the supermarkets, which doubled from 12 per cent in 2000 to 25 per cent in 2006. For this trade house, sales through the supermarkets accounted

Table 4. Sales by channel for a major UK trade publisher, 2000 and 2006

Channel	2000 (%)	2006 (%)
Waterstone's/Ottakar's	28	23
WH Smith	13	12
Other chains	11	11
Independents	8	3
Wholesalers	14	9
Library	4	2
Travel	8	9
Internet	2	7
Supermarkets	12	25

for a quarter of their sales in 2006, and the supermarkets had over-taken Waterstone's in terms of sales volume. Moreover, whereas Waterstone's share was declining over time, the share accounted for by online retail (Amazon) and by the supermarkets was increasing rapidly. These non-traditional outlets were the growth areas for this and other trade publishers, whereas the traditional bricks-and-mortar booksellers were either static or declining as sales channels.

In June 2011 the HMV Group announced the sale of Waterstone's to the Russian billionaire Alexander Mamut for £53 million. HMV was facing serious financial difficulties, with declining sales and high levels of borrowing, and the sale of Waterstone's was part of a broader strategy aimed at reducing its overall debt and securing new lending agreements with its creditors. The new owner of Waterstone's installed James Daunt as managing director. As the founder of Daunt Books, a small independent bookselling chain in London, Daunt had forged a reputation for running attractive, high-quality bookstores that served a loyal customer base. Managing a large nationwide chain of bookstores that face growing pressure from the supermarkets, from Amazon and from the growth of ebook sales will be a challenge of an altogether different order.

We shall return in later chapters to the consequences of these enormous changes in the retail landscape of bookselling in the United States and Britain. But first we must examine the other structural transformations of the publishing field.

2

THE RISE OF LITERARY AGENTS

The origins of the literary agent

The second factor shaping the evolution of English-language trade publishing in recent decades has been the growing power of the agent. The literary agent is not a new figure in the publishing field: the first professional agents appeared in London in the late nineteenth century.[1] The mechanization of printing technologies in the nineteenth century and increasing literacy had helped to create an expanding market for newspapers, periodicals and books, thus creating a growing demand for written material. Informal literary agents began to appear in the 1850s and 1860s, posting advertisements in periodicals like the *Athenaeum* soliciting stories for newspapers and other publications. But the first professional literary agent is a designation usually reserved for A. P. Watt, a Scotsman from Glasgow who began his career as a bookseller in Edinburgh before marrying the sister of publisher Alexander Strahan and moving to London to work as a manuscript reader and advertising manager in Strahan's publishing firm.[2] When Strahan's firm ran into difficulties in the mid-1870s, Watt began working as an advertising agent, a role that gradually evolved into a literary agent. His work as a literary agent appears to have begun around 1878, when he was asked by a friend, the poet and novelist George

---

[1] See James Hepburn, *The Author's Empty Purse and the Rise of the Literary Agent* (London: Oxford University Press, 1968); Mary Ann Gillies, *The Professional Literary Agent in Britain, 1880–1920* (Toronto: University of Toronto Press, 2007).
[2] Hepburn, *The Author's Empty Purse*, pp. 52ff; Gillies, *The Professional Literary Agent in Britain*, pp. 27ff.

MacDonald, to sell his stories for him. He did so initially as a friendly favour – something that others had done before him – but he soon saw the commercial possibilities. By 1881 Watt was advertising himself both as a literary agent and as an advertising agent. He began by charging his clients a fee for specific tasks but soon decided to switch to the system he used as an advertising agent, charging a 10 per cent commission on the money earned by his clients for the transactions he completed. For two decades Watt had the field pretty much to himself, and by the end of the nineteenth century he was representing some of the leading writers of the time, including Walter Besant, Thomas Hardy, Rudyard Kipling and Arthur Conan Doyle. But by this time other enterprising individuals – notably Albert Curtis Brown and J. B. Pinker – had seen the opportunities and entered the field, advertising their services and competing with Watt to act as authors' agents.

It was not uncommon for the early agents to act for publishers as well as authors – they were often, in effect, 'double agents', seeking to find publishers and outlets for their writers' work, on the one hand, and seeking to dispose of serial or book rights for publishers, on the other. Watt conceived of his job as that of selling or leasing copyrights, and he was content to act in this capacity for publishers as well as authors. The fact that Watt occasionally worked for publishing houses did not, however, endear him to all publishers, some of whom saw the agent as a threat who would disrupt the traditional relationship between the publisher and the author and debase literature by emphasizing the commercial aspect. It was undoubtedly A. P. Watt whom the publisher William Heinemann had in mind when he penned his scathing portrait of the literary agent in 1893: 'This is the age of the middleman,' wrote Heinemann. 'He is generally a parasite. He always flourishes. I have been forced to give him some little attention lately in my particular business. In it he calls himself the literary agent.'[3] Heinemann's contempt notwithstanding, by the beginning of the twentieth century publishers in London were forced to come to terms with the existence of literary agents – they had become a reality in the publishing field. By acquiring a specialist knowledge of the different publishing houses, newspapers and periodicals that were interested in acquiring written material and willing to pay for it, agents were able to provide a range of services to authors – including placing material with suitable publishers and periodicals,

---

[3] William Heinemann, quoted in Hepburn, *The Author's Empty Purse*, p. 1.

negotiating terms and contracts and collecting payments and royalties – that were valued by many authors, including some of the leading writers of the time.

Literary agents began to appear in the United States at roughly the same time as their English counterparts. Among the most important of the earliest American agents was Paul Revere Reynolds, who began his career working for the publisher Lothrop in Boston before moving in 1891 to New York, where he was offered a job working as the American agent for the English publisher Cassell.[4] While his main duties were to look for American publishers who might be interested in publishing Cassell's books in America and advise Cassell on American books that might be of interest to them, he soon began to look for American authors who might be interested in publishing with Cassell. By 1895 he was acting for authors independently, offering their books to publishers and charging a 10 per cent commission on the business he transacted. Like Watt, Reynolds was working as an agent for both publishers and authors. He thought of himself as a middleman, a broker in the literary marketplace, arranging deals between the buyers and sellers of literary properties regardless of who they were.

From their beginnings in late nineteenth-century London and New York, literary agents gradually grew in number and their roles became more sharply defined. Agents increasingly came to see that their interests lay with their authors, and the ambiguous role of the double agent gradually evolved into the modern conception of the literary agent as an intermediary whose primary allegiance was to the authors who, in effect, employed them. This did not mean that agents were uninterested in the well-being of publishers. They needed to work with publishers and to maintain cordial relations with them, even if they were no longer working directly for them. For the most part they saw their role as one of mediating between authors and publishers, serving their authors by negotiating deals that both parties – authors and publishers – would regard as fair and reasonable. As Curtis Brown put it in 1906, the literary agent 'stands between the author and the publisher, and he ought to uphold better than either of them the importance of the greatest truism in trade, viz., that no bargain is ever really sound and honest without being profitable to both parties to it.'[5]

---

[4] Hepburn, *The Author's Empty Purse*, pp. 73ff.
[5] Albert Curtis Brown, '"The Commercialization of Literature" and the Literary Agent', *Fortnightly Review*, vol. 80 (1 Aug. 1906), p. 359.

This modern conception of the literary agent continued to shape the development of the profession throughout the twentieth century, but in the 1960s and 1970s new factors came into play that helped to increase the power of agents and altered the way in which some agents understood their role. The most important of these factors was the massive expansion of the market created by the rise of the retail chains. Beginning with the mall bookstore chains in the US and then the superstore chains in the US and the UK, books were increasingly made available to consumers in ways and on a scale that had simply not been possible before. Books were sold like other commodities in shopping centres and high streets, and the chains used the same retailing principles to sell books as they used to sell music, videos and other goods. As a result, they were able to sell a much greater volume, and books that were commercially successful were successful on a scale that was unprecedented. With the stakes increasing significantly, especially for bestselling authors, agents were in a stronger position to negotiate a growing share of an expanding revenue stream for their authors. And the more their authors earned, the more agents earned too, enabling them to expand and grow their own businesses.

A second factor that came into play was the growth of opportunities to exploit the rights associated with a work. Hollywood was hungry for material that could be turned into movies and the publishing industry was providing a steady stream of well-plotted stories that lent themselves to screen adaptations. Moreover, the global dominance of the English language meant that books written and published in English had the potential to be exploited in a multiplicity of markets around the world, both by selling English-language rights into different territories (most commonly, selling North American rights separately from UK and Commonwealth rights) and by selling foreign language rights (which again, in some cases, could be split in territorial terms – Spanish rights for Spain could be sold separately from Spanish rights for Latin America, for example). But to exploit rights effectively required specialist knowledge of different markets and a good deal of administrative support. Many publishers lacked this specialist knowledge and were simply unable or unwilling to provide the kind of concerted effort required.

A third factor was the appearance in the 1970s and early 1980s of a new breed of literary agents who came into the publishing field from outside and were not in any way attached to the traditional practices of publishers and agents. They understood the role of the agent differently, not so much as a mediator between author and publisher but as an unadulterated advocate of the interests of their authors – whom they thought of as their clients. Traditional agents, in their view, were too imbued with the ethos of the publishing world; they took for granted the traditional ways of doing things and preferred moderation and compromise to the kind of forthright advocacy that might run the risk of rocking the boat. The new agents had no such compunction. Some, like Morton Janklow and Andrew Wylie, rose from nothing to become some of the most powerful players in the field; their rise is both a symptom of and a testimony to a profound shift in the nature of agenting and in the relations of power that structured the publishing field. Without too much exaggeration we could describe the emergence of this new breed as the rise of the super-agent.

The rise of the super-agent

Morton Janklow came into the publishing industry by accident. He was a lawyer by training and was working as a corporate lawyer in a large New York law firm in the early 1970s when an old college classmate, Bill Safire, called one day and asked if he could help him publish a book he wanted to write about Richard Nixon. Safire had been working as a speech writer for Nixon and, with his insider's knowledge of the workings of the White House, he was aware that there was more to the Watergate scandal than had become clear at the time; he wanted to leave the Administration, become a journalist and write a book. Janklow didn't know anything about publishing, but he agreed to represent his old friend and try to find a publisher for him. He knew two people in New York publishing and he called them up, took them to lunch and asked them to send over a copy of their standard publishing contract. 'I called each of them after having read their agreement and said to them, "Let me ask you one question: does any right-minded author sign this agreement?" And they said, "Everyone signs this agreement. What don't you like about it?" "Almost everything," I said. "The date and the parties are fine but after that it's a mess." So I did some research, not because I intended to be in the business – this was a one-off as far as I was concerned – but because Bill was an important friend and I wanted to make sure he was properly represented.' Safire produced an outline for a book on Nixon, Janklow invited a number of different publishers to his office to see the outline, a bidding war developed and they sold the rights for around a quarter of a million dollars – at the time, an exceptionally high advance for a non-fiction book.

By the time Safire finished writing the book, Watergate had become a full-fledged scandal and American politics was consumed by the affair. The political climate had changed and the publisher, who had bought the book with such enthusiasm a year or so earlier, got cold feet; they decided they didn't want to publish the book after all and they wanted their money back. Janklow was incensed. He threatened to sue the publisher. 'No one ever tries to force a publisher to publish a book,' the publisher said. '"Oh," I said, "I'm not trying to force you to publish the book, I'm only trying to force you to pay for it. You don't have to publish it. Just give me the quarter of a million dollars and don't publish it, and I'll find someone else to publish it."' Janklow served the publisher with papers, it went to arbitration, he won and they ended up keeping the money and selling the book to another publisher. 'My client was happy, his reputation had been preserved, his book was getting published and I could go back to my law practice. And then the floodgates started to open. People started calling me and said, "You know, my agent never would have done that. My agent is a mediator between me and the publisher, he doesn't advocate my interest."' More and more authors came to him and asked him if he would represent them, and pretty soon this was crowding out his other work in the law practice. So he decided to change professions and set up a literary agency.

At the same time, he became increasingly aware that many authors were more important than publishers in encouraging people to buy books. 'I walked into a bookstore one day just to get a sense of the retailing side of the business and I realized that nobody goes in and says, "What's the latest from Knopf?" "What's the latest from Simon & Schuster or HarperCollins?" They say, "Where's the new Crichton?" "Where's the new Tom Wolfe?" So the writer is the star, much like the movie business. Nobody goes to see a Paramount movie, they go to see a new Tom Cruise movie. So I began to negotiate from the perspective of someone who thought he was in control of the negotiation. That had never been done before in publishing, as simple as it sounds.' He didn't feel constrained by the traditional practices and courtesies of the publishing world, since this was not a world in which he himself had been brought up or to which he felt any particular affinity. 'The other agents at the time tended to be old-timers. They considered themselves partners of the writer; they were literary people, not lawyers. The writer would say "I want this" and they'd say, "You can't have it, the publisher would never give it to you," and that was the end of it. The last thing in the world they did was advocate. They just advised.' By contrast, Janklow took the view that the author, not the publisher, was in the position of strength and that his job as literary agent was to act as the author's advocate, revising contracts if he felt they were unfair to the author. For instance, Janklow was unwilling to accept that the publisher, once it had entered into a contract with an author, should retain the unilateral right to reject a manuscript delivered by the author on the grounds that it was unacceptable:

> I developed a clause where I insisted that a standard be applied to the acceptability of a manuscript. The publisher couldn't just decide on its own, it was unacceptable. So you pick books when you went into a contract. The author is the author of these three books and the publisher agrees *now* that if the book under contract is written to that standard it will be deemed acceptable, and that no change in economic circumstance between contract and delivery date can affect the acceptability. That was an entirely new concept, never been done before. People were outraged at this, and for two or three years some publishers wouldn't sign the contracts. 'Fine, don't take the author,' I said, 'I'll sell him somewhere else. I'll break this system.'

Thanks in part to the actions of outsiders like Janklow, the traditional pattern of relationships in the publishing field was disrupted. The rights of authors were championed more vigorously by agents who thought of themselves less as intermediaries, mediating between author and publisher, and more as dedicated advocates of their client's interests. They conceived of their task primarily in legal and financial terms, and they displaced the centrality of the publisher by asserting control over the rights of their clients' work and deciding which rights to allocate to which publisher and on what terms. In their eyes, the publisher was not the central player in the field but simply a means to get what they wanted to achieve on their clients' behalf, which was to get their work into the marketplace as effectively and successfully as possible. The traditional relations of power between author and publisher were gradually overturned. 'It went from the publisher being king and the author being grateful for the opportunity to have his work presented to the public, to the author being king and the publisher being used by me and my author as a tool to get the book into the marketplace.'

Morton Janklow built up an extremely successful agency on the basis of a no-nonsense legal and commercial attitude that paid little heed to traditional publishing practices. His agency typically retained dramatic as well as foreign rights and devoted a great deal of attention to managing these rights as effectively as possible – 'We *orchestrate* the use of these rights and how they are going to relate to one another. The day I finish a deal, every part of that transaction is a symphony, and every segment has to play on key and in time.'[6] Foreign rights, film rights, serial rights – all are part of the symphony that, if carefully managed, can help to make a book a commercial success. He increased the commission to 15 per cent to help cover the cost of running a large office with numerous staff working in foreign rights and royalty rights management – a commission that has now become more or less standard in the industry. The clients of Janklow & Nesbit, as the agency is now called, include some of the world's most successful writers of commercial fiction, like Danielle Steele, Judith Krantz and Jackie Collins, as well as many well-known writers of literary fiction and serious non-fiction.

Like Janklow, Andrew Wylie entered the world of publishing with the attitude of an outsider. Commonly referred to by journalists as 'the jackal', he is famous, if not infamous, for his willingness to poach authors from other agents and for his tough-minded pursuit of high advances, practices that have earned him the wrath and respect of his colleagues in roughly equal measures. When he decided to set up a literary agency in 1980, he had no background in publishing; his father was an editor at Houghton Mifflin and he had studied romance languages and literature at Harvard, but he was a novice when it came to the business of publishing. Given his academic background in comparative literature, he wasn't particularly interested in bestselling works of commercial fiction. What interested him were works of enduring value that would sell over time, and the question he asked himself was whether he could build a viable business by representing the authors who were writing works of quality. When he looked at the big agencies in New York at the time, he was struck by the cosiness of the relationships they sustained with the publishing houses:

> When I looked at the big agencies I saw that the money goes from the publisher to the agent to the author. And because of that process and the direction of the revenue, the big agencies had very close relationships with the publishers, they were basically in bed with the publishers, and these people over here, the writers, were uneducated, uninformed, sentimental, self-interested fools, children. And they were

---

[6] Morton Janklow, quoted in Whiteside, *The Blockbuster Complex*, p. 60.

employed by the agencies to keep the agencies going with the publishing companies. There were examples I came across that were jaw-dropping examples of agencies feeling a primary fealty to the publishing companies. And what I realized, which was at the time revolutionary – it sounds strange to say it but it's true – was that I was employed by the writer. And my job was to become strong enough by virtue of my employers – not by myself, my employers' strength – so that I could act directly in their interests with the publishing community who could do nothing except do what I wanted because of our strength, because of who we represented. So I needed a large number of employers. They had to be very high quality; we would corner the market on quality, as it were, and we would drive up the price.

The three key components of Wylie's strategy were to build up a critical mass of quality writers; to be extremely attentive and aggressive in pursuing their interests; and to be international. Unlike Janklow, Wylie self-consciously positioned himself at the quality end of the literary marketplace, partly because it concurred with his own literary tastes ('I wanted to enjoy my life, so I didn't want to read Danielle Steele'), partly because there was less competition and partly because he believed it was a better way to build a business in the long run. There was less competition because at that time, around 1980, most agents and publishers were pursuing bestselling authors whose books could be sold in large quantities through the retail chains. Tom Clancy, Stephen King and Danielle Steele were in great demand while Philip Roth, Saul Bellow and Salman Rushdie were, relatively speaking, neglected. It was a better way to build a business in the long run because it was backlist oriented: the sales were lower but they lasted longer, and therefore they delivered a more stable, less risky form of revenue in the long term. 'The best business is to have on your roster one hundred authors who will be read in a hundred years, not two authors who will be read in a hundred days. So I'm sorry but we're going to demand a better deal, a more accurate appreciation, of the value of the contribution being made to the bottom line of a publishing house by someone like Roth.'

So Wylie set out to build up a large client base of authors who were writing what he thought of as quality work, both fiction and non-fiction. Some were not represented but many were, and this is where his controversial practice of poaching authors came into play: he would call up authors whom he knew were already represented by other agents and point out the shortcomings of their current arrangements, calling their attention, for example, to the fact that

some of their earlier books were out of print and that, with the concerted effort of an agent, they could all be brought back into print,
or that their books were not available in languages and countries
where there could be a substantial market. For many agents, this
practice was regarded as beyond the pale: it infringed the norms to
which they believed the community of agents should adhere. 'It's
gross,' said one agent, clearly incensed by the practice; 'it's like steal-
ing someone's girlfriend.' But Wylie had no truck with moral com-
punctions of this kind:

> I think it's lazy or quaint or both to assume that one doesn't poach.
> It is pretending that publishing is a business peopled by members of
> a social elite who have a sort of gentlemanly game going, and the
> gentlemanly game was played to the disadvantage of the writer. If a
> writer as an independent contractor is paying an agent a fee to look
> after his or her business properly and that business is not being looked
> after properly, then it seems to me that the writer deserves to know
> this. They deserve to know the difference between an agency that is
> not aware that the writer's rights in the Netherlands are unexploited
> and one that is. They should be paying the agent who knows that
> these rights are available in the Netherlands and can sell them with
> one phone call, not the agent who doesn't have the systems to figure
> out that their books are not available in this country. So to hell with
> them frankly.

Wylie was not in business to make life comfortable for other agents
but to improve the position of authors who were writing the kind of
quality work he wanted to represent, and if he ruffled the feathers of
other agents in the process, as indeed he did, then so be it.

The second aspect of Wylie's strategy was to be extremely attentive
and aggressive in pursuing his client's interests. The needs and wants
of each client had to be carefully understood, since each person has
a different set of requirements, and their wishes then executed as
efficiently as possible and to their satisfaction. And the stronger his
client base as a whole, the more able he would be to achieve what
any individual client wanted. 'If a new writer says, "I want to jump
over the wall," I can say to them, "That can be arranged." And they
say, "But I'm this little person, how can you put me over that wall?"
I can say, "Well, you know, there are five hundred other writers we
represent and you're going to climb on all their shoulders."' Wylie
was also unapologetic about pursuing his clients' interests aggressively, especially when it came to negotiating advances. 'We get

criticized as an agency for being aggressive in getting Philip Roth and Salman Rushdie and Susan Sontag paid a lot of money. But they're not paid a lot of money at all. Paid a lot of money is Danielle Steele and Tom Clancy. Tom Clancy is getting $35 million a book. Michael Crichton is getting $22 million a book. Philip Roth is getting $22 million a lifetime. But 20 years from now the only one who will be selling is Philip Roth.'

So why was Wylie so determined to secure high advances for his authors? Like many agents, Wylie believes that the only thing that will ensure that a publisher gets behind a book and publishes it energetically is the size of the advance they pay: the more they pay, the more they will get behind the book, prioritize it, put resources behind it and try to make it a success – 'It's an iron law.'

> The only pressure a publisher reacts to is the pressure of the profit and loss statement that they sign up to when they acquire a book. And so if you're trying to sell a book you have to get a high advance. The number of copies printed is in direct relation to the advance paid to the author, not to the experience of reading the book and deciding, 'Ah, this is *The Magic Mountain* and this is not' but rather 'Ah, I paid Thomas Mann a million dollars and I paid him $100,000.' If I paid Thomas Mann a million dollars I'll print 200,000 copies. If I paid him $100,000, I'll print 30,000 copies. Everything is set based on the P&L, which is based on the price.

Many publishers would disagree with this cold assessment of the way that publishers determine their publishing priorities and allocate their resources, and editors and sales directors will cite numerous examples that appear to defy Wylie's iron law. But the fact that some agents proceed on the assumption that this law holds – and undoubtedly there are aspects of the way large publishing houses work which lend support to this assumption, as we shall see – means that the aggressive pursuit of high advances has become a guiding principle for some sectors of the agenting world.

The third strand to Wylie's strategy was to develop the agency on an international level. This was important because 'quality sells over time and it sells internationally', and if you have the systems in place to exploit rights effectively in the international arena then you can generate substantial additional revenue streams both for the author and for the agency. But most agents did not have good systems in place to exploit international rights. They either handled these poorly and inefficiently, or they relied on sub-agents who acted on their behalf in foreign language markets, or they ceded foreign rights to the publisher who acquired English-language rights. In Wylie's view, neither sub-agents nor English-language publishers are likely to be incentivized in the same way as the agent who is working closely with the author. 'If you understand the writer's aims you can actually make things happen around the world with the same level of commitment that you can make things happen here in the US.' So, for example, when Philip Roth writes a new book, an agent who is on the ball can do a foreign rights deal in Spain or Italy, not for one but for 27 books. By carefully managing the copyrights, he can ensure that, once the licences for the existing Spanish or Italian editions of his books have expired, the licences can be assigned to a new publisher. 'The new publisher now has 27 Roth books to publish and I can't tell you how incentivized they are. They paid a whole lot of money for the new book and a whole lot of money for all the old books. And all of a sudden you've got enough mass so that Philip Roth is approaching, in terms of the publisher's commitment to Roth, the level of Tom Clancy or Danielle Steele. All of a sudden the playing field is level, and if the playing field is level, Shakespeare wins.' As manager of his clients' copyrights, the agent is usually in a position to determine which rights to assign to which publishers. A publisher may want to acquire world rights in all languages and may signal their wish to bid for them, but it is the agent who has the power to decide, in consultation with the author, whether to cede world rights or to fragment the rights into different markets by language and region of the world. Doesn't this lead to fights with publishers? 'There are skirmishes,' says Wylie, 'but they are not of a seriousness that would allow you to distinguish their intention by calling it a fight.' The large publishing houses have become global corporations with subsidiaries operating in many different countries and languages, as we shall see; but in this new globalized arena of the printed word it is the agent, not the publisher, who controls the keys.

Andrew Wylie remains something of an outsider, a pariah even, in the world of literary agents, and his willingness to poach authors from other agents is viewed with contempt by many of his contemporaries. But even those agents who despise some of his methods are inclined to concede that he has changed the rules of the game. 'Andrew is completely outside the establishment,' observed one senior agent. 'He's a brilliant man and he's been brilliantly successful. He's operated outside the system and I think he's had a great influence, particularly on the way some younger agents operate. He's probably changed the landscape of agenting more in the past 15 years than any other single individual.'

The proliferation of agents

Morton Janklow and Andrew Wylie epitomized a new breed of literary agents who entered the field in the 1970s and 1980s as outsiders and developed an approach to the advocacy of their clients' interests that was much more assertive and aggressive than the approach that had been adopted by many agents in the past. Not all agents followed their lead or approved of their methods, but as their agencies grew in size and strength, it was difficult for other agents to ignore them. They were models – albeit controversial – of a new kind of literary agent and a new style of agenting, many of the features of which would become increasingly commonplace in the course of the 1980s and 1990s.

At the same time, the 1980s and 1990s witnessed an explosion in the numbers of agents operating in the metropolitan centres of English-language trade publishing – in New York and London. Surprisingly, there are no accurate statistics on the growth in the number of agents over the last couple of decades. The Association of Author Representatives – the professional association of literary agents – listed 424 members in 2008 but this tells us very little, since many agents and agencies, including some of the largest and most powerful agencies, are not members. One New York agent reckoned there were 1,500 agents in America, '97 per cent of them being based in New York which is where the heart of mainstream publishing is', but this was just a rough guess. The absence of accurate statistics is partly a reflection of the fact that literary agenting always was, and still remains, an unregulated profession. Anyone can set himself or herself up as a literary agent – all you need to do is call yourself an agent, hook up a telephone (and now an internet connection) and display some knowledge, however slight, of how the industry works.

While there are no accurate data on the numbers of agents operating in the US and the UK today and on how these numbers have changed over time, we can get some sense of the increase in numbers by examining the names of agents and agencies used in book deals in recent years. Publishersmarketplace.com – on online service that is well known for hosting *Publisher's Lunch*, a popular newsletter for publishers and agents – has monitored the names of agents and

Table 5   Numbers of agents and agencies in recorded deals, 2004–2008

	2004	2005	2006	2007	2008
Agents	811	954	1,019	1,006	1,018
Agencies	471	554	578	555	569

Source: Publishersmarketplace.com, 2009.

agencies used in deals in the US, Canada and the UK since 2004. Their data are not comprehensive: they cover only deals reported to them by a party to the transaction, plus a small number of deals gleaned from third-party publications, so agents doing small deals on the margins of the field are unlikely to show up in their figures; but their data represent the only large-scale compilation of information we have on book deals in the English-speaking world. Table 5 shows the number of agents and agencies involved in the book deals monitored by publishersmarketplace.com between 2004 and 2008. In 2004, 811 agents' names were used in deals; by 2008 this number had risen to 1,018 – an increase of 25 per cent. In 2004, 471 names of agencies were used; four years later this number had risen to 569 – an increase of 20 per cent. Even though the data are not comprehensive and relate only to a brief period between 2004 and 2008, they attest to a significant growth in the numbers of agents and agencies in the field.

So why has the number of agents grown significantly in recent years and decades? Part of the explanation lies in the increasing supply of well-qualified individuals in the publishing field who found themselves either without a job or dissatisfied with the direction their career was heading. The increasing supply was due largely to the changes that were taking place at this time in the publishing houses themselves (changes that will be examined more closely in the following chapter): in essence, the growing consolidation of publishing houses forced out many publishers and managers – including some very senior and experienced publishers who were very knowledgeable about the industry. There were others who were not forced out but who found themselves working for large corporations that were requiring them to work in new ways, and some chose to leave and set up shop as agents rather than adapt to a new set of practices with which they had little sympathy. 'There were many publishers like me who became agents in the 90s,' explained one London-based agent.

And we became agents partly because we were casualties of the consolidation of the industry and there weren't as many jobs for people like us, and partly through inclination. I wanted to see what it was like being an agent – that was 15 years ago and I can say that it's pretty good. You have a remarkable degree of freedom of action. You don't have to enlist the support of your colleagues for what you want to do. We do not, as agents here, consult each other about the authors we take on. In a publishing house, an editorial meeting has to make a collective decision. Here, provided you're paying the bills, provided you're paying for yourself, there is complete freedom of action. There's almost none of the bureaucracy which plagues publishing these days. And the other thing is that you're close to the source. I'm in publishing because I like working with authors, and as the agent you are, generally speaking, the first point of contact with the author.

But the increasing supply of well-qualified individuals is only part of the explanation: the other side of the story is that there was a growing demand for agents. There were various reasons for this but two stand out as particularly important. First, with the consolidation taking place in the publishing houses, editors became increasingly mobile. Some were forced out and some chose to leave; some were headhunted by the new corporations seeking to develop their publishing programmes and others moved to new companies in search of better salaries and better jobs. It was a time of turbulence and change and the traditional bonds between authors and editors were breaking down. 'Writers saw that their interests weren't being protected,' observed one agent. 'They either had to stay with the publishing house and lose their editor or they had to move with the editor and lose their backlist. So they needed someone who was really on their side.' The agent increasingly became the writer's primary point of contact with the publishing world. Most writers had neither the time nor the inclination to try to stay abreast of all the changes that were taking place in the industry – most were, as the same agent explained, 'absolutely clueless about this business they were tangentially involved in'. They needed an agent to look after their interests and deal with a world that was becoming less personal and more corporate, more complex and more businesslike, by the day.

There was another reason why writers increasingly needed agents: they did so because, in the course of the 1980s and 1990s, the agent effectively became the *necessary point of entry* into the field of trade publishing. In the 1970s and before, an agent was an optional extra for a writer; there were many authors who published with trade houses and worked directly with editors, without the mediation of an agent. By the late 1990s, however, an agent was a necessity: a writer who wanted to publish with a major trade house now *needed* an agent. Of course, there were exceptions. Even in the large corporate publishing houses in the early 2000s, there were cases of authors who signed contracts directly with the publishing house and didn't have an agent, though these cases were rare (and have become increasingly so). 'I only have one or two authors that I can think of who don't have agents and both of those are now getting agents,' said one senior editor at a major New York house. 'If I have a hundred books under contract, maybe 3–5 per cent would be without an agent or lawyer.' In fact, most of the major houses in New York and London will no longer accept submissions from authors who don't have agents, and if they do get submissions from unagented authors – perhaps passed on to them from one of their other authors – they will usually suggest to the author that they get an agent.

At first glance this may seem surprising: why should editors and publishers encourage authors to get agents when they know that agents are likely to up the ante and drive a harder bargain than most authors, left to their own devices, would be inclined to do? Part of the answer is that most editors and publishers don't want to negotiate financial and contractual details with authors. They prefer to differentiate between the creative process of writing and editing, on the one hand, and the business aspects of negotiating advances and contracts, on the other, and they find it easier and less awkward if the business aspects are handled by agents who, like them, are professionals in the business of publishing. The agent may be sitting on the other side of the table but they are at least sitting at the same table and they know the rules of the game. Dealing with agents simplifies the negotiation process even if it raises the stakes, because agents have been through the negotiation process many times before and they 'know what to ask for', as one senior editor put it. It is less likely that time and effort will be wasted discussing contractual niceties that are of little import. It also protects the editor from having to become too involved with authors in a day-to-day way. 'They don't have time these days,' explained one agent, 'so they don't want someone calling them up at night, they don't want someone calling them up in the morning and they don't want to listen to the ins and outs of someone's divorce. The agent filters out what can be relayed, explains some of the things that need explaining, and the editor gets a concise version of whatever the issue is rather than another 45-minute conversation with someone. I feel like I have the long conversations with authors so that the editors don't have to.' Many editors and publishers also recognize that a good agent can help an author to develop their ideas in ways that will improve the quality of the work, adding real value – something that may be of particular importance for new writers who are still finding their way. 'It's often better to have three heads working on it than two,' the same editor continued. But there are other reasons, more profound than either of these, that help to explain why publishers and editors in the major houses tend to prefer their authors to be agented.

As publishing houses have become increasingly consolidated, the workload of individual editors has tended to increase and they have come to rely increasingly on agents to provide the initial screening of projects: editors have, in effect, outsourced the initial selection process to agents. 'Publishers look at us as being their first readers,' said one senior agent, 'and they assume that if something is coming from this agency then it's going to be worth their while to look at it whether they make an offer or not.' This simplifies the editor's job in certain ways, as it means that they can rely on agents to do the initial scouting for new talent by scouring the pages of the literary magazines, travelling to conferences and literary festivals, visiting college campuses and so on. Just as importantly, it can be left to agents to wade through the slush piles of letters, emails and manuscripts, trying to find the occasional gem among the mind-numbing quantities of unsolicited dross. Agents provide the first filter in the system of selection through which new book projects get channelled into the publishing business. For the most part it is agents, not editors or publishers, who are expected to discover new talent, to find new writers whom they think are promising and to work with them to turn an idea or draft manuscript into something that an editor or publisher would recognize as an attractive project and potentially successful book. This can be a very demanding and time-consuming process. Often it leads to nothing, though occasionally a manuscript may turn up that, with a certain amount of guidance from the agent, can result in a project that will be taken on by publishers and may even turn out to be a great success.

However, the outsourcing of the initial selection process to agents is not simply a matter of reducing the workload for editors and publishers: it's also a matter of spreading the risks of judgement. As we shall see in a later chapter, one of the key characteristics of trade publishing is that, for a large part of the frontlist (leaving aside the brand-name authors), no one really knows how well a new book is going to do. It is a high-risk business in which serendipity plays a large role. Hence editors and publishers are constantly looking for ways to back up the risky judgements they have to make every time they decide to take on a book by a new author, or a book by an author who does not have a clear track record and established readership. In this context, the fact that an author and a book project have been taken on by an agent is in itself important, and who the agent is matters greatly, because editors and publishers come to trust certain agents as reliable sources of content. At the heart of trade publishing there is what I shall call a *web of collective belief* and, in the absence of clear-cut evidence to support judgements, the backing of a trusted agent lends credibility to authors and books. In a business where judgement is inherently risky and success is often dependent on a host of intangible and unpredictable factors, sourcing your new books from agents with whom you share similar tastes and sensibilities and who have a track record of success in spotting new talent is an entirely understandable – though eminently fallible – way of spreading the risks.

So while at first glance the interests of publishers and agents would seem to be diametrically opposed, in practice they are locked together in a system of reciprocal interdependency and mutual benefit that has certain advantages for both. Agents need publishers and ideally a multiplicity of them, so that they can place their authors' books, secure sizeable advances and ensure – or try to ensure – that their books are effectively marketed and sold. But editors and publishers have also come to see agents as necessary players in the field to whom they can outsource certain tasks which they no longer have the time or inclination to do, and whose judgements and track records provide them with a valuable resource for their own decision-making processes. Authors, for their part, are pretty much obliged today to try to find an agent if they want to be published by a mainstream trade house, since they have little chance of placing their book with a major publisher unless they have the backing of an agent (though this does not apply to authors who are content to publish with a small independent press on the margins of the field, as we shall see).

Agents and agencies vary greatly in terms of their size, power and influence: like the publishing world more generally, the world of agenting is hierarchically structured. Agencies range from well-established, multimedia agencies with numerous divisions, of which book publishing is only one, like ICM (International Creative Management) and Curtis Brown, to small boutique agencies run from small offices or even from the agent's home or apartment, with many variations and gradations in between. Even the largest agencies are, however, relatively small concerns, and few have more than a dozen agents dealing specifically with books, though with support staff their numbers will be more. (The total staff of Curtis Brown, one of the largest and most diversified agencies in London, comes to only 65, which includes 33 agents, 10 of whom are book agents.)[7] Just as with publishing houses, the standing of any agency in this hierarchical world is dependent on the kinds and quantities of capital they possess – on their economic capital (in most cases quite small), their human capital (their staff and especially their agents), their social capital (their networks and contacts), their intellectual capital (the rights and copyrights they control) and their symbolic capital (their prestige and the respect accorded to them by other players in the field). Any individual agent will be able to leverage some of the capital accumulated by the agency for which he or she works – not only its financial resources but also its networks and contacts and the reputation that the agency has acquired in the field – and this undoubtedly makes his or her job easier. But all agents, regardless of their standing, are expected to generate a revenue stream of their own by cultivating their own contacts, building their own client list and establishing their own reputation in the field. How do they do this?

Building a client list

The world of agenting is very diverse – there is no single, agreed set of procedures. The ways that agents operate vary from agent to agent and from agency to agency, and the problems they face depend on who they are, their background, their experience and the kinds of books they are selling. In some cases individuals with some standing in the industry are invited to join an agency by the existing owner or partners – this was often the case with successful editors who were either forced out by the consolidation within the industry or who became dissatisfied with their jobs and were looking for a change. These individuals brought with them a great deal of social capital, since they had been in the business for a long time and had many connections with editors and authors. They also brought with them a great deal of insider knowledge about the business of publishing, and a good feel for what editors and publishers were looking for.

---

[7] See Eric de Bellaigue, '"Trust me. I'm an agent": The Ever-Changing Balance between Author, Agent and Publisher', *Logos*, vol. 19, no. 3 (2008), p. 114.

When an individual like this joins an agency, they may inherit some clients from an agent who is overloaded or one who has retired or is about to retire, but they will also need to go out and actively search for new clients. One agent who had previously been an editor described the process like this:

> When I came here, I inherited about a dozen authors that were already here from an agent who had retired. That was really good for me because I had something to start with, but it wasn't enough. So I went out to look for more. I went to the creative writing schools, I used a contact that I had with the director of one of these schools and I would say to him, 'Can I come up and talk to the students?' and we would go out to dinner afterwards and he would tell me who was good and so on. Well, you know, everyone's playing that game. I wrote to promising people who I thought were writing interesting things. One of my favourite clients is someone I wrote to when he'd written a piece in a magazine and I wrote to him and said, 'You look to me like somebody who should be writing a book,' and out of that came a very successful book and the author is now an established novelist and so on and so forth.

In addition to finding clients through active initiatives of this kind, many agents will get new clients by taking on authors who are referred on to them by their established clients, who act effectively as scouts for them, or by other agents who are too busy to take on new clients, or even by publishers who refer authors to them. 'Publishers who feel that authors should have agents will say, "Ah, so-and-so has been at that agency for a couple of years, he's building his list – why don't you talk to him?"' added the agent quoted above. 'I think they think it's inevitable that these authors will have agents and that they'd like these authors to have the kind of agents they'd like them to have rather the kind of agents they wouldn't like them to have.'

The individual who becomes an agent after having been an editor or publisher will usually find it much easier to build a client list than the young agent who starts as an assistant and then slowly works his or her way up the ladder, although this is how many agents begin. The publishing industry – both in literary agencies and in publishing houses – remains largely an apprentice-based industry. 'You really have to work under a mentor in order to make inroads,' explained one young woman who started as an assistant and had been working as an agent for about a year. 'So much of it is connections. You can't take a class on how to become a literary agent. You have to work at an agency to learn it.' By joining an agency and working as the assistant to an established agent, an individual learns how the business works and picks up the tricks of the trade. They also tend to imbibe the ethos of the particular agency in which they are working or of the particular agent for whom they are working, learning their distinctive ways of doing things and making them their own. Each agency has a character and culture of its own, often shaped by the personal views and values of the founder or founders who remain active in many agencies, and the younger members of staff who aspire to become agents will tend to take their bearings from the agent or agency for whom they are working. While much of their time will be taken up by dealing with correspondence and handling contract work for their boss, promising assistants are often given some scope to start building a client list of their own. In addition to their basic salary, they may be given a small commission on any sales they make. Some of their clients may be overspill clients whom their boss passes on to them, some may be clients who have written to them or whom they've discovered in the slush pile and some may be clients they have actively sought out by going to writers' conferences or reading articles or short stories in magazines or newspapers. Aspiring agents of this kind are particularly hungry to find new talent because it is the only way that they will be able to advance their career in the world of agenting.

For some assistants, the opportunity to progress and become an agent in the agency where they are working will eventually come, though it may be a long apprenticeship. 'From the time you walk in the door and sit down as an assistant I truly believe that it's going to be five years before you can fully and confidently call yourself an agent,' explained one senior agent who had herself risen through the ranks and who has trained many younger agents. 'It doesn't matter whether you've sold five books or fifty books by then, it's five years before you get the nuances down.' Some assistants stick with it and are gradually given more latitude to build their own client list, but others find that they have to move elsewhere in order to create the time and space to develop their own career. 'I was making so little money and I wasn't able to figure out a way to fully have my own list,' explained one young agent. 'If one of my former boss's big clients called and she was out they were so used to having me as their assistant that they would ask for me, even though I was no longer the assistant, and they would say, "Oh, can you read my novel overnight," and of course I would do it because I still worked for the agency and that was our agency's biggest client. But it was really becoming a drain.' So this young agent moved to another agency which was recruiting for a junior agent position, where she found that she had more freedom to do her own work and build her client list, unimpeded by expectations that stemmed from her previous work as an assistant.

Some junior agent positions of this kind pay a straightforward salary, some pay a low base salary plus commission and some are commission-only posts. Where the agent is earning a commission, it will be on the basis of an agreed split with the agency – that is, the 10 or 15 per cent commission earned by the agency will be split on an agreed basis between the agent and the agency, which could be anything from a modest 20 or 30 per cent share to incentivize a junior agent whose primary job is administrative to 50:50 (50 per cent to the agent and 50 per cent to the agency), 60:40 or even, in the case of more experienced agents or those who work from home, 80:20. The commission-only agents either earn their commission as and when they sell their books, or earn it on a 'draw'. 'A draw means that your agency assumes you're going to earn $X,000 a year on commission and pays you as if you're going to earn that,' explained one young agent. 'If you earn more by the end of the year, it's almost like a bonus and they pay you the extra. If you earn less, depending on your agency, they will either ignore it or ask you to pay it back.' For those young agents who work on a commission-only basis, it is often very difficult to make ends meet. 'I've been here for a year,' this agent continued, 'and I'm not completely earning my living on my commissions yet. It's a business you have to grow.' She relied on savings, her husband's income and some freelance editing work to make ends meet. A year later she had moved to another agency where she was offered a better deal.

Given the task of building a list, young agents generally have a much tougher task than those agents who come into the business with some previous experience and standing in the world of publishing; they lack the social and symbolic capital of their more established colleagues and have to accumulate it more or less from scratch. Sarah had been working at a New York agency on a commission-only basis for about a year. She explained that, at this stage of her career, she was eager to build her client list and was trying to sign up one, possibly two, clients per month. She typically received over a hundred unsolicited queries a week from prospective writers, all of which she read but the vast majority of which she declined to pursue – less than 1 per cent were followed up. Occasionally one of the one or two clients Sarah signed each month came from the 400-odd unsolicited queries she received every month, 'out of the proverbial slush', which means that for this young agent, who was hungry to find new clients and paying more attention to unsolicited queries than most experienced agents would have time to do, the chances of a prospective writer getting taken on over the transom were less than a quarter of 1 per cent. Most of Sarah's new clients were the result of her own searches, but even this method was haphazard and usually resulted in disappointment. Magazines and journals were her principal source. She regularly read a host of women's magazines like *Marie Claire* and all the literary journals – the *New Yorker*, *Mississippi Review*, the *Missouri Review*, *Paris Review*, *Tin House*, etc. She would find writers whose work she liked but the chances of signing them as clients were slim:

> I spend maybe $50 a year on my *Tin House* subscription and maybe in all the issues I've read I'll find three writers I'm interested in, because they seem like they're at that point in their life where they're good writers and they're getting published and they haven't been discovered. So they're ready to be discovered. So I reach out to them. And out of those three what usually happens is that one is already represented, one doesn't have a book-length work to show and the third has a book-length work that I request, that I read and that I don't like or it's not ready or it's not saleable. So it's just very difficult. It's like looking for a needle in a haystack. It's a hustle – you're constantly hustling. You're constantly looking – especially when you're me, when you don't have a stable of clients who are bringing in regular income writing a book a year. You're constantly looking for the next great client and trying to get them before someone else does.

A young agent struggling to build a client list will constantly come up against the problem of poaching, since many of the good writers who are publishing in the literary magazines will have already come to the attention of other agents who are similarly seeking to add new clients to their lists. In most agencies, young agents will be careful to avoid overt poaching, not only because it is likely to be regarded as improper behaviour by the more established people in the agency and would be condemned by them but also because they fear that it would damage the one resource that they are most in need of at this stage of their career – their reputation. 'It's a very small business,' explained Sarah, 'and if you get a reputation for poaching clients, nobody's going to want to work with you. That kind of thing can spread to the writers' community, clients might not want to sign with you, authors might not want to come to you, editors might not want to work with you, agents might not refer clients to you. It's bad for your reputation, and the one thing you don't want is a bad reputation.'

While the taboo against poaching is keenly felt by most agents, and especially by the young agents who are struggling to establish themselves, it is a taboo that is sufficiently vague to allow every individual to find their own way of accommodating themselves to it. Sarah had worked out her own way of drawing the line between what she regarded as acceptable and unacceptable behaviour. 'I'm actually thinking of two writers now that I'd love to poach,' she confided, just after having explained with some conviction why she felt it was bad behaviour, 'and there are subtle ways of feeling out if they are unhappy in their situations.' She elaborated:

I read a short story in a literary journal that I loved and I said to myself, 'This writer has to be mine, I want this writer.' So I Googled him and I found the writer and his contact information and way down on the third page I found that he was agented. My heart sank. I saw that the agent was on the younger side, so I drafted an email to this writer which said 'Dear so-and-so, I loved your story, it touched me in so many ways. I'd love to take you out for lunch. Please tell me that you're not agented so that I can take you out.' That leaves the door open because the person could write back and say, 'I'm sorry but I'm agented and I'm happy with my representation,' in which case I'd write back and say, 'I'm so happy for you, I'm so glad you're in such good hands and I look forward to reading your next work.' Or this person could write back and say, 'I'm unhappy with my representation, I'm reconsidering it and I'd love to meet with you.' If they're already unhappy, I'd be willing to meet with them, even though I think it's dangerous. In other words, I'm going to pretend that I never got to the third page of that website and only stayed on the first two pages. That's a subtle way of doing it.

Even in this case, Sarah explained, she would wait for the writer to break things off with their existing agency and come back to her before she formally asked him if she could represent him. 'I would want them to make the decision independently and separately.'

For some agents who are seeking to build their client list, there is a pivotal moment, which often happens by pure chance, that suddenly gives their career a boost and puts them on the map of agents. It might be a surprise phone call, a writer who gets referred to them by a friend or a manuscript that comes in over the transom – many young agents live in hope that their careers will be suddenly transformed by a serendipitous event of this kind. One senior agent who had been in the business for 20 years reflected on the fortuitous occasion that launched her career:

> Fairly early in my career, I was an assistant to a very well-known literary agent and was working on a Friday afternoon in the summer – something which is unheard of in this industry – because I had stuff to catch up on. I answered a phone call and it was from an author who'd written a novel. He was not at all well known at that time – he had published a couple of non-fiction collections with a small Midwestern university press. We spoke for an hour and a half and at the end of the call he said, 'Can I send you the book?' I said, 'Sure you can, but I'll need to pass it on to someone else at the agency.' He said, 'That's fine, but I really think this book is quite good and I really enjoyed this conversation, so I think you'd be the right person to handle it.' I'd just started taking on clients so I read it and passed it around to the other agents at the agency who were more senior than I was and they all said, 'Go with God.' And that was X [a bestselling novel that went on to sell over 4 million copies in the US, was made into a film, translated into 25 languages and sold more than 50 million copies worldwide], and that got me started on my trajectory to agenting.

Not all agents are as lucky as this one was. Some struggle for years and never manage to sell a book for over $100,000, let alone happen upon a bestseller. 'I've been an agent for three years and I still have never made a six-figure deal. What can you do?' said one young agent. But at the end of the day, the standing of any agent in the field is indissolubly linked to the success or otherwise of the particular books they have sold and authors they have signed. Their client list is their CV, and their reputation as an agent, together with the trust they are able to elicit from editors and others, is shaped by the clients they represent and the rewards and awards – both financial and symbolic – that the books they sold have produced and received.

As an agent builds his or her list, the problems they face begin to change. They reach a point – and this may happen quite quickly with a successful agent, after four or five years of building a client list – when they have a good stable of authors and when the time and energy they have available to take on new clients is now much more limited. Most agents, including very senior and established agents, will say that they always try to remain open to new authors, even if admitting that it becomes more and more difficult. 'I'm much less open than I used to be,' said one well-established New York agent, 'simply because there are only so many hours in the day. I tend not to shed clients, I'm very loyal to the clients I've taken on, and mercifully very few clients have ever left me, so I don't have that many slots to fill. But I would never want not to be looking for new writers because there is a thrill to discovering an unpublished writer that is different from the thrill of the success of a writer that you'd already discovered.' For the established agent, the problem increasingly becomes one of balancing the interests of existing clients with the natural inclination of most agents to want to renew their lists by taking on new authors. Most agents' lists will effectively divide themselves into active and inactive authors, as some authors go quiet for a long time while they work on a new book or stop writing altogether. This enables the agent to concentrate their time and attention on those authors who are productive and whose work is selling well while allowing the less active authors to remain almost passively on their list. Most agents are reluctant to cut loose an author whom they've taken on, however inactive they may be. Partly this is because they see the bond with their clients as one of loyalty and mutual commitment: if an agent was prepared to cut loose their less productive clients, then what would stop their more successful clients from cutting them loose in turn? Partly it's also because even the most inactive author can, on occasion, surprise you. 'Authors you think have become inactive will suddenly come back with a wonderful new book,' observed one agent. 'It's five years since you last made a contract and now you're making a new contract and suddenly there's momentum again. The pleasures of the unexpected are of course one of the great pleasures of this business.'

While most agents are very loyal to their clients and hope for their clients' loyalty in return, there are occasions when agents and authors part company. There are occasions when an agent will come to the view that it is no longer worth their while to represent a particular client, usually because they find themselves investing a great deal of time and effort in reading drafts of material that ends up going nowhere, though they tend to present such parting of the ways as a separation by mutual consent. One agent described how he spent six years reading drafts of a second novel which never really worked, and eventually he decided to submit it to publishers because he didn't know what else to do with it. One by one, the publishers turned it down, 'and eventually [the author] and I looked at each other in the face and just realized that I wasn't doing him any good anymore. Certainly the idea of even looking at another draft of anything that he was ever going to write just filled me with dread. And he's gone to another agent.' The other side of this equation is that most agents and agencies are dependent financially on a relatively small proportion of clients whose books are exceptionally successful, and the possibility of losing one of these key clients is a constant fear. 'You look at any business in our neck of the woods and somewhere between 70 and 80 per cent of our income is generated by somewhere between 20 and 30 per cent of our clients,' explained the same agent. 'That's a scary equation and sometimes it's even worse than that, with the ebb and flow of people's successes. And then suddenly you look at it from behind my desk and think, "Jesus, if we hadn't had X and Y, we would be in real trouble."' There are different ways that an agency can lose a key client – they might become ill, die or simply decide to take a break from writing. But the possibility of losing them to another agency is always a risk:

> There is no doubt at all that there are certain circumstances at certain points in an agency's existence where a certain kind of client – and I've seen it happen, though never, thankfully, been on the receiving end of it – will go, 'I'm now such a successful author that part of what I need to demonstrate to the world is that I'm represented by a very successful agency. So however attractive your small boutique agency may seem, you know, seen from a distance, William Morris is my kind of place. I want to be up there with the big hitters.' Well, there's not much you can do to stop that, and hopefully you've been clever and perceptive enough in your selection of the client in the first place to guard against the possibility of that happening. And if you've been the one who, when they were really at their wits' end, said, 'We don't normally do this, but how would it be if I lent you a couple of grand just until the next book?' I'm not saying it's always about bribery but there are many ways in which you can be the one that was there when everybody else seems to have fallen away.

The agent's role

So how exactly do agents understand their role vis-à-vis their clients? In the broadest terms, most agents would describe their role as that of managing the long-term career development of their authors. 'It's about choreographing a career,' as one agent rather grandly put it. This breaks down into several different components, including the following: preparing proposals and manuscripts for submission; pitching; selling; managing rights; managing careers. Each is a complex subject in itself and the list is not exhaustive, but a brief account of these activities will go some way to clarifying the agent's role.

Once an agent has decided to take on a client, he or she must work with the writer to prepare the proposal or manuscript for submission to publishers. This is particularly true for the first book but, depending on the writer and the stage of his or her career, it may also apply to subsequent books. A great deal of thought and effort often goes into this process. It is not uncommon for a book proposal to go through six or more drafts, or, in the case of a novel, for the manuscript to be revised several times in the light of feedback from the agent, before it is presented to publishers. 'I have an author who is a well-respected journalist and he just couldn't get the proposal right,' explained one senior agent. 'We went through draft after draft and it took us a year. I probably could've sold it six months earlier but I really wanted him to get his head around exactly what he needed to be doing.' The good agent knows, or has some sense of, what editors and publishers will be looking for, and they want to present their client's offerings in the best possible light. 'I operate as if I only have one shot,' this agent continued, though she knew that, in practice, this wasn't strictly true. She cited the case of a younger agent at her agency who had sent out a novel more than 40 times over the course of four or five years and eventually sold it. She admired his tenacity but it wasn't her way of doing business. She also observed that some agents didn't put as much care and effort into preparing proposals as she did. 'There are some agents who have the shit-against-the-wall theory; they look at something and just throw it out there and if they sell it they sell it and if they don't, they don't. I don't believe in doing business that way and I don't train the people I work with to do business that way. I think it's putting your best foot forward.'

Preparing a proposal or manuscript for submission is not just a matter of polishing a text: it's also a matter of grooming the writer. How you present a writer can be just as important as how you present a text: what does this writer have to say that hasn't been said before? What unique traits do they bring to the table that others have not brought before them? Of course, in a media-saturated world where publicity can make a big difference to the sales of a book, the physical appearance of the author and how telegenic they are can become a factor, especially for topical non-fiction books, and it is not uncommon for agents to parade their authors from one publishing house to another, both for the authors to meet editors and other staff and gauge their enthusiasm for a book and for the staff at the publishing houses to meet the author and gauge their potential for promoting their book. But preparing an author for the submission process is about much more than appearance: it is also about what those in the business call 'platform'.

'Platform' is a term that has become particularly prevalent in the world of New York trade publishing in recent years, though the same considerations come into play in London even if the term is used less frequently. Essentially, platform is the position from which an author speaks – a combination of their credentials, visibility and promotability, especially through the media. It is those traits and accomplishments of the author that establish a pre-existing audience for their work, and that a publisher can leverage in the attempt to find a market for their book. As one agent put it, 'platform means what kind of built-in audience is this writer bringing that can guarantee a certain number of book sales.' Platform is important for all kinds of books but it is particularly important for non-fiction, especially for certain types of non-fiction like fitness and diet, where 'the author absolutely has to have a national platform to sell the book these days.' If an author regularly appears on national television or has a syndicated newspaper or magazine column, this gives them a high-profile platform which creates a pre-existing potential market for their book. As the marketplace for books becomes more crowded, the author's platform becomes more important for agents and publishers alike, because they see it as a basis on which they can build a market for a book, get publicity for it and make it stand out from all the other books that are competing for the time and attention of readers, buyers, reviewers and others.

Some writers come with platform; others have to get it. So how does an author get platform? Here is where a good agent can help out. An agent can advise an author about how to build their platform – where to publish articles, how to improve their website and so on. But well-connected agents – those with good quantities of social capital, accumulated through years of strategic networking – can also call on their friends and contacts in the media to help get exposure for their clients. As one agent at a large agency explained,

> There are occasions when I've called in favours for clients. One of my writers is an editor at a major newspaper who writes only human

interest stories for them. She was looking for a new project and I said, 'This guy is great, do a story about him and the publishers are going to flock to it,' and that's exactly what happened. That's what I call a sweetheart deal. It helps. And being at a big agency like this helps. Sometimes I'll go to another agent and say, 'Can someone at the *New York Times* write a story about this?' There's definitely a patronage system going on.

By putting their clients in touch with people in the media who can help to give them more exposure and visibility, well-connected agents can help them to build or extend their platforms, thereby strengthening their hand when it comes to pitching the proposal to publishers.

How an agent pitches a proposal or book depends very much on whether it is a new book by an established author who has already published one or several books, or a new book by a new author who is as yet an unknown quantity. Pitching a new book by an established author is often quite straightforward, especially if the author has a good relationship with a particular house and editor, everything is going well and the author is keen to stay with that house. In cases like this, which comprise a good proportion of the deals done by agents with an established client list, the agent is simply letting the editor or publisher know about the new book, explaining how it fits with the author's previous work, talking about how it should be positioned in the marketplace and discussing money and terms. However, there are many ways in which this seemingly straightforward negotiation can become more complicated. The author and agent might be looking for more money or better terms, the publishing house might be looking to reduce the advance in the light of the sales of the previous book or books, the author might be 'orphaned' at a particular house and so on. An author becomes orphaned when the editor to whom the book was originally sold leaves the house and the book is inherited by someone else – something that happens more and more often with the mergers and acquisitions among publishing houses. In such cases an author will often feel abandoned, lost. 'It mostly doesn't work out and you have to move the author,' explained one agent. 'It's such a personal business. You have to be with the editor who wanted your book and wanted you as a writer and the way you wrote and so on, and the person who comes in after that likes you but has other writers they like more. So mostly you're pitching to a publishing house thinking, "This isn't going to work and I'm going to try some other houses."'

With a first book by a new author, or a book by an author who is publishing a trade book for the first time or actively looking for a new house, the issues are somewhat different. The first question the agent has to figure out is: who is going to like this book? The agent has to work out a plan about which editors or publishers should be contacted about this specific book or proposal. There are many different elements that feed into this plan: partly it's based on the agent's view of what kind of book this is going to be and which publishing house or imprint would be a suitable home for it; partly it's based on their knowledge of who's who in the different publishing houses and what their tastes and inclinations are; partly it's based on their knowledge of what the different houses will typically pay and what they think they can get for this book; partly it's based on their experience of working with particular editors and publishing houses; and partly it's based on their assessment of how hungry any particular editor or publisher is at any particular point in time and how much support they can muster within their house. These are often elaborate judgements in which a great deal of experience and implicit knowledge, gleaned from countless conversations over lunch and elsewhere, is drawn upon by the agent in order to work out an appropriate strategy for a particular book.

Knowing the tastes of different editors and publishers is crucial, and this is part of the practical knowledge that an agent acquires by working with editors and talking with them about which books they like and which they don't – 'You talk about books all the time in this business, and you just slowly get to know people's tastes,' explained one agent. So in trying to figure out which editors to submit a new book to, the agent is always seeking to match the content of this particular book, its specific style and character, to what they perceive to be the tastes of particular editors: it is an exercise in the equilibration of tastes. But it's also about knowing who is looking for what at which point in time and how much power and support they have within the organization. One senior London agent put it like this:

> You've got to know what's going on, you've got to know who's up and who's down, you've got to know whose list is full and whose list isn't full, you've got to know who's looking for what kind of book, you've got to know which editors seem to be able to get their books through the system successfully and which editors don't seem to be able to, and you do that by talking to them all the time. You do that by going out to lunch, by going to parties, by reading the trade press

– that is, trying to figure out what's going on in the houses. It's spying in a sense – you're a spy in the house of publishing. But it's not really spying because spying implies that you're trying to get information from people who don't want to give it to you, whereas actually what happens when you sit down for lunch with a publisher is that they have as much interest in the trade of information as you do.

Since many agents have worked for publishing houses at earlier stages of their careers, they have a good sense of how the houses work. But they need to keep up with changes inside the houses and movements between them and try to get a sense of which editors are in favour and which aren't, and the only way to do this is to talk to the people who work in the houses and pick up whatever bits of information they can get.

All agents have a cognitive map of the field of the publishing houses, divided up into players of different size and strength, which are further divided into the imprints that are located within each house, and populated by the names of editors and publishers whom the agent either knows personally or knows of. The map is always hierarchical, in the sense that the large publishing corporations are always at the top, with their various imprints listed beneath, usually in order of size and importance, followed by the serious but less than major houses, followed in turn by a handful of smaller houses. 'There's definitely an A, B and C list,' said one senior New York agent. 'I hate to admit it but there is. I'm being honest with you. There's definitely a hierarchy. Part of it is who pays the most. Part of it is who has created the most bestsellers. And part of it is – and for me this is the number one concern – who ultimately is the best editor for this particular book.' When an agent is considering which editor or publisher to approach about a particular book, he or she will usually have some names in mind – often editors whom they've worked with before and whose tastes they know well. But they will also usually consult their cognitive map – their master list of publishing houses – and try to come up with other names. This New York agent explained how she does it:

I have a master list that I look at and I'll say, 'This would be a really good fit for such and such a place, so who should I send it to?' And I'll look at the master list and I'll say, 'OK, so-and-so would be a perfect fit for this at Penguin.' A lot of times at an agency this size we go around and talk to each other about it – you know, 'I've got this book; this is what it's about,' and we'll sit in each other's offices and jaw about it for awhile. And we also have an agents' meeting every week where, if we've hit a dead-end or are just at the beginning, we'll talk about different projects and throw around ideas.

For the most part, the author is not consulted in this process – unless, of course, the author already has a pre-existing relationship with a particular editor and a particular house and would like to maintain this, in which case the process of submitting the new book project will be shaped by this set of preferences. But for the vast majority of new books by authors without pre-existing relationships in the world of trade publishing, this process of selecting editors and publishing houses is entirely in the hands of the agent. 'The author doesn't know anything,' commented one senior New York agent. 'I mean if the author says, "You know, by the way, my uncle is Jason Epstein," I will listen. But otherwise the author is paying me to know these editors far better than he or she might.'

Once the agent has identified the editors to whom the book is going to be submitted, he or she has to contact them and tell them about the project – in other words, they have to pitch it. Often the first approach is by telephone – some agents always start by calling up the editor and trying to suss out the level of interest. 'I have to know where they are, I have to know what they're up to, I have to know what their reading schedule is like,' explained one New York agent. 'And my job as an agent is to get their blood pressure just a little higher after I've called them.' This is then followed up with a letter and a proposal which is emailed to them. Some agents do most of their pitching by phone and keep their follow-up letters very short and to the point, while others write more elaborate pitch letters. The pitch letter frames the book: it gives a little background about the author and the book, often points to other books with which it can be compared or contrasted, gives the editor a way to think about the book and perhaps some reasons why they should take it seriously. 'I try to give them a way of describing the book to their colleagues,' this agent continued. 'I'm telling them how to position this book.'

Sometimes the agent will make the drawbacks explicit in the pitch letter, with the intention of deflecting in advance potential reservations and focusing the editor's attention on what the agent sees as the book's real strengths. 'There are several things I can't offer you,' begins one pitch letter. 'I can't offer you a particularly promotable author. X is not a sexy 28-year-old looker who photographs well in black. He's a shy man who remains a little awestruck by my passion for his book. To make matters worse, I can't offer you a high concept plot which can be described efficiently.' The letter then goes on to compare the author to several hugely successful writers and adds, 'I've read four drafts of this first novel in as many months and my conviction about the freshness of writing here remains stolidly unchanged. There are scenes here I've never read before and metaphors that belong to X alone.' What matters above all with new fiction, explained this agent, is plot, character and voice. She knew that this author was a shy, reticent man and that his book lacked a strong plot. But the characters were well developed and the author had a fresh and original voice, so these are the features she chose to accentuate in her pitch.

How the agent pitches the book matters, but it also matters who the agent is. Experienced agents with good track records tend to be listened to with more attentiveness by editors and publishers than young agents who are struggling to make a name for themselves. 'Certain agents have greater leverage, greater clout and greater credibility than other agents,' explained one senior New York agent who began her career on the other side, working for a major publishing house. Their credibility is based on their track record, their ability to spot talent and sign up authors whose books turn out to do well – either becoming bestsellers or gaining critical acclaim or both. A track record of success gives an agent a degree of credibility, a quantity of symbolic capital, which helps to ensure that the books he or she is pitching will be taken seriously by editors and publishers. This doesn't mean that editors and publishers will necessarily want to buy the next book pitched by a well-regarded agent, but it does mean that they are more likely to take it seriously, look at it more quickly and be more positively predisposed to it. 'He's someone whose taste I trust, therefore I'll take him seriously when he says he likes something I haven't read' is how one senior agent described the way he thought that editors generally responded to his submissions.

For younger agents who lack the track record of their more established colleagues, it can be much harder to get editors and publishers to pay attention to their submissions. 'Some editors will take longer to read your work because they don't know you,' explained one young agent, though it helps if you are working for an agency that is well known and respected. Young agents often tend to form lateral connections – based on age and relative newness to the game – with young editors at the publishing houses, both because they find that they share more in common in terms of their tastes and also because they find it easier to get their attention. It's a strategy that serves both parties well, since the young editors find it just as difficult to get submissions from the well-established agents as young agents do to be taken seriously by well-established editors. Their lack of symbolic capital in their respective domains of the field gives them a certain commonality of purpose. They form relationships with their opposite numbers that will evolve with time and the success of one can help to build the success of the other, thus cementing the system of mutual benefit that ties agents and editors together.

Having pitched a book, the agent then needs to sell it if they can. In essence, there are three different ways of selling a book: a one-on-one submission, a multiple submission and an auction. If an agent has a book that they know needs a lot of work and they have in mind an editor and a publishing house that they think would be a good home for it, they can send it to the editor exclusively in return for them undertaking to look at it quickly and to give it the attention it needs – 'You honour them with a single submission.' More commonly, an agent will send the proposal or manuscript to a carefully selected group of editors – the multiple submission. In some cases only one editor expresses an interest and makes an offer, in which case the agent does what he or she can to raise the terms, though their bargaining position is weak. If more than one editor is interested, the agent can decide to have an auction. There are basically two ways of running an auction – the traditional auction, where the agent asks for the first offer by a particular time and date, after which the agent goes back to those who bid below the highest offer and asks them if they want to increase their offer and continues this process until bidders drop out; and the best-bid auction, where the agent asks everyone to give their best offer by a particular time and date. Whichever method you use, 'you also always reserve the right to have the author's decision be based upon all the terms,' explained one agent. 'So if you have $30,000 more from a publishing house that the author really doesn't like, you can go elsewhere. You know you'll still offend and aggrieve the publisher who's offered more money, but it is the author's right.' At the end of the day, continued this agent, it's the author's decision. 'But', she added, 'they depend very greatly upon my opinion.'

So do agents always advise the author to go with the highest bid? Some do, some don't. There are some agents who subscribe to Andrew Wylie's view that the advance is the only mechanism the agent can use to get the publisher to commit themselves seriously to a book and to sell and promote it aggressively, so going with the highest bid is the only rational thing to do. But many agents will adopt a more nuanced position. The size of the advance is important, no agent would deny that, but there are also other considerations to be taken into account, such as which editor and publisher would be the best for this particular book, how they propose to 'position' the book in the publisher's list, what kind of marketing and publicity plans they have for the book, how much enthusiasm they express and so on. When asked whether the financial conditions were the most important factor when deciding which publisher to go with, one senior New York agent responded like this:

> Absolutely not. If I can get you a deal where you can do what you want to do, and can put food on your table and pay your rent and stay relatively happy and sane, then I'm doing my job. If that deal is for $100,000 and you love your editor and you love the people who are helping you get where you need to get in your career, then that's a perfect deal. Whenever I run an auction, one of my rules – and I have the most straightforward set of rules, there are five of them – is that at the end of the day it is up to the agent and author to decide what constitutes the best deal. So for me that's not only the advance and the territories that come with the advance, it's the actual editor, who may or may not be there by the time the book is published, as experience shows us, it's what they're talking about in terms of publicity and marketing muscle, and just overall enthusiasm. I've had people pay a lot more for books and let them die, for whatever reasons, and that's something I'm very cautious about now.

So would this agent be happy to accept a significantly lower advance if other things seemed to warrant it? 'Happy? No, never happy.' But yes, on occasion, willing to do so. Most agents tend to subscribe to this more holistic view of 'the best deal', where the aim is to find 'the best home' for the book and where the size of the advance is one factor – albeit a very important factor – in an overall package. At the same time, most will also acknowledge that, while the largest advance does not always win the day, in practice it usually does, and that other factors tend to come into play most often when the differences between the final bids are small.

When an agent has three or four publishers who are seriously interested and who have all put in bids which hover around the same figure, the agent might arrange to take the author around to meet the editors and perhaps also the sales, marketing and publicity directors – what is commonly described in the business as 'the beauty contest'. From the agent's point of view, the beauty contest is an opportunity for the agent and author to meet the people they would be working with, get a sense of how committed they are and how they are think-ing about the book, and assess their marketing and publicity plans. Of course, it's also an opportunity for the publishers to meet the author and gauge how effective he or she would be in helping them to promote the book, but at this stage of the acquisitions process it's really the publisher whose beauty is on show. 'If you've made the level where you've offered, say, $500,000, you've made the decision as a publisher that you want this person on your list,' explained one marketing manager at a major publishing house. '"Beauty contest" is a little slim of a term because it just suggests tarting yourself up, but really what you're trying to do is say "We are the best house for this book and here's why we think so. Here's how we would publish your book, it would be a lead title in our catalogue, we would focus on it at Bookseller Expo, we would do this kind of online campaign, we would have that advertising component, we would want you to be on the road and do an eight-city tour." You try to give them some sense of how you would promote their book.'

Once the agent and author have decided which offer to accept, the agent has to negotiate the details of the contract and deal with those rights that have not been assigned to the publisher. Agents vary in their ways of thinking about rights: some are willing to assign rights for other territories and other languages when they do a deal with a publisher, while other agents will always hold on to these rights and make it clear to publishers when they submit a book to them that rights for other territories and other languages are not available. The agents who are willing to assign these rights may, in the case of a sought-after book, ask publishers to submit two offers – one for restricted rights (either North America or the UK, depending on where the auction is taking place) and one for world rights or world English-language rights – and they will weigh up the pros and cons of the two offers and form a judgement about whether they and their client would be better off if they were to hold on to foreign rights and dispose of them directly. In those cases where the agent holds on to foreign rights, whether these are for North America (in the case of an agent in the UK), Britain and the rest of the world (in the case of an agent in the US) and/or foreign languages, the agent has to come up with a strategy for disposing of the rights they have retained, something which agents do with varying degrees of efficiency and dedication. Some agents will contract sub-agents to try to sell rights in other territories and languages, while other agents will handle these rights themselves and put considerable thought and effort into selling them.

The major book fairs, like Frankfurt and London, play an important role in the selling of rights – these are, essentially, rights fairs – and every agent and agency will have their Frankfurt strategy and their London Book Fair strategy, but the selling of rights is a continuous process that extends well beyond the planning for particular fairs. An agent will often use the size of the advance they were able to achieve in their domestic market as leverage to try to maximize advances in other markets and may try to 'prime the pump' by selling some foreign rights first. 'Generally speaking you're selling British rights first,' explained one senior London agent, 'but that's not always the case. Some agents have been known to sell rights in Germany first before selling British rights because they know a particular editor in a German house that they've dealt with before and think is going to be receptive and the buzz is created in Germany or possibly in Italy or America first.' By carefully orchestrating the sale of rights, the agent can create a snowball effect, with each sale serving to increase the leverage they have in subsequent sales. They may also draw scouts into this process, since they know that scouts are hungry for information about forthcoming books and they may calculate that by providing them with certain selected bits of information or even entire texts at certain points in time, they may be able to generate excitement about a book in foreign markets before it is sold in the domestic market. 'Before he's sold a manuscript here, quite often an agent will think, "If I slip this manuscript to a scout and the scout is enthusiastic and alerts publishers abroad, then I've got momentum, I've got buzz."' And this snowball effect may happen whether the agent actively seeks to create it or not, simply because the world of potential buyers is small and they talk to one another constantly. 'It's a very leaky business,' this agent continued. 'We all go back and forth between London and New York all the time, we all know each other extremely well, we all pick up the phone to each other all the time. An American editor will call up a British editor and say, "So-and-so has just sent me this book, I see you bought it, how much did you pay for it, what are you going to do with it, when are you going to publish it?" and so on, and that will condition their response.' Success breeds success. Buzz generates more buzz. Of course, doing a big deal with a British publisher does not guarantee a big deal in the US, nor does a big deal in the US guarantee a big deal in the UK – the markets are different and much depends on the author, his or her platform in the different markets and what kind of book it is. But if you do a big deal in the UK, 'your chances of making a big deal in the US, depending on what kind of book it is, are greatly improved', and vice-versa.

In addition to helping authors prepare proposals and manuscripts, pitching and selling books, negotiating contracts and managing rights, most agents understand their role as one of managing the long-term careers of their clients. Part of this role is trying to secure enough money for them to become full-time writers and live from their pen. 'You have a client because you believe they have a career,' explained one agent. 'And if you're only making X amount of money in a year and I'm not helping you become a full-time writer because you're not making enough money, I'm not doing my job well enough.' She saw it as part of her job to get enough money for her clients to enable them to write full-time, 'and most of them do'. This doesn't necessarily mean that they are only writing the kind of novels or non-fiction books they want to write – they might have to do other kinds of writing as well, such as writing for newspapers or magazines or perhaps even ghostwriting. 'I'm happy if my writers are just writing on a regular basis,' this agent continued. 'I think writing is the great lost art, or will be the great lost art, and the only way we're going to sustain it is for people to continue with the written word.'

As part of managing their authors' careers, most agents will spend time with their clients discussing their next book, and may read draft chapters and give them advice and feedback. Depending on the writer, some novelists will start to work on something, send a couple of draft chapters to their agents and say, 'Should I carry on or should I dump this now and not waste the next two years turning it into a novel?' Other writers will have a very clear idea of what they want to do and will simply send their agent the final manuscript when it's done. In the case of non-fiction, agents may suggest ideas for books to their clients and work with them to shape the proposal before sending it out. With both fiction and non-fiction writers, agents will sometimes actively encourage a writer to change direction if their career seems to be in a rut. Most commonly, this is simply a matter of channelling a writer's energies in one direction rather than another, of using one's experience and knowledge of the market to temper the inclinations of the writer and encourage them to pursue a more promising path. But sometimes it can involve more radical changes – even to the extent of suggesting, in some instances, that a writer changes his or her name.

One senior agent in London described how one of his agency's clients – call her Sarah Jones – had been writing novels for many years, each selling somewhere between 40,000 and 45,000 hardback. 'So everybody thought they knew how much she was worth. That's how much she sold so everything became geared to that. Despite the enthusiasm of the publisher, despite their relentless attempts to persuade the trade that they'd got it wrong, she was labelled.' Then one day the author decided she wanted a change of pace. She made a couple of suggestions to her agent about what she wanted to do next and the agent's response was lukewarm – 'We said, "I really don't think that's going to work but, most importantly, I don't think that's where your heart lies."' The agent encouraged her to move in a different direction, to write something frothier and aimed at a slightly younger audience, and, crucially, to submit it under a different name. Why?

> Because it feels different, but mostly because if we go back to the marketplace with another Sarah Jones novel, they'll say 40,000 copies. I'm not even going to tell your existing publisher – who will get preferential treatment – who this is by. In other words, I want to create for you that absolutely 'magic moment'. It's like the first date, before you realize that the girl you think you've just fallen in love with is going to irritate you terminally because she keeps leaving the top off the toothpaste tube. It's that blissful moment when everything is possible, we're not constrained by any previous history and it's just blue sky ahead.

Coming up with a new name – 'this manufactured authorial name', as the agent put it – gave this writer a new lease of life and created a completely new publishing presence, untainted by the settled assumptions in the marketplace that were inseparably linked to Sarah Jones. The new novel went on to become a huge international bestseller and spawned a series of highly successful sequels. The agent insisted that it was not the agent who reinvented this author, but rather the author who reinvented herself with the help and active encouragement of the agent. 'One of the things we all need to remind ourselves of in this business is a wonderful phrase of a much lamented late colleague of ours who said, "What we're here to do is to publish the gleam in the author's eye." And I think we forget that at our peril. But that doesn't mean to say that we just let that gleam bounce off as many mirrors as it wants to – it needs to be directed.'

While an agent who takes on a client is investing in principle in their long-term career development, it is not always easy to strike the right balance between long-term interests and short-term gains. It can be very difficult for agent and author alike to resist a very large advance for a first novel, especially when it represents, as one agent put it, a 'life-changing' sum of money, even though they know that, if the book turns out to fall far short of the publisher's expectations and comes nowhere near to earning out, this may make life more difficult for the author when it comes to selling his or her next book. This is an issue about which there is a varied range of opinions and attitudes in the agenting community. 'There are agents who say, "You always want the publisher to overpay wildly, you want to get them to overpay by as much as you can possibly manage,"' explained one agent. 'But you have to keep an eye on the fact that in the long term an author is judged not on their books but on their sales. I think that you want them to pay as much as you can get but not to the extent that someone looks at their sales figures when their next book comes around and says, "Well, that was a flop." Then they either move on or they make no effort for the second book. There's a sort of middle ground you're aiming for where you're trying to get them to dig deep but not so deep that it's impractical and the book can't possibly come anywhere close to fulfilling their hopes.' Caution of this kind may sound sensible and reasonable but in the heat of an auction it's not easy to put a lid on the bidding. There are some agents who do it but it's difficult. In a field where the dynamics are shaped by different players competing against one another and pursuing interests that coincide in some respects and diverge in others, and where the value of a book proposition is determined as much by passion and belief as it is by any clear-cut evidence or firm knowledge of likely sales, there is enormous scope for the imagination to run wild and for enthusiasm to drive up prices to levels that, with the benefit of hindsight, can be seen to have been excessive and, in some cases, undoubtedly damaging to the long-term careers of authors.

While most agents work very hard to nurture the careers of their authors and secure the best deals they can for them, there will always be cases where authors feel let down by their agents, either because they feel that their agents failed to get the kind of deal they expected (or were led to expect), or because they feel that their agents advised them poorly (or failed to advise them at all), or for some other reason. The world of writers abounds with horror stories about incompetent and duplicitous agents who lavished attention on young and promising writers and then dumped them as soon as the going got tough, who failed to return their calls or respond to their emails, who misled them, lied to them or ripped them off by charging fees for reading and other things. One Brooklyn-based writer described how he had been through six agents in 15 years, including one – his first agent – who worked for a big agency, read his first book and was enthusiastic about it, signed him up, sent the book out to the top editors in the big houses and then, when she failed to sell it, quickly dropped him:

> It got to a point where she said 'You know what, I think I've sent it to the people that I can send it to,' and at that point I said, 'Well, how about trying smaller presses?' And she just flat out said 'I'm not going to do that because there's not enough money in it for me as an agent, at this big agency.' So she didn't do it. And then her attitude just completely flip-flopped. She went from being incredibly nice and kind and enthusiastic to suddenly not returning my phone calls. I called someone else at the agency and they said, 'Oh, you're a non-client.' And I said, 'What do you mean?' Because she didn't tell me that she was dropping me as a client. I found out just by accident. So that was my first experience with an agent.

His experiences didn't get much better. The next agent he signed with lied to him about the foreign rights he had sold for the book, while another, when asked by an author clearly desperate for some career advice, replied by saying that he couldn't help because he had no idea how the business worked. Maybe this was just bad luck. Certainly it is rare for a writer to go through six agents in 15 years, and for every story like this you will hear another of a writer who has remained happily with the same agent throughout his or her career. But the experiences of this writer do highlight the fact that, in a field where anyone can become an agent and there are no common standards and regulations, finding a good agent is a treacherous undertaking and often depends on an elusive mixture of good connections, good chemistry and good luck.

3

THE EMERGENCE OF PUBLISHING CORPORATIONS

The emergence of large publishing corporations is the third factor that has shaped the evolution of English-language trade publishing in recent decades. For many observers, this is the most striking change that has taken place in the world of publishing, so it may seem odd that we come to it only at this stage; but I have postponed until now the analysis of this development for good reasons. It is vital to see that the field of trade publishing does not consist only of publishers: there are other players who inhabit this field and who exercise a great deal of power within it, and we will never understand what happens within publishing firms unless we see that their actions are to some extent responses to forces and developments that lie outside their direct control. Large publishing houses may seem to be the major players and to have a great deal of power (and, indeed, they do); but in the book supply chain, the publisher is in many ways just another intermediary, a player in the middle, and the power of the publishing house, however large it is, is always hemmed in by and traded off against the power of two other key players in the field: the power of the retailers, on the one hand, who largely control access to the customers, that is, the readers; and the power of the agents, on the other, who largely control access to the content and to the creators of content, that is, the authors. The publishers themselves are middlemen who, thanks to the developments that have transformed the field, are in the position of players who have to compete with others for access to the most highly valued content and for the attention of consumers, and those who decide which books should be brought to the attention of consumers, in an increasingly crowded marketplace.

The rise of the modern publishing corporation has to be understood in this context. Of course, the growing role of large corporations is not unique to the publishing world: large corporations have become increasingly important players throughout the media, information and communication industries, and indeed throughout the economy as a whole, and many of the corporations that have acquired major stakes in publishing are diversified media conglomerates with interests in other sectors of media and entertainment.[1] But the way that consolidation has occurred in the field of trade publishing, the reasons for it and the consequences of it are in some respects unique and are closely interwoven with the two other developments that have shaped the evolution of this field.

There can be little doubt that the rise of large corporations has transformed profoundly the landscape of trade publishing, so much so that today it bears little resemblance to the publishing world that existed half a century ago. In the 1950s and before, there were dozens of independent publishing houses in New York, Boston and London. Among the better-known American houses were Random House, Simon & Schuster, Scribner, Doubleday, Harcourt, Harper, Boni and Liveright, Henry Holt, Dutton, Putnam, Viking, Alfred Knopf, Farrar, Straus & Giroux, William Morrow, W. W. Norton, Houghton Mifflin and Little, Brown, to name just a few. London had its own plethora of independent trade houses, including Macmillan, Longman, John Murray, Routledge and Kegan Paul, Heinemann, Allen & Unwin, J. M. Dent, Chapman & Hall, Gollancz, Jonathan Cape, Faber, Secker & Warburg, Michael Joseph, The Bodley Head and Penguin. Many of these houses were run by individuals who either owned the company outright or had a substantial stake in it, and other members of the family were commonly involved in the business. These publisher-owners were often men of strong character and opinion – and they nearly always were men. They knew what they wanted to publish and they built their lists on the basis of their own judgement and taste – and, as they grew larger and delegated more responsibility to editors, on the basis of the judgement and taste of their editors.

---

[1] On the rise of the media conglomerates, see Ben H. Bagdikian, *The New Media Monopoly* (Boston: Beacon Press, 2004); Edward S. Herman and Robert W. McChesney, *The Global Media: The New Missionaries of Corporate Capitalism* (London: Cassell, 1997); Robert W. McChesney, *Rich Media, Poor Democracy: Communication Politics in Dubious Times* (New York: New Press, 1999); Anthony Smith, *The Age of Behemoths: The Globalization of Mass Media Firms* (New York: Priority Press, 1991).

Editors tended to work at the same publishing house for many years, often for their entire career, and authors tended to remain loyal to the house that published them. In some houses meetings were rare and decisions were taken by publisher-owners or editors or both. 'We have a rule at Random House', explained Bennett Cerf in his memoirs, 'that our senior editors can accept any book they want without question, unless an enormous advance against royalties is involved, in which case we have a discussion about it. There are two ways of doing this at Random House. One is regular meetings, committees, which I loathe and detest and won't go to. The other method is, when I want a meeting I call together the people I need, and we talk – which is the way I think a publishing business should be run.'[2] These businesses were run with varying degrees of efficiency and financial discipline. Some, like Random House, flourished and grew into large and successful publishing companies, while others fared less well. Horace Liveright, Bennett Cerf's former employer and the publisher of many celebrated authors from Ezra Pound to William Faulkner, famously squandered his resources on everything from lavish parties and excessive advances to Broadway musicals and Wall Street speculation; he was eventually forced out and died penniless in 1933, the same year that the firm was declared bankrupt.[3]

By the early 1960s the landscape of trade publishing in the United States and Britain, which had been characterized by a plurality of independent publishing firms, had begun to change. Large corporations began to take an interest in the publishing industry at the same time as many of the owners of publishing houses became interested in selling. A wave of mergers and acquisitions swept through the industry, beginning in the early 1960s and continuing through to the present day. By the 1990s the shape of the industry had changed dramatically: in a field where there had once been dozens of independent publishing houses, each reflecting the idiosyncratic tastes and styles of their owners and editors, there were now five or six large corporations, each operating as an umbrella organization for numerous imprints, many of which still bore the names of previously independent houses that were now part of a larger organization, operating with varying degrees of autonomy depending on the strategies and policies of the corporate owners. How can we explain this dramatic transformation of the field?

---

[2] Bennett Cerf, *At Random* (New York: Random House, 1977), p. 221.
[3] See Tom Dardis, *Firebrand: The Life of Horace Liveright* (New York: Random House, 1995).

The rise of the publishing corporations is a complex story which defies simple explanations. To make sense of this transformation we have to see that there were many different factors involved, some personal, some structural, and that each merger and acquisition involved some specific combination of these factors depending on the circumstances of the individuals and organizations involved. We also have to see that there were 'push' factors and 'pull' factors, in the sense that there were some factors that inclined or impelled a publishing house to sell and other factors that made a corporation interested in buying. Among the push factors was the fact that many of the great trade houses in both the US and the UK were founded in the early part of the twentieth century by entrepreneurial individuals who, from the 1960s on, were beginning to think about retiring from the business and about how best to secure the future of the publishing house in their absence, while at the same time enabling them to realize some value from the time and effort they had invested in the firm over many years. Another push factor that played a role in some cases was the fact that some of the traditional, family-owned trade houses began to find it increasingly difficult to operate in a financially viable way, because the business was being run inefficiently, or because it was undercapitalized or because it was unable to compete effectively in changing circumstances (or some combination of these elements); in short, they were struggling, and the sale or merger of the firm was seen as a way of solving what had become an intractable set of financial problems. The pull factors were a range of strategic considerations that varied from one corporation to another and changed over time; they included, among other things, the search for synergy, the drive for growth, the desire to expand overseas and, more specifically, the wish to establish or increase a foothold in the English-language market, whether that was the US or the UK or both.

Although it involves a degree of oversimplification, it is helpful to distinguish two main phases in the process of consolidation, the first extending from roughly the early 1960s to the early 1980s, the second from the early 1980s to the present. Each was characterized by its own distinctive set of pull factors which encouraged large corporations to take an active interest in acquiring trade publishing houses. These two phases display some elements of continuity but also demonstrate how fickle business strategies can be, with large-scale corporate acquisitions soon followed by disillusionment and divestiture. As one perceptive commentator remarked, 'The history of the book illustrates generously the paradox – by no means confined to this industry, however – whereby strategies that dominate one period are replaced by others, which can go all the way to representing a total reversal of policy.'[4]

The 'synergy' phase

The first phase was characterized by the active involvement in the publishing field of large corporations that had substantial stakes in other industries, including information, entertainment, education and the emerging computer industry. For senior managers in these corporations, publishing houses looked like attractive acquisitions because they seemed to offer the prospect of providing content that could be repurposed for other sectors of the business and vice versa – in the way, for example, that books might be turned into movies or movies into books, or the content of books might be adapted for the 'teaching machines' that were being contemplated by some of the key players in the nascent computer industry. This idea of 'synergy', whether it was between different media formats or between equipment ('hardware') and content ('software'), provided a compelling and seemingly cogent management rationale for large corporations to acquire publishing houses: it was a powerful pull factor. At the same time, many of the successful trade publishers in the 1950s and 1960s were houses that had been founded by entrepreneurial individuals in the 1920s and 1930s who were reaching an age when they were contemplating retirement and considering how best to deal with the problem of succession, sometimes in the absence of obvious family heirs to continue running the business. Merging with a competitor and/or selling to a corporation were, from the viewpoint of some publishing houses, ways of solving the succession problem: they were powerful push factors.

The history of Random House in the late 1950s and early 1960s illustrates the interplay of these factors very well. Having been founded by Bennett Cerf and Donald Klopfer in 1925, Random House had grown into a large and successful publishing company with many well-known writers on its list – James Joyce, Sinclair Lewis, William Faulkner, Gertrude Stein, Truman Capote, John O'Hara and many others. But by the late 1950s Cerf and Klopfer were becoming concerned about what would happen to the company

---

[4] Eric de Bellaigue, *British Book Publishing as a Business since the 1960s: Selected Essays* (London: British Library, 2004), p. 3.

if one of them died. 'Donald and I knew that the real value of the company had increased each year, but nobody knew by how much,' wrote Cerf in his memoir.[5] 'If its value was too high, how could the survivor afford to buy the other half, and how could the widow of the one who died raise enough cash to pay the estate tax?' They began to think seriously about changing the financial standing of the company. The first major change came in 1959, when they arranged for a financial institution on Wall Street to sell 30 per cent of their stock to the public. 'This marked a big change,' reflected Cerf, 'since the minute you go public, outsiders own some of your stock and you've got to make periodic reports to them. You owe your investors dividends and profits. Instead of working for yourself and doing what you damn please, willing to risk a loss on something you want to do, if you're any kind of honest man, you feel a real responsibility to your stockholders . . . From then on, we were publishing with one eye and watching our stock with the other.'[6] Six months later, flush with cash from the stock issue, the next significant change in Random House's fortunes occurred: they bought Knopf. Cerf had long admired Alfred Knopf and the list that he and Blanche Knopf had built since Alfred had founded the firm in 1915; with a talent for finding the best European authors and an unwavering dedication to high-quality production standards, Knopf was widely regarded as the very definition of quality publishing. In 1959 Alfred and Blanche's son, Alfred A., Jr ('Pat' as he was generally known), left the family firm to found Atheneum Publishers with two friends, depriving Alfred and Blanche of an obvious successor. They knew that Cerf and Klopfer were interested in buying Knopf so they invited them to make an offer; they did in April 1960 and the Knopfs accepted. A year later Random House acquired Pantheon, which had been started in 1942 by two German refugees, Kurt and Helen Wolff.

With the business expanding, large corporations began to take an interest in Random House. 'Big computer houses and business-machine companies were going into education with their teaching machines and saw the potential value of having a publishing company in their fold – especially one with a list like ours . . . so approaches began to be made by huge companies. Everybody was listening, and so were we.'[7] Discussions with Time-Life were called off when it

[5] Cerf, *At Random*, p. 276.
[6] Ibid., p. 278.
[7] Ibid., p. 285.

became clear that the US Department of Justice would be likely to oppose a merger on antitrust grounds. When they were approached by RCA, they responded positively, 'because it was one of the great corporations of the country'. Cerf held out for $40 million and the deal was done in late December 1965. Random House was now owned by RCA, whose principal interests were in radio and television technology and who was, in the early 1960s, one of the major corporate players in the emerging computer industry.

With the sale to RCA, Cerf stepped down as president and ceased to be the towering presence in the publishing house that he had been since its beginnings in the 1920s. Under his successor, Bob Bernstein, Random House grew rapidly during the following decade, tripling its sales to $97 million by 1975. But as with many of the early corporate takeovers of publishing houses, RCA eventually grew tired of its new acquisition and decided to sell Random House in 1980. The large corporations that became involved in publishing during the first phase of mergers and acquisitions became disillusioned for two main reasons. In the first place, it soon became clear that the hoped-for synergies were not going to materialize in anything like the way that some senior corporate managers had persuaded themselves they would. They discovered that 'teaching machines' were a figment of the technological imagination at the dawn of the digital revolution, so the need to control content that could be fed to these machines quickly vanished. They also discovered that, while the idea of turning books into movies sounded good in principle, in practice the movie rights were increasingly controlled by agents rather than publishers, so owning a publishing house was no guarantee that the parent corporation could convert successful books into successful movies. In short, synergy turned out to be a myth.

The second reason why some of the large corporations became disillusioned is that growth and profitability in trade publishing proved to be consistently modest. Large corporations that took over publishing houses often did so in the belief that by introducing stricter financial controls and more professional business practices, they could achieve double-digit growth and profitability. However, despite determined efforts, they generally found that the levels of profitability in trade publishing remained stubbornly low, often below 10 per cent (in contrast to some other sectors of publishing, like educational, professional and STM – scientific, technical and medical – publishing, where profit margins of 20 per cent and above were not uncommon). Corporate managers were also frustrated by the cyclical and unpredictable nature of trade publishing and the strains this placed on cash flow. A trade publisher can have a big hit that produces a sudden influx of cash and can then have a fallow period when they are paying advances and suppliers but the money is not coming in. This makes it very difficult to manage cash flow and very difficult to budget for steady growth from one year to the next. With synergies failing to materialize and financial returns well below levels that could be achieved in other sectors, trade publishing did not seem like such a good investment after all. Patience faded and some of the large corporations bailed out.

The growth phase

The second phase of mergers and acquisitions in trade publishing, which began in the early 1980s and has continued to the present, was characterized by a different set of push and pull factors. Solving the succession problem remained a push factor for some publishing houses, but by the 1980s the field of trade publishing had begun to change in ways that put growing pressure on those houses that remained independent and gave them additional reasons, of a structural rather than personal kind, to sell to a large corporation. With the growth of the retail chains, the volume of sales that could be achieved with bestselling titles increased dramatically, but the costs and the risks increased too. Agents had become key players in the field and they were able to play publishers off against one another, and many successful authors expected to be rewarded with higher advances. As the scale of the advances increased, it became harder and harder for those independent publishers that remained to compete for the best authors. 'When you had 40 smallish companies all paying as little as possible for books, the competition was over something else,' explained one senior manager who lived through the changes. 'But when money became king, the colour of your petticoat was a lot less important. We always had a very beautiful petticoat, but you have to be within shooting distance of the competition.' The owners and managers of those companies that remained independent could see that they were being squeezed out of the market for content. In earlier decades, they could deploy both their symbolic capital and their economic capital to attract and retain authors, but with the changes taking place in the field, they now needed a much greater quantity of economic capital to stay in the game. The colour of their petticoat was not enough – they had to have deep pockets too. Selling to a large corporation, which would give them access to much greater resources, was a means of survival in a field where the stakes had risen so high that it was difficult for them to continue on their own.

On the pull side, the kinds of corporations that were interested in acquiring trade publishers in the US and the UK changed, as did the reasons for wanting to acquire them. While large American public corporations became increasingly disillusioned with trade publishing and sought to divest themselves of the houses they had bought, various international media conglomerates, often based outside the United States and Britain and in most cases with an existing interest in publishing, became increasingly interested in acquiring them. Two German media conglomerates, Bertelsmann and Holtzbrinck, both with large stakes in the publishing industry in Germany and elsewhere, became key players in the field of English-language trade publishing, as did the French conglomerate Lagardère, owner of the largest publishing house in France, Hachette Livre. Other key players were Pearson, the British-based media conglomerate, and News Corporation, the multimedia conglomerate founded by Rupert Murdoch. The reasons why these media conglomerates wanted to acquire trade publishing houses in the United States and Britain varied from one conglomerate to another but three factors were particularly important.

First, media conglomerates with substantial publishing interests in German or French were always going to have limited growth opportunities, both because they would reach a point where antitrust legislation would prevent them from expanding further in their domestic markets and because their opportunities to expand overseas would be limited by the restricted use of their languages. For these conglomerates to grow their publishing businesses, they would need at some point to expand beyond their original domestic fields; and given the global dominance of the English language and the importance of the American and British publishing industries in the global arena, acquiring a major stake in the US and/or UK publishing field was a particularly attractive way of achieving this growth. Second, for those media conglomerates that operated in English but originated outside the United States, such as Pearson and News Corp, acquiring a major stake in the US was always going to be important, given the sheer scale of the US market and its importance as a creative centre. This was just as true in trade publishing as it was in the other sectors in which these conglomerates were involved, whether it was educational publishing (as with Pearson) or newspapers, film and television (as with News Corp).

The third reason why these media conglomerates became highly acquisitive in the fields of English-language trade publishing is rather different and stems from what we could call 'the growth conundrum'. The conundrum arises because every corporation needs to grow and to generate a good level of profitability. The precise way in which this imperative is articulated and experienced will vary from corporation to corporation and will depend on whether the corporation is publicly quoted or privately held, among other things. But there is no escaping the imperative. The problem with trade publishing in the US and the UK is that these are very mature markets which have been largely static for many years; total sales of trade books in these markets tend to increase by about the rate of inflation year on year, but not much more. So the basic challenge that senior managers have to face in these corporations is this: how do you achieve significant growth year on year when the market is essentially static? That is the growth conundrum.

There are various ways of trying to deal with this challenge but three strategies are particularly important. First, you can try to take market share from your competitors. There are several ways to do this: you try to improve your hit rate and publish more bestsellers than your competitors; you try to squeeze your competitors in certain genres or subfields where you think you can grow your market share by strategically expanding your publishing activity; you try to bring a bestselling author to your list by outbidding his existing publisher when the agent goes out with his new book; and so on. Second, you can look for ways to achieve incremental growth within your principal market by opening up new channels and selling into non-traditional outlets (sometimes called special sales), like museums, gift shops, clothing retailers, etc., and by increasing sales outside your principal market – for example, by increasing your business overseas. And third, you can acquire other publishing houses. Most of the large publishing groups do all three of these things simultaneously. They constantly try to increase their market share by improving their hit rate, etc., they're constantly trying to poach bestselling authors from their competitors and they're always on the lookout for new acquisition opportunities.

The great advantage of acquiring other publishing houses is that it enables a conglomerate to grow and increase its market share very quickly. It provides a rapid growth spurt that bypasses the long and laborious process of investing in new publishing initiatives and growing organically. Depending on the acquisition, it might also enable the conglomerate to expand in areas where it is relatively weak, thereby producing a more rounded publishing programme. Growing through acquisitions not only enables you to solve the growth conundrum (at least temporarily) and meet the growth imperatives of the corporation, it also can bring other advantages that come with increasing scale, like giving you more leverage in the marketplace when negotiating with retailers and suppliers. But there are many potential drawbacks too – the quality of the list may be uneven, the price may be too high and the costs involved in merging the companies may be excessive, just to mention a few. Moreover, as the process of consolidation continued through the 1980s and 1990s, the pool of available companies to purchase became smaller in both the US and the UK, and hence the opportunities to grow through acquisition became ever rarer.

In addition to the growth conundrum, there was another structural factor, alluded to in an earlier chapter, that played an important role in the mergers and acquisitions of publishing houses: the need to achieve vertical integration between hardback and paperback lines. As the paperback revolution that began in the 1930s and 1940s gained momentum in the 1950s and 1960s, it became increasingly clear to the larger publishing houses that they needed either to develop their own paperback lines or to acquire paperback houses so that they could issue their own paperback editions rather than licensing them to external paperback houses. Not only would this enable them to build their backlist and increase their revenue in the long term instead of ceding control of the copyright to a third party, it would also put them in a much stronger position vis-à-vis agents and authors, since they could pay full royalties on paperback sales rather than 50 per cent of the royalties (as was normally the case if paperback rights were licensed to a paperback house). However, the more that the hardback houses began to develop or acquire their own paperback lines, the more important it was for the paperback houses to protect their own supply chain either by acquiring hardback houses or by launching their own hardback imprints and developing the capacity to publish hardback or paperback originals in-house. Stand-alone paperback houses found that their sources of supply were drying up, while hardback houses that had traditionally relied on the sale of paperback rights to offset high advances and provide large injections of cash found themselves in an increasingly vulnerable position, placing further pressure on those that remained independent to join forces with a vertically integrated group.

While I have divided the process of consolidation in trade publishing into two phases involving different players and different strategies or rationales, it is important to stress that these phases do not fall neatly into the two time periods I distinguished. There are some major trade publishers, like Simon & Schuster, that continue to be owned by a large American corporation (CBS in this case), and others, like Little, Brown and what is now called Grand Central Publishing, that have only recently been sold by a large American corporation to a foreign conglomerate (Time Warner sold them to Hachette in 2006). Nevertheless, while there are legacy corporate structures in the field of trade publishing, this should not obscure the broad structural shift that has taken place. (The rumour has circulated for years that CBS would be happy to sell Simon & Schuster if they could get the asking price, said to be $1 billion.) The process of consolidation in trade publishing has been underway since the early 1960s, but the world of corporate trade publishing in the early twenty-first century is not the same as the world that began to emerge with the first corporate takeovers in the 1960s and 1970s.

So why are large American corporations uninterested in trade publishing today, whereas European media conglomerates are willing to acquire and retain trade publishing houses in the US and UK? 'It's a Wall Street thing,' explained one senior executive of a large US publishing group. 'Since publishing was a slow growth or no growth, low margin, capital intensive business, Wall Street would look at whoever it was – Paramount, CBS, Viacom, Time Warner – negatively if they felt they were trying to build that asset. They always pretended to be trying to get rid of it, which kept Wall Street at bay.' For Wall Street, book publishing is not just old media, it is old, old media – 'Compared to a Google or whatever, commercial television is perceived as old media. So we are labelled as really old media.' Moreover, for these large American corporations, book publishing was a very small part of their portfolio – 'We were hardly a blip on their radar,' said another senior executive. 'I mean if we had a bad year it wouldn't have made any difference to them.' Why hold on to a business that represents a tiny fraction of your overall revenue, where margins are much lower than in your other businesses and where the prospects for growth are minimal? Not easy for a corporate executive with his eyes focused on Wall Street to give a convincing answer to that question. For the European conglomerates, by contrast, book publishing is a big part of what they do. For them, investing in American and British trade publishing is an effective way of achieving growth outside their domestic European markets, of gaining access to the American and British markets and of acquiring a foothold in publishing fields that operate in the English language, thereby enabling them to sell into all those parts of the world where English is used either as a primary or as a secondary language. In some cases the European conglomerates remain in private ownership – the German media group Bertelsmann, for example, is majority owned (76.9 per cent) by the Bertelsmann Foundation, a non-profit organization set up by the founding Mohn family, and the remaining 23.1 per cent is owned by the family itself. They don't have to deal with the Wall Street quarterly mentality and they can afford to take a longer-term strategic view. So the large American corporations and the European media conglomerates have very different orientations that are rooted in their different circumstances and the differing financial pressures they face.

The dominant publishing groups in the US

The outcome of this process of consolidation was that by the end of the 1990s there were four large and powerful publishing groups in the field of US trade publishing. The largest group by a considerable margin was Random House. RCA sold Random House for $60 million in 1980 to S. I. (known as 'Si') Newhouse, a wealthy business-man who owned a range of newspapers, magazines and cable televi-sion stations. Newhouse made further acquisitions in the course of the 1980s and 1990s and then sold the entire Random House group for just over $1 billion in 1998 to Bertelsmann. Bertelsmann had already entered the field of US trade publishing by acquiring Bantam Books in 1980 and Doubleday in 1986, merging them into the Bantam Doubleday Dell publishing group (Doubleday had acquired the paperback publisher Dell in 1976). With the acquisition of the Random House group, Bertelsmann became the largest trade publish-ing group in the US and, indeed, in the world. By 2007 Random House's global revenues for trade and mass-market publishing were around $2.39 billion; $1.27 billion of this, or around 53 per cent, was accounted for by sales in the US.[8] Random House's numerous imprints in the US now include Bantam, Delacorte, Dell, Doubleday, Broadway, Crown, Knopf, Pantheon, Anchor, Vintage, Ballantine and Modern Library (see appendix 1 for a more extensive list of the imprints of the major publishing corporations).

The three other large trade publishing groups in the US were Penguin, HarperCollins and Simon & Schuster. Penguin is owned by Pearson, the UK-based media conglomerate. Pearson had acquired

---

[8] Data provided by Open Book Publishing, 2008.

Penguin in 1971. In 1996 they bought the Putnam and Berkley publishing group, which had been owned by MCA since 1975, and merged it with Penguin in the US to form Penguin Putnam, subsequently rebranded as the Penguin Group. By 2007 Penguin's global revenues for trade and mass-market publishing were around $1.69 billion, and Penguin's US revenues were around $1 billion or 60 per cent of the total. Apart from Penguin and Putnam, Penguin's many US imprints now include Viking, Gotham, Riverhead, Dutton, Berkley and New American Library.

HarperCollins is owned by News Corporation, the international media conglomerate controlled by Rupert Murdoch. HarperCollins was formed through the merger of Harper & Row, which News Corp acquired in 1987, and the old British publishing house William Collins Sons & Co., the remaining shares of which News Corp acquired in 1989 (News Corp had already acquired a 30 per cent stake in Collins in 1981, through its subsidiary News International). By 2007 HarperCollins's global revenues in trade and mass-market publishing were around $1.29 billion, of which US revenues were around $903 million or 70 per cent of the total. HarperCollins's US imprints include William Morrow, Avon and Ecco; it also owns the religious publishing house Zondervan, publisher of the hugely successful book by Rick Warren, *The Purpose Driven Life*.

The fourth major trade publishing group in the US is Simon & Schuster, which has been through a number of ownership changes since the mid-1970s. Founded in 1924 by Richard Simon and Max Schuster, Simon & Schuster was acquired in 1975 by Gulf & Western, a large and diversified American corporation with interests in many different industries, from construction and manufacturing to leisure and film. In 1989 Gulf & Western was restructured and renamed as Paramount Communications, which was itself acquired in 1994 by Viacom, a large American media conglomerate. In 2000 Viacom purchased CBS, but in 2005 Viacom/CBS split into two companies and CBS inherited Simon & Schuster. While Simon & Schuster ranks fourth among the large trade publishers in the US, its business is much more US-focused than is the case with its three larger competitors. In 2007 Simon & Schuster's global revenues in trade and mass-market publishing were around $886 million, of which $730 million or 82 per cent were in the US. This strong focus on the US market is linked to the fact that since 1975 Simon & Schuster has been owned by publicly quoted US corporations that did not see further acquisitions in trade publishing, whether domestic or overseas, as an investment priority. With the acquisition of Macmillan in 1994,

Scribner and The Free Press were added to Simon & Schuster's trade division, but much of Simon & Schuster's growth in consumer publishing was organic and they were not able to acquire overseas assets to expand internationally. 'The inability to acquire continued to plague us through the 1990s and early part of this century,' explained one senior executive at Simon & Schuster. 'So we have never had the opportunity to buy in the way that our major competitors did.'

Beneath these four large publishing groups, there are a number of medium-sized groups and companies that are active in the field of US trade publishing. These include what was until 2006 the Time Warner Book Group, which was the book publishing division of the Time Warner media conglomerate. Before Time Inc. merged with Warner Communications, Time Inc. had acquired in 1968 the old American publishing house Little, Brown, which had been founded in Boston in 1837. When Time and Warner merged in 1990 to form the Time Warner multimedia and entertainment conglomerate, Little, Brown was combined with Warner Books to form the Time Warner Book Group. In 2001 Time Warner merged with AOL, the giant internet services and media company, and in the reorganizations that followed the merger Time Warner sought to divest itself of various assets, including its book publishing division. The Time Warner Book Group was eventually sold to the French media conglomerate Hachette for $537 million in 2006. Hachette retained the Little, Brown imprint but changed the name of Warner Books to Grand Central Publishing. Hachette was already the largest publisher in France, the UK and Australia and New Zealand, and the second largest in Spain; with the acquisition of the Time Warner Book Group, it was now a serious player in the field of US trade publishing as well.

Another medium-sized player in US trade publishing is the family-owned Holtzbrinck group. The Holtzbrinck group was founded in Germany in the late 1940s, when Georg von Holtzbrinck collaborated with others to start a book club. In the 1960s this book club took over S. Fischer Verlag, one of Germany's leading publishing companies, and subsequently acquired other publishing interests in Germany. Holtzbrinck entered the field of US trade publishing in 1985, when it acquired the trade book division of Holt, Rinehart & Winston, which it renamed the Henry Holt Book Company. In 1994 it bought Farrar, Straus & Giroux, which Roger Straus decided to sell to Holtzbrinck after having held out against the corporations for many years. Holtzbrinck purchased a 70 per cent interest in the Macmillan Group in 1995 and acquired the remaining shares four years later. Holtzbrinck's US trade imprints now include Henry Holt, FSG, St Martin's Press and Picador.

The French media conglomerate Vivendi made a brief foray into the field of US trade publishing by acquiring the Boston-based publisher Houghton Mifflin in 2001. With its origins dating back to the 1830s, Houghton Mifflin was one of the older American publishing houses. In the nineteenth century it published some of the best-known American writers including Henry Wadsworth Longfellow, Ralph Waldo Emerson, Nathaniel Hawthorne, Harriet Beecher Stowe, Mark Twain and Henry David Thoreau, and throughout the twentieth century it maintained a trade division alongside a rapidly expanding programme of educational publications for schools and colleges. In 2001 Houghton Mifflin was acquired by Vivendi Universal for around $2.2 billion. However, Vivendi's growing financial difficulties forced it to sell off some of its assets, and in 2002 Houghton Mifflin was sold for $1.66 billion to a consortium of private investment firms led by Thomas H. Lee Partners and Bain Capital and including funds from the Blackstone Group. In 2006 Houghton Mifflin was sold again, this time to the educational software publisher Riverdeep for $3.36 billion. Founded by the Irish entrepreneur Barry O'Callaghan in 1995, Riverdeep entered the field of US educational publishing in the late 1990s with several acquisitions, including The Learning Company. In 2007, following the acquisition of Houghton Mifflin, the group acquired Harcourt Education, which includes the Harcourt trade publishing division, from the Anglo-Dutch publishing corporation Reed Elsevier. The group created from Riverdeep Software, Houghton Mifflin and Harcourt was then renamed Education Media and Publishing Group. The position of the Houghton Mifflin Harcourt trade division within EMPG remains somewhat unstable. It was offered for sale in March 2009 but withdrawn from the market when the offers received – rumoured to have been in the region of $250 million – were lower than expected.[9] A restructuring of the company's finances in 2009 and 2010 helped to reduce the large burden of debt that had been accumulated by EMPG and eased some of the financial pressure on the trade division.

Table 6 shows the 12 largest players in the field of US trade publishing in 2007–8. Bertelsmann-owned Random House remained top with US trade revenues of $1.266 billion; Penguin ranked second with US trade revenues of $1.015 billion; HarperCollins ranked third

[9] *Subtext*, vol. 14, no. 11 (1 Oct. 2009), p. 2.

Table 6   The 12 largest trade publishers in the US, 2007–2008

Rank	Publisher	Parent company	US trade/mass-market revenues 2007 ($m)	World trade/mass-market revenues 2007 ($m)	% growth since 2006 (world)	US sales as % of total	% of total US trade/mass-market[1]
1	Random House[2]	Bertelsmann	1,266	2,388	−5.6	53	13.1
2	Penguin[3]	Pearson	1,015	1,692	0	60	10.5
3	HarperCollins[4]	News Corp	903	1,290	−1.7	70	9.4
4	Simon & Schuster[5]	CBS	730	886	+9.8	82	7.6
5	Hachette Book Group USA[6]	Lagardère	507	1,687	+8.5	30	5.3
6	John Wiley & Sons[7]	John Wiley	390	469	+2.8	83	4.0
7	Scholastic[8]	Scholastic	389	423	+112.0	92	4.0
8	Holtzbrinck Book Group[9]	Holtzbrinck	225	350	+2.9	64	2.3
9	Rodale	Rodale	193	193	+3.2	100	2.0
10	Thomas Nelson[10]	InterMedia	190	190	−13.6	100	2.0
11	Houghton Mifflin Harcourt	Education Media and Publishing Group	180	197	−1.5	91	1.9
12	Sterling	Barnes & Noble	150	150	−6.2	100	1.6
	Total		**6,138**				**63.7**

Includes adult hardcover and paperback, children's hardcover and paperback, and mass-market paperback.
All sales are estimated with the exception of Random House and Wiley, and with the exceptions noted below.
[1] Combined trade/mass-market revenues for 2007 were $9,645 million according to the Association of American Publishers.
[2] Fiscal year (FY) ended 31 Dec. 2007.
[3] World revenues are actual; breakout of US revenues is estimated.
[4] FY ended 30 June 2007. Includes Zondervan.
[5] World revenues are actual; breakout of US revenues is estimated.
[6] Formerly Time Warner Book Group. Worldwide trade/mass-market revenues for year ended 31 Dec. 2007 are estimated. Total global sales for Lagardère Publishing were €2,130 million ($3,132 million) in 2007, of which trade/mass-market revenues accounted for around 54 per cent.
[7] Worldwide professional/trade segment for FY ended 30 Apr. 2007.
[8] Estimated trade sales only for FY ended 31 May 2008.
[9] Estimated worldwide trade revenues for FY ended 31 Dec. 2007.
[10] Estimated sales of books and Bibles only for FY ended 31 Mar. 2008.
Source: Open Book Publishing, 2008.

with estimated US trade revenues of $903 million; and Simon & Schuster ranked fourth with US trade revenues of $730 million.

There is a significant drop down to the next group. Following the acquisition of the Time Warner Book Group, the Hachette Group ranked fifth in the field of US trade publishing, with estimated US trade revenues of $507 million. The largest independent player in the field of US trade publishing is John Wiley, with US revenues in its professional/trade division amounting to $390 million (although this figure will include revenue from the sale of professional and academic books as well as trade titles). The educational and children's book publisher Scholastic moved up to seventh in 2007–8, thanks to the phenomenal success of the seventh and final volume of the Harry Potter series, *Harry Potter and the Deathly Hallows,* which was released in July 2007 and became the fastest selling book of all time, selling 11 million copies on the first day in the UK and US. This one title alone more than doubled Scholastic's revenue for the year, adding $270 million to a revenue line which, without the new Harry Potter, would have stood at $153 million; in 2008–9 Scholastic slipped back down to tenth place. The Holtzbrinck Group, with estimated US trade revenues of $225 million, ranked eighth. Rodale, an independent publisher based in Pennsylvania which is particularly well known for its health and fitness books and which published the hugely successful *The South Beach Diet* in 2003, ranked ninth, with estimated US trade sales of $193 million. Thomas Nelson, which ranked tenth with estimated US trade sales of $190 million, is a religious publisher based in Nashville; it was bought by the private equity firm InterMedia in 2006. Following the acquisition of Harcourt, the Houghton Mifflin Harcourt Group ranked eleventh, with estimated US trade sales of $180 million. Sterling, which publishes a range of how-to and general interest books and was bought by the superstore chain Barnes & Noble in 2003, ranked twelfth, with estimated US trade sales of $150 million.

In terms of market share, Random House had around 13 per cent of the US trade market, Penguin around 10.5 per cent, HarperCollins around 9.4 per cent and Simon & Schuster around 7.6 per cent. Taken together, these four groups accounted for around 40.6 per cent of US trade sales in 2007–8. The Hachette Group and the Holtzbrinck Group are commonly ranked as fifth and sixth among the 'big six' US trade publishers. Taken together, these top six publishing groups, all owned by large media corporations and conglomerates, accounted for just under half – 48.2 per cent – of total US trade sales. The top 12 publishers taken together accounted for 63.7 per cent of the total.

The dominant publishing groups in the UK

A similar process of consolidation occurred in the field of UK trade publishing from the early 1960s on. The notion of synergy was less prominent in the UK context, where large diversified corporations like RCA and Gulf & Western did not become heavily involved in book publishing. But while the mergers and acquisitions in British trade publishing had their own characteristics and the changes that took place were labyrinthine in their complexity as houses were bought and sold (sometimes numerous times) over a period of some 40 years, the overall trajectory of consolidation, as well as the overall outcome, were broadly similar.[10]

By the 1960s and early 1970s, a generation of entrepreneurial British publishers – Jonathan Cape, Michael Joseph, Jamie Hamilton, Stanley Unwin, Victor Gollancz and Allen Lane, among others – were reaching the ends of their productive careers and the publishing companies they had started or reinvigorated faced succession problems and uncertain futures. At the same time, North American corporations with existing interests in publishing began to look acquisitively at British trade houses, attracted by the common language and a weakening pound. One of the first North American corporations to do this was the Canadian-based Thomson Organization, as it was then known. Roy Thomson had begun his career in the media industries by starting up a local radio station and buying a local newspaper in Timmins, Ontario in the early 1930s. During the next two decades he expanded the business by acquiring a stable of Canadian newspapers and other companies. In the early 1950s Thomson turned his attention to the UK, acquiring the *Scotsman* and a range of other national and regional newspapers. He also diversified into other areas, including book publishing, buying Michael Joseph in 1961, the Scottish publisher Thomas Nelson in 1962 and Hamish Hamilton in 1965, though his company would subsequently divest itself of these as it shifted its focus to information, educational and professional publishing.

The paperback publisher Penguin, which had been founded by Allen Lane in 1935 and had grown into a major force in British

---

[10] In this section I've drawn heavily on Eric de Bellaigue's excellent essays on the transformation of British trade publishing; see de Bellaigue, *British Book Publishing*. See also Christopher Gasson's very helpful *Who Owns Whom in British Book Publishing* (Bookseller, 2002).

publishing by the 1950s, went public in 1961 and soon found itself
the object of growing interest from the American publisher McGraw-
Hill, which increased its holding in Penguin from 10 to 17 per cent
in the course of the 1960s.[11] Shortly after Allen Lane died in 1970,
Penguin was merged with Pearson Longman, partly in order to avert
an American takeover, which Lane had feared. Pearson had begun as
a small construction company in Yorkshire, in the north of England,
in 1844, and had expanded into the media business in the 1920s by
acquiring a group of provincial newspapers. In 1968 Pearson acquired
the book publisher Longman, which had been founded in 1724 by
Thomas Longman and passed down through several generations of
the Longman family until it became public in 1948. Following the
Longman and Penguin acquisitions, Pearson increased its international stake in educational publishing, acquiring the educational
businesses of HarperCollins, Simon & Schuster and Prentice Hall,
and provided Penguin with the resources to expand in the field of
trade publishing. Penguin bought Viking Press in 1975, an acquisition
that both greatly increased Penguin's US presence (Viking, with sales
of $15 million, was three times the size of Penguin's US business)[12]
and greatly strengthened Penguin's position in the world of American
hardback publishing, which made up three-quarters of Viking's business. In 1983 Penguin acquired Frederick Warne, which gave it
control of the copyrights of Beatrix Potter's children's books, and two
years later it bought Hamish Hamilton and Michael Joseph from
Thomson, two hardback houses that enabled Penguin to achieve a
much higher level of vertical integration in the UK. In 1986 Penguin
bought the New American Library, one of the top five US paperback
houses with a strong presence in mass-market publishing, and ten
years later it acquired Putnam Berkley, which had been bought by
MCA in 1982 and was now being divested by them. Putnam Berkley,
with its strong emphasis on frontlist commercial fiction, brought a
new range of highly successful authors to Penguin's US list, including
Tom Clancy, Patricia Cornwell and Dick Francis. With the financial
backing of Pearson, Penguin had transformed itself in three decades
from a leading UK paperback publisher into a major international
publishing corporation with a diversified, vertically integrated list and
a strong presence in both the US and the UK.

---

[11] Jeremy Lewis, *Penguin Special: The Life and Times of Allen Lane* (London: Viking, 2005), p. 397.
[12] de Bellaigue, *British Book Publishing*, p. 41.

The distinguished and once-independent British publishers Chatto & Windus (founded in 1855) and Jonathan Cape (founded in 1921) merged in 1969, following the death of Jonathan Cape in 1960. The aim of the merger was to achieve certain economies of scale by providing centralized warehousing, distribution and infrastructural services, while maintaining the distinctiveness and editorial autonomy of each house. In 1973 they were joined by The Bodley Head (founded in 1887) to form Chatto, Bodley Head and Jonathan Cape or CBC, and in 1982 the group acquired the feminist publishing house Virago (founded in 1972). This unique constellation of British publishing houses survived until 1987 when, following several years of disappointing financial results and mounting debt (the group reported pre-tax losses of 2.5 per cent in 1985 and 1986 and net debt of £3.4 million by December 1986),[13] the group was sold to Random House for £20 million. For Random House, which was seeking to expand its overseas presence, the acquisition of CBC provided an excellent foothold in the UK. (Virago extracted itself from the sale through a management buyout and remained independent until it was sold to Little, Brown, then part of the Time Warner publishing group, in 1996.) Random House further strengthened its presence in the UK by acquiring Century Hutchinson in 1989 for £64 million. Century Hutchinson had been formed in 1985 when Century Publishing, a start-up founded in 1981 by Anthony Cheetham, acquired Hutchinson, founded in 1887, from London Weekend Television, which had bought Hutchinson in 1978 in the hope – largely disappointed – that it could be productively combined with its television interests. When Bertelsmann acquired Random House in 1998, Bertelsmann's existing UK interests, which included Transworld, became part of Random House UK, turning it into one of the largest UK trade publishing groups.

The companies that eventually came under Hachette's control in the UK evolved through a complex series of mergers and acquisitions. Like Century Hutchinson, some of these were instances where a relatively youthful start-up took over an old established house, either because the older house was facing succession problems or because it had fallen on hard times and was looking for ways to strengthen its position. In 1991 Anthony Cheetham, who had started Century and merged it with Hutchinson before selling it to Random House, founded a new company, Orion, and acquired Weidenfeld &

---

[13] Ibid., pp. 145–7.

Nicolson, the prestigious house which had been founded by Lord Weidenfeld, a refugee from Austria, in 1949; Weidenfeld, who was in his seventies, was attracted by the idea of selling the company, 80 per cent of which he owned, to someone with whom he had had business links in the past. In 1998 a majority of the shares of Orion were sold to Hachette, who acquired the remaining shares in 2003. In 1998 the group acquired Cassell, whose imprints included Victor Gollancz, and in 2002 Hachette greatly increased its stake in the UK market by acquiring the Octopus Publishing Group.

Octopus had been founded in 1971 by the publishing entrepreneur Paul Hamlyn. Hamlyn had gained some experience with start-ups, having established Paul Hamlyn Books as a remainder merchant in 1949 and expanded it into a leading mass-market publisher before selling it to the International Publishing Corporation in 1964 for £2.275 million. With Hamlyn's commitment to publishing books for the widest possible market ('I only understand one kind of publishing and that is books of wide appeal that improve the quality of life from the stomach to the mind'),[14] Octopus grew rapidly, from a turnover of £1.85 million in 1972 to £30.75 million in 1982.[15] Octopus went public in 1983, with Hamlyn retaining 67 per cent of the capital. In 1985 Octopus acquired William Heinemann, a house that had been founded in London in 1890, had acquired Secker & Warburg in 1956 and had been taken over by Thomas Tilling, an industrial conglomerate, in 1961; Tilling was itself taken over by BTR, another industrial conglomerate, in 1983, and BTR sold Heinemann to Octopus two years later for a 35 per cent stake in the newly merged company. Two years after that, in 1987, Octopus was sold to Reed International for a hefty £535 million, 'at the peak of the acquisitive euphoria sweeping over publishing'.[16] Following Reed's merger in 1993 with Elsevier, the large Dutch STM publishing corporation, and after several years of disappointing results, Reed decided to dispose of its trade publishing interests. The adult trade division, including Heinemann and Secker & Warburg, was sold to Random House in 1997 for a relatively modest £17.5 million, while the illustrated books division was reborn as the Octopus Publishing Group through a management buyout. In 2001 the Octopus Publishing Group was acquired by Hachette.

---

[14] Paul Hamlyn in *Sunday Telegraph* (Feb. 1984), quoted in ibid., p. 92.
[15] de Bellaigue, *British Book Publishing*, p. 98.
[16] Ibid., p. 110.

The third strand to Hachette's British stakeholding came through its acquisition of Hodder Headline from WH Smith in 2004. Hodder Headline was created through the takeover of an old English publishing house, Hodder & Stoughton, founded in 1868, by a start-up, Headline, which was founded in 1986 by the publishing entrepreneur Tim Hely Hutchinson. Hodder & Stoughton was a family business, 80 per cent owned by the descendants of the founder, Matthew Hodder. In the late 1980s it found itself in difficult financial straights, in need of additional capital and with no institutional shareholders to call on. For Headline, which had launched in 1986 with an avowedly commercial frontlist and had gone public four years later, the attractions of acquiring an old house, nearly half of whose revenue was backlist, were evident enough. Headline acquired Hodder & Stoughton for £49 million in 1993, despite the fact that it was much smaller than its older acquisition (Headline's turnover in 1992 was around £16 million, compared to Hodder & Stoughton's turnover of around £56 million).[17] The newly formed Hodder Headline was subsequently sold to WH Smith, the high-street retailer, for £192 million in 1999. In 2002 WH Smith added John Murray to Hodder Headline. Founded in 1768, John Murray had remained a family-run business for over two centuries and had published some of the greatest English authors, including Lord Byron, Charles Dickens and Jane Austen, but with an annual turnover of around £8 million it was no longer in a position to compete with its larger and better-resourced competitors. However, as WH Smith found itself facing increasingly tough competition in the retail marketplace, it decided to sell Hodder Headline, which was bought by Hachette for £223 million in 2004, with Tim Hely Hutchinson remaining as CEO. With Hachette's acquisition of the Time Warner Book Group in 2006, Time Warner's UK book businesses, including Little, Brown, were added to Hachette's UK operations.

Table 7 summarizes the top ten UK publishers by revenue in 2007, using data from Nielsen BookScan.[18] Hachette's estimated UK trade revenues in 2007 of £298.8 million made it the largest player in the field of UK trade publishing, giving it a market share of 16.6 per cent, its numerous imprints in the UK now including Hodder & Stoughton, John Murray, Headline, Octopus, Orion, Weidenfeld & Nicolson, Gollancz, Phoenix, Little, Brown and Virago. Random House, with

---

[17] Ibid., p. 63.
[18] *The Bookseller* (24 January 2008).

Table 7   The ten largest trade publishers in UK, 2007

Rank	Publisher	Parent company	Estimated UK trade revenues (£m)	% growth since 2006	% of total UK trade market
1	Hachette Livre UK[1]	Lagardère	298.8	+5.1	16.6
2	Random House[2]	Bertelsmann	263.4	−2.5	14.6
3	Penguin	Pearson	177.3	−0.8	9.8
4	HarperCollins	News Corp	142.7	+0.6	7.9
5	Bloomsbury	Bloomsbury	74.7	+140.0	4.2
6	Pan Macmillan[3]	Holtzbrinck	61.4	+12.0	3.4
7	Oxford University Press		33.1	+0.3	1.8
8	Pearson Education	Pearson	32.3	+0.3	1.8
9	Simon & Schuster	CBS	26.9	+12.1	1.5
10	Egmont	Egmont Group	24.9	+8.9	1.4
	Total		1,135.5		63.0

Compiled from Nielsen BookScan's Total Consumer Market (TCM), which covers more than 90 per cent of UK book retail and internet sales, for the 52 weeks ending 29 Dec. 2007.
[1] Includes full-year sales and backdated previous-year sales for Piatkus, acquired by Little, Brown on 20 July 2007.
[2] Includes full-year sales and backdated previous-year sales for Virgin Books and BBC Group, acquired by Random House in 2007.
[3] Includes full-year sales and backdated previous-year sales for the children's publisher Kingfisher.

estimated UK trade sales of £263.4 million in 2007, occupied second place with a market share of 14.6 per cent; its more than 30 imprints in the UK now include Jonathan Cape, Chatto & Windus, William Heinemann, Harvill Secker, Bodley Head, Century, Hutchinson, Ebury, Transworld, Doubleday, Bantam, BBC Books and various paperback imprints like Vintage, Arrow, Corgi and Black Swan. Penguin ranked third with estimated UK trade sales of £177.3 million in 2007 and a market share of 9.8 per cent; in addition to Penguin, its imprints in the UK include Allen Lane, Viking, Hamish Hamilton, Michael Joseph, Dorling Kindersley and the Rough Guides. Harper-Collins, with estimated sales of £142.7 million in 2007, ranked fourth with 7.9 per cent of the market; its imprints include Harper Press, Collins, Fourth Estate, Voyager and Avon. Together, these four corporate groups accounted for nearly half – 48.9 per cent – of UK trade sales in 2007 (retail and internet).

The fact that independent publisher Bloomsbury occupied the fifth position in 2007 was due largely to the tremendous success of the seventh and final volume of the Harry Potter series, for which Bloomsbury controls the UK rights. Bloomsbury had estimated sales of around £74.7 million in 2007, but roughly half of this (£37 million) was accounted for by *Harry Potter and the Deathly Hallows* alone. The sales of this book pushed Bloomsbury up to fifth position in 2007 and increased Bloomsbury's market share to 4.2 per cent, though by 2008 Bloomsbury had fallen back to sixth place, with sales of £43.3 million, and its market share had fallen to 2.4 per cent.[19] The Holtzbrinck Group, which acquired a 70 per cent stake in Macmillan in 1995 and purchased the remaining shares in 1999, would normally occupy the fifth spot (to which it returned in 2008), but with estimated sales of £61.4 million in 2007, it is considerably smaller than the four main groups. In addition to Macmillan, Holtzbrinck's trade imprints in the UK include Pan, Picador, Tor and Sidgwick & Jackson. The top ten publishers, taken together, accounted for nearly two-thirds (63 per cent) of UK retail sales.

The four largest publishing groups in the field of UK trade publishing are also among the five largest trade publishing groups in the US. The only significant differences are that Hachette is much more dominant in the UK than it is in the US (although the acquisition of the Time Warner Book Group has moved it up to number five in the US) and Simon & Schuster is a much more significant player in the US

---

[19] 'Review of 2008', *The Bookseller*, 23 Jan. 2009, pp. 26–9.

than it is in the UK (a consequence of the fact that its American corporate owners did not historically make available the resources it would have needed to expand internationally, as noted earlier).

Concentration and creativity

For the large publishing corporations, the main advantages today of further acquisitions are twofold: they enable them to achieve quick top-line[20] growth in a mature and relatively static market, thereby increasing their market share and providing them with the benefits that stem from that (such as greater leverage in their negotiations with suppliers and retailers); and they provide opportunities to improve the bottom line by streamlining and rationalizing back-office operations and publishing services, such as finance, production, sales and distribution. But there are risks associated with the increasing size of publishing corporations, one of which is the danger that it will impinge on and damage the creative activities that lie at the heart of the publishing firm. This is one of the key questions that all large publishing corporations have to face: how to reconcile the economies that can be achieved through greater scale and rationalization with the creative editorial work upon which the future success of the corporation ultimately depends. How do they deal with it?

Different corporations have responded to this question in different ways. In a somewhat oversimplified fashion we could distinguish two basic approaches – what we could call the centralized model and the federal model. Each model is an ideal type in the Weberian sense – that is, an idealization of reality that highlights some features at the expense of others. The centralized model was probably more prevalent in the early phases of corporatization, when acquiring corporations were inclined to try to rationalize and reshape the publishing houses they acquired. In more recent years the federal model has come to be seen by many senior managers as a more effective way to organize a corporate publishing group, although in practice there are many different gradations of federation.

The centralized model seeks to achieve the maximum benefits of economies of scale by combining forces wherever possible and reor-

---

[20] 'Top line' refers to the total revenue generated from the sale of goods and services, before all costs, expenses and other charges have been taken off to show the net income or profit, also known as the 'bottom line'.

ganizing all aspects of the publishing operation, from back-office systems and publishing services to sales, marketing and editorial. Following a merger or acquisition, the company acquired is relocated to the premises of the parent company (or, in the case of large-scale mergers or acquisitions, new shared premises are found), thereby achieving significant reductions in overheads. The business and financial operations are merged, often leading to redundancies and further cost savings. The sales forces are also merged to create a single integrated sales force for the whole company, again with further savings. The editorial operations will also be restructured; lists will be recombined and possibly rebranded to reflect a new vision for the publishing company. Different types and genres of publishing may be reassigned to new or different imprints – e.g. an imprint for literary fiction, one for commercial fiction, one for science fiction, one for non-fiction, one for lifestyle, one for sport, and so on. The old names of acquired companies may be given a new identity in this process – what was once a general trade publisher may be rebranded as a publisher of a particular type or genre of books. Some of the old names might disappear, or be retained only as part of a new name. The company that emerges from this process of reorganization will be restructured from top to bottom. It will not be a continuation of the old companies under different ownership but will be a new company with a new vision of itself and of the way it is seeking to position itself in the field. It will also be much leaner and more efficient than the old companies, operating as separate entities, would have been – in terms of overheads and operating costs, not $1 + 1 = 2$ but $1 + 1 = 1.5$ (or less).

The federal model is less radical in terms of the extent of restructuring. It seeks to reap the benefits of economies of scale while at the same time preserving some of the autonomy of the old publishing units. As one senior manager put it, reflecting on the way they set out to restructure the organization following a major acquisition, 'We had to be big and small at the same time. We needed to be really big where it mattered and we needed to be really small where it mattered.' It matters to be big when you are dealing with suppliers like printers and negotiating with retailers, where size gives you leverage and power. It also helps to be big when it comes to providing publishing services like warehousing, distribution, finance and IT, where you need to invest substantial sums of money in order to gain efficiencies and where you can achieve real economies of scale. However, in a creative industry like publishing there are areas like editorial where it matters to be small:

The benefits of being small are that you're working with creative talent and they don't want to feel like they're working with a sausage machine. So they need to have their editor, the publicist, the production person who cares about them, etc. – the person they know they can speak to. They need the personal contact; they don't want to feel that they're working with just anyone. The other thing about being small is if you're a small group of people passionate about a small range of books then each one will get attention, whereas if you're a big organization that looks at books just in terms of which are the biggest, and spends all of its time on the ones that are the biggest, there will be lots of books that don't get attention in terms of publicity, marketing, etc. So you need to be big where it matters and small where it matters.

Another reason why it matters to be small in a business like trade publishing is that there is a large element of judgement and personal taste involved in the acquisitions process – in deciding which books to buy and how much to pay for them – and a large element of luck involved in which books turn out to be successful. Not everything is a matter of luck, to be sure, and there are things you can do to inform and guide acquisitions decisions – you can look at the historical performance of similar titles, you can introduce more formalized budgeting procedures, you can give sales and marketing directors some role in acquisitions decisions, and so on. Most of the corporations (and indeed most trade publishers, whether they were part of corporations or not) introduced procedures of this kind in the course of the 1980s and 1990s. But at the end of the day there is an inescapable element of judgement and taste involved in the acquisitions process, especially when it comes to taking on new authors who lack an established track record, and an ineliminable element of luck involved in the success or otherwise of certain books, and if you try to standardize and rationalize the acquisitions process too much you run the risk of inhibiting the very creativity upon which the success of the organization depends. Sometimes an editor's decision to follow his or her instincts and take on a book that has been rejected by others turns out to be an inspired move and the book turns out to be a huge success. The small independent trade houses are particularly well attuned to benefit from this kind of serendipity – the story of Harry Potter is the classic example but is by no means an isolated case. But there are many in the corporate groups who believe that in a creative industry like trade publishing, the devolution of editorial decision-making to small editorial teams operating with a high degree of autonomy within certain financial parameters is the best way to

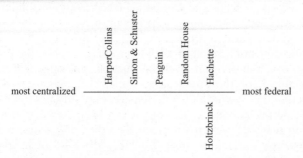

Figure 5 Major publishing corporations on the centralized–federal
spectrum

maximize your chances of success. As one senior manager in a large
corporation put it, 'We're giving somebody a playing field and we're
putting fences around the edge of it and saying, "If you want to cross
one of those fences, you have to ask a question. But if you're playing
in the field you can do what you like." You give people a lot of scope,
but you provide a framework within which they operate.'

Any particular publishing corporation at any particular point in
time can be situated somewhere along the centralized–federal spectrum, from highly centralized at one extreme to a loose federation of
publishing units with minimal centralization at the other (see figure
5). HarperCollins has traditionally been situated near the centralized
end of the spectrum, whereas groups like Hachette and Holtzbrinck
have tended to situate themselves at the federal end, with corporations like Simon & Schuster, Penguin and Random House somewhere
in between – Simon & Schuster and Penguin probably being a little
more centralized than Random House (at least in the UK, where the
senior management of Random House publicly advocates a federal
model). The most decentralized of the federal groups allow some of
the publishing houses they own to retain their own premises and they
maintain separate sales forces for different imprints or divisions, even
though these arrangements increase the cost base. 'You can't do a
halfway house on this federal thing,' explained a senior manager at
one of the most decentralized groups. 'You can only maintain the
imprints separately if they are totally separate, by which I mean if
they control their own sales, their own marketing, their own art, their
own publicity. So they have to have a very different flavour.'

Most of the large corporations don't go this far, since the more you
decentralize, the less you are able to reduce the cost base and gain

the economies of scale that can be achieved from consolidation. So typically they will organize the imprints into clusters or divisions that are treated as separate profit centres. Each imprint may have its own marketing and publicity staff, although in some cases these may be centralized at the division level. Production and sales will typically be centralized for the group as a whole, although some divisions might retain their own production department and sales force – many different permutations are possible. It is a balancing act with profitability on one side and creativity on the other, and senior managers are constantly looking at how to achieve the kind of balance they think would be best for their organization. They keep this question under constant review and may change their position over time, depending on the financial pressures they face and on what they see, at any particular point in time, as the most effective way to structure their organization. Moreover, the way that one branch of a corporation in a particular country, such as the UK, positions itself on this spectrum may not be the same as the way that another branch of the same corporation in another country, like the US, positions itself – these branches may operate with considerable autonomy and the senior management may be given a large degree of latitude by their parent corporation to organize their branch as they see fit.

Given that different corporations, and even different branches of the same corporation, position themselves differently along the centralized–federal spectrum and that the more federal groups devolve a great deal of autonomy to their imprints or divisions, it follows that there is a great deal of variability in the ways that the different corporations and imprints operate. The world of corporate publishing is, in practice, a plurality of worlds, each operating in its own way. Certain procedures are common to them all but the ways in which editors and others operate vary considerably from one corporation to another, and even from one imprint to another within the same corporation. A corporate headquarters, like Random House's imposing skyscraper at 1745 Broadway in New York, may look to the casual observer like the house of a well-ordered bureaucracy where all procedures have been formalized and standardized, but in reality it is more like a conservatory that houses a plurality of micro-environments, each of which is allowed to grow its own exotic varieties of vegetation provided that it meets certain conditions.

Let us step inside one of these micro-environments for a moment. 'Star' is an old imprint that was acquired some while ago by a house that has gone through several changes of ownership over the years and is now part of a large international corporation with a major stake in publishing. Star is a prestigious imprint that once had its own offices in midtown Manhattan but now occupies one of the upper floors of a large corporate building. It is unique in some ways, partly because of its history and its standing: in terms of symbolic capital, it is richly endowed. But it now lives alongside numerous other imprints in one of the worlds of corporate publishing. Many of those who work for Star have lived through two or three changes of ownership, they've seen corporate bosses come and go and experienced various cycles of reform. But for the most part they've successfully buffered themselves from it all. 'There is an unspoken rule,' explains one senior editor who has worked at Star for some 30 years, 'put one toe out of the elevator to interfere with us and we will cut you off at the knees. And the only thing that enables us to take that attitude is profitability. As long as we make the money, we can tell them to go fuck themselves. It's as simple and as old-fashioned as that. The second that goes wrong, we've had it. If we stop being profitable, the incursions will start.'

At Star, editors continue to have a great deal of latitude to buy the books they want, and decisions about what to buy are taken in one-to-one discussions between the editor and the publisher – that is, the head of Star. 'Our editorial meetings – which happen once a month if X [the publisher] can be bothered to have it, and he has always had a deep dislike of meetings, so months can go by with no meeting at all – these meetings exist only for the editors to announce what they have bought. The editorial meeting does not exist to have a discussion about what we should buy.' When an editor wants to buy a book, he or she must prepare a case. This will include doing a profit and loss sheet or 'P&L'. The P&L is a financial summary of the likely revenue that will be generated and costs that will be incurred in publishing a book. It typically uses a standard template into which certain variable numbers are plugged – e.g. first-year hardcover sales, subsequent paperback sales, prices, etc. The template applies certain fixed charges, such as cost of sales, royalties, discounts, returns, marketing costs, overhead charges, etc., and shows the projected financial contribution of the book – that is, the net profit or loss.[21]

---

[21] For a helpful breakdown of the typical elements of a P&L for a trade book, see Albert N. Greco, Clara E. Rodriguez and Robert M. Wharton, *The Culture and Commerce of Publishing in the 21st Century* (Stanford, Calif.: Stanford University Press, 2007), pp. 121–4. However, what one doesn't get from a formal analysis of this kind is any sense of the role that the P&L actually plays in the day-to-day lives of editors and publishers.

By estimating the royalties that would be paid if the sales forecast turned out to be accurate, the P&L also gives the publisher some indication, in theory at least, of the level of advance that he or she might sensibly pay for the book. But the P&L is at best a rough approximation of the financial performance of a book; it may provide some helpful guidelines but for many editors and publishers the P&L is a kind of corporate fabrication. 'They're a total fabrication, on top of which nobody looks at them,' said the former publisher of Star, now retired. The corporate managers introduced P&Ls as a way of trying to instil a greater degree of financial discipline into the acquisitions process, but editors and publishers know that the numbers can be made up to reflect what you want to do. Here's what happens, explained the former publisher of Star:

> I'm going to buy a book. To justify buying a book we have to fill out a profit and loss statement. Now suppose I am buying your biography of Vanessa Bell, and you're just about to start five years of research and three years of writing about her. And I'm supposed to justify the $50,000 advance. So I'm supposed to know how many copies we're going to print, how many pictures we're going to have, what paper's going to cost, what the price of a book is going to be, and most important, how good it is. Well, it's clearly a wank – there's no way that any possible person can do it. And so you say to your assistant, 'We're spending $50,000. Work up figures that make sense and stick them in.' Everybody knows they're lies.

While not irrelevant, the P&L is not the crucial part of the case the editor has to make. Much more important is simply the editor's judgement of the quality and importance of the book and its likely sales based on a reading of the proposal or manuscript and her experience and knowledge of the market. Commercial considerations will come into play as an integral part of the assessment of the project and its potential, but not to the exclusion of quality. 'Sure, I think very much of commercial considerations,' said one senior editor. 'If we don't make money as a company, nobody will be here. But at the same time, I never walk away from talent. If I see terrific talent, even if I don't believe we're going to make money on that book, I wholeheartedly embrace it.' The editor might ask one or two colleagues down the corridor to look at some material to get some other opinions, she might consult with someone in publicity or sales to get their views on promotion prospects and she might talk with the paperback publisher to get his view of the book's paperback potential – this additional input will help her to form a judgement about whether to press ahead with the book and, assuming that the feedback from colleagues is positive, build a case. The purpose of building the case is to persuade the publisher that she should be allowed to buy or bid for the book – this decision is taken in discussion with the publisher, but ultimately it is the publisher who has the final word. The former publisher of Star put it like this:

> An editor would come to me and say, 'I've just read this book, I really love it, I think we should do it.' I say, 'Fine, give it to me.' I read it that night. The next morning I would say, 'Fine, I don't like it as much as you do but you love it so let's buy it.' And she would say, 'What can we spend?' And my head would be the P&L statement. After 30 seconds I'd figure out what I thought it might sell, what the paperback rights might go for, whether it had a bookclub chance, whether we might sell foreign rights and I'd say 'You can spend $35,000.' That was the P&L. Publishing was a very simple matter: a successful publisher or editor is right more often than he's wrong. No one is right 100 per cent of the time, or even 80 per cent of the time. That's the business. And if you don't lose too much money on the ones that don't work and if there's an opportunity to make a good deal of money on some of the ones that do work, you're in profit.

So long as Star is profitable and meets its financial targets, then the business and finance people will leave them alone. 'If you make your numbers, you'll be fine. If you don't make them, all the rules are off and that's very clear,' explained one senior editor. Those at the top of the corporation value the imprint both for the financial contribution it makes and for the quality of its books, quality as measured by things like prizes, Nobel Laureates, front-page reviews in the *New York Times Book Review* and so on – there are many different ways of attesting to quality. This is part of the mystique of the imprint, 'and the one thing corporate owners are scared shitless of is messing with mystique,' said another senior editor. 'Mystique is what they don't understand. All they know is, if it works, don't break it.' The experience of the former publisher reflected this:

> I had lunch the other day with [AB], who was the president of the corporation when I was there. I said to him, 'You know, [A], in my 19 years of working with you, you never once asked me a question about [Star]. All you wanted was my advice on how to run the corporation.' He said, 'Well, I don't think that's true.' I said, 'Believe me,

I would've noticed. Nor did you ever bother to say "Well done."' He said, 'Well, that's true, because I knew you were running it wonderfully and it was making a profit and you knew far more about how to do it than I did. I couldn't contribute anything, so why would I even think about it?'

Of course, not every imprint will have the same experience as Star, nor will their procedures be the same. Star occupies a unique position in the field, thanks in part to the prestige attached to its name and its consistent record of success in both financial and symbolic terms. The culture of the house has been maintained with a remarkable degree of continuity over four decades and several changes in corporate ownership, a continuity linked to the fact that it has had very few changes at the head of the house and many of its senior editors have remained in place despite the changes. Not all trade houses have been so fortunate.

Let us step inside another trade house, 'Cedar Press', which now occupies several floors in an attractive office building in central London. Cedar was bought by a large corporation some while ago. For many years Cedar was left to get on with what it was doing, with minimal interference from the corporate owners. But as the company began to make further acquisitions, it grew too large to operate as a single entity and it was broken into separate divisions, with different imprints clustered into different divisions. A difficult period financially coincided with retirements at the top and new senior management was brought in. Some of the publishers and senior editors who had been at Cedar for many years left at that time; others were encouraged to go. Individuals from outside were brought in to head up some of the divisions and imprints, which helped to instil a new culture in the organization. What had been a very male culture – 'sharp, clever, slightly cynical' – became something quite different: younger, more female, more oriented to success. One senior editor who lived through the changes and still works for Cedar today described the transformation like this:

It's become more success-oriented, more figures-driven; I would say that the commercial enterprise has moved much more to the centre. There probably was a sense that by the 1980s we had become rather remote and elitist and that some of our competitors had taken the commercial ground from under us, and we probably did need to rediscover that. And I think that's been the main force of the last ten years or so – to build up again the core commercial popular fiction area. One of my colleagues once said to me that our job was to manage [Cedar's] decline gracefully, and I thought that was a rather charming thing to be doing, whereas there's none of that here. It's very success-oriented. You get an email at 4 o'clock most afternoons saying 'We're number one with this' or 'We sold 100,000 of that.' There's a constant celebration of commercial success.

In this new, more commercial culture, it is much more difficult for an editor to buy a book. In the past, if you were an editor of a certain seniority, you could almost certainly buy a book you wanted to buy. It had to go through the publisher but he would almost always say yes. But now it is much harder, the hurdles at the beginning are much higher. Why? 'Because they want to cut down on the numbers being published and they're only interested in really big books. There's not much truck for or patience with small books any more. There was a time when it would have been fine to publish a book that sold four or five thousand copies in hardback and then went on to sell eight to ten thousand paperbacks, but now it's like why did we bother?' There are exceptions. An editor might still be allowed to publish some poetry books, for example, even though no one expects them to sell more than a few thousand copies. But these are exceptions. Even if books often turn out to do less well than you hoped when you bought them, you have to start out thinking they might be big. 'Some time ago I published books which I knew were going to be small, in the hope that in some ways they were either classic books potentially or might backlist at high levels, or that the author might go on to write big books, whereas now I think there's a feeling that if you know it's going to be small than we shouldn't do it.'

In the past, Cedar was very much editorially driven, and sales and marketing were rarely involved in the acquisitions process. 'I remember a meeting – this is going back a very long way – that was attended by the head of sales and marketing, a very nice man named [MN]. I was unsure about a proposal and I happened to say in the meeting, "[M], I'd like to talk to you about this proposal I've got." The head of the company, who happened to be at the meeting, asked me to stay behind, and he said, "[Philip], I'm going to teach you one thing: you're the editor and you don't ask sales and marketing what books to publish." That's unimaginable here now.' Now an editor has to make a case for a book he or she wants to buy, and has to get a few key people to sign up. The proposal has to go through a local editorial meeting and then an acquisitions meeting that is attended by the managing director of the division and the publishers of the various imprints but also by the head of sales, the head of marketing and various other people. It can be a tough meeting – 'It's certainly not a pushover.' Proposals can get turned down. Editors try to avoid mishaps by preparing the ground as well as they can in advance. 'I think politically the best thing to do is to make it a shoo-in by having enough people on your side before you go to that meeting, and particularly the guy who chairs it, the MD, because if he's on your side then you're fine. Even though the little meeting liked your proposal, if you take it along to the big meeting without any support it could go anywhere, you're just opening it up to anything – I mean I've seen people humiliated there. It's not quite as bad as I understand some newspaper meetings are every morning but it can get a bit rough.'

From the viewpoint of the management at Cedar, subjecting proposals to more intensive scrutiny is all about refining judgements and balancing risks. It's not a matter of replacing the power of the editor with the power of sales and marketing, let alone the power of the accountants. It's more a matter of clarifying what kind of book it is, what its market is likely to be and what sales prospects it can realistically be expected to have. One senior manager at Cedar put it like this:

> I think all acquisitions decisions still start with the editor. Editors are still allowed to do something on a whim and that's right; they need to exercise judgement and taste and be entrepreneurial and risk-taking. But I think it's no bad thing that the voice of sales and marketing has become more powerful so that those acquisition decisions can be more informed. If someone is buying a book, the sales person wants to know what kind of book it is and how much the editor loves it, and then the sales person can say, 'Well, given the type of book, the best scenario is X and the worst scenario is Y. I can give you those two levels, then it's up to you.' But a publishing house where the acquisitions decisions are entirely run by sales and marketing would be a complete disaster, and not least because you have to spot new trends and some authors and books invent new markets. And at the end of the day, if you're talking about a piece of brilliant literary fiction, what can a sales and marketing person say? You've got to rely on the taste of the editors.

The publishing manager who is responsible for the division sees the acquisitions process as the building of a portfolio of risk. There are some areas of the portfolio where you have to take big risks on new writers, 'because tastes and fashions constantly evolve and brilliant new talent can emerge from anywhere'. But this has to be counterbalanced by books that have much more predictable sales. 'I don't know how one would quantify it,' the manager explained, 'but perhaps 20 per cent of your commissioning is very risky and new and some of it will work and some of it won't.' While the house can and should continue to take on new writers, the books have to be carefully chosen and there can't be too many, simply because they represent one of the riskiest categories in the publisher's portfolio of risk.

We have briefly stepped into two micro-environments in the world of corporate publishing, each unique, each very different from the other and each characterized by its own culture, procedures and practices. Every imprint and micro-environment displays its own peculiar traits; even within the same publishing corporation, two imprints or divisions on different floors or different parts of the same building may operate in very different ways. Publishing corporations are far from being faceless bureaucracies where everything has been standardized and homogenized, and the more the corporation adheres to a federal model, the more variability there is likely to be. Nevertheless there are certain common themes that can be discerned across the different publishing corporations – let me highlight a few.

In the first place, all publishing corporations are organized into divisions or companies, and imprints are generally clustered together in these divisions. The management structure varies from corporation to corporation and it tends to be more complex in those corporations that are organized along more federal lines, but there is always a clear line of power and authority, so that, for example, the editors report to the heads of the imprints (often called publishers), the publishers report to the head of the division, and the heads of the divisions report to the president or CEO.

Depending on the corporation, publishers or heads of division are vested with a great deal of power in terms of deciding which books to take on and how much to pay for them. In some houses or imprints, decisions about which books to buy are taken by the publisher in discussion with the editor; in other houses they are taken by the publisher and the editorial director in discussion with the editor. It is up to the editor to sift through the submissions from agents, read proposals and manuscripts and decide which books he or she is interested in buying. The editor may ask one or two other editors for their opinions (especially if the editor is relatively new or junior) but they will very rarely (if ever) go out of house for an opinion. The editor may consult with sales and marketing staff, especially when the stakes are high, and may also consult with the publisher of the relevant paperback imprint whose support can be crucial for some books (namely, those for which the sales in paperback are expected to account for a substantial part of the book's revenue); the more commercial the imprint or house, the more important the views of sales and marketing staff tend to be. These consultations are all part and parcel of making the case for buying a book. The editor has to persuade the publisher (or the publisher and editorial director) that they should be allowed to buy the book, and learning how to make this case effectively is a central part of the editor's craft. 'It's a bit like fly fishing,' explained one editor at an imprint in a large corporation. 'You have to pick your spot and pick your moment, look at the light on the water, choose your fly carefully, drop it in at exactly the right place and hope something happens. It's like that here. You have to pick your moment and present a book in a way that will catch the publisher's imagination and enable her to see how it could work and how it could help build the list.'

Editorial meetings, or acquisitions meetings, exist in many divisions or imprints but their role varies considerably from one corporation, division or imprint to another. Often these meetings are formal occasions in which decisions that have already been taken are simply reported; editors may also report on the proposals or manuscripts they have received from agents and which they are actively pursuing, report on the outcome of auctions, etc. No decisions are actually taken at the meetings and the discussion is primarily an exchange of information. However, in some divisions or imprints, the acquisitions meetings do have a more substantive role. In some divisions, acquisitions decisions taken at a lower level – e.g. between the editor and publisher in an imprint of the division – have to be presented at an acquisitions meeting of the division where sales and marketing directors as well as publishers may be present; editors may have to line up outside, wait their turn and then go in and make their pitch. In meetings of this kind it is vital for editors to do their homework in advance, get key people on board before the meeting and, crucially, make sure that their publisher is fully behind them. But even when everything has been carefully prepared the outcome cannot be guaranteed, since a great deal can depend on what happens in the meeting itself and how the head of the division, who in this setting has the ultimate power to decide, responds to the book and the pitch.

In all publishing corporations – and, indeed, in independent trade houses too – editors are expected to complete a P&L for each book they buy. However, while the completion of a P&L is a routine part of the acquisitions process, financial calculations of this kind generally play a less important role than many outside observers tend to think. All publishers and editors may not be as cynical as the former head of Star but many share his view that calculations of this kind are procedural formalities that have little bearing on the actual process of deciding which books to buy and how much to pay for them. Most experienced editors and publishers have an intuitive idea of how much they should pay for a book and they don't need a P&L to tell them what the numbers should be. 'Usually the number I give my boss is just based on my ballpark sense in my head of what it's worth,' explained one senior editor. 'I think we can all do a P&L backwards in our head.'

In every corporation there are rules that govern advances and stipulate how much can be authorized by whom. A publisher or head of division will have the authority to approve an advance up to a certain level, say $200,000 or £100,000. After that, he or she will have to get the approval of someone higher up the chain of command, such as the president, who may have the authority to approve an advance up to another level, say $500,000 or £250,000. Anything more than that will have to be authorized by someone higher up the chain, such as the CEO. There will also be rules governing competition between the imprints or divisions. In some cases different imprints or divisions of the same corporation will be allowed to bid for the same project, provided that there is at least one outside bidder; in other cases the corporation will make a house bid, on the understanding that if they are successful then the agent and author can choose which imprint to be published by; and so on.

Every publishing corporation operates with budgets. The budget is the key place where the financial requirements of the corporate owners intersect with the practical business of running the publishing organization. It is a central feature in the life of the publishing corporation and a great deal of time, effort and thought goes into the annual exercise of constructing it. The budget also places considerable financial pressure on the heads of divisions or imprints, to whom specific financial targets are allocated each year on the basis of the final budget that is agreed with the corporate owners. One of the key tasks and responsibilities of senior managers in the publishing corporation is to translate the budget into concrete financial targets and decide how to distribute these targets among the heads of the various divisions or imprints. For the heads themselves, this means that every year they are presented with targets that they have to try to meet, and they in turn have to work with the publishers for whom they are responsible to decide what they can do to meet their targets.

It follows that middle management – the publishers and heads of divisions – are often those who experience the greatest pressure in publishing corporations. They are the switching points, as it were, where the financial requirements of the corporate owners are translated into the practical need to generate extra sales, either by buying new books or by extracting more out of the books that have already been bought. Editors, for their part, are often shielded from this pressure and left to get on with their jobs; it is not uncommon for editors to be completely oblivious to, or only dimly aware of, larger financial issues. 'Part of my role is to protect other people in the company from that pressure everyday,' explained one division head, 'because I think it's wrong to put too much pressure on commissioning editors and publishers. It can paralyse them.' But for the middle managers, focusing on the budget and doing everything they can to meet their targets is a constant source of pressure – 'It is definitely a stressful process and I know my numbers every day.'

Five myths about publishing corporations

We shall probe further into the workings of publishing corporations in later chapters but first I want to dispel a few myths about them, some of which have been perpetrated or perpetuated by the memoirs of some former employees.

Myth 1: The corporations have no interest in publishing quality books. All they are interested in publishing is commercial bestsellers. Of course, the corporations are interested in publishing commercial bestsellers (and so too are many of the independent publishing houses). But to say that they are not interested in publishing books of quality is simply wrong. Of course, 'quality' is a slippery term; even in commercial fiction, there are good thrillers and bad ones. But leaving aesthetic questions aside, it is important to see that all of the large publishing corporations have imprints or divisions that are explicitly concerned with publishing literary fiction or serious non-fiction. These imprints or divisions are unlikely to be the biggest and the best resourced, but the mere fact that they exist at all attests to a certain commitment on the part of the large corporations to publishing books of quality. Why do they do this? Why don't they simply axe those parts of the list that are less commercial in character and concentrate their resources on publishing books that are likely to sell in larger numbers?

Three reasons. First, quality books can sell well if you get the right ones. They can also sell for much longer than many of the more commercial books, which means that they can help to offset the reliance of the large corporations on frontlist publishing. So there are good financial reasons for publishing quality books. Second, most of the publishing corporations seek to develop a balanced list, where commercial fiction and popular non-fiction are complemented by books of a more serious kind. To some extent this is a matter of personal taste and predisposition on the part of senior managers, but it is also a matter of creating a diversified portfolio of risk. Since it is very difficult to know where the next runaway success will be or which author will become successful in five years' time, it makes sense to hedge your bets by spreading your risks. Third, symbolic capital matters to most large publishing corporations; it is not just a matter of financial success. Winning a major literary prize is not quite as good as getting picked by Oprah or getting on the bestseller list, but it does matter. It reaffirms the judgement of the editor or publisher and it brings some kudos to the organization. If it is a major prize, it can also increase the visibility of the author and the book and have a significant impact on sales. So to varying degrees, the large publishing corporations are committed to publishing books of quality, and it would be difficult to argue that the rise of publishing corporations has resulted in a clear decline in the quality of books being published, or that today books of quality are being published only by the independents – there are countless examples that would belie the latter claim. Having said that, it is undoubtedly the case that the sales thresholds that quality books have to meet in most corporations are high (and have got higher in recent years) and that current market conditions make it increasingly difficult for the large corporations to do this kind of publishing, as we shall see.

Myth 2: The owners of large corporations exercise a baleful influence on the editorial content of the publishing houses they own, obliging them to realign their editorial output so that it is consistent with the political values and beliefs of the owners and censoring content that might be perceived as contrary to the corporation's interests. There are cases where corporate owners have sought to influence the editorial output of publishing houses – a notorious example being the decision by HarperCollins to cancel the book by Chris Patten, the former governor of Hong Kong, which was critical of the Chinese government.[22] This was undoubtedly a clumsy and ill-judged move on the part of HarperCollins and they paid heavily in terms of bad publicity, but instances of this kind are rare. Corporate owners are generally content to remain at a distance from the editorial activities of the publishing companies they own. They want and expect their publishing houses to deliver good financial results, but they do not want to get involved in day-to-day decisions about whether to publish a particular book or author. To the extent that there is pressure on the editorial autonomy of a publishing house, it is more likely to take the form of a kind of mild nepotism (such as an expectation that the house will publish a book by the owner or a senior figure in the corporation) or a subtle kind of self-censorship on the part of publishers and senior managers rather than overt pressure from corporate bosses. Publishers and senior managers simply avoid taking on the kind of book that could give rise to friction. They have enough to worry about in terms of maintaining good relations with their owners, and they don't want to add to their list of worries by publishing books that could ruffle feathers in the corporate HQ. ('You need to be sensitive,' is how one former CEO put it. 'If you worked for Disney, would you publish a book that was anti-Mickey Mouse?') The senior managers of the publishing houses owned by large corporations very rarely, if ever, experience pressure that could be interpreted as a clear threat to their editorial independence, though the absence of pressure of this kind is no doubt due in part to the fact that senior managers adjust their publishing practices in ways that minimize the risk of conflict of this kind.

Myth 3: The corporations don't experiment with new authors. They're only interested in publishing established authors who write books according to tried and tested formulas. Nothing could be further from the truth. Indeed, the really surprising thing about the large publishing corporations is not that they are unwilling to

---

[22] In 1998 the London branch of HarperCollins sought to cancel Chris Patten's book, which it had signed the previous year for £125,000. Patten's editor at HarperCollins, Stuart Proffitt, stood by his author and was suspended from his job; he subsequently resigned and moved to Penguin. The book, *East and West*, was published later that year by Macmillan. HarperCollins is owned by Rupert Murdoch's News Corporation, which has substantial financial and media interests in China, including Star TV, a major satellite television network based in Hong Kong that serves mainland China and other parts of Asia. It is widely believed that Murdoch objected to the publication of Patten's book on the grounds that Patten's forthright criticism of the Chinese government could harm his business interests in China, although Murdoch's precise role in the affair remains a matter of debate.

experiment with new authors but, on the contrary, that they are willing to do so with such reckless abandon. They are desperate to find new talent and are willing to pay very large sums of money for books by first-time authors when they think they have the potential to sell well. We'll get a better idea of why this is so when we examine the factors that shape the buying decision in chapter 5. But here let us simply note that when we've understood these factors, we'll see that the real problem is not with new authors, who in some ways are in a privileged position in the field, but rather with those authors who have published one or two or several books that have not sold as well as the publishers had hoped. The publishing corporations are not uninterested in new talent, but they are impatient with talent that has not proved its mettle in the marketplace.

Myth 4: In the large publishing corporations, editors have lost the power they once had in the traditional publishing houses. Sales directors, marketing directors and accountants are the new power brokers and they decide what gets published. There is an element of truth in the first sentence, but the second sentence simply doesn't follow. It is true that in many traditional publishing houses, editors often had a great deal of scope to decide what to publish, and sales and marketing staff were generally not involved in these decisions. The publishing model was essentially linear: editors and publishers decided what to publish, marketing staff marketed it and sales reps sold it. In the course of the 1980s and 1990s, this traditional linear model was replaced in many publishing firms – not just in the publishing corporations but in many independent houses too – by a more dialogical and consultative model in which the views of sales and marketing staff were actively taken into account in the acquisitions process. Editors were encouraged to get the views of sales, marketing and publicity staff for certain kinds of books, especially when it was clear that the stakes would be high. If acquisitions meetings were introduced, sales and marketing directors were commonly asked to attend. Partly this was in order to inject a sales and marketing perspective into the deliberations – what kind of market is this book likely to have? which channels can we sell it into and in what quantities? what kind of publicity could we get for it?, and so on. Partly it was also in order to ensure that the house was behind the book and that the enthusiasm was widely shared so that the chances of turning it into a success were maximized. But none of this implies that the editor has become powerless in publishing corporations and that the key acquisitions decisions are now taken by sales, marketing and financial staff.

Practices vary from corporation to corporation and imprint to imprint but in all corporations and imprints it is still the editors who are the driving forces behind new book acquisitions. They are the ones who scrutinize proposals and books and decide which ones they want to buy. They will generally have to make a case for buying the book, and in some imprints or divisions they will have to present the case at an acquisitions meeting, as we have seen. In many imprints, editors no longer have the kind of free hand to acquire books that they once had. But this does not mean that sales and marketing directors are the new power brokers. The more commercial the imprint, the more power the sales and marketing directors are likely to have, but even in avowedly commercial houses it is the editors and publishers who drive the acquisitions process. If there is anyone who has acquired an enhanced range of powers in the acquisitions process, it is the heads of the imprints or divisions, who in most cases are the individuals whose support is now vital. And many of these individuals have risen through the editorial side of the business and are as attuned to editorial matters as they are guided by sales, marketing and financial concerns.

None of this is to say that sales issues have not become more central in the acquisitions process – they have. But editors have become much more conscious of sales issues too, and have incorporated an awareness of sales figures and an understanding of changing market conditions into their own modes of assessing new book projects. The importance of sales and the market is not something that is simply imposed on recalcitrant editors by an increasingly powerful triumvirate of sales, marketing and finance directors; it is something that editors themselves have internalized and incorporated into their own practices.

Myth 5: Editors no longer edit. It is a common charge that editors in the large publishing corporations no longer edit in the way they once did. It is said that, with the rationalization and bureaucratization that usually follows mergers and acquisitions, editors are now handling too many books and are too busy going to meetings and preparing material for sales and marketing to have time to edit. Whether it is structural editing or line editing, there is simply no longer the time for editors working in imprints or divisions in the large publishing corporations to do this properly. The result, it is said, is that quality invariably declines – inconsistencies go unnoticed, errors are not picked up and the text does not benefit from the careful eye of an editor who knows how to turn a promising manuscript into a good book. If authors want their books to be properly edited today, they would be better off asking their agents to edit or employing a freelance editor to do the job. Is there any truth to this charge?

It is undoubtedly the case that editors vary in the degree of their conscientiousness when it comes to editing: some are known to be careful editors, whereas others have a reputation for being cavalier. Houses vary too: some are known for the care and attention that their editors give to their books, whereas others have a reputation for churning out large numbers of books and hoping some will catch on – the proverbial spaghetti against the wall. It is also undoubtedly the case that most editors in all publishing houses – large or small, corporate or independent – are expected today to do a lot more administrative work and this makes growing demands on their time. And there will always be individual cases where authors may feel let down by their editor, sometimes because the editor who had originally signed up the book has moved to another house, leaving the author and the book with someone who did not acquire it and may not have the same degree of commitment to it or share the author's vision. But it is difficult to see any substance in the view that, as a general trend, editors in the large corporations do less editing today than editors did in the past, let alone that they no longer edit at all.

At many imprints in the large New York publishing corporations, it is common for an editor to edit around 8–12 books a year – at most, one a month. Of course, they have many other things to do; much of their time is spent reading proposals and manuscripts which are being offered by agents, and for each book they buy there will be many that they lose to other houses. But an editor will typically invest a good deal of time and effort in the 8–12 books that they will be putting into production each year. How much time they will put into a book depends entirely on the book – some need a lot of work, others may need relatively little. Most books go through at least one rewrite at many imprints. It is not uncommon for an editor to read a manuscript once very carefully, write a letter to the author with comments – this can vary from two pages to 30 or 40 pages, with an average being 8–10 pages. The editor may read a revised manuscript and provide a further set of comments before deciding whether the manuscript is ready to go into production. This is a part of the job that most editors take very seriously. If, after one or two edits, they are reluctant to do more work on a manuscript, it may be because they feel they've reached a point where the author just couldn't make the book any better, not because they no longer have any time to edit.

My intention in dispelling these myths is not to offer an uncritical defence of corporate publishing or to suggest that all criticisms are unfounded. It is simply to suggest that some of what passes for criticism is cloaked in misunderstanding and uninformed by what actually happens in the day-to-day activities of those who work in the large publishing corporations. The corporations come in for a lot of flak but there is a great deal of fine publishing that goes on within them. Later I shall offer a critical reflection on the current state of trade publishing but I shall seek to do so in a way that is grounded in a careful analysis, developed in the following chapters, of how the industry works.

4

THE POLARIZATION OF THE FIELD

Up until now we have been analysing three developments that have shaped trade publishing in the English-speaking world – the growth of retail chains, the rise of literary agents and the emergence of publishing corporations – but we haven't yet considered how the interplay of these three factors has created a field that has a certain structure and dynamic. The aim of the next five chapters is to do just that.

When we examine the field of trade publishing, we are immediately struck by the fact that there are a small number of very large corporations which, between them, command a substantial share of the market, and a large number of very small publishing operations, ranging from small indie presses to a variety of trade associations and educational institutions, with a small and dwindling number of medium-sized players. This polarization of the field is apparent in both the US and the UK – and, as we have seen, most of the large corporations are the same on both sides of the Atlantic. Why does the field of trade publishing become polarized in this way? Why do large corporations become so dominant in the field of trade publishing? Why are there still so many small publishing operations – why aren't they simply eliminated by the large corporations? And why is it so difficult to be medium-sized?

The benefits of scale

One of the main reasons why large corporations have come to occupy such a prominent role in the field is that there are real benefits of scale that can be achieved in trade publishing. Although any analysis of this kind involves some simplification, there are six main areas where the benefits of scale can be found.

The first area – and the one where economies are most quickly achieved following a merger or acquisition – is the rationalization of the back office, the reduction of overheads and the consolidation of sales forces, warehouses, distribution and other publishing services. All of the large publishing corporations, even the most federal and decentralized, involve some degree of rationalization and consolidation in terms of central services. Business operations like finance, royalties, rights, etc., are commonly centralized, thereby eliminating duplication and reducing headcounts. Warehouses are consolidated into a single distribution service and sales forces may be wholly or partially combined into a single, integrated sales group, generally organized in terms of sales channels and territories. In some cases attempts will be made to reduce overheads further by relocating all or most of the staff to a single building, where different imprints may occupy different floors or may sit alongside one another on the same floor, with different floors or spaces being allocated to editorial, sales, marketing, etc.

The two areas where economies of scale are less easy to achieve are editorial and marketing/publicity. Editorial for reasons we examined in the previous chapter: the creative edge of the business tends to work best in small groups, where editors can be left to work on their own or in collaboration with a few colleagues, and maintaining a multiplicity of editorial units is one way of spreading the risks of trade publishing. Smaller editorial groups also provide a human scale where you most need it – where the organization interacts with authors and agents. Publicity and some aspects of marketing also tend to be decentralized in most publishing corporations and attached to particular imprints or divisions. This is partly in order to maintain a close connection between marketing/publicity and editorial, both for the purposes of acquisition and for the purposes of promotion, and partly to ensure that the imprints or divisions have a human face in one of the other key arenas where personal contact and relations of trust are vital: the media. Even the largest publishing corporations recognize the need to be small where it matters.

The economies achieved through rationalization and consolidation can make a real difference to the profitability of a trade publishing house. Partly because of the high discounts given to retailers (at least 47 per cent, but it can be considerably higher in the UK for reasons we shall examine later), the high advances (a large proportion of which – some put the figure at 85 per cent – never earn out), the high level of returns (on average around 30 per cent, though it can be 60 per cent or more for some frontlist titles) and the need for substantial marketing spend, trade publishing is a low-margin business. To achieve a profit margin of 10 per cent is considered by most senior managers in trade publishing to be an exceptional performance; 6–8 per cent is more typical, 3–4 per cent is not uncommon and 12–15 per cent is rare. This contrasts with higher education publishing or some areas of professional and technical publishing, where the discounts to retailers are much lower (typically 20 per cent for textbooks and 32 per cent for professional books) and profit margins above 20 per cent are considered normal. Hence the economies that can be achieved through rationalization and consolidation can make a real difference to profitability, since any savings in terms of costs will be reflected in an improved bottom line.

The second area where the benefits of scale can be realized is in dealing with suppliers. Publishers work with a variety of different suppliers, including typesetters and printers, and the terms they can get will depend on the volume of business they do – the more business, the better the terms. So a large publisher which can consolidate its business with a few key suppliers will be able to secure much better terms, thereby driving costs out of the supply chain. 'When I arrived here we were dealing with about 70 printers across the world, printing in different formats,' explained one senior manager who was responsible for streamlining a large publishing corporation which was making a loss when he arrived. 'You consolidate into ten and suddenly you can take a lot of cost out of the business. Scale is a great facilitator to turning a business around and making it more profitable.'

Not only does scale enable you to negotiate better terms with suppliers, it also enables you to exact certain advantages which can have a significant, though less obvious, impact on sales and profitability. Given the volume of business they do, the large publishing corporations can put pressure on their key printers to turn around an urgent reprint in three days, whereas a small publisher might have to wait several weeks. In a business where the supply side is characterized by a great deal of uncertainty and wastage and where publishers typically print many more copies than they end up selling, the ability to shave several days off the reprint cycle gives the large publishers a crucial advantage. It means that they can afford to print in smaller quantities, knowing that they can resupply quickly if they need to, and they can put off reprint decisions until they have more information about sales. Enabling the publisher to make more accurate printing decisions by cutting down the time of the reprint cycle reduces the risk of being left with large quantities of unsold stock, which has to be written down and therefore reduces profitability, while at the same time reducing the risk of being temporarily out of stock and unable to fulfil orders, which may result in sales permanently lost.

The third area where large publishers enjoy the benefits of scale is in the negotiation with retailers. With the growth of the large retail chains, the distribution of power in the relation between publishers and retailers shifted decisively towards the retailers. The more market share a retailer has, the more power they have vis-à-vis their suppliers – that is, the publishers – when it comes to negotiating discounts, payment terms, resources for various forms of in-store promotions and marketing, and so on. This shift in the balance of power is particularly evident in the UK, where, unlike in the US, discounts are typically negotiated on a retailer-by-retailer basis; but even in the US the large retailers are able to use their market muscle to negotiate better terms and more money for promotions, among other things. The large publishers are in a much stronger position to resist the pressure for better terms from retailers, and are therefore in a better position to protect their margin when higher discounts and more marketing spend would threaten to erode it. The continued growth of large publishing corporations through further consolidation is in part a response to the shift in the balance of power from publisher to retailer that has occurred over the last couple of decades: it is, in part, a defensive reaction to the growing power of the retail chains.

The large publishers are also in a stronger position when it comes to getting their books into the main retail channels and securing positions of visibility within these channels. They will have dedicated sales teams of sufficient scale to call regularly on the key buyers at all the major retail chains, both bricks-and-mortar and online, specialist booksellers as well as general retailers, discount clubs and supermarkets. They will also have field sales forces to call on the independent booksellers that are spread across the country. While the independents represent a diminishing share of total sales, they remain very important for certain kinds of books, so the capacity to reach them with travelling sales reps gives the large publishers a crucial advantage. Small publishers – especially in the United States with its huge distances – simply cannot afford to maintain a sales force capable of calling on independents up and down the country. They are obliged either to ignore the independents, or to call selectively on a limited number of independents in certain parts of the country, or to buy in sales representation from another publisher or sales and distribution provider, which will give them reach but will not give them the same kind of dedicated sales representation that a large publisher, with its own in-house sales force, can count on.

The large publishers also have the resources you need to achieve high levels of visibility within the key retail channels. All the major bookselling chains – Barnes & Noble, Borders, Waterstone's, etc. – charge publishers to display books in the key retail spaces at the front of the store. This is very costly, and the more visibility you want – that is, the better the location within the store and the more stores of the chain in which the book is displayed – the more costly it is. The larger the publisher is, the more easily they will be able to absorb these promotion costs. Small publishers will find it difficult to afford the costs of in-store promotions and, if they do it at all, will have to be very selective about the titles they decide to support.

The fourth area where large publishers enjoy benefits of scale is advances. As noted earlier, publishers are competing in two markets: they are competing in a retail market, where they are trying to get their books noticed, stocked and bought by booksellers and readers, and they are competing in a market for content, where they are competing with other publishers to acquire the rights for new books. And just as the growth of the retail chains has shifted the balance of power from publishers to retailers in the retail market, so too the rise of the literary agent has shifted the balance of power from publishers to authors and their agents in the market for content. A publisher who is unable to compete effectively with other publishers in the market for content will lose out; and a fundamental part of being able to compete effectively in this market is the ability to offer advances that compare favourably with what the other major players are able and willing to offer. An imprint or division that is part of a large publishing corporation will have access to corporate resources to pay advances, and this puts them in a much stronger position than that of the small or medium-sized publisher which must fund advances out of their own relatively modest cash reserves. This gives the imprints owned by large corporations a clear competitive advantage in auctions, and it puts them in a strong position to hold on to successful authors or to woo successful authors from elsewhere. Most bestselling authors will migrate to the large corporations (if they are not already there) and, if they move publishers, will usually move from one corporation to another, because it is only the large corporations that can afford to pay the level of advances which these authors and their agents can command.

A fifth benefit of scale is that it enables the large publishers to take hits. It provides them with the kind of financial cushion you need in order to take risks, to invest in books which could do very well but where success is by no means guaranteed. The loss on a seven-figure advance that doesn't earn out can be absorbed by a large corporation, whereas a write-down of this magnitude would be disastrous for many smaller firms. Similarly, large corporations can afford to print 100,000 or more hardcover books and take the chance that a substantial proportion may not sell. If 80 per cent come back as returns they will not be bankrupt, whereas 80,000 unsold copies of a single title could cripple a smaller firm. Of course, the existence of a financial cushion can lead to a kind of excess, helping to drive up advances and encouraging the large publishers to overprint and push many more books into the marketplace than are likely to be bought. But it also enables the large publishers to take risks, and therefore to benefit from success on those occasions when the risks pay off.

A sixth benefit of scale is that it enables the large publishers to invest in IT and in the infrastructural systems that are so vital for publishing houses today. One consequence of the digital revolution – well known to those who work in the industry but less visible to those outside it – is that most aspects of the publishing process, from the preparation of manuscripts and the typesetting and design of books through to the processes of selling and marketing, the provision of efficient distribution and the management of the supply chain, as well as all the back-office systems like finance, royalties and rights, have been extensively digitized. Re-engineering publishing processes, maintaining IT systems in a state of continuous renewal and providing dedicated IT support staff are costly undertakings, and large publishers are able to invest much more than smaller houses in these less glamorous but extremely important aspects of the publishing business. They are also better able to invest in the kind of infrastructural work, such as creating data archives and digitizing their assets, which will enable them to take advantage of new and emerging revenue streams.

The virtues and vulnerabilities of being small

So in a field characterized by large retail chains and powerful agents who control access to customers and content respectively, there are clear advantages to being big. But the fact that the field of trade publishing is dominated by a handful of large corporations that are

Table 8 Estimated number of active publishers in the US by size, 2004

2004 publishing revenue	Estimated number of companies	Estimated % of companies
$50 million+	502	0.8
$1 million–$50 million	3,580	5.7
$50,000–$1 million	11,872	18.9
0–$50,000	46,860	74.6
Total	**62,815**	**100.0**

A 'publisher' is defined here as the owner of an ISBN. BISG estimates that, of the 85,000 US publishers in the Bowker database with active ISBNs, 62,815 (or 73.9 per cent) were 'active publishers' in 2004, that is, reported that they had revenues from book publishing in 2004.
Source: *Under the Radar* (Book Industry Study Group, 2005).

able to reap the benefits of scale does not mean that there is a dearth of small publishers today – on the contrary, the rise of large publishing corporations has gone hand in hand with the proliferation of small publishing operations. At first glance this might seem paradoxical: why haven't the small players been either swept up by the large corporations or forced out of business? What is it about trade publishing that allows for, perhaps even encourages, the proliferation of small publishing operations?

Let us look more carefully at what these small publishing operations actually are. It is not as easy to document this region of the field as it is to identify the large publishers, since many small publishing operations remain invisible to governmental organizations and to the main trade associations – they are 'under the radar', as a recent report commissioned by the Book Industry Study Group put it.[1] Focusing on the United States, the BISG report estimates that, of the 62,815 active publishers in 2004, 93.6 per cent (or 58,795) had publishing revenues of less than $1 million, and 74.6 per cent (or 46,860) had publishing revenues of less than $50,000 (see table 8).[2] While publishers with revenues less than $1 million represented over 90 per cent of active publishers, they accounted for less than 10 per cent of total book sales (around $2.7 billion, out of total book sales in the US of around $29 billion in 2004). However, publishers in the next group up, with publishing revenues between $1 million and $50

---

[1] See *Under the Radar* (New York: Book Industry Study Group, 2005).
[2] Ibid., pp. 15, 21.

million, generated about \$11.5 billion in sales, or around 40 per cent of total book sales. BISG estimates that there are around 3,580 companies that fall into this group of small to medium-sized publishers.

What are described as 'publishers' in this study are a very diverse array of organizations and entities. The definition of a 'publisher' used in this study is based on the ownership of an ISBN (an International Standard Book Number, which, following the introduction of the Standard Book Number (SBN) in 1967, has become the standard code for identifying a book), and an 'active publisher' is defined as the owner of an ISBN who reports revenue from book publishing during the year. At the lower end of the scale, many publishers are, in fact, self-publishers – individuals who acquire an ISBN in order to publish a book or pamphlet on their own, or with the help of the numerous self-publishing services that can be found on the internet. Of the publishers earning less than \$50,000 per year, 46 per cent were self-publishers (the other largest group being small independent publishers, who also represented 46 per cent). As revenues increased, self-publishers declined as a proportion of the group, and independent publishers, trade associations, educational institutions and corporations became more important. For example, among the active publishers earning between \$500,000 and \$1 million in 2004, 75.8 per cent consisted of independent publishers, 11.3 per cent were university presses and educational institutions, 8.1 per cent were associations of various kinds and 3.2 per cent were corporations whose core business is something other than publishing.[3]

The BISG study does not give us an accurate picture of the distribution of economic capital in the field of US trade publishing, nor does it aim to do so. The figures are based on responses by a relatively small proportion of the total number of publishers in the US (3,234 out of 85,000), so the estimates of the total number of companies in each category are very approximate at best. The study does not deal specifically with trade publishing but covers all forms of book publishing, from adult trade and children's books to professional, scholarly and college textbook publishing. Moreover, the definition of a 'publisher' as the ownership of an ISBN takes no account of who owns the owners of ISBNs: a number of imprints which own their own ISBNs, such as Random House, Knopf, Ballantine and Doubleday, may be owned by the same corporation (and, in this case,

---

[3] Ibid., p. 26.

they actually are). Hence the estimated number of companies is unlikely to be an accurate reflection of the number of autonomous publishing entities. Nevertheless, the study very helpfully underscores the fact that consolidation within the publishing industry has not precluded the existence of a large number of smaller publishing operations.

Why are there so many small book publishing operations? One reason is that entry costs to the field are very low. This has always been the case, but the digital revolution has lowered the entry costs even further. The development of cheap desktop publishing software has made it possible for authors to publish their own work, and a variety of self-publishing organizations – Book Guild, AuthorHouse, Lulu, Xlibris, YouPublish, iUniverse, Matador, to mention just a few – have sprung up online to offer self-publishing services to authors. ISBNs can be obtained easily and inexpensively online. Printing can be done either through small traditional offset printing or, if the print run is low, through short-run digital printing or print on demand. Given the ease of self-publishing in the digital age, it is not surprising that self-publishers comprise nearly half of the publishers with annual revenues of less than $50,000 in the BISG study.

But the digital revolution has reduced costs for small independent publishers too and made it easier for them to start up and survive in the field of trade publishing. Over a period of two or three decades, the entire book production process, from the creation of the original text to the typesetting, design and printing of the book, has been transformed by the digital revolution. The role of typesetters changed and their costs fell dramatically; and with the growing availability of desktop publishing software, one could, if one wished, bypass traditional typesetters altogether. The rise of the internet also made it much easier for publishers to work with suppliers in India and the Far East, which reduced costs still further.

Small publishing operations are also facilitated by the fact that so much of the publishing process can be outsourced. A publisher does not have to employ its own copy-editors and designers – these tasks can be outsourced to freelancers or small companies. Nearly all publishers today, small and large, outsource typesetting and printing. Distribution and sales representation can also be outsourced, either to specialized organizations like Consortium, a sales and distribution company based in St Paul, Minnesota which offers sales and distribution services to publishers and charges a commission on sales, or to existing publishers which take on other publishers as clients and provide sales and distribution services for an agreed commission charge. Marketing and publicity services can also be bought in, although this is less common and less effective. The ability to out-source most of the publishing functions means that a small publisher can set up and operate with very little initial outlay and expertise. A computer, a telephone line, a kitchen table, a small amount of working capital and a name – that's enough.

To a large extent, this world of small presses exists as a parallel universe to the world of the large corporate publishers. The worlds don't overlap very often because the gulf between them, in terms of the scale of resources they have at their disposal, is just too great. The world of small presses is itself very diverse and comprises many different kinds of organizations, ranging from small operations run by one or two people working out of their own apartment or house and doing this in their spare time, in the evenings and weekends, to well-established businesses that have their own premises and employ several members of staff on a full- or part-time basis. In addition to private businesses, they include a variety of not-for-profit organiza-tions, like The New Press in Manhattan, Archipelago Books in Brooklyn and Graywolf Press and Milkweed Editions in Minnesota. The financial constraints on not-for-profits are different from the constraints operating on small publishers acting as private businesses. Not-for-profits are tax-exempt and most receive grants from founda-tions, trusts and individuals; grants can comprise half or even two-thirds of their income, which cushions them to some extent from the harsh realities of the marketplace.

Whereas the large publishers benefit from an economy of scale, the small publishers benefit from what we could call an *economy of favours*. This economy of favours operates in many different ways. One way it operates is that small presses commonly share knowledge, expertise and contacts with one another. They see themselves as part of a common vocation and shared mission. Their competitive rivalries are overshadowed by the affinities that stem from their common sense of purpose, their shared understanding of the difficulties faced by all small publishers and their collective opposition to the world of the big corporate houses. They will recommend designers to one another, share sales figures with one another and so on. 'They're all good for different kinds of questions,' said one small publisher based in Brook-lyn. '[X] is very good with numbers so we'll ask him, "Oh, you did this book last year, we're thinking of doing a similar book, did it do well?" He'll give us the exact figures. [Y] is good because he's given us designers and things like that. [Z] is just kind of friendly and we hang out most with him.' The fact that there are clusters of small indie presses in the same area – such as Brooklyn, where real estate is much cheaper than Manhattan and there is a vibrant cultural scene – facilitates the exchange of information and the intermingling of experience.

Another way that the economy of favours operates is in terms of the rates charged by freelancers for providing services to small independent publishers. In practice, a dual economy operates within the field, with many freelancers charging (and expecting to be paid) one rate by the large corporate publishers, while agreeing to work for small indie presses at a much lower rate. 'We have the best book designers in the country,' explained the owner of one indie press. 'They can do a job for Random House and they'll charge them $4,000. We'll get the same book cover for $300.' The contrast here may be slightly overstated. One freelance designer who works for both the large corporate publishers and the small indie presses explained that the going rate for the corporate publishers is $2,000–$2,500 plus the artwork for most books (and if you're a well-known designer you can charge more), whereas the small independents typically pay $700–$1,000, and sometimes freelancers will do jackets for indie presses for as little as $200 (or even for free if they really want to do it, or want to build their portfolio). Whichever way you look at it, the small indie presses pay much less for freelance design – at least half, but probably more like a third or less – than the large corporations.

Why are freelancers willing to accept so much less from the small independents? Some freelancers are willing to work for less (or even for free) because they need the work and the experience and they don't yet have the connections you need to get freelance jobs from the large corporations. But even those who do jobs for the large corporations are often willing to work for the small indie presses at lower rates because they share the ethos of the indie presses and/or they find it rewarding to do so. Some freelancers see themselves as part of the same cultural and political project, sympathizing with their radical political views, their countercultural values and their anti-corporate stance. 'Ethically I support independent publishing companies and I respect what they're doing,' said one freelance designer. 'I feel that if anybody deserves good design to sell their books and compete, they do, and I'd love to be able to give it to them. If we can continue to offer our services to small companies and offer the same services to a big company then at least it will level the visual playing field of the business.' Others are happy to work for less for the small indie presses simply because they like the books or the authors and they find it satisfying, both professionally and personally, to design the covers. Their reasons are more aesthetic and professional than political. 'Here's one I did for $200,' said one well-established freelance designer who earns his living by working for the large publishing corporations but still does work for much less for indie presses. 'I did it because of the subject matter – I just think it's an important book and I'm very happy that they're publishing it.' He continues to work for the indie presses because he sees it as a creative challenge and he likes the content, even though he could make more money if he only accepted work from the large corporate publishers. 'There are all kinds of different designers, but I do it because I love to do it. I don't do it for the money, I do it because of the satisfaction of making things.'

The economy of favours can also operate at the retail level. 'There's definitely an affinity between independent bookstores and independent publishers,' said the owner of one small publishing house in Brooklyn who regularly organizes events with several independent bookstores in the New York area. 'They love what we do, they love how we do it, they love what we stand for.' But it's not just the independents – 'We have a strong affinity with Barnes & Noble too.' He explained how one of the buyers at Barnes & Noble had read and really liked one of his books, and loved the cover too. 'So she put this book at the front of Barnes & Noble and kept it there for two years.' They paid some co-op money to Barnes & Noble, 'but had we been Simon & Schuster, Barnes & Noble would've demanded a lot more money than they demanded from us'. Thanks in part to the heavy exposure it got in Barnes & Noble, this book went on to become this publisher's bestselling title, selling over 70,000 copies in Barnes & Noble alone. 'The buyers at Barnes & Noble don't want to think they're crushing little companies,' explained this small independent publisher. 'They care about books and they care about the literary landscape, so they want to support independent presses. A lot of floor managers at Barnes & Noble's are young people, young college graduates who notice our books and care about our books. So even in Chicago or LA, we're really well represented in Barnes & Noble and it's coming from the top but also from the bottom.'

The small independent presses do not just exist in a different space and benefit from a different kind of economy than the large corporate publishers, they also tend to operate in different ways. At the outset they often depend on an injection of cash from the founder-owner(s), in some cases supplemented by resources from family and/or friends, which provides the necessary working capital. The company is commonly subsidized by the unpaid, or only partly paid, labour of the founder-owner(s), who may have savings or other resources to fall back on or who, in some cases, may have other jobs to pay their bills. Costs are often kept to a minimum by working from home or renting offices in low-rent premises such as disused factories. If there are paid employees, they often work long hours for modest salaries, and much of the routine work is done by unpaid interns. 'There's a daily scrimping process,' explained one owner. 'With every encounter that involves money, I'm angling for ways to cut the costs because there's just no cushion or room to manoeuvre.' Some small publishing houses have benefited from one or two books that became unexpected successes and generated a windfall that temporarily eased the cash flow, enabled them to clear debts and invest in future growth. But in financial terms, most small publishers live from hand to mouth, constantly worried about cash flow, juggling bills and in some cases funding the business by running up debts on personal credit cards. 'We printed a whole season on credit card debt,' said one small publisher in Brooklyn.

In editorial terms, small publishers are much less dependent on agents than the large houses, for the simple reason that they are unable or unwilling to pay advances at a level that most agents would regard as minimally acceptable. So when agents go out with a new book, the small indie presses are very unlikely to be on their 'A' list or even their 'B' list. There are exceptions. There are occasions when an agent may feel that a particular book would be a good fit on the list of a certain small press, and there are some small presses who are willing to pay modest but significant advances for a book that they really want to publish. But it is more commonly the case that agents will turn to the small presses only when they have failed to sell a book to one of the large or medium-sized houses which are able and willing to pay substantial advances. Some agents, especially the younger ones, may then be willing to sell to a small press for a small advance because, at this stage, there may be no real alternative apart from dropping the project altogether, and they may feel that it is better to place the book with a small press for a small advance in the hope that it will help to build the author's career and lead to better deals with bigger presses in the future.

Since the small presses cannot rely on agents to provide them with new content, they have to devise other acquisition strategies. How they do this varies from press to press. Some use strategies very similar to those of young agents: they go to literary festivals and writers' events, read literary journals, magazines and newspapers, scouting for new talent and looking for new authors and ideas to pursue. Some rely more on their own personal contacts and networks, their accumulated social capital, following up recommendations from existing authors, friends and acquaintances. 'A lot of the books we get are through friends,' commented one small publisher. 'So I sort of rely on my social world to be the agents for the books I publish.' Others seek to commission books from individuals who have developed a presence and a following in the blogosphere. 'We were personally very involved in the political blogosphere,' explained the owner of one small press, 'so we thought we should start doing books out of the blogosphere. It's kind of a new movement that most publishers don't understand because you've got to kind of be part of it to really know who's big and who's not big and what ideas sell and what ideas don't sell.' Most small presses rely on some combination of these methods, together with an element, especially with non-fiction, of good old-fashioned brainstorming – thinking up ideas that would make good books and then trying to find authors to write them. Small presses also receive a large amount of unsolicited material and, while they may initially look through this material conscientiously, many soon realize that they have to close the doors – 'It took me about five or six years to realise how many hours were spent reading manuscripts that we weren't publishing, because if you have a slush pile the percentage that you're going to end up publishing of unsolicited manuscripts is really small.' The more established a small press becomes, the more likely it is that it will receive submissions from agents and that the proportion of agented material will grow, but the relation between agents and small presses is generally less harmonious than the relations between agents and editors or publishers at the large houses simply because the gulf between the financial aspirations of agents and the economic realities of small presses is so great.

Most small presses tend to be strongly editorially driven and to publish books about which the founder-owner(s) feel passionate. This is a world in which passion, commitment and belief play a crucial role – whether it is political commitment, countercultural beliefs or a passion for certain kinds of writing and literature. That the books taken on should sell and make money matters, of course, but this is rarely the most important consideration. 'We had a staff meeting yesterday where I introduced to the staff four novels that I've recently read and that I want to consider for publication because I like all four of them to varying degrees,' explained the founder-owner of one small indie press which has achieved some success. 'None of those books have bestseller written on them and I'm proud of that. To me that's grounding and I love that, I need that because it lets me know that I'm still in it for the reasons why I got in it. I hope we can succeed with any of the four books but truthfully none of the four is likely to sell very well. But I'm really excited about them.' Commercial success is not frowned upon, and most small publishers would be only too pleased to have a book that was a runaway success – 'You want the books to be read. That is the goal. And in fact I would love it if we sold a million books and suddenly had lots of cash in the bank.' But most books are taken on not because the founder-owner(s) thinks they actually will be very successful in commercial terms, but for other reasons. And the fact that commercial success is generally a secondary concern gives the small presses a leeway to experiment with what might be seen as small, more marginal and offbeat books in a way that the large houses are less likely to do.

The downplaying of commercial considerations in many small presses is often coupled with a view, articulated with varying degrees of passion, of the shortcomings and inadequacies of the world of the big corporate publishers. For many small indie presses, the world of corporate publishing is seen as a sphere of commodification in which money reigns supreme and where cultural values and commitments have been sacrificed to commercial ends. The founder-owner of one small indie press put it very well:

A lot of people are dismayed by the direction that publishing and culture in general have moved, particularly in the United States – by the corporate commodification of all culture. Whether it's the music industry or the book publishing industry, every year decision-making processes are controlled more and more by the bottom line and I think people find it refreshing that we're driven by an editorial imperative, an aesthetic imperative, and the bottom line takes a back seat. And I think that in a culture moving in a different direction, people like to see what we're doing and therefore support us. Even people at Random House and Simon & Schuster will talk about how noble what we do is. Having said that, I don't think of myself as out of sync with the direction our culture is heading. And in fact, when I hear people in publishing pining about the good old days when people cared more about books, I reject that, because to me it's actually a very conservative mode of thought. I embrace the fact that culture changes, pop culture develops. I don't have a problem with the number of readers there are in society; I think the burden is on us book publishers to engage people in transforming society. So we are very countercultural.

A lot of our books explore things on, or are written by authors who sort of fancy themselves on, the periphery of mainstream society.

Of course, not all small publishers see themselves as countercultural, or position themselves in opposition to what some see as the commercialization of mainstream publishing. There are some small publishers who see themselves as more mainstream, seeking to publish the same kinds of books as larger houses and taking some of the more successful independents (or former independents) as their models. 'Fourth Estate was a real model to me,' recalled the co-owner of one small independent house in Britain. 'They were the house I looked at with huge admiration for brilliant, creative, innovative publishing, doing a lot of books I liked. Harvill and Faber remained the lists that I really cared about in terms of the deep backlist and the fiction.' This small publisher was motivated not by radical political beliefs or countercultural values – 'I'm not some freak who has strange tastes' – but simply by the love of good literature and a firm belief in his own ability to recognize quality when he sees it. Being small has its limitations in terms of the resources that are available for new acquisitions among other things, but this is offset in his view by the intimacy and personal touch that only a small house can provide. 'To me, the very reading experience is one of the most intimate things there is, and therefore I think the place that books come out of should be an intimate environment. And I think you can affect things in more minute detail if you're working in a smaller house, and just more care and love goes into the actual publishing.' He is happy to remain small or to grow at only a modest rate and he values the fact that, as a small privately owned independent, he doesn't have to publish for the bottom line – 'I'd never want to be going down that route.'

Regardless of the differences in the beliefs and aspirations that motivate small publishers, they all share one thing in common: vulnerability. Their smallness gives them a degree of freedom and creativity – they can be nimble, move quickly, experiment with unconventional books, or simply publish books they like, without having to pay as much attention as large publishers to the prospective financial contribution of a book they want to take on. But their smallness also renders them vulnerable in several ways – consider five.

In the first place, most small publishers are undercapitalized and they experience cashflow problems more or less constantly. Given the long production cycles, advances must be paid to authors, and bills from typesetters, designers and printers must be paid, well before a book is actually published; and even when it is published, the payment terms with retailers and wholesalers generally mean that a publisher will be paid 90 or 120 days after the stock is shipped to the customer. Hence a publisher needs substantial working capital simply to fund work in progress. Every advance paid locks up capital in a new book project which may or may not materialize and, even if it does materialize, may or may not earn out. Every print run decision locks up capital in stock which may or may not sell, or which may be provisionally sold to a retailer or wholesaler only to be returned some months later for full credit. For large publishers with substantial cash reserves, these cashflow issues are important but they are not life-threatening. For small independent presses, however, they are a constant source of anxiety. Most small publishers will say that the hardest thing about running a small press is money, capital, cash flow, 'because the whole business is predicated on being able to finance something nine months out, or 12 months out'. 'I would love to have a line of credit,' said one small publisher in Brooklyn. 'We are totally desperate for a line of credit. Basically it's really difficult to get financing for new publishers because banks really don't understand why young publishers need so much capital to start out and why it's such a heavy cashflow business where you bottom out and then you have money coming in all sorts of times and you don't have a constant cash flow. So you need large amounts of capital and then you don't see that returned for a while. We need a line of credit – that's the hardest thing.' In the absence of cash reserves and good credit arrangements, many small publishers find themselves juggling bills and deciding which to pay and which to keep on hold. In some cases they may find themselves relying on a bridging loan from their distributor, who may be prepared to lend them money against future earnings. Some small presses may have to curtail new book production simply because they are not in a position to pay the printer's bills. And for some, the risk of bankruptcy is ever-present.

A second source of vulnerability for small presses is that they often find it difficult to get the kind of attention for their books in the media that they need in order to drive sales. Many small presses are not in a position to pay for a full-time publicity manager – in many small houses, the owner-founders take on the responsibility of dealing with the press and invest a good deal of their own time and energy in this. But even those small houses that can afford dedicated publicity staff often struggle to get the kind of media attention that the large publishers or more established imprints are able to get. 'If there's a book review editor that's on the edge, like should I do this book by this small publisher or this book from Knopf, I mean which one's going to be more important? Which one's going to look better on the book page? Probably the Knopf book, and ours will get pushed back,' commented a publicity manager at one small house. He felt that even on those occasions when their books were covered in the media, the reviews tended to appear much later than they did with books from the major imprints at the large corporations, so that the momentum you need in order to drive sales when the books are actually in the bookstores was dissipated. 'If the review runs late and then people see the review and want the book but they're being returned, it just becomes a nightmare. And that has happened over and over.'

Others are even more despondent. 'It seems to be incredibly difficult for independent presses to get serious book reviews,' said the owner of one small publishing house. 'And when I say serious book reviews I mean in the serious publications like the *New York Times* and the *Washington Post* and the *New York Review of Books* and so forth. They tend not to review a lot of little independent press type books, they tend not to review many trade paperbacks, and they tend not to review outsider authors – people that don't have any kind of track record or literary credentials. They like to review books by known names.' This small publisher has more or less given up trying to get reviews in newspapers like the *New York Times* or book review supplements like the *New York Times Book Review* – 'We almost don't even bother.' He has been publishing for seven years and he has never had a review in the *New York Times* or the *Washington Post* or the *New York Review of Books*. Their books have been reviewed in other major newspapers, like the *Boston Globe*, the *Dallas Morning News* and the *Houston Chronicle*, 'so it's not that it's a complete lock-out by major newspapers'. But like many small publishers, he has found that focusing on other forms of publicity, like radio and internet, has proven to be a better use of his time.

A third source of vulnerability is the dependence that many small presses have on one or two highly successful books. The growth pattern of many small trade houses is like this: sales tick over very modestly for a number of years and the company is loss-making; then suddenly, and usually quite unexpectedly, they have a book that takes off, perhaps because it wins a major prize, gets picked by Oprah or the Richard and Judy Book Club[4] or gets a big review in a major

---

[4] The Oprah Book Club and Richard and Judy Book Club are discussed in more detail in ch. 7.

media outlet like the *New York Times Book Review*; this surprise success produces a sudden influx of cash that increases the company's revenue by a multiple of two, three or even more; after years of running at a loss, they suddenly find themselves profitable and with cash in the bank. Now the problems they face change: they are profitable and successful but success in trade publishing is short-lived. A successful book, whether fiction or non-fiction, may continue to sell well as a backlist title, but the spike in sales that it produced as a bestselling frontlist title will fall off very quickly. The publisher will need to find new ways to try to prevent revenues from falling back to where they were before their unexpected success. The newer the publisher is, the smaller their backlist will be and the more they will depend on finding another exceptionally successful book to sustain their growth. Given that there is often an element of luck in success of this kind, the task is not easy and there is always a risk that, in the absence of another bestseller, sales will plummet.

Those small publishers who are fortunate enough to have a surprise success respond to this dilemma in different ways. Some use the proceeds of their success to acquire other small companies or lists, partly in an attempt to build up their backlist. Others use the resources to grow organically, taking on new staff and buying more – and more expensive – books. Either path increases overheads and accentuates the need to maintain revenues (or prevent them from falling too far). Moreover, achieving success with one or two books changes the way that other players in the field view the house. A small publisher that was not even on the radar screens of agents will suddenly find themselves receiving submissions from them, with the expectation that they will be able to pay competitive advances. A small house that previously eschewed agents and advances may find itself drawn into a game that it can ill afford to play, and the risk of overpaying in the hope of generating another success is a constant danger. 'Your success leads you to being more above the parapet,' explained the head of one small house which had enjoyed enormous success a few years earlier with a novel that had been turned down by all the big houses and went on to win the Booker Prize. 'The dangers now are that we overpay for books, we spend too much money and we have to write off not only lots of stock but big advances too. You have to be extremely focused in your publishing and make sure that everyone in the house is similarly responsible in their different ways.'

A fourth source of vulnerability for small houses is losing their authors. A small house may be willing to take a chance with an author who is overlooked or turned down by the bigger houses and may then find that, if the book is successful, the author and his or her agent want to 'test the market' for the next book and see what other publishers are willing to pay. This may force the small house either to pay an advance which is higher than is sensible for them, given their limited cash reserves, or to back out of the competitive situation and allow the author to go elsewhere. This makes it very difficult for small houses to hold on to authors and to build their careers in the way that larger houses can, and therefore makes it difficult for them to reap the long-term rewards of their willingness to take risks at the beginning of an author's career. Most small publishers can cite examples of how an author whom they published when the big houses were not interested, or whose work they came across and actively supported, subsequently decided, often with the encouragement of an agent, to move to a bigger house which was able to pay a much larger advance for their next book (or even for the book that the small publisher had been urging the author to write).

Small publishers respond to this predicament in different ways. Some take the view that this is perfectly understandable and a natural consequence of the structure of the field. 'I respect my authors and they treat us with respect,' said the founder-owner of a small publishing house in Brooklyn. 'So if they're in a situation where they write a new book and I'm interested in publishing it and there's another publisher, like Random House, who is going to give them $75,000, that's their decision. And they know what's best for them a hell of a lot more than I know what's best for them. I think it's really arrogant when any publisher gets mad at their authors for leaving them because if you respect your authors, then you have to respect their ability to make the best decision for themselves.' However, even this publisher admitted to feeling used and betrayed on occasion. He cited the case of a foreign author whom he had gone out of his way to meet and whom he had helped a great deal, reading and revising the text in minute detail – 'literally touching every single sentence, essentially rewriting every sentence in the book' – and then, when the author was named as a finalist for a big award, 'we were suddenly small beans. And that was just awful. I felt betrayed. None of it would've ever started had I not gone to meet him, had I not edited every sentence of his book to make it what it was.'

Small publishers can try to minimize the risks of authors leaving by forging close relationships with the authors they want to keep – making up in human and social capital for what they lack in economic capital. The owner of one small house put it like this:

If an author decides to go, that's ultimately their decision. But you can try and decrease the chances of that happening by publishing them in a way that the bigger houses can't. They have a relationship with you – not just me as the publisher but also with the editorial director, with our publicity director, our rights director, with all the different people that are part of this small company, people who are enormously talented and really good to work with. And you have to hope that authors are going to recognize that and appreciate it and feel that that's worth a lot more than just being offered more money up front by another publisher.

While this small publisher worked hard to keep his authors by trying to provide them with the kind of personal attention and care – 'intimacy' was his way of describing it – that they would be less likely to get at a larger house, he was under no illusions about the risks. Already he had lost several authors to larger houses, and the dangers are common knowledge to all small publishers. 'It's like M [the owner of a medium-sized independent house] always says to me, "Just you wait, the more books you've got, the more times you'll be fucked over by agents."'

A fifth source of vulnerability is the dependence of small publishers on third-party sales and distribution arrangements. Sales representation, warehousing of stock and distribution (or order fulfilment) are areas where economies of scale in publishing really do matter. Although the growth of the retail chains and the centralization of buying in the chains, coupled with the decline of the independent bookstores, has reduced the need to maintain large sales forces which travel the country and call on a myriad of bookstores, it is nevertheless vital for publishers to have a team of sales reps who can call regularly on the national accounts and on the most important independent bookstores; and if they wish to sell their books in international markets, they need sales reps who can call on accounts overseas. All of this is very costly and it is very difficult, if not impossible, for a small independent publisher to maintain a sales force on a scale that would enable it to achieve good representation on a national level, let alone internationally. Similarly with warehousing and distribution: these are specialized functions that require high levels of staffing and investment in order to be run in an efficient, state-of-the-art way, and small publishers are simply not in a position to support staffing and investment of this kind. Hence, most small publishers will find themselves turning to third parties in order to buy in sales and distribution services.

There are two main sources of sales and distribution provision to which small publishers can turn. On the one hand, there are organizations, such as Consortium, which are specialized in providing sales and distribution services to small publishers. They have many clients – Consortium represents over a hundred small presses – and they produce composite seasonal catalogues that present new titles from all of the presses they serve. The other source of sales and distribution provision is large or medium-sized publishers who have their own warehouses and sales forces and who are willing to take on third-party clients; at a time when sales growth is hard to achieve and when it is becoming more and more difficult to justify maintaining a field sales force (that is, a sales team that calls on the dwindling number of independent bookstores), the extra revenue that can be generated from taking on third-party clients is a welcome addition for some of the large and medium-sized houses.

For small publishers, contracting out sales and distribution can work well, but it has several downsides. First, it means that the small publisher's books are being sold by reps who are also selling books by other publishers and who are therefore not able to give their undivided attention to the books of the small house. There is always the worry among small publishers who have third-party sales arrangements that their books are being overlooked or are not being given the priority that they would be given if they were being sold by reps employed by the house itself – 'You're always a stepchild,' as one publisher put it.

The second downside is that sales and distribution services of this kind are expensive. The organizations which provide sales and distribution services generally charge their clients a commission on sales. The commission can vary widely, depending on the service provided and the size of the client among other things, but it commonly ranges between 20 and 26 per cent for full sales representation and distribution. This amounts to a serious drain on the already very limited resources of small houses. If they are selling their books at a full trade discount of, say, 48 per cent, and they are paying 20 per cent for sales and distribution, then the sale of a book retailing for $15 will provide them with revenue of only $6.24, from which they must pay royalties and cost of sales as well as marketing expenses and other overheads. 'You just can't run a profitable business if you're paying 20 per cent out for your sales and distribution function,' said one small publisher. 'And if you're operating on 26 per cent, you're probably really losing money.' In his view, the need to contract out sales and distribution was the single most important limitation they faced as a small independent house: 'We've had our ups and downs with sales but we've made some really good books. All said and done, we should be doing a lot better than we are, and I think the removal of sales and distribution from within the walls of your own house is the explanation – you know, the financial numbers are not there, and also just the kind of control and input isn't there either.' He may be overstating the debilitating effect of these costs, but there can be no doubt that the commissions charged for sales and distribution are onerous for small publishers.

Contracting out sales and distribution also means that small publishers, whose position is precarious already, are dependent on the financial stability of a third party who holds their stock and is responsible for collecting their revenue. Some distributors guarantee receivables for their distributees but not all do, and if a distributor were to encounter financial difficulties or go bankrupt then the position of the small publishers who were its clients could become critical. This hypothetical situation became a grim reality for many small and medium-sized publishers in the US in 2007, and some were forced into bankruptcy following the collapse of Advanced Marketing Services, the parent company of Publishers Group West which distributed books for more than 130 independent publishers. PGW was founded in Berkeley, California in 1976 by a young Stanford University graduate, Charlie Winton, as a sales, marketing and distribution collective for small publishers. Over the years it built up a substantial client base which included many well-known small and medium-sized trade houses like McSweeney's, Soft Skull, Milkweed and Grove Atlantic. Winton established a reputation as an active supporter of small presses, frequently advancing money to his clients to ease their cash-flow problems. But in 2002 Winton sold the business to Advanced Marketing Services, a large distribution company based in San Diego, so that he could focus on his own publishing activities. Following the discovery of irregularities in AMS's accounting practices, the company filed for Chapter 11 bankruptcy on 29 December 2006. This meant that the end-of-year sales revenues of the publishers who were clients of PGW were frozen. In early 2007, the Perseus Books Group, based in New York, took over many of PGW's clients, offering them a 70-cents-on-the-dollar settlement for revenues owed. But for some small publishers who were already living from hand to mouth, the temporary collapse of PGW and the freezing of revenues proved to be the last straw. 'The independents got fucked by the Enron of publishing,' as one small publisher, forced into bankruptcy by the affair, graphically put it.

A train wreck in slow motion

Let us make these considerations more concrete by walking into the offices of a small publishing house, 'Sparrow Press', on the outskirts of New York. Sparrow's offices are located in one of the old disused factories that are scattered across areas like Brooklyn, Hoboken and Jersey City. The red brick walls, chimney stacks and narrow corridors lined with heating pipes and strip lighting attest to a building designed in another age for another purpose, but now the machinery is silent and the floors have been divided into loft spaces for small businesses and artistic collectives of various kinds. Sparrow has an open-plan loft space that is notionally split into separate offices by free-standing bookshelves and screens. Now they have two full-time employees and a couple of unpaid interns working for them but when they began it was a two-person, husband and wife, operation. They started, five or six years earlier, with no knowledge of publishing – 'It's really amazing how little we knew' – and very little capital. They were motivated to publish a book that had arisen out of specific political circumstances, and they wanted to publish it themselves because this was, in part, a way of taking a stand against the established media – 'A lot of what we were doing was saying "screw the media".' Publishing the book themselves rather than going to an established publisher was a way of intervening in a public debate and public arena without having to rely on existing media organizations. 'Books still have a power here and they're a part of the media that nobody really acknowledges as part of the media.' They thought of themselves more as artists than as business people, and making a book was more like an art project than a commercial venture – 'We were artists and we didn't think a lot about money. We did it for art's sake.'

They learned how to publish a book by calling friends and getting advice and help from others, but much of it was learning by trial and error. 'You would not believe the errors we made – it's just astonishing.' With the first book the colour of the cover came out wrong and they made the printer rip off every single cover and redo them – 'It was like one debacle on top of another.' Like many small presses, they funded the first and subsequent books by using personal savings, gifts and credit cards – 'We printed on credit cards.' After a couple of years they took on investors, family and friends who were willing to put a modest amount of capital into the venture, and they got a line of credit from a bank. But 'like most small businesses, we were totally undercapitalized and we've never recovered from that. We're always a day late and a dollar short.' Their output nevertheless grew rapidly, rising from two books in the first year to 20 or more by year four. They worked from their apartment for the first couple of years before taking space in the old factory. Their early books sold modestly; some got a certain amount of media attention and did better than others but sales were modest and, in financial terms, they were living from hand to mouth. And then suddenly they had a big success – a book that other houses had turned down, they took on and, when it was published, it struck a chord. They sold 20,000 in cloth before releasing it in paperback. This success generated an influx of cash but the reprieve was temporary and the success of this book highlighted the problems they faced as a small publisher in the field. 'We would need to have a series of bestsellers every year to really be able to make this system work,' but it's difficult for them to achieve this for various reasons.

In the first place, they don't have the money to print the books. If the retail chains get excited about a book and want to take 5,000 or 10,000 copies, this becomes a huge outlay of resources for them. They will also have to pay co-op to the chains in order to get the books displayed in the stores. They will have to price it at a level that will reduce their profit margins. And then, even if the book sells well, they are likely to be faced with high returns, at least 20 per cent, possibly as high as 50 per cent, which will be credited to the retailer and deducted from their receivables by their distributor, though they still have to pay the printer's bills. 'We call it "feeding the beast". You have to feed the goddam beast and it just doesn't work.' As the returns come back they undo much of the gain they thought they had achieved with a book that seemed to be selling well – 'I think of them as little time bombs planted along the way.' Of course, the big houses get high returns too, but they can afford to take the hits in a way that Sparrow cannot. As a small house with limited resources, they have to try to reduce the risks of overprinting and high returns by printing more cautiously – 'We have to print very close to the bone. We can't afford to over-print on the off chance that the book will hit and start moving fast.' But then they find themselves running the risk of being out of stock at the very moment when a book starts to sell and, unlike the large publishers, they don't have the clout to get the printers to deliver a reprint in a few days. 'If we'd been Random House and we could print in a day and ship in a couple of days, we would have sold 300,000 copies of this,' said one of Sparrow's owners, holding up a brightly covered paperback novel. 'This thing was hot. But we simply couldn't make the books. We couldn't make enough books and we couldn't make them fast enough. I was literally on my knees, I was begging the printers, but the fastest we could get them out was three weeks. We really missed a lot of the heat of the thing.'

Many of the books they signed up emerged out of their own commissioning. They would think up an idea for a book and then try to find an author or set of authors to write it, or they would read an article or hear an author speak and then ask them if they would be interested in turning it into a book. Once they had a bestseller they were on the radar screens of agents who began sending things to them with ever-greater frequency, but they preferred not to work with agents because they found that the expectations of agents, both in terms of advances and in terms of controlling rights, were not financially manageable for them. 'It's about accelerated money. They need a lot of money, they need it up front, they need accelerated schedules, they need to control rights – all the things the big houses have slowly granted them over the years. We're always trying to slow down the money, to work with the cash flow.' There have been occasions when they came up with the idea for a book and approached an author, or worked with a writer to develop a book they were writing, only to find that as soon as an agent got involved they would lose the book. 'The author will love the idea and they'll say, "That's fantastic, let's do it, just call my agent and tell her I said it's a go." And you call the agent and the agent will say, "Well, we're gonna need $20,000, we're gonna need it tomorrow and we're gonna keep all the rights." We tend to avoid them. The pie just isn't big enough for that third person. That's the flat out economic reason for it.'

They also found it very difficult to get media attention for their books. In the first few years they did a lot of books on topical, newsworthy issues and they thought they would get plenty of review coverage in the media, but they soon came to realize that this view was naive. As they now see it, the main print review media are in cahoots with the big publishers and it's very hard for small publishers to get their attention. 'It's a very exclusive club and it's very hard to break into. They don't take things from outside all that seriously.' The big houses are able to build a book in the media through a combination of promotion and publicity. 'In the big houses, if something begins to go, you pour fuel on the fire and make it burn faster. But you're just not able to do that with a house this size.' Now they don't bother much with the mainstream print review media, and often don't even send their books to them. They concentrate on radio, internet marketing and events in bookstores and elsewhere.

Sparrow's sales and distribution were handled by a third party and their problems were compounded when their distributor was taken over. Following the takeover, there were lots of problems with the billing system and the operation of the warehouse – 'They lost shipments of books, entire deliveries of books and things like that.' Sales declined and returns skyrocketed. Since their distributor was virtually their only source of revenue, they felt more vulnerable than ever. Suddenly there seemed to be some truth to the saying that every independent publisher is just one crisis away from bankruptcy. The situation became so dire that they eventually decided they had to change distributors in order to survive. For a business that was living hand to mouth, this was in itself a highly risky move, since it creates a temporary hiatus in revenues which a small press like Sparrow is ill-equipped to manage. Their debts grew and they fell back on goodwill – 'the kindness of strangers' – in order to tide them over, all the time hoping that the new sales and distribution arrangements would eventually bring a significant uplift in sales (and, fortunately for Sparrow, they eventually did).

Sparrow continues to publish some very good and innovative books and the founder-owners take pride in the books they have published, even those that have sold only 200 or 300 copies – 'They were mistakes but they're mistakes we were proud of,' said one; 'they're beautiful mistakes,' said the other. For them, publishing is a kind of calling, a personal, cultural and political commitment with which they persevere even though it is tough, a way of participating in cultural and political life and giving expression to something that might not otherwise get brought into the world – 'You feel you're doing a very worthy thing. It's exhilarating at the same time as it's deeply heartbreaking.' But in purely financial terms their situation remains precarious. 'We're tired, we're worried, our credit cards have maxed out and we've used up every resource we had – just every single one.' They live on the edge, constantly worried about whether they will be able to pay their staff and keep their creditors on hold for another week or two. 'It feels like a train wreck in slow motion': this is how one of Sparrow's founders summed up their first five years as a small independent press.

Of course, every small publishing house is different and each has its own unique characteristics, depending on its history and on the personalities and commitments of the individuals involved, but all face similar pressures and difficulties that stem from the structure and logic of the field. Some small houses limp along from one year to the next, supported in part by the labour of love invested by their founder-owners, who may themselves survive by earning their salaries in other jobs. Some eventually run out of cash and go into liquidation or are taken over by other small or medium-sized houses. There are some founder-owners who decide that, after having run their company on a shoestring for a number of years and grown it to a respectable size, it's time to bail out – either to join forces with another press or to sell up and retire or make another life for themselves. If the company is profitable and has a good list, they are likely to find a number of suitors among those middle-sized and even large houses that are looking to grow. But there are also some small houses that flourish, thanks to a combination of luck, clever publishing and good financial backing. They find a niche and develop a reputation for innovative publishing. They have the occasional success, which produces a spike in sales and eases the cashflow problems, and their books get shortlisted for prizes and sometimes win, which raises their profile and augments their symbolic as well as their economic capital. Their title output increases and their revenue grows; after years of loss-making and debt they find themselves generating a modest profit. Over time a few of these houses find themselves moving from the world of small publishers into a grey zone where they are neither big nor small but 'medium-sized'.

Why it is so difficult to be medium-sized

There are a handful of large corporations in the field of trade publishing and a large number of small publishing operations of one kind or another but the space in between – the space of the medium-sized publishing house – is thinly populated. Of course, 'medium-sized' is a loose term – what is medium-sized in the eyes of one person may be small in the view of another. Here I'm using the term to refer very loosely to publishing organizations that have annual revenues from trade publishing of around $20 million or above but less than $500 million (or, in the UK context, more than £10 million but less than £100 million). Many of the medium-sized publishers that do exist tend to operate within a specialized niche like health and fitness, practical guides and how-to books, religious publishing or children's publishing – this is the case with Rodale, Thomas Nelson, Scholastic, Workman and Egmont, for example. There are other medium-sized publishers who are significant players in the field of trade publishing and who combine this with a presence in another publishing field, such as higher education publishing and/or STM publishing, which provides greater scale and helps them to counterbalance the unpredictability and low profitability of trade publishing – such is the case with Wiley and Norton, to mention two. But the number of independent publishers who are focused exclusively or substantially on mainstream adult fiction and non-fiction trade publishing and could be regarded as medium-sized is relatively small. In the US, Norton and Grove Atlantic fall unambiguously into this category (Houghton Mifflin and Harcourt would count as medium-sized trade publishers, although they are no longer independent). In the UK, Faber and Bloomsbury are probably the two most significant trade houses that are medium-sized and still independent, although Bloomsbury's position is unusual in that their growth in recent years has been accounted for overwhelmingly by the books of one author (J. K. Rowling).

So why are there so few medium-sized independent houses in the field of trade publishing? In the first place, it's not easy to grow a trade publishing business from small to medium-sized. The field is crowded and the market is saturated, so any growth beyond inflation that one company achieves is largely at the expense of someone else. There are very few, if any, backlists left to buy, since nearly all of the older publishing houses have been bought up by the conglomerates, so you are heavily dependent on frontlist successes to maintain revenue and growth. 'It requires you being lucky at such a disproportionate level that it is unrealistic,' observed the publisher at one of the medium-sized independents. When those legendary publishers like Bennett Cerf, Alfred Knopf, John Farrar and Roger Straus built their companies, they did so at a time when the state of the field was very different. Agents were not a major force and they didn't have to compete with large corporations for content and attention. They could acquire new books without having to pay high advances and they had time to build a backlist. Today these conditions no longer apply. Now more than ever, it takes a special combination of entrepreneurial flair, publishing nous and sheer good luck to steer a trade publishing house from a small start-up into the ranks of the medium-sized and keep it there.

Being medium-sized in the field of trade publishing is in some ways the most difficult place to be. You have much higher overheads than the small publishers and you cannot benefit from the economy of favours that is part of their world, but you don't have the size and resources of the large corporations and therefore you cannot achieve the same economies of scale as they can, nor can you wield the same clout with suppliers and retailers or reach into pockets that are as deep. You are now on the agents' radar screens and you find yourself competing with imprints at the large corporations for new books, but you don't have the resources of the large corporations to draw on when you're making a bid. For the occasional title you can afford to splash out, but the risk for you is much greater than it is for the imprint at a large corporation, which can afford to take more hits when the advances fail to earn out (as many invariably will). Moreover, every expensive acquisition of this kind has an opportunity cost for you that it doesn't have for the large corporations. You can only afford to take so many chances of this kind, so you have to call your shots very carefully, whereas the imprints at the corporations can always go back for more if a special book comes along that seems to warrant it.

Not only will you find yourself at a disadvantage in the acquisitions process, you will also find that holding on to your successful authors will become one of your greatest challenges. You need one or two books that do exceptionally well every year in order to maintain revenue levels and be profitable, but your most successful authors – often with the encouragement of agents – will be tempted to 'test the market' and move to larger houses that can pay significantly higher advances. The large corporate publishers can afford to pay more not only because their pockets are deeper but also because they can, and routinely do, overpay on advances in the knowledge that they will have to write off a proportion of the unearned advance, regarding this as part of the game they have to play in order to sign the most sought-after authors and books, and this is something that the medium-sized house can ill afford to do. And if you lose your successful authors to bigger houses, then you have to reinvent success from scratch every time. William, the publisher of one medium-sized house, put it like this:

What I'm finding increasingly difficult, having grown from $7–8 million to around $20 million, is that we're losing our authors after we make them successful. And it's very difficult, psychologically and emotionally and in all other ways, but business-wise it's very difficult, because now we've got to go back and start all over and find another one, and hope to be lucky and have a hit. The authors get more money and I can't afford to pay it, and I'm making mistakes by paying it sometimes and the book's not earning out. Often authors will give us a 20 or 30 per cent break, they'll go into business with us if we get within 20 per cent [of what the large groups will pay]. But sometimes the number is so high that I shouldn't even be getting within 50 per cent of the number because it's foolish. And sometimes I go ahead and do it and I lose money. The large groups will write off between 5 and 8 per cent of net revenues in unearned author advances each year. That's a giant amount of money. If I did that I'd be out of business. They are still able to do it and make a profit, and part of the reason they can is because of the economy of scale they have. They're doing their own sales and distribution – they're probably saving 6–8 points right there. So what it means is that they're using different currency than I'm using. They're playing with monopoly money, I'm playing with real money. And that's what I see as the most daunting task ahead for me.

The large corporations are, in effect, paying higher royalties to certain key authors because they know that a proportion of the advance will have to be written off and they build this into their calculations as part of the cost of doing business. They can do this and still be profitable because their size enables them to achieve economies of scale and to squeeze costs out of the supply chain elsewhere.

So how can William compete with the large corporations? There are various things he can do. First, he has to try to be quicker and smarter than the editors and publishers at the large corporations, finding things before they do, seeing potential where they don't and getting promising new books under contract before the large corporations get involved – 'I've got to be smarter and quicker and faster. I've got to be more active than reactive. I've got to take more chances, and I'll buy books before other people read them or see them.' Second, he has to create a set of relations with authors that some authors will value more than they will value the extra money they could get if they were to go to a larger house, and create a list with which they want to be associated. William has a special way of describing this: publishing good books has a 'psychic equity', by which he means, first, he enjoys doing it – 'It's part of why I'm in this business rather than being in real estate or a bond salesman' – and second, 'it creates some value for your imprint.' People look at your list differently – book reviewers, retailers but also other authors, the kind of authors you want to publish. In other words, it creates symbolic value for the house, which becomes a vital weapon in his struggle to acquire and hold on to successful and sought-after authors in the face of competition from large corporate publishers who have access to much greater quantities of economic capital. William described the case of a successful fiction writer he wanted to publish and who was being courted by a number of the big houses. 'I wrote letters over a year and a half, two years, and sent her catalogues and books. And finally she agreed to sell us the books at a reasonable price, very fair. We've now sold over 300,000 copies of her books. But when I finally had dinner with her I said, "What persuaded you?" And she said, "Well, you know, I saw your catalogues and I liked the books. I thought what an interesting list. I'd be pleased to be, proud to be, part of this list."'

A third thing William can do is be inventive in the way he tries to recover advances. If he can persuade the agent to grant him world rights, then he can earn back part of the advance – in some cases, quite a substantial part of the advance – by selling translation rights into different languages. He will want to hold on to paperback rights if at all possible, since this is the only way he will be able to build his backlist over time, but in exceptional circumstances he may also consider doing a deal with another house to split the hardback and paperback rights and share the advance in order to secure a book or prevent a successful author from moving elsewhere. Even this strategy doesn't always work, however. Perhaps the best example, well known in the publishing industry, is Charles Frazier, whose first novel, *Cold Mountain*, was a tremendous success, selling more than 1.6 million copies in hardcover. The hardcover sales of this book, together with the sale of the paperback rights to Random House/Vintage, lifted what was then a small New York publisher, Atlantic Monthly Press (now Grove Atlantic), into the ranks of the medium-sized trade houses. For Frazier's second novel Grove Atlantic joined forces with Knopf and Vintage to split the hardback and paperback rights and were able to offer a combined advance in excess of $5 million. It wasn't enough, however. Under the guidance of his new agent, the author held out for more – and got it from another division of the Random House group, which was prepared to offer $8.25 million for *Thirteen Moons* on the basis of a short proposal. As it turned out, the loss of this author was a blessing in disguise for Grove Atlantic (and a small disaster for Random House and the editor who bought it), since actual sales of the second novel were far below the level that would have been necessary to recoup even the more modest (but still very sizeable) advance that Grove Atlantic was willing to offer.

So these are the key problems faced by the medium-sized publisher: you are not on an equal footing when it comes to competing with the big corporations for new books and you are vulnerable when it comes to holding on to your most successful authors. And that is the main reason why it is so difficult to be medium-sized. Your problems are exacerbated by the fact that you will not be able to achieve the economies of scale that the large corporations can achieve and you will have less clout in your negotiations with suppliers and retailers, and this will give you even less room to manoeuvre when it comes to competing with the corporations and writing off unearned advances.

Clubbing together

One way for small and medium-sized publishers to try to counter some of the difficulties they experience in the field of trade publishing is to join forces and collaborate in various ways – to club together. The area where there is likely to be the most obvious gains from collaboration of this kind is sales and distribution: if a small or medium-sized publisher were to bring together a number of small publishers and offer a sales and/or distribution arrangement to them, or if they were together to work out a collective sales and/or distribution arrangement, then they might be able to offset some of the disadvantages they suffer as small players in the field. The two main examples where this kind of clubbing together has occurred are the Perseus Group in the US and Faber's so-called 'Alliance' in the UK.

The Perseus Group is a hybrid model. Founded in the mid-1990s by a wealthy financial investor, Frank Pearl, who liked good books and was worried that they were being increasingly sidelined by the large corporations, Perseus has evolved into two closely linked but distinct businesses. On the one hand, the Perseus Book Group comprises a number of publishing houses and imprints that are either wholly owned by the private equity firm Perseus LLC or are a joint venture with them. Some of these houses, like Basic Books, were cast-offs of the large corporations, while others, like Da Capo Press, Running Press and the Avalon Publishing Group, were straightforward acquisitions of stand-alone companies. Public Affairs and Nation Books have more complex joint-venture arrangements with Perseus. On the other hand, Perseus also developed a sales and distribution service that could be offered to a whole range of small and medium-sized independent publishing houses that were not part of the Perseus Book Group. This side of the business grew dramatically between 2005 and 2007 with the acquisition of three other distribution services, CDS, Consortium and Publishers Group West, making Perseus the leading provider of sales and distribution services to independent publishers in the US.

With Pearl's financial backing, Perseus has been able to develop a sales and distribution service for small independent publishers that is much more extensive and sophisticated than they would be able to develop by themselves. 'Independent publishers need a platform to support them that's much more robust than what they needed a generation ago, to level the playing field with both the giant conglomerate competitors and the giant conglomerate booksellers which are dominating the industry,' said one senior manager at Perseus. They see themselves as specialists in selling and distributing the kinds of books that are aimed at specialized, well-defined markets – 'our strategy is to succeed by reaching target markets rather than compete for the giant blockbuster hit.' But occasionally a targeted book will catch on and explode into the broader market, and when that happens 'you have to have the scale and sophistication to be able to chase that and exploit it fully.' And that's what Perseus seeks to provide in terms of its sales and distribution services – 'the distribution range and the power in the marketplace and the ability to make a million-copy bestseller happen, and we're doing it on behalf of an independent publisher'.

This is undoubtedly a hugely important, indeed invaluable, service for small and medium-sized publishers in the US; without it, these small presses would be much worse off, and many would be unable to survive. However, the danger for the small presses is that, with the consolidation of CDS, Consortium and PGW in the hands of the Perseus Group, the Group has now become the dominant provider of sales and distribution services to small presses in the US, and this has strengthened their hand in negotiating terms with small presses, for whom the cost of sales and distribution is one of the critical factors affecting their survival and competitive position. And some small presses fear that the consolidation of sales and distribution services will be followed inexorably by the rationalization of sales forces, with sales forces being merged and independent sales reps being laid off, leading to poorer and less comprehensive representation for the small presses who are their clients. 'I think it's a very dangerous moment,' said one small publisher, 'and I think it's very unhealthy for the culture at large.' Whether this publisher is right to be worried or is being overly pessimistic remains to be seen.

Faber's 'Alliance' is a much more modest undertaking but is of equal significance for small independent publishers in the UK. Faber is a medium-sized independent trade publisher with an outstanding backlist in literary fiction and poetry, but as a relatively small player it didn't have the same access to the major retail channels as the large corporate publishers – 'We weren't really at the races,' as one senior manager put it. It had provided third-party sales representation to a number of small independent houses, but the idea of the Alliance was born in 2004 when Faber began talking with a number of other British independent publishers about providing sales representation for them in Europe. 'They said, "Europe, yeah, that's fine, get on with it, but what we really want to talk with you about is the UK," and at that point the Alliance was born,' explained one of the people who was involved at the outset. Faber joined together with several key independents (Atlantic, Canongate, Icon, Portobello, Profile and Short Books, subsequently joined by Quercus, Serpent's Tail and Granta), providing different levels of sales representation for different houses, depending on whether they wanted to do their own major accounts. 'At one stroke, all of a sudden, we were worth dealing with.' By 2006 they had become the sixth largest group in Britain, roughly comparable to Pan Macmillan in terms of total sales. They were now able to gain access to the supermarkets and other non-traditional retailers, such as discount clubs and motorway service stations, in a way that simply hadn't been possible before. 'From their point of view, they knew the independent sector was producing good books but at the same time they never really bothered to get ahold of them – OK, the occasional flash bestseller happened that they had to get involved in. But at last there was one place they could go for all that different stuff, all the variety, with a fantastic track record and people who were quite fun to do business with.' They soon began to collaborate on other aspects of the business. All the publishers moved to the same distributor and they used their collective strength to negotiate better terms for everyone. Similarly with printers and other suppliers, and recently they've begun to collaborate on rights. 'It started as a set of sales arrangements, which doesn't sound very glamorous, but it's become a very big idea and it's become, front-end and back-end, extremely valuable to all the companies concerned.'

As a consortium of independent publishers, the Alliance was a very clever and effective way to respond to changes in the market-place. By clubbing together they were able to get a seat at the table of the big retail chains – and especially at the table of the super-markets which were becoming an increasingly important channel to market in the UK. It raised the profile of the independent sector in a way that no single independent could do alone – with the possible exception of Bloomsbury, at least while it was riding high on the success of Harry Potter. But the success of an alliance of this kind depends very much on getting the right balance between the interests of the different parties and there is always the danger that the central player – in this case, Faber – will be perceived as dominant, wielding more power and gaining more from the Alliance (and the commission it charges) than the others gain from it. There are even some senior managers at Faber who fear that the Alliance may compromise the interests and autonomy of the smaller companies who are party to it: 'I worry that we're replicating what Random House did by sort of sucking up these different companies. Of course, they did it in a very different way, by buying them and making them imprints, and in order to compete we've had to do the same thing in our own way. I wish it was different really.' But the realities of the marketplace are such that clubbing together is one of the only ways that small publishers can gain effective access to the major retail channels.

On the margins of the field

We have concentrated in this and the previous chapter on analysing the positions of three types of publishing house that occupy the field of trade publishing – the large publishing corporations that are dominant players in the field, the myriad of small publishing operations and the handful of medium-sized trade publishers. But there are also a variety of publishers who are situated on the margins of the field and who regularly publish trade books, even if trade publishing is not their primary concern. The university presses are one such set of players.

The university presses belong primarily to another publishing field – that of scholarly publishing.[5] Their principal output is scholarly monographs, that is, high-level academic books that are written by academics and researchers and intended primarily for other academics and researchers. Their remit as university presses is to publish works of scholarship, mostly written by academics, and to make available the results of scholarly and scientific research. They are first and foremost educational institutions that are concerned with the development and transmission of knowledge rather than commercial enterprises, and it is for this reason that they are recognized in law as not-for-profit organizations (charities in the UK) and exempted from corporation tax.

---

[5] For a full analysis of this field, see Thompson, *Books in the Digital Age*, part 2.

However, many university presses have long been involved in other publishing fields, including reference publishing, journal publishing and ELT (English-language teaching) publishing, as well as trade publishing. Harvard University Press was one of the first of the American university presses to become a serious player in the field of trade publishing. This was largely the consequence of the appointment of Arthur Rosenthal as director in 1972. The founder of Basic Books, Rosenthal was a New York trade publisher who had a great deal of experience publishing books by scholars and scientists for a general readership. He arrived at Harvard at a time when the Press was in serious financial difficulties, having suffered a deficit of more than half a million dollars in 1970–1 on sales of around $3 million, and a deficit of $350,000 in 1971–2.[6] Rosenthal reoriented the activities of the Press and gave it a new profile as an up-market trade house, publishing 10 or 12 titles per season (out of a total of around 50–60 titles per season) that had the potential to get national review coverage and to do well in the trade.

Harvard's success in ploughing the ground between academic and trade publishing provided a model that other university presses have sought to emulate with varying degrees of dedication and success. The key assumption of this model is that high-quality books with a scholarly content, often (but not always) written by scholars, have the capacity to sell into a general trade market if they are developed and marketed properly – that is, they can 'cross over' from academic to trade. Hence an academic publisher, if they choose their books well and develop and market them effectively, can reach an educated readership beyond the academy. This fits well with the self-understanding of the university presses, many of whom see their mission not just in terms of serving the scholarly community but also in terms of making scholarship available to a wider readership and contributing to the broader public debate.

Since the late 1980s, the attractions of this model in the eyes of many in the world of the university presses have been accentuated by three developments. First, as a result of a dynamic internal to the field of scholarly publishing, the sales of scholarly monographs – the staple output of the university presses – have declined dramatically. At the same time, many university presses were expected by their host institutions to become more robust financially and less dependent on

---

[6] See Max Hall, *Harvard University Press: A History* (Cambridge, Mass.: Harvard University Press, 1986), p. 186.

subsidies and other forms of support. So many university presses began to look for other forms of publishing where they might be able to generate revenue and compensate for the declining sales of scholarly monographs. Regional publishing – that is, books about the history, culture and environment of the region, including cookbooks, travel books and books about flora and fauna – was one type of publishing to which many of the American university presses turned. Trade publishing was another.

The second development that made trade publishing look increasingly attractive to many university presses was the fact that, as the once-independent trade houses were bought up by the large corporations, the kinds of books they were seeking to publish began to change. Their sales expectations were higher, and the kinds of books they might have taken on in the past were being passed over by many of the imprints in the large corporations. Moreover, many of these imprints were publishing some authors whose books were selling less well than they had in the past – not necessarily because the books were less good or less interesting, but simply because the market had changed. So there was a growing pool of so-called 'mid-list' titles that were in search of new homes, and publishers with mainly academic lists were able to move into this space. While a mainstream trade publisher might be looking to acquire books that would sell a minimum of 10,000 or even 20,000 hardcover copies and consider anything less to be marginal, many academic publishers would be delighted to sell 3,000 or 4,000 copies of a non-fiction hardcover before bringing out a paperback edition. The sales thresholds and expectations of the university presses were much lower, and therefore they were able to move into a space in the field of trade publishing that was being increasingly vacated by the big trade houses.

A third development that favoured the migration of university presses into trade publishing was the rise of the retail chains. The rapid growth of the chains created an increased demand for books that were needed to stock the newly opened superstores, and many academic publishers found that they could secure substantial orders from the chains for books that were perceived to have some trade potential. In sharp contrast to the declining library market for scholarly monographs, the late 1980s and 1990s were a period of more or less steadily expanding demand for scholarly books that crossed over into the general trade, particularly in the US. Many American university presses saw this as an opportunity to increase sales and devoted more attention to commissioning books which they thought they could sell into the chains, from which they were deriving a growing proportion of their revenue.

These three developments explain why university presses have become increasingly involved in trade publishing since the late 1980s, and some university presses – especially Oxford University Press, Harvard, Princeton and Yale – now have a recognized presence in the field. But even the largest and most active of the university presses are still marginal players. For the university presses, trade publishing is a sideline, it's not their raison d'être, and they don't have the resources to compete at the upper levels. Even the largest of the university presses will seldom pay over $100,000 and will generally prefer low five-figure advances. 'Most of our advances are around $10,000,' said the director of one university press; they will occasionally pay significantly more than this, partly in order to let the agents know that they are able and willing to go higher ('You want to be seen to be able to play in that league'), but this is rare. They simply don't have money to throw around. This means that, in practice and for most books, the university presses will not be on agents' 'A' lists but may be on their 'B' or 'C' lists (if they appear at all). When they find themselves in competitive situations, it is generally other university presses, and occasionally the more serious medium-sized independents or imprints like Norton, Basic and Farrar, Straus & Giroux, with which they are competing. Given their relative weakness in the market for content, the university presses generally prefer to use a different acquisitions model, relying less on agents and more on their privileged access to the academic community to try to persuade academics to write books that stand a chance of crossing over into the trade. But like all small and medium-sized publishers, the university presses run the risk of losing their more successful authors to bigger houses, especially since some agents have actively sought to recruit successful and promising academic authors for their client lists.

Just as university presses lack the resources to compete with the major trade houses in the market for content, so too they lack the clout and the resources to get their books into the big retail chains and make them visible. 'We don't have money to spend and we aren't in the world [of trade publishing] vigorously enough to market the book,' observed the director of one of the university presses which is most active in trade publishing. 'We can't buy the real estate at Barnes & Noble.' For most of the university presses, Amazon is their biggest customer rather than Barnes & Noble and the other retail chains. When the university presses do have big successes in the field of trade publishing, more often than not they are books that surprise everyone, themselves included. They are home runs that come seemingly from nowhere, lifted out of relative obscurity by historical events, unexpected reviews or just some strange concatenation of circumstances. Ahmed Rashid's *Taliban*, published by Yale in April 2000, was a modest-selling backlist title imported from the UK when the events of 9/11 suddenly turned it into a runaway success. When Princeton published Harry Frankfurt's *On Bullshit* in 2005 – a short essay that had originally been written as an article for an academic collection some years earlier – no one at the press imagined that it would sell more than a few thousand copies at best; when the book found its way on to the *New York Times* bestseller list and sold over 360,000 copies in cloth, everyone at the press was surprised.

Despite the disadvantages they suffer, participating in the field of trade publishing remains worthwhile in the eyes of some university press directors. It can help to raise the profile of the press in the review media and in the public arena more generally, and the sales that can be achieved in trade publishing can make a significant financial contribution if you get things right. The key is to participate modestly and to recognize that, whatever success you may occasionally have, you are and always will be on the margins of the field. 'We have no illusions that we're in the game with HarperCollins, Simon & Schuster and so on,' explained one university press director. 'We think of ourselves as competing at the lower end. A bestseller for us would be five figures and that's really the range that we're looking to strike at – 10,000 copies plus is a very good thing for us. Most of our books don't achieve this but that's the goal. So we see ourselves as a bigger fish in the university press world but not really pretending to be with those other guys who are throwing away six-figure advances on a regular basis.'

While the university presses cannot compete at the same level with the big trade houses, they sometimes find themselves picking up established authors who have, in effect, been cast off by the trade houses, or who feel undervalued by them. The sales of these authors' books may be declining with each new book and the trajectory of their careers may appear to be downwards, so the big trade house may lose interest. The books themselves may be getting better and their careers may be maturing but the sales are just not good enough to retain the interest of the big trade houses – 'The romance is over, the buzz is off,' as one university press director put it. But what the large trade house sees as a declining asset may look to the university press like a valuable catch. They will be quite happy to sign an established author knowing that they are unlikely to sell more than 10,000 copies in cloth. 'Everyone's happy in a sense because there's no false expectation. We can't be burned and he's not out there on a limb.' Some established authors writing high-quality non-fiction, especially if they are professors with a career investment in the academic world, will self-consciously migrate to the margins of the field where a university press may offer them a more commodious home.

— 5 —

BIG BOOKS

We've seen how, with the rise of publishing corporations, the growth of the retail chains and the increasing power of agents, the field of trade publishing becomes polarized. On the publishing side, the large corporations become the dominant players in the field, and the imprints and houses that are owned by the large corporations feature prominently on the 'A' lists of agents who are seeking to sell what they regard as their most highly valued assets. Some small independent presses will also occasionally feature on an agent's 'A' list, depending on the author and the book, but they will rarely feature on the 'A' list for a book for which an agent has high financial expectations: in these cases the agent will focus his or her selling activities on the imprints in the large corporations in the knowledge that they will be able and willing to pay an advance at the sought-for level while the small independent presses will not. Depending on the author, the book and the level of financial expectation, the medium-sized publishers may or may not be on the agent's 'A' list. Some of the medium-sized publishers, especially the larger ones, are perfectly able and willing to pay six-figure advances for the right book, and this is often sufficient to get them included on an agent's 'A' list if the author and the book seem to match what the agent perceives to be the editor's taste and the profile and strategy of the house.

Within this highly structured space of collaboration, competition and reciprocal interdependency between agents and editors/publishers, the 'big book' plays a particularly important role. Agents, editors and publishers all speak frequently and unselfconsciously about 'big books': they are the prized assets on which all of these actors are focusing their most dedicated attention. What counts as a 'big book' may differ from one agent to another and one house to another, but all agents and all houses want them. They are constantly in search of big books. But what exactly are big books and why are they so important in the field of trade publishing? Why does the preoccupation with big books become a key feature of the logic of the field?

The growth conundrum

We spoke in chapter 3 of the growth conundrum that confronts the senior managers of all of the large publishing corporations: how do you achieve significant growth year on year when the market is essentially static? Now there is one way of answering this question that the senior managers of most large publishing corporations have come to reject: they generally reject the view that they should try to achieve growth simply by increasing the number of books they publish. Why do they reject this view? Partly because increasing the number of books they publish would increase the demands on an already over-stretched sales force. As the large publishing corporations absorbed more and more houses, most of the corporations (apart from the most decentralized) sought to achieve some economies of scale by amalgamating and rationalizing the sales forces. One consequence of this is that the sales teams ended up carrying more and more books – with every merger and acquisition, the number of titles they had to sell grew. It became increasingly difficult for them to give time and attention to all of the new books that were being launched each season.

Most of the large corporations responded to this problem in three ways. First, they increased the number of selling cycles. Rather than the traditional two cycles, spring and fall, most of the large corporations moved to three or more selling cycles per year. Three cycles became the general norm in the industry and other smaller houses followed suit. But for the major national chains, selling cycles became shorter still, and the reps for the large corporations began to call on the central buyers for the national chains as frequently as once a month.

Second, the large publishing corporations moved to a system of title prioritization. Not all new titles were treated equally, and the sales directors worked with the publishers of the various imprints and houses to work out a prioritization of the new books in each selling cycle. The sales forces of the largest publishing corporations in the US today will be dealing with 5,000–6,000 new titles each year – in effect, 5,000–6,000 new 'product lines'. If they are working to three sales cycles, this means they will be selling around 2,000 new titles in each cycle. Given that they have a relatively short amount of time to sell the new books to any particular buyer, they have to prioritize; they can't possibly deal with 2,000 titles in a single meeting, or indeed with anything like this number. So how do they establish their priorities? Tom, the sales director of a large US publishing corporation, put it like this:

> Each day of the sales conference we'll have a session with a core publisher from one of the groups. They come into a conference room, we show covers and so on. Let's say the summer list will be 2,000 titles. We have our meetings and first of all, we don't cover every title in the meetings. The publishers don't even cover all their titles. So if the total number is 2,000, they will cover, say, 1,500. Then what I do is I sit down with my divisional directors, we take the 1,500 and I come up with what we call our 'priority titles', and that's going to be about 500.

Which books feature among the priority titles and in which order depends on which part of the sales force it is – the reps calling on the big national chains will be prioritizing different titles from the reps calling on the independent booksellers. The easiest books to deal with are those by brand-name authors, the John Grishams and Michael Crichtons and Stephen Kings – these books are 'pure numbers, we put out 60,000 of this here, we're going to put out 35,000 there and that's it, you don't have to talk about it,' explained Tom. The author's name, the cover and the historical record of the sales of the author's previous books in different channels are all you need to know. Then you have the books where the publishers have some reason to think that they have real potential in some particular channel, such as the independent bookstores. The publishers will say that this title – say a work of literary fiction by a promising novelist – is a priority title for the independents, and so the field reps will 'work' these titles in the independents, whereas a John Grisham or a Michael Crichton will not be a priority for them because they know that Barnes & Noble and Borders and the price clubs will take these books in large numbers. The final factor that helps them come up with their priority titles is feedback from the sales reps. The sales reps are not just selling: they are also the eyes and ears of the corporation in the world of the publisher's most immediate customers, the bookstores and the retail chains. 'We have an electronic bulletin board,' continued Tom. 'We've got all these reps out there meeting buyers and giving manuscripts and galleys to booksellers and things bubble up to the surface. All of a sudden we may get a sense that the buyers and booksellers like a particular book and that we should make it a priority.'

Given that the list of priority titles might include only a quarter of all the titles being published in that season, this means that as many as three-quarters of the books being published by the corporation are not being prioritized; they are not completely neglected, but they are not given the kind of attention and concerted sales and marketing support as the prioritized titles. This doesn't mean that none of the non-prioritized titles will sell. Some will sell modestly. There will also be the occasional title that will surprise everyone – the 'black swan', the outlier, the singularity that lies outside the realm of normal expectations.[1] With the benefit of hindsight it's always easy to spot the bestsellers and to argue backwards from success – '*The Da Vinci Code*, that's easy, we can do that again.' But in advance it's much more difficult and there are always going to be some books that confound expectations. 'Why is it that this book we're really hot on turns out to be an absolute bomb and then something we just didn't expect at all takes off?' reflected Tom, who has been in the business all his professional life. 'We don't know, *we just don't know*,' he repeats with emphasis. Like movies and other products of the creative industries, many books display what Caves aptly calls the 'nobody knows' property.[2]

Given that trade publishing is to some extent a 'black swan industry' where serendipity plays an ineliminable role and given that for many if not most books nobody really knows just how well they're going to do, every trade publisher has to be prepared to gamble on some books where success is by no means clear. Every experienced publisher will know that bestsellers can emerge from quarters where you least expect them. This is why the story – recounted by an editor at one of the large houses – of the external management consultants who are invited in to advise senior managers about how to improve productivity and profitability in a publishing house after a merger is a standing joke among trade publishers:

---

[1] Nassim Nicholas Taleb, *The Black Swan: The Impact of the Highly Improbable* (New York: Random House, 2007).
[2] See Richard E. Caves, *Creative Industries: Contracts between Art and Commerce* (Cambridge, Mass.: Harvard University Press, 2000), p. 3 and passim.

Millions of dollars have been spent, untold numbers of hours have been chewed up analysing and arranging and rearranging. And eventually a report this high and this square gets dropped on the CEO's desk and there is a cover sheet on top. And in some form or another within the first four bullet points, what it announces is that the management consultants involved in this study have finally solved the riddle of publishing. They've worked it out and here it is. You've given us 5 million dollars, here's the answer: only publish bestsellers.

The ineliminable serendipity of trade publishing makes the management consultant's solution risible, but the equally inescapable truth is that a large proportion of the books published by trade publishers – both the large corporations and the independents, medium-sized and small – turn out to sell in small numbers. 'If the field reps don't work it, if Barnes & Noble don't go for it, it's likely to be tough,' said Tom. 'I've sat through print meetings where we'll look at the numbers and we'll say, "Jesus, nobody likes this book." But, you know, the publisher's paid and they've got an advance out there, they go ahead and publish it. The likelihood is we will wind up getting 70–80 per cent of it back in returns.'

While recognizing that they must always allow for the possibility of the black swan, most large trade publishers have responded to the harsh reality of the marketplace by trying to reduce the number of titles they publish. This enables the sales reps to focus their efforts on a limited number of titles, and reduces or limits the number of titles that are going to be relegated to the non-prioritized list. It also allows the marketing budget to be divided up among a smaller number of titles, and enables the marketing and publicity staff to focus their energies. 'The game is to maximize,' said one sales director in a large house. 'We try to maximize sales in the least number of books.' Publish fewer books and sell more of the books you publish: this is the mantra that is chanted in nearly all of the large publishing houses, and in many of the medium-sized and small publishing houses too.

Now if you're going to publish fewer titles and still achieve your growth targets, you're going to have to do your best to ensure that some of the books you do publish sell exceptionally well. This is the basic organizational necessity that underlies the preoccupation with 'big books'. You're going to have to try to buy some 'big books', and you're going to have to try to discourage your editors from buying too many 'small books'. Some 'small books' are fine; they can add diversity to the list, they might win a prize and add lustre, or symbolic capital, to the house. Moreover, you need a certain quantity of books 'just to keep the machine going' – to create a critical mass of frontlist titles, to feed into the paperback lines and so on. But too many 'small books' will dissipate energy and fill the list with books that are unlikely – even allowing for the possibility of a black swan – to fulfil your growth targets. One London agent put it like this:

> What the publishers are doing is that they're putting more and more of their eggs in the baskets of well-known celebrities – the Robbie Williams, the Steven Gerrards – where they feel they can get a lot of media attention and can sell in large quantities. They want a small number of big books in order to meet their ambitious sales targets and it doesn't help them to play around with these small books, as it were, because they just may go nowhere and you're going to find it hard. The sales process of your reps going out there, talking to Tesco's and talking to Waterstone's, they can sell Robbie Williams like that, but to get them to sit down and listen to the story of a sprinter at the time of the Boer War is hard. It's breathing too valuable oxygen. I was talking with an editor at one of the big houses recently and he said, 'I don't like having this conversation with you because I want to publish this book, I love the story but I know what's going to happen when I go to the acquisition meeting. They're going to say, "Why are we bothering with these little books that are going to breathe all this valuable oxygen both creatively and promotionally." And also, if we buy it at that level, we can't afford to spend anything in the marketing budget. Tesco's won't even bother to take it. Whereas Lewis Hamilton, OK, sure, we've paid a million for it but the door's already open when I arrive; I don't have to bruise my knuckles trying to get it through.'

While some aspects of this account are specific to the UK, where the supermarkets have become such an important retail outlet for trade publishers, the dynamic that leads the large houses to focus more and more on big books, and to pass over the 'small books' that 'breathe valuable oxygen', is the same on both sides of the Atlantic.

So what are big books, exactly? Simple, you might think: big books are bestsellers. Intuitively plausible though that may seem, in fact it is wrong. Big books are not bestsellers for the simple reason that, for most big books (though not all – more on the exceptions below), at the time when they are being sent out by agents and bought by publishers and are being treated by both as big books, they have not yet been published and no one knows whether they will actually *become* bestsellers. 'We don't know, *we just don't know*.' So big books cannot *be* bestsellers. At most they are *hoped-for bestsellers*, which is not at all the same thing. The difference between a big book and a bestseller is the difference between aspiration and reality. The difference is the outcome of the temporal gap between acquisition and publication coupled with the inescapable indeterminacy of trade publishing. The big book exists in the space of the possible, nourished by hope and expectation; the bestseller exists in the space of the real – hard numbers that can be scrutinized by everyone *post factum*, an incontestable fact.

Given the organizational need for the large publishers to focus more of their attention on big books, and given that big books are not bestsellers but merely hoped-for bestsellers, there is a great deal of room in the field of trade publishing for what we can call 'buzz'. Buzz is a performative utterance,[3] a type of speech act that is a pervasive feature of the field of trade publishing (and of other creative industries too). As a performative utterance in the field of trade publishing, we can give it a precise definition: buzz is talk about books that could be big. It is not the same as 'hype'. Hype is also a performative utterance which is common in trade publishing, but there is an important difference between buzz and hype. Hype is the talking-up of books by those who have an interest in generating excitement about them, like agents; buzz exists when the recipients of hype respond with affirmative talk backed up by money. Hype is like fishing with the most attractive fly you can find: the agent tries to present his or her book in the most favourable light, stressing its positive features and overlooking any possible blemishes. Buzz happens when you start to catch fish: editors and publishers react positively, respond to the agent's speech acts with affirmative speech acts of their own that may either put money on the table or begin serious talk of money. It is, in this very specific sense of the term, pecuniary talk. And the higher the figure, the greater the buzz.

It follows that at the heart of trade publishing there exists what we could call a *web of collective belief*. Since for many of the new books that are being offered by agents and bought by editors and publishers, no one really knows just how well they will do, a great deal of time and effort is invested in one party seeking to persuade

---

[3] I borrow this term from J. L. Austin, *How To Do Things With Words*, 2nd edn, ed. J. O. Urmson and Marina Sbisà (Oxford: Oxford University Press, 1976). A performative utterance is one in which 'the issuing of the utterance is the performing of an action – it is not normally thought of as just saying something' (pp. 6–7).

the other that the book being offered is, indeed, a big book, or at least sufficiently big to warrant a serious degree of attention from editors, and a great deal of weight is placed on what other people – especially trusted people – think and say about the book and how big it is. Big books do not exist in and by themselves: they have to be *created*. They are social constructions that emerge out of the talk, the chatter, the constant exchange of speech acts among players in the field whose utterances have effects and whose opinions are trusted and valued to varying degrees. In the absence of anything solid, nothing is more persuasive than the expressed enthusiasm (or lack of it) of trusted others. So the more buzz there is, the more excitement there is around a book, and the more that excitement is backed up with offers of hard cash, the more likely it is that others will become excited by it. This is the contagion effect in the field of trade publishing, and it is hard for those involved in the field, even those on the margins of the field, not to be seduced by it.

Valuing the valueless

So if you are an editor or publisher in a trade house, how do you form a view about a book or a project when there are few solid anchor points? How do you determine the indeterminate? How do you place a value on the valueless – on that which, at the time when you're considering it, has no clear and specifiable value?

First and foremost, you rely on your judgement based on a reading of the proposal or the manuscript. You will be looking for certain things depending on the kind of book it is, but ultimately it is a very personal reaction on the part of the editor, 'your instinctive passionate embrace of the item that is on offer', as one agent put it. If it is a debut novel by a new writer you will typically look for the familiar traits, character, plot and 'voice', placing different weights on them depending on the kind of novel it purports to be. In the case of non-fiction, topicality is obviously important, but so too is freshness, originality and the distinctiveness of the authorial voice. 'To me it's always about voice basically,' said a senior editor who acquires both fiction and non-fiction for one of the imprints of a large publishing corporation. 'To me it's not that much different if it's fiction or non-fiction; I work on it the same way. Even if it's fairly analytical or something, it still has to be an author who you feel like you're kind of in good hands with, and they have this, whatever, special spark of genius that you want to be stuck with for 300 pages. The sense that they're brilliant both in the way they're thinking and the way they're putting words together. You know you don't always get 100 per cent of both and so you're trying to find the balance.'

However, even in those cases where you sense a distinctive voice, that 'special spark of genius', you have to be able to combine your passionate embrace of the book with a vision, a practical sense, of how you would publish, market and sell the book to turn it into a success. This includes a vision about how many copies you think you could sell at what price and how much you should pay for it. A book that sells only 4,000 copies can be profitable if you don't pay much for it, but for most editors at the large houses in New York, 4,000 copies would be a worst-case scenario. 'I would never go into a project thinking that if we do everything right, that's our ceiling.' Although specific targets are seldom discussed, a senior editor at an imprint in a large US publishing corporation may be notionally expected to buy 8–12 new books a year, most of which could be expected to ship out between 20,000 and 50,000 in hardcover and at least one of which could be expected to do much better. 'At the level I'm at now,' said one senior editor who had been in the business for just over 12 years, 'I think I'm expected to bring in one book a year let's say that is legitimately a blockbuster that's going to ship over 100,000 copies.' In practice, if you're projecting that you're going to ship more than 50,000, you're assuming that you're going to get up to 100,000, 'so anything over 50 becomes 100'.

When an editor reads something and feels inclined to pursue it, he has to make a case for buying it. Whether this case needs to be presented to an acquisitions meeting or simply to his boss varies from imprint to imprint and corporation to corporation, as we noted in an earlier chapter; but regardless of the specific procedure for decision-making, the case needs to be made. In part the case will be based on the ability of the editor to convey what is special about the book and the vision he has for it. One editor put it like this:

I'm bringing [the publisher] something where I'm interpreting where it can go and who I think will come to it. And, you know, sometimes he'll have issues about where I think it can go, where he doesn't see the magnetism of the voice. Sometimes I'll just be asking him 'Do you see that? Do you see what I'm saying here?' and if he says no, that's just fine. I think in these cases it's the idea itself – I sort of imagine there's a market and he doesn't. But I guess more often what happens is we can both sort of come to terms on agreeing that there's a market but someone else across town sees a different, bigger market, or they're willing to lose money on that project for whatever reason. Normally what will happen is he'll ask me, 'What do you want to do? How much do you want to pay?' I'll come up with a number and he'll either say, 'Mm, I was thinking of something higher' or 'Are you crazy?'

The number this editor comes up with 'is just based on my sort of ballpark sense in my head of what it's worth'. Of course, he can do a P&L, but the P&L all depends on the numbers you plug in to the spreadsheet and most experienced editors don't need to go through the motions. If he sees this as a big book then sales and publicity or marketing will get involved at the acquisitions stage. 'You don't call on them if it's just, you know, a novel that's going to sell 7,000 copies. But if you're going to have to be asking them to get out this many hundreds of thousands of copies, and if from the very beginning they're saying that's going to be a big problem, then at the very least you need to know now that you're facing resistance.'

So a great deal depends on the editor's reading of the proposal or the text and his ability to articulate, to the publisher or to those in the acquisitions committee or both, a vision for the book which they can be persuaded or induced to share. Of course, the editor may fail, and may fail for different reasons:

> There are certainly times when I brought my boss a series of books where, if every time I'm sort of estimating that book's commercial prospects higher than he is, it just kind of makes sense that at a certain point he's going to have to say, 'Look, the last five we're taking flyers on, we can't do it this time.' That's not that frustrating to me. What's more frustrating I guess is when I feel like I have a sense of what it can do that's not necessarily borne out by the past history of book publishing and I'm not able to convince him. For the most part I think that it's my responsibility to be articulate enough to present that vision. But there are definitely times when I feel like I've been articulate well enough and he's just not going for it. That's the most frustrating. The rest is a sort of slow, low-level frustration.

While a great deal depends on the editor's ability to articulate a vision for the book and sell this vision to his boss and to others within the organization, there are certain things that the editor can draw on in order to help form a judgement and build a case for the book. It's not all just a matter of what the editor and others see in the text. So what are these other things, and how do they help to determine the value of something which, at the time when it is being offered by agents and considered by editors and publishers, is a mere hypothetical asset whose value is strictly unknown?

There are at least four things that an editor can draw on and that will help to determine the value of this valueless hypothetical asset, apart from the editor's own reading of the text and the vision he can articulate for it.

The first thing, hugely important in trade publishing, is the track record of the author – the 'track', as it's commonly known in the business. Before 2000, the track record of an author was a restricted form of knowledge – restricted to the author, to his or her agent and to the publisher who had published the author's previous books. The partial exceptions were the books that made it onto bestseller lists like that of the *New York Times*, which surveyed hundreds of retail outlets to estimate which books were selling the most copies and published the rankings but not the figures. The retail chains and bookstores themselves would have their own records of the sales histories of an author's books, records that became increasingly reliable with the computerization of the retail sector and the introduction of EPOS – electronic point of sale – systems, which record all cash register transactions. But the sales records of the retail outlets were incomplete, since they captured only the sales made by the retailer whose records they were, and they were not available to those outside of the retail organization, such as editors and others in the publishing houses. In those circumstances, there was a great deal of scope for agents to inflate the sales of an author's previous books when they were going out with a new title. They could exaggerate the sales of an earlier book when they were pitching a new book to a publisher who had not published the earlier one, in the knowledge that it would be difficult for the publisher to confirm or dispute the sales history (unless the new publisher was on good terms with the previous publisher and could call them to check the figures). The track record of an author was a contestable variable that was known to some, surmised by others and always subject to exaggeration in the interests of inflating value.

With the advent of BookScan, all of this suddenly changed. Book-Scan is a service provided by the Nielsen Company, an information and media company that was originally founded by Arthur Nielsen in 1923 and acquired by the Dutch group VNU in 1999. Nielsen specialized in market research, in developing methods for tracking the volume of sales in the marketplace and in measuring the size of radio and television audiences (the so-called 'Nielsen ratings'). The rolling out of EPOS systems across different retail sectors from the 1970s on opened up the possibility of providing much more accurate information on actual sales by collating point of sales data from a plurality of retail outlets. Following the success of SoundScan, which tracked point of sales information for music, Nielsen launched Book-Scan in the UK in December 2000 and in the US in January 2001. In essence, BookScan works like this: Nielsen purchases point of sales data from as many significant book retail outlets as it can, collates, regularly updates and manipulates this data so that it can be presented online in a clear and easily navigated way, and then sells access to the collated data by charging subscription fees to publishers and other clients in order for them to access the data on their website, varying the fee according to the size of the company. All the collated data on the website is accessible to all the clients who subscribe to the service, which means that the weekly and cumulative sales figures for every title are viewable by every client.

Thanks to BookScan, the sales history of any book published after 2000/1 is now public knowledge and the track record of any author is transparent to all – or, to be more precise, is transparent to everyone who has access to BookScan, which in practice means individuals who work for organizations that subscribe to the service. The game of concealment, selective disclosure and calculated inflation is over. Now there is nowhere to hide. Authors carry their sales histories around with them like a noose around their neck – although, curiously, this is a noose that they may not see, or may not know just how loosely or tightly it grips their neck, since they often know less about the sales histories of their books, and less about the consequences of different sales histories, than those in the industry do. But noose it is. If your first few books do well and show a nicely upward trend in terms of sales, you will be just fine, but if your first book disappoints and the second one tanks, you're in trouble: you're going to have a hard time persuading anyone that your next book is going to be a bestseller.

The advent of BookScan has undoubtedly changed the rules of the game, and in making the case for acquiring a new book an editor will routinely check the sales history of the author's previous books and build this into their calculations. They know that their publisher and sales and marketing directors will have access to the BookScan figures and may check the editor's expectations against the track. They also know that, when it comes to selling the book into the retail chains and bookstores, the buyers are likely to consult BookScan as well as their own in-house computerized sales records. So there is no point ignoring this: BookScan provides the one form of hard data available to everyone, the statistical common currency, that can defuse an agent's hype and temper an editor's imagination. But there are significant limitations.

The most important limitation is that BookScan does not collate data from all retail outlets. The UK version is more complete and reliable than the US version. BookScan UK's 'Total Consumer Market' (TCM) collects sales data from all major high-street chains, independents and supermarkets as well as internet sites, from Amazon to travel and other specialist sites; it claims to cover over 90 per cent of all retail book purchases in the UK. BookScan in the US collects sales data from the retail book chains, including Barnes & Noble and Borders, from a sample of independent bookstores, from Amazon and other internet companies, from Follett, Costco, Target and various other retail outlets. However, BookScan does not have access to sales data from Wal-Mart and Sam's Club and from other outlets like food and drug stores which, for certain kinds of mass-market books, can account for a substantial proportion of overall sales. 'On a new general interest hardcover release we're probably 70 to 75 per cent of the total market,' explained one senior manager at Nielsen's US office; 'on the mass market, we're probably around 50 per cent.' BookScan's figures are most reliable, in terms of providing an accurate picture of total sales, when dealing with books that sell primarily through traditional book retailing outlets, like Barnes & Noble, Borders and the independents, as well as through Amazon. 'For a lot of publishers on a lot of books, mid-level books, we could have 90 to 95 per cent of the market because they don't sell those books in food and drug stores and they're not in the Wal-Marts.' But the more commercial the book is, and the more likely it is to sell through non-traditional book retail outlets, the smaller the proportion of the overall market their data will capture.

Apart from the incompleteness of the data, there are obvious dangers and limitations in relying on the sales histories of an author's previous books when it comes to thinking about a new book by the same author. Historical sales can be an unreliable guide and can lead you to underestimate or overestimate the sales potential of a new book by the same author. The industry is awash with examples of both. Dan Brown is probably the most famous example of an author whose track record was a very unreliable guide to the future. His previous books had sold modestly in hardcover and paperback –

'There was no Dan Brown readership,' as one senior publisher observed. Based on the historical track record, the advance that was offered by Doubleday for his new book was very modest by industry standards – $400,000 for a two-book deal. The fact that this new book, *The Da Vinci Code*, went on to sell over 18 million copies in cloth in the US alone is a poignant reminder of how misleading it can be to rely on the historical track record of an author.

The other limitation of BookScan data from an acquisition's point of view is that there are of course some authors who have never published a book before and therefore have no track record. Does this mean that, in the brave new world where hard BookScan data have redefined the rules of the game, the first-time author is in a structurally disadvantaged position? An aspiring writer with no numerical credentials: how can he or she hope to be taken seriously by an industry seemingly fixated on numbers?

Ironically, in a world preoccupied by numbers, the author with no track is in some ways in a strong position, considerably stronger than the author who has published one or two books with modest success and muted acclaim, simply because there are no hard data to constrain the imagination, no disappointing sales figures to dampen hopes and temper expectations. The absence of sales figures sets the imagination free. The first-time author is the true tabula rasa of trade publishing, because his or her creation is the book for which it is still possible to imagine anything and everything. He or she could become the next Dan Brown or the next Patricia Cornwell or the next Ian McEwan. Or could vanish like a meteor in the summer sky.

This does not mean that, with the first-time author, there is nothing on which the editor can draw to help build a case – there is, and we shall come to this in a minute. But does it mean that the author who is already up and running will always be judged through the lens of the sales figures of his or her previous books, that their sales history is their fate? Yes and no. The sales figures are there as a public record and editors and others will always familiarize themselves with the sales performance of an author's previous books before bidding on a new one. But it is also always open for an editor – and, indeed, an agent – to make the case that a new book by an author is the exception that will break the mould. There are many different ways in which this can be done – the author has decided to write a different kind of book for a different kind of reader; the publisher of the previous books didn't understand the author and didn't have the right vision for the books and their market; or, simply, this new book is just much better than the previous books and in a different league.

Here's an agent in New York describing a case when she went out with a new book by an author whose previous two books had not sold well:

> The first one sold not many and the second one sold next to nothing and he wrote a third manuscript after a long gap, much struggle and despair and knowing that it was his last throw of the dice. I sent it out and the editor at one house said, 'Just don't fudge, what are his sales? I can get them from BookScan, you know.' 'You don't want to know them,' I said, 'you really don't want to know them.' But I told her the numbers and she came back and she said, 'Oh yeah, I checked and you know, you gave me accurate numbers. They're terrible!' 'I know, can we just pretend they never happened?' They decided to buy it, they paid a lot of money and they just decided to ignore his track record. They put a ton behind it and went out to booksellers saying 'I know he hasn't sold and I know he has a lousy track record but trust us, this is the book.' It's admirable when a publisher will do that because they're running against all sorts of numbers and what everyone says is going to happen to that author's career and just saying, 'Well, we love it.' They can do it when they have something that's flamboyantly exceptional in some way. They have to be able to tell a story about it, in-house as much as anything, and if someone brings up the past they go, 'I know, I know, but now he's written his masterpiece.' But then that puts more pressure on the book and makes it more important that it works out. And in turn, if it doesn't, God only knows. Last throw of the dice.

The second thing an editor can use to form a judgement and build a case is 'comps' – comparable books. Considerable time and energy is invested by agents and editors in trying to come up with other books to which the new book they want to sell as an agent or buy as an editor can be compared. The comparisons can be made in many different ways – plot, style, genre, voice, subject matter, argument or some combination of these and other factors. There are few clear-cut rules, but the one rule that does matter is that the book chosen as a comp should be a successful book. There is no point choosing as a comp a book that bombed out – it would simply defeat the purpose. Identifying comparable titles is essentially an exercise in building best-case scenarios by analogy. The selection of comps can't be so simple and brazen as to be implausible because then it will carry no conviction, but it serves no purpose unless the book chosen as a comp has excelled in some way. It's a fine line to tread. 'The tricky thing is

that you know you can't really compare a book to a runaway success,'
explained one senior editor. 'Like you have to find a sort of solid
success.' Solidly successful, but not so successful that no one will
believe you. So you can rule out *The Da Vinci Code* straightaway.
But a solid success, like *The Lovely Bones* or *The Memory Keeper's
Daughter*, would be an attractive comp.

Everyone knows that there is an element of speciousness in the
citing of comparable books but everyone plays the game nonetheless.
Why? Agents obviously do it because they want to sell their books
to editors and publishers and citing comparable books is a way of
putting a positive gloss on a new book, getting potential buyers to
think of it in terms of another book (or other books) whose eye-
watering sales figures are available to everyone on BookScan. But
editors do it too. Sometimes they use the comps cited by agents, but
more often than not they come up with their own, and they do this
for various reasons. First because they too have to have a way of
getting a handle on the potential sales of a new book, and how else
can they do this except by referring to the sales of the author's previous books or by looking at the sales of other books that share some
significant features in common with the new book, even if they were
written by others? But equally importantly, the editor does it because
the editor is, fundamentally, a salesperson within his or her own
organization. An editor who wants to buy a book has to be able to
sell it to others within the organization – not just his or her immediate boss, the publisher, but also to sales, marketing and publicity staff.
They have to be able to persuade others that this is a book worth
doing and that they should get behind it. And a crucial part of making
the case is to be able to see not just what is special and unique about
a new book, but also what it shares in common with other books
whose track records are known or knowable. 'So if you think a book
is really just special because it's so special, it can be hard to make the
case,' the senior editor explained. 'But the fact is you're going to have
to make that case all the way along the line. Not just to your boss
but to the sales people, to the publicist to make sure they get the good
publicists working on it, and so on.'

While every new book is in some sense unique and its future sales
are strictly speaking unknowable, those working within organizations need to find ways of hedging the indeterminacy in order to
attach some value to the new book in advance of knowing what
the real value is. Thinking by analogy is one way of hedging the
indeterminacy of the new. It gives the editor a way of trying to
estimate sales, gives the publisher a way of trying to assess whether

the editor's vision for the book is realistic or feasible, and gives sales and marketing staff a way of thinking about the book, assigning priorities, allocating resources and, eventually, selling the book to buyers, review editors and others outside of the house on whose fate the book will to some extent depend. All the way along the line, those who are dealing with the book will be thinking in terms of comparable titles, because thinking by analogy is one of the few tools available to them for hedging the intrinsic indeterminacy of the not-yet-published book.

The third thing that the editor can use to form a judgement and build the case for a book is the author's platform. We encountered the notion of platform in chapter 2 when we examined the way that agents prepare a book and an author for submission: platform, we said, is the position from which an author speaks, a combination of their credentials, visibility and promotability, especially through the media. We noted that this factor is particularly important for non-fiction books, and especially certain types of non-fiction like fitness and diet books, but it is also relevant to works of fiction. Why is platform so important for an editor when he or she is seeking to form a judgement about a new book and to build a case for buying it?

It is important for two reasons. In the first place, the author's platform creates a pre-existing market for a book. If the author is a prominent journalist, news anchor, politician or TV personality, then he or she will already be known to a large number of people who constitute a potential market for the book and to whom the book can be promoted. So the importance of the media for trade publishers is not simply that they provide the means for marketing and publicizing books: the role of the media is more fundamental than this. For the media are the milieu in which an actual or potential author creates a platform, that is, demonstrates their ability to reach an audience and becomes to some extent – however modestly – a visible and identifiable persona in the public domain. So-called 'celebrity publishing' is simply an extension of this fundamental dynamic, a special case where the 'author's' platform becomes not just one factor to be taken into account but the overriding factor, indeed the principal reason for publishing the book ('author' being in inverted commas because many celebrity books are in fact ghost-written by others).

The second reason why platform is important to an editor, especially for non-fiction books, is that it matters to those within the organization to whom the editor has to sell the book – the publisher and the sales, marketing and publicity staff. And it matters to them not only because it creates a pre-existing market for the book but also because it gives them the basis for building the marketing and publicity campaign. Trade publishers rely on publicity and marketing to drive sales. Getting books into the bookstores is one thing, getting consumers to go into the bookstores and buy the books is another, and the difference between the two is returns. Anything the author can bring with him or her in terms of platform is going to help the marketing and publicity staff build a campaign aimed at driving sales and reducing returns. For certain kinds of books it helps if the author is presentable, articulate and telegenic, would perform well on radio or television, and so on. These things matter in trade publishing because visibility is the oxygen of publicity and, in an increasingly crowded marketplace where the spaces of the visible are shrinking for publishers and authors (a theme to which we shall return), you need all the help you can get.

The fourth thing that an editor can draw on to help form a judgement and build a case is what other people think. And at the end of the day, this is the most important factor. Of course, the editor's own opinion of the proposal or manuscript and his or her vision for the book matters greatly, and the weight they carry tends to vary with the seniority and track record of the editor. A new editor will often have a honeymoon period when they are given considerable leeway to buy new books, but generally speaking, the more senior the editor and the better their track record in picking books that turn out to be successful, the more weight the publisher and others will give to the editor's opinion. The power and influence of the editor tends to be directly proportional to their track record of success, where 'success' is measured primarily in terms of sales and secondarily, depending on the imprint and the house, in terms of prizes or other forms of recognition. Numbers matter – the sales record of the author's previous books as well as the sales of books that could plausibly be considered as comparable titles. Platform matters too. But at the end of the day, it is a specific combination of judgements and opinions, of who thinks what and what they think about it, that determines whether a house will buy a book and, if so, how much they will pay for it. This is the web of collective belief.

The web operates in different ways from house to house and book to book – it could be thought of as a net with varying degrees of extension. The net is made up of opinions, beliefs, judgements and talk about these opinions and beliefs, whether that talk is expressed orally or in writing (which, these days, usually means email). The

least extended version of the net may involve just three individuals
– the agent, the editor and the editor's boss (usually the publisher).
Each will have an opinion, usually based on a reading of the proposal
and all or part of the manuscript plus a consideration of the three
other elements, analysed above, that are commonly involved in judgements of this kind. The weight accorded to the opinion depends on
whose opinion it is and on their respective power, both real and
symbolic. If it is an imprint or house in which the ultimate power
to decide is vested with the publisher, then his or her power will
override the beliefs or opinions of the editor. But if the editor is
a senior and experienced colleague who has been at the house for
many years and has a good track record of picking successful books,
then the publisher may well defer to the editor's judgement on a
particular project; even if the publisher has reservations, he or she
may give the editor the benefit of the doubt on this occasion. It is a
negotiation in which the editor makes a case and the publisher con-
siders it, forms his or her own judgement by looking at some of the
material and decides, in discussion with the editor, what to do –
sometimes in an informal meeting in the publisher's office, sometimes
in an impromptu conversation in the corridor, sometimes in a brief
email exchange.

However, even in this smallest version of the web, there is always
a third party who contributes to the deliberation – the agent. From
the perspectives of the editor and the publisher, the value of the agent
is not simply that they provide the initial filter that selects some
authors and books and screens out others: the very fact that they are
supporting the book, and the way that they support it when they are
sounding out the editor's interest on the telephone or over lunch and
when they send the proposal or manuscript with a cover letter or
email, are vital contributions to the web of collective belief. In the
first place, *who* the agent is matters: some agents carry much more
weight in the field than others. Some agents have built a reputation
and accumulated large stocks of symbolic capital by virtue of the
authors they have managed to sign and the books they have chosen
to support. Others, especially those young agents who are new to the
field, will have much less symbolic capital and their support of a
project will mean much less, though their lightweightedness in the
field can be offset to some extent by the reputation of the agency for
which they work. An editor will always take account of who the
agent is when they are considering a new book because they know
that agents have different track records, that their track records are

part of what makes up their reputation and that their reputation matters when it comes to making the case for buying a book.

This is particularly true at the large publishing corporations where nearly all new books are agented. Chris was the publisher at a small independent house in New York before he moved to become an editor at an imprint in one of the large publishing corporations. He had previously tried to avoid agents whenever possible: as the publisher at a small independent, he tended to view agents as a source of trouble who, as soon as they became involved in the acquisitions process, tended simply to up the ante. But now that he was working for one of the large publishing corporations, he saw agents very differently. When he wanted to sign up an author he had published in the past, he actively encouraged her to get a well-known agent, and when he told his boss that the author was represented by this agent, his boss was much more enthusiastic about buying the book. Of course, it meant that they would have to pay more – the author, who had previously published with the small independent, would have been delighted with an advance of $25,000, but now, with this well-known agent involved, they would have to pay $100,000 or more. But that didn't matter. The fact that this well-known agent was representing this author, lending his reputation and accumulated symbolic capital to the author and the book, was in itself a sign that the book was worth buying. His support was an integral part of the web of collective belief, was used as such by the editor and seen as such by the publisher. 'When I was at [the small independent house] I always thought of agents as my enemies,' said Chris; 'now I see them as my friends.'

The problem for new or young editors at the large houses is that they generally will not be the first port of call for those established agents who have the most credibility in the web of collective belief. When the established agents have a big book, or even just a book for which they have reasonably high expectations, they will tend to go first to those editors or publishers in the various imprints and houses with whom they have established relationships and who they think will have the most clout within the organization – that is, the greatest capacity to sell the book within the organization and get others to back it with enthusiasm, commitment and cash. New and young editors generally find themselves receiving submissions from the newer and younger agents – that is, through the lateral networks that develop in the field between editors and agents of the same cohort or generation. This may put them in good stead for the future, since they will form strong and lasting relationships with some of the agents who may eventually become powerful figures in the field, but it weakens their position in the present. The only way around it is to work, slowly and steadily, on building relationships with those agents who carry more weight – try to have lunch with them, explain the kinds of books you'd like to buy and, from time to time, show them that you're capable of getting the support of the organization by making an offer on a scale they would regard as serious.

While the least extended version of the web of collective belief involves at least three players, the editor, the publisher and the agent, it very often involves many more. The web is often extended by the fact that an editor will commonly consult others within the organization. He or she will often ask another editor, a colleague, to have a look at the proposal or read part of the manuscript, just to get another opinion from someone whose opinions they value and whose judgement they trust. The bigger the book, the more people they are likely to consult – not just other editors but also, for bigger books, sales directors, marketing and/or publicity directors and, for those books that have paperback potential, the publisher of the paperback imprint. All of this consultation is done in-house; very rarely does an editor at an imprint in the large publishing corporations consult someone outside of the house. It is simply not done – 'It's considered bad form,' as one editor put it. Why? Why do editors in the large publishing corporations rarely if ever send proposals or manuscripts to external readers? Partly it's because they are pressed for time: they often have no more than a couple of weeks to consider a proposal or manuscript and it would be difficult to get reports from outside readers in that time. But more importantly, the opinions of external readers are just not the kinds of opinions that matter in the web of collective belief that characterizes trade publishing. Unlike academic publishing, where the intellectual quality and originality of a book is a major consideration and consulting external readers is a routinized way of assessing quality, in trade publishing it is assumed that satisfying a good editor (or good editors) is a sufficient test of quality. If a proposal or manuscript passes this test, then what matters most in the deliberative process is the assessment of the market for the book and its sales potential, and those working within trade houses generally assume that the views of external readers are unlikely to be of any help in this regard. 'An academic can often make a much more pointed and acute judgement than I can about the strengths and weakness of an historical argument,' explained a senior editor at one of the imprints in a large corporation, 'but I also have to think about the commercial appeal. It isn't an industry where you have to have the highest possible intellect to succeed as a good writer and good publisher. We're not a rarefied kind of club for the elite; it's just not what publishers are. So you're going to rely on your instinct about what a book could sell or whether we can sell it. It's not going to come from an academic.'

So how does an editor know how many people they need to consult in-house? Partly that depends on how big the book is. But how do they know how big it is? For any editor who knows their job, the signs are there at an early stage – who is the agent, what is the buzz, who is the author and what is his or her platform, what is the track record of the author's other books, what are the sales figures of comparable titles, what expectations were signalled by the agent when he or she sounded out the editor or submitted the proposal or manuscript?, and so on. There are many different ways that an agent can signal expectations. If the agent is showing it to only one publisher in the first instance, he or she will often indicate how much the publisher would have to pay to pre-empt a book and 'take it off the table'. If the agent is going for multiple submissions, he or she will often say something along the lines of 'we're looking for support in the mid-six figures'. These and numerous other signals, some explicitly stated, others conveyed by a wink and a nod, help to define the bigness of the book and determine the value that the agent expects it to have. But they pale in comparison to the one mechanism that serves more than any other to define the bigness of books and determine their value before anyone knows what their value really is: the auction.

The auction is commonly seen as an economic mechanism that is used by the agent to maximize the advance paid by the publisher, and it does indeed perform this economic role admirably. But the auction has another function that is symbolic rather than economic: it is a device for generating buzz and extending the web of collective belief – in short, a buzz machine. Indeed, the very effectiveness of the auction as an economic mechanism actually depends on its effectiveness as a symbolic device for generating buzz and collective belief. If a book is submitted to multiple publishers and only one publisher expresses an interest in buying it, there will be no auction. The possibility of an auction arises only when it becomes clear that a plurality of publishers are seriously interested in acquiring the book, in which case it is immediately apparent to each of the publishers that there are other houses that ascribe sufficient value to the book to want to bid for it. In the web of collective belief that characterizes the world of trade publishing, this in itself helps to validate the editor's judgement – it shows, as one editor put it, 'that you're not the only one'.

When the auction gets underway, the agent may go back to the bidding parties and tell them what has been offered by another (nameless) party, asking them if they want to reconsider their own offer in the light of their competitor's bid, and may continue this process until they have found the highest bidder before presenting the options to the author. Each time an agent does this, the publisher is, in effect, reconsidering their own assessment of the value of the book by taking account of the value perceived by one of their competitors in the field. The auction is a continuous process of re-evaluating the value of a book, testing one's own judgements and opinions against the judgements and opinions of others and adjusting them in this light. The higher others are prepared to go, the more likely it is that you will be inclined to think that you should go higher too. Since the value of the book is at this stage intrinsically indeterminate – it could always be worth more, though it could be worth less too – it can be difficult to draw a line beyond which one is no longer prepared to go. Auctions have an addictive quality, precisely because the value of the book is indeterminate and the assessment of its value is shaped by the web of collective belief.

In deciding whether to go into an auction, to stay in and how high to go, an editor is concerned not just to win a competition for a book and add it to their list but also to nurture and protect a set of relationships that is vital for their own success – namely, their relationships with the key agents in the field. Here the interests of the editor don't always coincide with the interests of the publisher or the head of the division, since the editor is also competing with other editors in the same house, a competition that can be stressful and intense. 'My God,' said one senior editor working for an imprint in a large corporation, 'the biggest competition around here is which editor is going to get the submission from the important agents. And that's why turning things down is hard, because you just know that if you turn something down that's kind of a big-deal book for them, they're probably not going to submit their next book to you. They're going to pick one of your colleagues.' In a field where agents control access to content, an editor's relationships with the key agents are their lifeline: they simply cannot afford to screw this up. So they may find themselves deciding to bid for books, and asking for permission to bid at levels that even they feel are excessive, simply because they don't want to offend important agents and they want to be seen and known around town as somebody who bids, and who can, if need be, bid high. 'If I have a book that there's a lot of interest in and I could go either way on, I'm probably going to go forward with it because I want to be a player,' this editor added. 'Often you've been in an auction and you just hope you won't win. Everybody does it.'

The more a publishing house ends up paying for a book, the bigger that book tends to be for the house concerned. This is not exactly an 'iron law', as Andrew Wylie would have it, but it is probably as close to an iron law as you're likely to find in this field. There is undoubtedly a correlation – albeit rough and always susceptible to exceptions – between the scale of the advance paid and the bigness of the book. Much more is riding on a book for which $500,000 has been paid than is riding on a book for which $50,000 has been paid, and the expectations, preparations and prioritizations within the publishing house are adjusted accordingly. Ironically, this creates a perverse incentive within the large publishing corporations to pay more for books rather than less, because the more you pay, the bigger the book is and the more likely it is that it will be seen and treated as a big book all the way down the line, from positioning within the catalogue and the allocating of marketing spend to prioritization by the sales directors and the way the book is worked by the reps.

There is only one hitch: a big book is not a bestseller; it is merely a hoped-for bestseller. It is the editor's and publisher's best guess, a judgement based on their personal response to the proposal or manuscript that is filtered through their experience and supported by various things including the author's track record and platform, the sales of comparable titles and the web of collective belief. But it could be wrong. 'In a world where the value of a thing is not established,' said one agent, 'it's not like somebody says "Here is a diamond of this size with this many facets." You look at the diamond and you go, "Ah, that means it's worth this much." The book that you've just paid $300,000 for could be worth a million. Or it could be worth $25,000. That's the risk you take.'

More often than not, the guess is wrong. It's a gamble, a roll of the dice, which pays off in some cases and fails in others, and the challenge for the publisher is to try to ensure that you win enough times to compensate for the books that fail, and that, when you do win, you are able to turn it into a success on a scale that will make up for all those failures and make a serious difference to your top and bottom lines. 'Book publishing is a business of hope to a great extent,' observed one former CEO. 'You have to be an optimist, you

have to believe that the occasional investment will have a disproportionate payoff and some do.' So what proportion of new books succeeds and what proportion fails in the typical output of the large
publishing corporations? The answer to this question depends on
how you understand 'success'. If success is understood from a strictly
financial point of view in terms of profitability, then the broad answer
is probably around half and half, though only a much smaller proportion of frontlist titles do really well. The business managers at the
different corporations have different views on the precise breakdown,
but this account, summed up by the business manager at one of the
large New York houses, is probably a fairly accurate picture of the
industry as a whole: 'On the new hardbacks we're putting out each
year, probably half lose money and half make money, but only 30
per cent really exceed what we're looking for. And it's really the top
10 per cent that make all the difference. A smaller number of books
are now accounting for a larger share of the revenue.'[4] Of course, no
editor or publisher will buy a book with the intention of losing
money, but roughly half of the books they buy will. For many of the
books they buy, they really don't know in which percentile it is going
to end up – whether it's going to be in the 50 per cent that lose money
or the 50 per cent that make money, or the 30 per cent that exceed
expectations, or even the 10 per cent that sell exceptionally well and
make the difference. They may have a good hunch but there are
always books that surprise even the most seasoned editors and publishers, either by exceeding their expectations or by selling much more
poorly than anyone thought. Fortunately for trade publishers, not all
is serendipity.

The comforts of the brand

While frontlist publishing is inherently risky, there are two areas
where trade publishers can count on more reliable revenue streams
– brand-name authors and backlist. Both forms of publishing are
extremely important for trade publishers because they provide the

---

[4] Greco, Rodriguez and Wharton give a slightly different account of the breakdown
between success and failure on the frontlist of trade publishing: 'Our research indi-
cates that 7 out of every 10 frontlist hardbound books fail financially (i.e. they do
not earn enough to cover the author's advance and other editorial, marketing, and
overhead costs), 2 books break even, and 1 is a hit' (*The Culture and Commerce of
Publishing*, p. 30).

counterweight – the ballast, as it were – to offset the inherent riskiness of frontlist publishing.

Brand-name authors are important for two reasons: first, their sales are predictable, and second, they are repeaters.

Their sales are predictable because they have readerships that are loyal to them. Readers become 'fans' of a particular writer, or of a series of books by a particular writer, and they want to read more. The publisher can therefore count on a market that is to some extent captive, and the sales of the author's previous books become a good guide to the sales of the author's next book. If the author's career is developing satisfactorily, the publisher can count on cumulative growth: each new book will sell more than the previous one, and the overall trajectory will be a steadily climbing curve. In a world where so much frontlist publishing is a crapshoot, predictability of this kind is a gift.

This kind of loyalty is more common in fiction than in non-fiction, and more common in commercial fiction than in literary fiction. It is more common in fiction than non-fiction because many readers buy non-fiction books for other reasons – for example, because they heard the author speak or they read about it and are interested in the topic. And it is more common in commercial fiction because this is an area where genre publishing is normal – thriller, detective, romance, science fiction, etc. – and where brand loyalty can be developed particularly effectively. Readers of literary fiction tend to be more selective in the books they buy and read, and will move from one author to another with less sense of loyalty to a particular writer. Hence the development of brand-name authors is primarily a feature of fiction publishing, and the more commercial the fiction, the more common the practice. But there are exceptions. There are some non-fiction writers who display the characteristics of a brand, especially if they are media celebrities who have an established fan base, such as celebrity cooks with a regular TV show, like Jamie Oliver and Nigella Lawson. Brand-name non-fiction writers of this kind can be just as valuable to trade publishers as the more common brand-name commercial fiction author.

Brand-name authors are also repeaters. They write a book a year, or maybe a book every two years. This means that the publisher with a number of repeaters can plan their future programme with much more accuracy and reliability than a publisher who is relying on the normal hit-and-miss business of frontlist trade publishing. They know when each of their repeaters will deliver and they can plan their publishing strategies for each author and each book in order to maximize their sales potential – each year a new hardcover, which is subsequently relaunched as a trade or mass-market paperback, etc. The regular, predictable output of repeaters enables the publisher to build the author's brand over time, feeding new books into the marketplace at regular intervals to maintain the interest and loyalty of existing fans and to recruit new readers. It also enables the publisher to build the backlist, since the better known the author is, the more valuable his or her backlist will tend to be, as new and existing fans turn to earlier books in order to sate their appetite for their favoured author's work. So the publisher with brand-name authors wins on both fronts: predictable frontlist hits that can be turned into staple backlist titles.

There are some trade houses that were built on the development of a programme of brand-name authors. Putnam is one. An old American house dating back to the middle of the nineteenth century which had published some celebrated books in the 1950s and 1960s such as *Lolita* and *The Godfather*, Putnam was taken over by MCA, the multimedia entertainment conglomerate, in 1975. MCA wanted steady growth and steady cash, and Phyllis Grann, who was brought in as publisher in the late 1970s, delivered this by importing into the world of trade publishing a model that was used by MCA in other sectors of their entertainment empire. 'I was in the repeater business,' explained Grann. 'Putnam was built on repeaters. It was incredibly profitable.' She found commercial fiction writers who were publishing with other houses, brought them over to Putnam by paying good advances and lavishing personal attention on them, and then worked closely with them to build their brand and their sales. 'It was like the old MGM studio system. We made it very hard for them to leave.' They wrote a book a year and publication was spaced out so that new books by big-name authors were not competing in the same slot. The sales force developed strong relationships with the accounts and worked hard to push each new book up the bestseller lists, so that the author, not just the title, became more and more visible. At the same time they kept the author's backlist constantly in front of the public. The model was hugely successful. 'We had 33 per cent growth in some years. I mean we really did grow.'

The model pioneered by Putnam in the 1980s and 1990s was soon imitated by others. Some houses sought, as Putnam had done, to poach established writers with clear track records of success, but some also tried to create stables of new writers who would become successful repeaters, developing a kind of 'nursery' in which an author's brand and career – and, at the same time, their readership – could be nurtured over time. One senior editor at a commercial fiction house in the UK which used the nursery model explained how she had helped to develop the career of one of her more successful writers – let's call her Sandra Post. When she received Sandra's first novel as a submission from an agent, she read it not only for the intrinsic interest of the material but also with a view to whether Sandra was someone whose career they could develop, whether she could work with her and whether Sandra would respond to the kinds of comments and criticisms she would be making. When the first novel was published, the emphasis was placed on the cover image and the title – 'the most important thing is the atmosphere, your relationship to the feeling that it evokes in you – good title, good image.' The author's name was in small letters and discreetly positioned at the bottom of the jacket. But once the hardback had had a good reception, the cover for the paperback edition was completely redesigned. The author's name was now positioned at the top of the cover and printed in bold and embossed lettering, SANDRA POST – 'Now we're starting to build.' A shout line was added to the front cover and extracts from glowing reviews of the hardback were printed on the back cover and in the prelim pages. They also took the author to their customers by bringing her to sales conferences where she could meet and talk to the buyers for the major chains, 'because if you have her in your room with your five buyers, that's it, that's 90 per cent of the trade in that one room. And so you start to build her profile in the trade and get them to buy into it.'

The first book was a great success in commercial terms with over a million copies sold, in part because it was picked by the Richard and Judy Book Club, but the publisher then faced the question of how to build on this with the second book. One thing they did with Sandra's second book was choose a very similar title – two words, same number of syllables in each title. The cover was designed in a similar way with a similar script, the author's name was bold and embossed at the top of the cover but the shout line was different to avoid confusion.

There has to be that subliminal connection to the people who read [the first book]. Hopefully we'll get the readers of [the first book] to come to it and maybe some new ones who didn't. And as time goes on her name will get bigger as she becomes a brand rather than the title being the brand. And once you're in a brand so to speak, or in work where you're building a brand, then every time you publish a book you have to try to find the new readership. You're constantly trying to find new readers. So first of all you're having to transfer some of your paperback fans into hardback buyers, and then you have to replace those paperback fans that you've moved over and add some more. We have to analyse how to do that, and for each author the plan is different. And it's even down to the tiniest detail about when you publish and which week you publish and who's up against it and the space you get in the shops and the marketing you can do.

By developing a carefully orchestrated strategy for each author, the publisher tries to build the author's brand in the minds of their customers – the key buyers at the retail chains – and in the minds of readers, endowing the author with ever greater name recognition and, if all goes according to plan, gradually expanding the fan base of loyal readers.

While the repeater business is an effective way to build a publishing programme, especially in commercial fiction, there are two significant downsides for the publisher. First, advances. The more successful a brand-name author is, the stronger the position the author and the agent are in when it comes to negotiating advances. The agent knows perfectly well how valuable the brand-name author is to the publisher and is able to use this to leverage higher advances. What this means, in effect, is that the advance ceases to be a guarantee on future royalty earnings and becomes an 'over-guarantee', that is, a premium paid to the brand-name author for the benefits that accrue to the publisher from having him or her on the list. This reduces the profitability of the author's books and puts pressure on the publisher's margins, since it means that the brand-name author is taking a larger share of the publisher's revenue.

'As a rough rule of thumb,' explained the CEO of one large publishing corporation in New York, 'I would say that 15 or 20 years ago, the author and the publisher were much closer to splitting the revenue after costs of producing a title at 50:50. Now it's much more like 75:25, or even 80:20, in favour of the author.' In contractual terms, the author will typically get 15 per cent of retail price on a hardcover book, which is essentially 30 per cent of the net revenue (assuming a discount to the trade of 50 per cent). 'But if the book doesn't earn out – which is frequently the case, in fact usually the case with the major authors – there is what I call an over-guarantee,' the CEO continued, 'which means that although your contractual royalty is 15 per cent, you're probably actually paying 20–25 per cent, which means that right off the top, half of the revenue that's coming in is going to the author. And the publisher still has to pay for manufacturing the book, all the promotion and everything else. So the author is coming out way ahead of the publisher at this point. It's no longer a 50:50 split.' In this respect, the trade publishing business has some similarities to the movie business, where the big stars get enormous sums of money off the top, which can run to $15 or $20 million in a picture that might cost $50 million to produce. 'And it's the same in the book business, because the economics of the business are such that every publishing house needs blockbusters. They in the long run do produce income. They are the surest form of income. But the blockbuster author is getting a bigger and bigger piece of the pie because of that.'

While the brand-name author produces the most reliable form of income for the publisher and can therefore make a big difference to the top line, their contribution to the bottom line is constantly being squeezed by the capacity of the author and their agent to command higher and higher advances, and therefore a higher and higher proportion of the revenue. The more successful the author becomes, the more important it is for the publisher to hold on to them, since to lose them would create a revenue hole that would be hard to fill; and yet holding on to them means that the publisher is likely to experience intensifying downward pressure on their profitability, since the margins they are able to achieve on their books will be squeezed more and more over time. A large publishing house can absorb this downward pressure on profitability, provided the revenue is high and they don't have too many of these 'subperforming margin people', as one CEO described them, on their list. 'A big author, even if it's throwing off a 10 per cent margin where your average is 40 or 45, eventually gets you through your overhead – 10 per cent of a big number is a big number. And then you can afford a 10 per cent margin book because it's incremental. But the challenge is not to kid yourself that you can afford a whole bunch of 10 per cent books, since pretty soon you'll have a 30 per cent loss.' This CEO put a limit on the number of 'subperforming margin people' his publishers were allowed to have on their lists. 'We're giving each publisher an allowance. You can have so many lower performing ones, and then either you have to find a way to get them to be higher margin or you're not going to be able to buy. Then once you use your allowance up, that's it, don't come to me because I'm not approving any more of those that year.' You may need some of these big-name authors in order to achieve your top-line revenue targets and maintain the standing of the house, but the more you have on your list, the more your bottom line will suffer. That, in short, is the price publishers pay for the comfort of the brand.

The second downside of publishing brand-name authors is that there is always the risk they will leave. Brand-name authors are in a strong position in the field, and their agents can play publishers off against one another in an attempt to get them to pay over the odds for the revenue streams that will be generated by their future books. Thanks to BookScan and other sources of data, a publisher seeking to acquire a brand-name author will have a pretty good idea of the historical track record of sales and will be able to calculate by how much they would need to increase the author's market share in order to justify the premium they would have to pay to wrest the author away from his or her existing publisher. If the author is dissatisfied with some aspect of the services provided by his or her existing publisher, the hand of the predatory publisher will be strengthened, but in this highly commercial sector of the publishing field, the scale of the advance – and therefore the size of the premium that the publisher is willing to pay – is of paramount importance. From time to time, the big brand-name authors will move houses – in 1997 Stephen King moved from Penguin Putnam to Scribner, an imprint of Simon & Schuster, having turned down an offer of $21 million from Penguin Putnam for his next book; in 2001 Michael Crichton moved from Knopf to HarperCollins, signing a two-book deal reported to be worth $40 million; in 2006 James Patterson changed his publisher in the UK, moving from Headline, an imprint of the Hachette Group, to Random House in a deal that committed the author to deliver eight co-written books in a year. High-profile moves of this kind are a testimony to the poaching game that is played out constantly in that sector of the field where brand-name authors are leveraged by large corporations seeking to grow their revenues and increase their market shares in a market that is largely static. While poaching clients is viewed as foul play by most agents, poaching authors is seen as part of the game by publishers – with the important proviso that, for the brand-name authors, it is only the large corporate publishers, or imprints owned by the large corporations, who can afford to play.

The managing director of an imprint at one large publishing corporation explained how she'd successfully poached a brand-name author only to find, some years later, that he was poached by a competitor:

I thoroughly enjoyed his thrillers and I didn't think they were reaching anything like the market they ought to. So I talked to the agent because I knew he was being underpublished. And they said, 'Mmm . . . may be interested.' And months later they sort of said, 'Actually, you know, would you like to discuss it?' He wasn't happy with the publisher he had – he's a very strong-minded man. So he came to us for a not insignificant amount of money. We got him straight onto the hardback bestseller list with our first outing, we got him to number one with the second book and completely transformed his career. We set ourselves hurdles that we knew we needed to over-take. Because the significant thing if you are poaching is: only do it if you believe you can do something better than the current publisher. Because if it's just a question of poaching the turnover, actually it's going to go horribly wrong, because you're going to overpay for the current turnover. So if you can't increase the sales, don't do it, leave it – and that's not a rule everyone follows.

Having got him to number one on the bestseller list, it wasn't long before other publishers were wooing him in turn. At a certain point one of the large corporations offered him 'X percentage more' in terms of the advance for each of his books, an increase that his existing publisher didn't feel able to match, not because they didn't have the resources – their pockets were certainly deep enough – but because on their reckoning this would tip it over the point at which it was a profitable publishing proposition. But of course the loss of such an important brand-name author left a significant hole in the sales of the house that lost him. So what did they do to fill the gap? 'About two years before he left we knew that day would come,' explained the managing director, 'so we put in place strategic plans to replace that turnover at a profitable level.' This meant working hard to attract new thriller writers and build them up. Every major house has a wish list of authors they would love to publish and the departure of a major brand-name author opens up space in the list for the house to promote authors whose brands are not yet so well established. But in the short term, the revenue gap created by the loss of a brand-name author can be difficult to fill. 'I won't deny that it's challenging,' the managing director reflected, and she expected to take a big hit on the top line in the short term. But her hope was that by promoting some of their existing authors and perhaps poaching a few from elsewhere, as well as expanding their publishing programme in other areas where they felt there was some unmet demand, they would eventually be able to make up the lost revenue and at the same time do so in a more profitable way.

The virtues of backlist

The second area where trade publishers can count on reliable revenue streams is the backlist. The virtues of the backlist are numerous: the revenue is relatively predictable and stable from one year to the next; the major investment costs have already been made and any unearned advances have usually been written off by the time a book becomes a backlist title (and certainly by the time it becomes a deep backlist title); marketing expenditure and promotion costs are minimal; and returns are generally low. With backlist titles the publisher is simply reprinting books to meet ongoing demand and the only costs they incur are the costs of printing, the costs of warehousing and distribution and the royalty payments to the author (and, in the case of books no longer in copyright, not even the latter). Backlist publishing is therefore much more profitable than frontlist publishing. Not only does it make a relatively stable contribution to the publisher's top line; it also makes a disproportionately large contribution to the bottom line. It is the closest thing there is in publishing to printing your own money.

So why don't publishers do more of it? The simple explanation is that building backlist is a slow and laborious process, especially in trade publishing. It takes a long time to build up a list of books that backlist well. Good backlists were built by publishing houses that were founded in previous centuries, or in the earlier part of the twentieth century, when the conditions of the field of trade publishing were very different. Most of those backlists have now been acquired by the large publishing corporations, which bought up houses and imprints partly in order to acquire the kind of backlist that would be very difficult to create *ex nihilo* today. 'Everybody's out looking for little niche backlist companies that you could just lay into your company because you could do it for nothing, you know, almost no additional expense,' said the CEO of one of the large publishing corporations. 'But those are now pretty much gone.' So there are very few opportunities left for the large publishing houses to grow their backlist by acquisition. They have to build the backlist organically, which takes much longer and is much more difficult to do.

But there is another factor that has tended to depress the value of the backlist in the world of trade publishing – namely, the revolution in the retail sector. The rise of the retail chains has set in motion a series of changes that have tended to reduce the value of backlist publishing to houses. Let me highlight three.

In the first place, the hardback revolution, which we analysed in chapter 1, has led to a long-term erosion in the sales of mass-market paperbacks. The traditional trade publishing model – whereby a new title sold in the thousands, possibly in the tens of thousands and only in rare cases in the low hundreds of thousands in cloth, and was then released in a mass-market paperback edition which could go on to sell in the hundreds of thousands and sometimes millions – was increasingly replaced by a new model in which the initial hardcover edition was itself mass marketed and could sell in the hundreds of thousands and even in the millions. But this meant that the market for the subsequent mass-market paperback was being cannibalized by the initial hardcover edition. Hence most trade publishers have generally experienced a significant long-term decline in the sales of mass-market paperbacks.

Second, publishers who had invested heavily in developing lists of classic titles that were out of copyright, like Penguin's Classics and New American Library and Random House's Vintage Classics and Modern Library, found themselves facing growing competition from the retail chains themselves, in particular Barnes & Noble, which began publishing its own editions of out-of-copyright classics. As a retailer turned publisher, Barnes & Noble was able to compete with the big trade houses on advantageous terms. Since they owned their own retail space, they could undercut the prices of their competitors – Barnes & Noble's Classics edition of Daniel Defoe's *Robinson Crusoe*, for example, sells for $4.95, and $4.45 to those who belong to Barnes & Noble's membership scheme, compared to $7.95 for Random House's Modern Library edition and $8.00 for Penguin's Classics edition. They could also give their own books greater prominence and visibility in their stores, and allow them to stay on the shelves and display racks for longer. Barnes & Noble's move into the publishing of classics undoubtedly hurt those trade houses who were publishing classic editions – 'They simply stopped buying our classics,' commented the CEO of one of the large houses, which now had to rely on other retailers to sell books that had previously sold well through Barnes & Noble. With Barnes & Noble's acquisition of Sterling Publishing, they began to compete with publishers in other areas too, such as generic four-colour books like 'The Book of Horses', 'The Book of Roses', etc. As illustrated reference works, these books had traditionally backlisted well, but publishers like Penguin's Dorling Kindersley found that competition from Barnes & Noble was eroding sales of generic books of this kind.

The third reason why the retail revolution has tended to depress the value of the backlist is that the major retail chains have become increasingly frontlist oriented, and the discount stores and supermarkets, which have become increasingly important players in the retail market for books, are strongly oriented towards frontlist bestsellers. The field of trade publishing as a whole has become increasingly focused on frontlist bestsellers, and the amount of time that any particular title has in order to prove itself in this highly competitive arena has diminished over time. To some extent this development has been compensated for by the rise of Amazon and other online booksellers, which have proved to be ideal outlets for older backlist and more specialized titles that are unlikely to be routinely stocked by bricks-and-mortar stores. But whether the migration of backlist sales into the online retail space will fully compensate for the marginalization of backlist titles in the bricks-and-mortar chains remains to be seen.

Despite these developments, backlist publishing remains hugely important, indeed vital, for trade publishers, and it helps greatly to offset the inherent serendipity and unpredictability that characterizes so much frontlist publishing. But trade publishers vary enormously in the extent to which their revenues break down by frontlist and backlist. Some trade houses like Hyperion, the publisher owned by the Disney corporation, are overwhelmingly frontlist driven; they have relatively small backlists, amounting to no more than 20 per cent of their sales, and they are hugely dependent on their ability to publish a number of frontlist bestsellers every year in order to meet their sales targets. Other publishers like Workman, whose *What to Expect When You're Expecting* has become the standard work on pregnancy with more than 14 million copies in print, are largely backlist driven; backlist sales account for as much as 75 to 80 per cent of their revenue and frontlist bestsellers play a much smaller role in their publishing programme. The big corporate publishers lie somewhere in between. For those corporations with large backlists, like Penguin and Random House, backlist sales typically account for between 30 and 40 per cent of total revenues; for those with smaller backlists, like Simon & Schuster, the proportion is more like 25 to 30 per cent. This means that for the large corporations, somewhere between 60 and 75 per cent of the revenue generated each year must come from new books. 'Every year I have to reinvent 70 per cent of my revenue,' as one CEO put it. That creates a pretty powerful incentive to acquire big books and do everything you can to turn them into bestsellers.

EXTREME PUBLISHING

I arrived at the New York offices of 'Olympic', a large publishing corporation, at 9:40 on a Wednesday morning in March 2007, well in advance of the meeting that was scheduled with the CEO at 10:00. In the management offices on the top floor of this towering office block in midtown Manhattan, the CEO's personal assistant kindly offered me a cup of coffee while I waited. Just before 10:00, she ushered me into the CEO's office, warning me to watch out for the step as I entered. I looked down and noticed a mat on the floor with the words 'Mind the Gap' woven into it. As I greeted the CEO and shook her hand, I commented light-heartedly on the mat. 'I like the mat. You must've picked that up in London,' I said, thinking that she must have bought it as a souvenir of the London underground and courteously placed it at the entrance to her office in order to call attention to a step that could easily trip up an unwary visitor. 'Oh no,' she laughed, 'that has nothing to do with London. The gap is what we live with every day around here.' 'Really?' I said. 'Tell me about the gap – I've never heard this before.' And so began my initiation into the budgetary finances of large publishing corporations.

Minding the gap

'Well, so what happens, is this,' she continued. 'It's June, and every publisher in the company says, "OK, what's coming in for next year?" – they lay it out.' They look at what is in the pipeline for the next year and they estimate the likely sales of each book on a title-by-title basis. Then they add it all up and it gives them X amount of sales. Senior management then amalgamates all these figures, takes account of costs and produces a draft budget for the coming year – let's say it's $800 million of revenue with a profit of 8 per cent. The CEO then takes this draft budget to the corporate bosses in the parent corporation and they say, 'That's fine, but you're planning to do $800 million this year. Next year we want $800 million plus 10 per cent.' And that extra 10 per cent of revenue is the gap: it's the difference between what the publishers think they will sell on the basis of the books that are in the pipeline for next year, on the one hand, and what the corporate bosses say the company has to achieve, on the other. 'My expectation', explained the CEO, 'comes from what [the parent corporation] tells me I have to do.'

By September the size of the gap for the coming year will be clear, and the task of the CEO and other senior managers will then be to divvy it out among the publishers – 'to apportion misery', as one former CEO of another house put it. In a corporation of this size the gap could easily be $100 million. If there are, say, six divisions and six publishers in the corporation, then each of these publishers will be assigned a share of the $100 million gap. Usually it's not divided up equally – some publishers might be expected to do more to fill the gap than others, simply because they are more likely to publish the kinds of books that are good for filling gaps. There might be some to-ing and fro-ing ('discussions that are not negotiations') but the allocation of gap-filling targets is essentially a top-down process. Once each publisher has been assigned a target for the coming year, they have to focus a great deal of effort on trying to meet it. They may talk with some of their editors and urge them to go out and find potential gap-filling books, or to come up with ideas for books that could help to meet the target they've been assigned. Progress against this target is monitored carefully at all levels of the organization, both by the publishers and by the CEO and other senior managers: in the world of corporate publishing, this is what 'minding the gap' means.

So how do publishers set about trying to meet the gap-filling target? 'They find books,' explained the CEO curtly. But remember that it is now September, and the revenue gap must be filled before December of the following year, which means that the publishers only have six to eight months to find the books that will enable them to meet their share of the gap-filling target. So 'they have to find books that are finished or can be finished in a quick amount of time, can be published quickly, fast to market. That means a book that is easy to define, easy to sell and easy to communicate.' It can't be too complicated because the gap-filling book – or 'instant book', as one

publisher aptly termed it – will, in all likelihood, be published outside
of the normal publishing cycle. It will probably have missed the seasonal catalogue in which it would normally be expected to appear;
it might even have missed the sales cycle in which it would normally
have been presented to buyers. Almost everything about the gap-
filling book is abnormal, exceptional. It is an add-on to the normal
publishing cycles and schedules. 'This company has in fact perfected
what we call "extreme publishing",' continued the CEO. 'What it is
basically is this: it's adding books into the process that are not
normal.'

So, for example, in April of any given year, this company will have
a sales conference for which they have a seasonal catalogue and in
which the sales reps will be told about the books that will be published in the fall, right up to January. The reps will then go out and
sell these books to the buyers at the key accounts and at the independents, 'so by the end of May the world will think they know what
we are publishing till January. But they know already that they don't
know, because we will add books right up until September.' Obviously it's desirable for the publishers to try to find the gap-filling
books as early as possible, once they've been told what their target
is, so the period from September to March will be particularly important in the quest to fill the gap. But the search will go on right into
the summer – though the later the book is acquired, the more pressure
it will place on the publisher's systems and schedules in terms of
getting the book out before December. In practice, a parallel set of
systems has to be created that will enable these crucial gap-filling
add-ons to be published in a very short time-period – not just produced, but also marketed and sold. 'We've created a system whereby
our sales people have a way of communicating with accounts and
getting orders fed back in. We've developed a way of adding these
books into production. We've perfected a whole way of doing it,
because these books are out of cycle,' the CEO explained. 'So a
financial necessity has in fact become a publishing advantage.'
Olympic has become known in the trade as a publisher who is able
to move books through the system very quickly and to bypass the
normal publishing cycles. It has become known, and its senior managers are proud to think of it, as a publisher who excels in the art of
extreme publishing.

Not every kind of book lends itself to extreme publishing. In fiction
you can't do it, unless it's one of your repeaters who is delivering a
new book ahead of schedule that you can rush through in order to
ship it before the end of the year. 'But if you have an author you're

making, you have to take the time – if you don't take the time, it won't happen. So everybody knows there are different rhythms. You can't do it for every book,' explained the CEO. Extreme publishing works particularly well with certain kinds of non-fiction books: celebrity books, topical books, the 'quirkier gift humour books' and so on. It works with celebrity books because the author has the kind of name recognition that will enable the major accounts to sell the book without having to put much effort into it. 'They don't have to do anything. They put the book out, they make money. So for them, that's ideal.' If it's the kind of celebrity book that will be of interest to the Christmas shopper and they can get the book into the major accounts by December, that's even better. The reps will have to go to the accounts and explain that this is a late Christmas add-on which didn't appear in the catalogue. 'But you know, the accounts won't care. They'll be joyous to hear that we're going to give them another book that they can sell well at Christmas.' You can also do it with some topical books. 'When 9/11 happened we had a book on Al-Qaida that was supposed to be publishing in the spring. We crashed it out and it became a huge bestseller.' So the principal way of managing the gap is to acquire several major pieces of commercial non-fiction that are already written, or can be written quickly, and published fast.

She gives an example: a couple of years ago several of their imprints received a submission from an agent in March for the autobiography of a well-known celebrity. The book consisted mainly of four-colour pictures of the celebrity in question, with a minimal amount of text that was written tongue-in-cheek. 'We thought, this woman's going to have a two-second life so we said "We'll publish this book in September." Six months later, a four-colour book. We crashed the book. We added it in September, we sold 200,000 copies. That's over $2 million of volume by the way for the end of that year. Turned out it kept on selling. Now it's still selling in paperback because it turned out she didn't have a half-life of six months which we thought. That's a perfect example because everybody knows who she is, it was easy to add, you could say, "Here it is and here's why it should be crashed." Made sense, right? You want to get it while it's hot, right?'

When it comes to the search for gap-filling books, the attention of publishers and editors is therefore naturally focused on big books. There is no point trying to close the gap with small and mid-list titles, since by this stage in the publishing cycle most lists will already have more than enough titles of this kind; there is no room to add more and, in any case, they would not generate the kinds of numbers you need to make a serious contribution to the gap-closing task. 'The middle and the bottom of the list fills itself up naturally through the process of your editorial meetings,' the CEO continued. 'If you've got, say, five or six editors and they all buy five small books, suddenly you have 25 books, plus you have continuing authors who turn in their next book. So there's a certain amount of the list that just comes naturally by the process of people working. What you're looking for now is how to fill in your big ones.' Some big books will be in the works already – new novels by some of your brand-name authors, some major non-fiction titles that were bought some while ago and are now coming to fruition, etc. But these books will already have been taken into account in the budgeting process, so they will not be available to you when it comes to filling the gap (unless you can speed up some other titles of this kind and 'crash them out' before the end of the year). So for the most part you will be obliged to look to your normal sources of supply – that is, the agents – for new big books that are already finished (or nearly so), or to come up with ideas for big books that can be put together quickly and fast-tracked through the systems of extreme publishing. And since all the large corporate publishers are in the same boat and are working to broadly similar schedules, the process of closing the gap tends inexorably to raise the stakes in the already overheated market for big books.

Buying new big books that can be published quickly is the best way to manage the gap but it's not the only way. You can also try to squeeze more out of the books that are already in the pipeline by marketing them more aggressively and looking for ways to maximize their sales potential. If a book starts to sell well, you can push it harder and put more resources behind it in the hope that it will take off and sell beyond your initial budgeting expectations – for example, you can do extra advertising, you can extend the publicity tour, you can go back to your major accounts and say, 'Look, Barnes & Noble have got a 50 per cent market share on this book – you're missing out here,' and so on. 'You keep on re-promoting,' explained one senior manager. 'Really, so few books work, the trick is making the books which do work even bigger then they already are.'

While filling the gap accounts for perhaps only 10–15 per cent of the total revenue of the publishing corporation in any given year, it is a crucial 10–15 per cent – 'crucial because you don't make money till the end', explained the CEO of Olympic. Once your overheads are fixed, you have to be able to drive additional revenue through the system in order to meet your financial targets – both top line and bottom line. 'The main thing is the bottom – you've got to make the bottom line. But there's nowhere else to make it except increased sales. You could be lucky and get a big subrights deal but in today's world that's very unlikely. So sales is the only place.' If you can't get the top-line growth, then either you're going to fall short on the bottom line or you're going to have to scramble to cut costs in order to try to rescue a margin under pressure. The incentive to close the gap is experienced by senior and middle managers as a corporate imperative, and in the more performance-oriented corporations their bonuses are tied to it, 'and bonuses are a big portion of our salaries'.

So what are the downsides of extreme publishing? For the CEO of Olympic, the main danger is that, if you're not careful, you can end up publishing things too quickly. 'The danger is that you try to do it too quickly. That's what you don't want to do. What you want to do is schedule it right. That's what [Olympic] has perfected – the scheduling of it.' Are there other dangers? Might they be losing money on these books, given the extra costs that might be involved in acquiring them and rushing them through the systems? 'We thought maybe we were losing money on add-ons because we were adding them on to make budget and were overspending, so a few years ago we did a whole study. One of the amazing things we discovered is that we made more money on our add-ons than we made on our regular books.' So how did she explain that? 'We decided it was because we were closer to market, so we actually knew what we were doing. So you said, "I'm going to sell 20,000 copies," you sold 20,000 copies. Whereas when you buy from a proposal, the book comes in three years later. The public doesn't care any more; the book's not as good as you thought. With add-ons you're often buying from finished manuscripts – it's like a completely different animal. There's an excitement to the fact that you do it and then boom, you have a book in short order.'

So no worries there. What about quality? Is there a danger that many of the books published as add-ons might be rather poor books for which you tend to overpay and then rush through simply in order to meet the budgetary demands imposed on the organization by the parent corporation? 'I don't have a lot of sympathy for that,' replied the CEO. 'I've always been of the school that publishing is a business; people give you money to do it and they deserve to get their money back. So this idea that the corporatization of publishing makes it dirty has always annoyed me.' She concedes that the practice of extreme publishing stems from financial demands that are external to the publishing house and imposed on it by its corporate owners, but she rejects the suggestion that this, in and by itself, leads to bad publishing – 'It all depends on your judgement going into it.' You can overpay for a book that you're buying to fill the gap and you can overpay for a book that you're planning to publish in two or three years' time – either way you can lose a shedload of money, whether it's extreme publishing or not. So the CEO of Olympic has no qualms about extreme publishing as such. 'My only reservation is about whether I'm making good judgements, and sometimes my judgement is good and sometimes it's bad. I'm perfectly willing to admit that.'

In search of the unknown

While Olympic has perfected the art of extreme publishing and turned necessity into a virtue, all the large publishing corporations experience similar pressures and proceed in broadly similar ways. They have all developed their own in-house jargon to describe the gap that arises every year, as sure as night follows day, between the sales they expect to achieve on the basis of their ground-up projections and the revenue targets that are handed down to them by their corporate bosses. 'In this company they're called "unknowns",' explained Jim, a publisher in another corporation across town. 'I've worked in enough of these places and it's the same everywhere. Every one of us is given a certain number of unknown, unbought titles that you have to find for the next fiscal year to be able to make your number.' As a middle manager who's saddled every year with the task of finding a certain number of unknowns, Jim takes a less sanguine view of this process than the CEO of Olympic.

Jim runs an imprint at one of the large publishing corporations. Every year he goes through the same budgeting exercise described by the CEO of Olympic, though modified in ways that are specific to his corporation. 'We look at what we have in the pipeline. With our director of sales we budget them title by title in terms of what we can get out initially. We add all that up and we say, "OK, here's the budget for next year." And they say that's not good enough. So they give us a higher number, and the way to get to the higher number is to say, "Now you have unknowns of 500,000 copies of a $25 hardcover book," or whatever it might be. And then our task as a publisher is to whip the editors to find those books.' Given the importance of unknowns for meeting the budgetary targets, the task of finding unknowns assumes a huge significance in the working lives of middle managers in the large corporations. 'Every time I see my boss she will say to me, "Have you filled your unknowns yet?" or "Where are you filling your unknowns?" That's all she cares about.'

Like all the publishers of the different imprints, Jim is under a lot of pressure to find unknowns. He searches himself, and he also puts pressure on his editors to search. How do they search? Where do they look? 'You literally call an agent and say, "I need a book for next fall." That's basically it. We also think of ideas and think of people who we can go after and that kind of thing.' Of course, since the agents know exactly what's going on and understand the pressure that the publishers are under, they know that they're in a strong bargaining position and can raise the stakes, or allow the stakes to be raised by letting publishers from different companies, all in a similar situation, compete against one another. 'It really is cheque book publishing,' explained Jim. 'It definitely has an effect on the stakes and inflates the prices of things, because you have a short-term need.'

The need to fill the gap also exacerbates the inefficiencies that are built into the supply chain, 'because the push is to ship a lot of books to make the short-term profit. It's what you can ship in the fiscal year, not what you can sell.' For the purposes of making budget, the key is to ship out as many as you can and record the sale before the end of the fiscal year, even if a substantial proportion of these eventually come back as returns. Jim explains: 'The way the accounting is done in this business is that we operate on reserves: everything is reserved at a certain level. For next year that will be whatever we ship less 40 per cent. And then you deal with the returns in the following years, either on the plus side – you have a book that might sell through at 90 per cent, so you take back from the reserve – or on the negative side, you know, you have titles that you ship and they come back at 60 per cent, so at some point you have to recognize that extra 20 per cent.' Since the reconciliation of returns is pushed into the future, managing the gap tends to create an incentive to ship out as many books as possible in order to maximize short-term revenue and short-term profit.

Desperate enthusiasm

The CEO of Jim's corporation, 'Galaxy', worries about the pressure put on his publishers by the need to manage the gap ('tremendous amount of pressure, yes'), but he also worries about the pressure put

on senior management 'to make sure these people [that is, the publishers and editors] don't get so desperate'. If the search for unknowns
begins around September, by March it is drawing to a close, since
from March on it's going to get harder and harder to buy books and
get them published before the end of the year, however good your
systems are. 'So in a year when they were looking to buy this book
as just another book in their list it would be worth this much. And
now, as they're getting closer to that March date, they start looking
at this book that they wouldn't have bought a year ago for that price
– they might buy it now, saying, "What else am I going to have? Am
I going to have nothing? Or I'll have this." So a sort of desperate
enthusiasm takes over. They get so desperate that they start to make
bad acquisition decisions. And when we look at those kinds of books
that were bought late in the cycle, they're almost never profitable,
almost never.'

Having paid more than they should for these gap-filling books, the
temptation is to ship out more than is wise in the hope of getting
your investment out of them. 'People tend to ship more copies than
they would be prudent to,' explained Galaxy's CEO. 'You know
there's a phrase "stack 'em high and let 'em fly" – that if there isn't
a substantial display of books in a store people won't see it, and if
they see it they'll think, "Oh, well, they have so many because this
is a hot book." But sometimes that doesn't happen.' Of course, this
temptation doesn't just affect gap-filling books – it is a feature of
trade publishing across the board, for reasons that we'll examine
in more detail later. But the temptation is particularly strong with the
gap-fillers, precisely because the main reason for publishing
these books is to fill a budget gap, so everyone in the organization,
from editors and publishers through to sales and marketing staff, is
focused single-mindedly on trying to maximize the revenue they can
generate from them (coupled with the fact that the high returns, if
and when they come, will be a problem postponed for another fiscal
year).

The CEO of Galaxy often finds himself at odds with his parent
corporation when it comes to budgeting and managing the gap. The
parent corporation is publicly quoted, and Galaxy's CEO has come
to the view that 'a trade publishing house is not a good fit for a public
company'. He elaborates:

> If you're going to be in the trade business, certainly you should expect
> growth, but the growth will not be quarter on quarter – you know,
> what Wall Street is expecting or the City of London is expecting. It

will be like this [he traces a wavy line, up and down, with his index finger], and if you try to go like this [he traces a steadily upward plane], you will ultimately affect your profitability, because there is no way to make up for a *Da Vinci Code* in the next year. It's like *Star Wars*: when *Star Wars* comes out, it does $500 million, and when it doesn't, it doesn't. It's a good analogy, because for that $500 million picture you might have to do 100 movies, or 50 movies, with all the associated expenses. And it's the same in books. So to make up for a $20 million or $30 million or $50 million book when the average book generates probably under a million dollars, you have to do 50 pieces of art and 50 typesettings and all that shipping and all that paper and people have to sell it 50 times and keep it in stock, and the chances are you're not going to get there anyhow. So I am usually at odds with our management on this, because they have to view things from a shareholder-value point of view, and my point is that we could be increasing the shareholder value by letting our sales go down, and not trying to make up for the aberrational books. So if the board of directors see a declining line, even though it'd be a wavy declining line, then they should get rid of this management, but if they're seeing this line going like that [he traces a wavy line from left to right], then they shouldn't. So [the parent corporation] is sort of coming around now to where revenues are becoming less important to them than margin. I'm saying that I can keep increasing our margin and our profits but I can't keep pushing the top line too.

Despite the pleas to his corporate bosses, the CEO of Galaxy has to manage a gap every year – in this corporation it's called a 'task'. Every year he sits down with the senior manager to whom the various publishers of the imprints report, they look at what they did last year and they assign them a task for the coming year. 'So everybody gets a task by imprint and they're always trying to work their numbers. So they either buy or they come up with other ideas from books they own from previous years that can generate incremental sales. They have the same problem on the micro-level that I have, so if they had a big book last year and they don't have it now, they've got to get as close as they can. And then we'll chart the progress. Every month when the financials come in we'll sit down and look at how we're doing against the task.' But as the CEO of a publishing company owned by a publicly quoted corporation, he faces another constraint – working capital. In financial terms, their performance is assessed not just in terms of top-line revenue and bottom-line profit but also in terms of working capital, and 'advances are a gigantic portion of my working capital. So the leaner I run on inventory [which in this context means new books purchased], the better from that standpoint. On the other hand, it makes you nervous not to own any books and say, "Where am I going to get this?"' In other words, controlling the expenditure of working capital means that less money is available to pay large advances for books that will come out in two or three years' time, and that means that there are fewer big books in the pipeline that can be counted on for next year's budget. Hence there is more pressure on publishers and editors to buy big books late in the budgeting cycle in order to fill the gap, raising the levels of anxiety among senior and middle managers as they move further into the cycle and increasing the likelihood of desperate enthusiasm setting in.

Public vs private corporations

Publishing companies that are owned by privately held corporations may be insulated to some extent from the financial pressures faced by companies like Galaxy, but they too will be expected to grow year on year and to deliver a respectable bottom line. The main advantage of being owned by a privately held corporation is that, depending on who the owner is, the privately held corporation can afford to take a more lenient attitude towards the vicissitudes of the trade publishing business. 'Any publishing personality understands that this year's good and next year's bad and there are going to be good years and bad years,' said the former CEO of a large publishing house owned by a privately held corporation. 'Whereas corporate people don't understand that, or if they do understand it – and they probably do because they're not fools – they don't care. When they're publicly owned all these businessmen fall back on the excuse "But I am responsible to shareholders." I think it's bullshit for the most part; it's an excuse. But they have that excuse and maybe it's real for all I know.'

But the publishing houses owned by privately held corporations will still be expected to grow year on year and will be subjected to similar budgetary pressures – they too will have a gap they have to fill every year and will assign specific tasks or financial targets to each of their imprints. The growth and profit targets may be a little more modest and the parent corporation may be less unforgiving if the targets are not met, but the pressure to perform to certain financial goals is just as much a part of daily life in the house owned by a privately held corporation as it is in the house owned by a publicly quoted one. 'Basically we're given a target from our parent company and then it's disseminated through the organization,' explained the CFO (chief financial officer) of 'Mosaic', one of the large publishing companies owned by a privately held corporation. 'There are certain groups that are stronger than others and based on that they may be given more. Everybody is tasked because if you don't task groups they're not going to perform up to the level you require. I'm a firm believer that the only way to get growth is to give them a task and give them something to work towards. If you just basically say you've got to grow 2 or 3 or 4 per cent each year, it's not going to amount to anything. You've got to stretch it.'

From the point of view of the publishers and business managers of the imprints in the privately held corporations, the budgetary process is very similar to that in the publicly quoted corporations. A budget is first prepared from the ground up, looking at all the titles that are in the pipeline and estimating sales for the coming year, estimating production costs and marketing spend, and then submitting the draft budget to corporate finance by around September. 'We throw it all together, come up with where we think we're going to be on a realistic basis, and then we know exactly what they're expecting of us and that's our gap or our bridge, and that's what we try to fill going forward,' explained the business manager at one of the imprints in Mosaic. Although they are not formally told what their task is until they have submitted their draft budget, he has a good sense in advance – 'We kinda have an idea now what they're going to expect for '09,' he said when we spoke in March 2008. 'We had the '08 budget, we know it's not going to go down or it's not like we really get relief, OK. So we know it's either going to be the '08 number or 5 per cent above – in that range.' In Mosaic, the emphasis is on bottom-line profit rather than top-line revenue growth, so the target they are given is defined primarily in terms of profit rather than sales. 'So we could fill the gap with inventory savings or advertising savings, or we could fill it by increased sales. How we get to where they want us to be is up to us. They say, "We want this amount of profit, that's what we expect of you, deliver it." Where we get it from is up to us.' So if the profit of this imprint in 2008 was, say, $4.8 million on a turnover of $80 million, then their target for 2009 could be $4.8 million plus 5 per cent, or $5.04 million. And if their draft budget for 2009 showed a provisional profit of, say, $4.6 million, then the task for 2009 would be to find an extra $440,000 profit, either through increased sales or increased savings or some combination. In a bottom-line driven corporation, that's the gap.

Managing a profit-based gap means that 'you have to worry about every single line of the P&L, because every one directly affects the bottom line.' You start by trying to increase sales – 'We will go to each publisher and say, "Look, you know what? We need an extra X amount of sales out of you, OK?", and we hope that by the time we get into the next 12 months, they can fill that gap,' whether through new title acquisitions, special promotions, more focused marketing and so on. But if that doesn't seem to be working (or is not working well enough), you can cut costs – '"You know what? We're going to stop doing your *Times* ads for the next three months unless the book hits the bestseller list" or something like that. If we see that the sales number is not going to be achieved, we'll look at other things. We've got promotional items we can live without, tighter printing, less special effects on the cover, anything we can do to affect the bottom line.' You can even change formats for some titles – release them in trade paperback rather than mass-market paperback, because you're likely to get fewer returns on trade paperback and the royalty is slightly lower, so that too will help.

One type of book that has worked well for this house as a gap-filling title is adaptations of screenplays for new movies. 'If we see a movie coming out, we run by the screenplay and get the adaptation. It's a novelization of the screenplay. Even if it's not a huge movie, at least the movie's going to come out and we'll have a book out there.' They'll typically publish the novelization of the screenplay as a mass-market paperback and may be able to ship out 100,000 copies, even for a small movie. This is relatively quick, relatively easy, gap-filling publishing. 'So there are things we can do that can move the needle.'

Even though Mosaic is owned by a privately held corporation, the pressures are just the same – 'The pressures are tremendous to hit your target, to make more and more every year with less.' They maximize the number of titles they can do in a year with the same or fewer staff, putting more pressure on everyone, and everyone is under pressure to do what they can to meet the profit target either by increasing sales or cutting costs or both. If they fail to meet their targets then everyone will suffer in terms of compensation, because bonuses are tied directly to meeting targets. Jobs may even be threatened. 'I think about it every day and night, to be honest with you. We employ 180 people here and we want to make sure that we employ 180 people tomorrow and next year and the year after. Eventually, if you don't hit the targets, they'll have a new business manager – you know, it's one of those things.'

So whether the parent corporation is publicly quoted or privately held, the budgeting process in the publishing houses owned by the large corporations imposes a financial discipline on the publishing imprints and divisions that obliges them to strive for certain targets through a combination of gap-filling acquisitions and cost-cutting measures. Buying big books late in the cycle, coming up with ideas for new books that can be put together quickly and crashed out, squeezing more revenue out of existing books through extra marketing and promotion and, if all else fails, looking to cut costs wherever you can in order to improve the bottom line even though top-line revenue may not be growing in line with corporate expectations – such is the normal struggle that characterizes life in the large publishing corporations, provides a constant source of anxiety for senior and middle managers and further raises the stakes for new books that are perceived as big in the web of collective belief.

On not minding the gap

While all publishing houses owned by large corporations will find themselves minding the gap in one way or another, this is a practice that is alien to the small and medium-sized independents. Many (though not all) independents will prepare budgets for the coming year and many will look for growth year on year, but the independents are not subject to the kind of external pressure for growth that governs the corporate publishing houses and they don't generally try to meet their budget targets by exhorting their publishers and editors to acquire gap-filling books that can be published quickly. Indeed, the absence of the gap-filling dynamic is one of the key features that distinguish independents from corporate publishers: it is not a daily fact of life for those who work in the independents in the way that it is for senior and middle management in the publishing corporations. 'I have never, ever heard that kind of discussion here and I would never expect to,' said the head of one well-established, medium-sized independent house. 'We own ourselves. If our sales drop 5 per cent in the upcoming year and our profits drop 20 per cent, I mean my fellow directors and I are going to get really concerned about it. If we're looking at a three-year trend line or a five-year trend line, we'll start to do some things, probably about cutting expenses over time. But we are never going to go out to acquire a book that doesn't belong on our list just because it fills a gap in the upcoming sales budget; it's just not gonna happen here. Never. I'm proud to say that I've never been part of a discussion like that here.'

For this publisher, the fact that they don't get involved in the kind of gap-filling publishing that is common in the corporations is a source of pride; it is part of what makes his house special, in his view, and marks it off from the world of corporate publishing – 'This is one of the points that, to me, tells you why [X] is a special place.' For other independents, not minding the gap is just the way business is done. It's not that they explicitly reject the idea that acquiring books should be governed by the need to meet a budget target, it's simply that most of what they do isn't done with a budget in mind. 'We don't have budgets,' explained the founder-owner of one of the most successful of the medium-sized independents. 'We're not unaware of money and we're not unaware of expense, but it's not through budgeting. It's all experiential. We simply go by precedent and knowledge of when we vary from precedent, and we have controls to keep us within the same guidelines.' Of course, this founder-owner wants to see his company grow every year, not because he needs to meet the expectations of corporate bosses but simply because he wants to be able to meet his financial commitments and reward his staff. 'How bright do you have to be to know that if you do less well this year than last, that's a bad thing? Or if you do the same as last year and inflation adds 3 per cent to your cost, that's a bad thing?' But he has never set a specific growth target for the company and never instructed his publishers and editors to try to achieve it by going out and acquiring more books. For this particular house, as for many small and medium-sized independents, that's just not the way that business is done.

— 7 —

SHRINKING WINDOWS

Walk into any Barnes & Noble or Waterstone's and, as you stand there in the entrance and cast your eyes over the racks of books displayed face-out and the tables stacked high with new hardbacks in their glossy covers or three-for-two paperbacks, you are surveying one of the key battlefields where the struggle for visibility in the book business is carried out. The front-of-store area that is in your field of vision is a thoroughly commodified space: most of the books you see will be there by virtue of the fact that the publisher has paid for placement, either directly by means of a placement fee (that is, co-op advertising) or indirectly by means of extra discount. Roughly speaking, it costs around a dollar a book to put a new hardback on the front-of-store table in a major chain, and around $10,000 to put a new title on front-of-store tables in all the chain's stores for two weeks (typically the minimum period). When you take account of the fact that a new hardback might be selling at $25 with a 50 per cent discount to the retailer, thus netting $12.50 to the publisher, a cost of $1 a book means that the publisher is spending 8 per cent of the revenue from this book just to put it on the table at the front of the store – and that's assuming that the book is actually sold. Visibility does not come cheap.

So why are publishers willing to spend so much to display their books? And what are the consequences of the fact that it is so expensive to do so? More generally, how do publishers try to make potential readers aware of the books they are publishing? Are their methods different from those that were used by publishers 20 or 30 years ago – and if so, why? In many ways it is the struggle to get your books seen, heard about, talked about – in short, made visible in an increasingly crowded and noisy marketplace – that is where the real battle in publishing is taking place today. As one publisher succinctly put it, 'It's become easier to publish and harder to sell – that's the paradox. Any old sod can publish a book now, but actually getting it out to the public has become much trickier.'

The struggle for visibility

Consider some simple statistics. Although the methods used to calculate title output were different in the past[1] and there are reasonable grounds for debate about what title output data are actually measuring, it is nevertheless clear that the number of new books published each year has increased dramatically over the last decade in both the US and the UK. The number of new books published in the US each year prior to 1980 was probably under 50,000. Throughout the 1980s and 1990s, the number of new books published greatly increased, reaching nearly 200,000 by 1998. By 2004 the number had risen to over 275,000 (see table 9).[2] After falling off in 2005, the total climbed to over 284,000 in 2007 and continued to rise in the following years, reaching an estimated 316,000 by 2010.

However, the full picture is more complicated than these figures would suggest, as there has also been an enormous increase in the

---

[1] In the US, the principal source of data on new title output used in the publishing industry has for many years been the data gathered by the R. R. Bowker Company and published in the *American Book Publishing Record* (ABPR); this data is also the basis of the listings which appear in the trade journal *Publishers Weekly*. The ABPR is essentially a record of the titles and editions passing through the Library of Congress Cataloging in Publication (CIP) programme. From the early 1970s until the mid-1980s, Bowker regarded this as a reasonably accurate basis on which to produce its statistics on title output, but in the 1980s it became increasingly clear that the totals were not reflecting what was actually happening in the American book industry. The ABPR numbers were more accurate as a picture of the CIP's workload (which levelled out at around 50,000–60,000 titles a year) than as an account of overall industry activity. American book title production was being undercounted, particularly in relation to trade paperbacks and the output of small presses. In an attempt to produce a more accurate portrayal of industry activity, Bowker began in 1998 to compile data on new title output from its more comprehensive Books in Print database. These data are based on new ISBNs issued in each calendar year, and therefore include paperbacks and modified re-editions as separate titles. They also include books published by publishers outside the US provided the ISBN is being made available to the public in the US.

[2] The data for the period 2002–10 are taken from 'New Book Titles and Editions, 2002–2010', at www.bowkerinfo.com/pubtrack/AnnualBookProduction2010/ISBN_Output_2002-2010.pdf

Table 9   US book title output, 1998–2010

1998	198,961
1999	212,953
2000	265,541
2001	224,853
2002	215,138
2003	240,098
2004	275,793
2005	251,903
2006	274,416
2007	284,370
2008	289,729
2009	302,410
2010 (projected)	316,480

This table is based on the total number of ISBNs for any kind of printed book (including reissues but excluding audiobooks and ebooks) made available through publication or distribution in the US in a given year. A book is 'new' if that ISBN has not previously been available in the US; the publisher or distributor can be located anywhere and the date is the date reported to Bowker as to when this ISBN will be available in the US. In 2006 Bowker introduced a new methodology to obtain a more accurate picture of annual title output; this enabled them to include ISBNs that have not been assigned a subject ('unclassified items'), ISBNs without prices and ISBNs with unusual bindings, such as stapled and laminated. To provide comparable data, the numbers for 2002–5 were recalculated using the new methodology. Numbers before 2002 are based on the old methodology and are therefore not strictly comparable.
Source: R. R. Bowker.

publication of reprints and titles printed on demand – what Bowker classifies as 'non-traditional' outputs. The data from Bowker suggest that the number of non-traditional outputs rose from 21,936 in 2006 to a staggering 2,776,260 in 2010, which, if added to the traditional books published in 2010, would give a total output of more than 3 million titles. The non-traditional outputs include books released by companies specializing in self-publishing, like Lulu and Xlibris, but the vast majority of these non-traditional outputs are scanned versions of public domain works that are being marketed on the web and made available through print-on-demand vendors. Indeed, one of these publishers, Bibliobazaar, an imprint of the historical reprints publisher BiblioLife, accounted for 1,461,918 ISBNs in 2010 – more than half of the total of the non-traditional output; and three publishers – Bibliobazaar, General Books and Kessinger Publishing, all specializing in reprints of public domain works – accounted for 2,668,774 ISBNs, or 96 per cent of the total.[3] These titles are not being 'published' in a traditional sense: the publishers are simply generating cover and text files, obtaining ISBNs and creating metadata to enable the titles to be sold and printed on demand. But the activity of the reprints publishers is increasing the volume of available ISBNs by several orders of magnitude and muddying the picture of what it means to measure new title output today.

The pattern for the UK is very similar. Prior to 1980 there were probably fewer than 50,000 new books published each year in the UK. By 1995 this number had doubled to more than 100,000, and by 2003 it had increased to nearly 130,000.The total number fell off slightly after that, though by 2009 the number of new books that were published in the UK had risen to more than 157,000 (see table 10), spurred on by the growth of print-on-demand, digital and self-publishing.[4]

Of course, gross figures like these don't tell you anything about what kinds of books are being published and where the main increases are occurring. Undoubtedly a large share of the new titles being published each year are accounted for by academic monographs and other books of a specialized kind; only a proportion, perhaps even a relatively small proportion, are accounted for by new trade titles that are aimed at a general readership and sold through the retail trade. Nevertheless, the huge increase in the number of new titles being published each year – an increase in the US of more than fivefold in less than three decades – has helped to create a marketplace that is saturated with new product. More than 50,000 new fiction titles were published in the US in 2007, double what it was in 2003. That's roughly 1,000 new titles a week, and that's just fiction.

And that's not all: books are just one media product among others, and over the last three decades the world of media and entertainment has witnessed a veritable explosion of media products, from videos, CDs, cellphones and iPods to the plethora of products and time-consuming activities that are available in a rapidly changing online

---

[3] 'Print Isn't Dead, Says Bowker's Annual Book Production Report', at www.bowker.com/index.php/press-releases/633-print-isnt-dead-says-bowkers-annual-book-production-report.
[4] 'More Books Published in 2008', at www.nielsenbookdata.co.uk/uploads/press/1NielsenBook_ProductionFigures_Feb09.pdf; 'Nielsen Book Releases 2010 Book Production Figures', at www.nielsenbookdata.co.uk/uploads/press/1NielsenBook_2010ProductionFigures_Feb11.pdf.

Table 10   UK book title output, 1994–2010

1994	93,475
1995	104,118
1996	112,627
1997	111,348
1998	122,922
1999	128,115
2000	124,423
2001	120,895
2002	124,940
2003	129,762
2004	121,556
2005	108,086
2006	112,865
2007	115,816
2008	120,947
2009	157,039
2010 (projected)	151,969

This table shows the total number of titles recorded as being published by a UK-registered publisher or made available from a UK distributor for the first time within the year. The definition of 'book' is based on the issuing of an ISBN and therefore includes some book-related products where an ISBN can be used as a legitimate identifier.
Source: Nielsen BookScan.

environment. In 2004 the National Endowment for the Arts in the US published a report called *Reading at Risk* that sent tremors, if not shock waves, through the publishing world: based on a survey of 17,000 individuals carried out in 2002, it appeared to show that reading is declining among adults and the rate of decline is accelerating, especially among the 18–24 age group.[5] The percentage of the US adult population who had read any work of literature in the previous 12 months fell from 54 per cent in 1992 to 46.7 per cent in 2002, and the percentage who had read any book in the previous 12 months fell from 60.9 per cent in 1992 to 56.6 per cent in 2002. In 1982 young adults (the 18–24 age group) were the most likely to read literature (59.8 per cent, compared to an average for all ages of 56.9 per cent); by 2002 young adults were among the least likely to

---

[5] *Reading at Risk: A Survey of Literary Reading in America* (Washington, D.C.: National Endowment for the Arts, 2004).

read literature (42.8 per cent, compared to an average of 46.7 per cent). At the same time, spending on audio, video, computers and software increased from 6 per cent of total recreational spending in 1990 to 24 per cent in 2002, whereas spending on books fell slightly from 5.7 to 5.6 per cent over the same period. A subsequent report by the NEA confirmed these broad trends and appeared to show not only that Americans are reading less, but also that they are reading less well: among high-school seniors, the average reading level declined between 1992 and 2005 for all but the very best readers, so that by 2005 little more than one-third of high school seniors were reading proficiently.[6] Even among college graduates, the percentage of those with a Bachelor's degree who were proficient in reading prose fell from 40 per cent in 1992 to 31 per cent in 2003.

With an avalanche of new titles being published every week, the reader is confronted with a plethora of books to choose from – just walk into any bookstore to test this proposition. With the proliferation of new media products and the rise of the internet, the consumer is faced with many new demands on their time and their disposable income. Books are just one type of media product, jostling for attention with many other flashier, noisier, brasher products of the electronic age. And the data on the decline of reading suggest that this is a competition that the traditional print-on-paper book is not particularly well positioned to win.

For the publisher, the challenge is how to get your books noticed among the mêlée, picked out by readers as sufficiently worthy of their time and attention to be bought by them. 'There's more competition out there; it's more of a buyer's market than a seller's market,' commented one marketing director. 'It's great that you can walk into a Barnes & Noble and have 30,000 titles to choose from. If I want a book on, say, Vietnamese cooking, I can go find 20 books about it. If I want a book on how to make a salad, I can go find 50 books on that. What a great thing for the consumer, but what a challenge for the publisher.'

So how do trade publishers deal with this challenge? How do they make their books stand out and get noticed despite all the competition and noise in the marketplace? This is the traditional domain of marketing and publicity, but over the past 30 years the parameters of the marketing and publicity effort have changed in

---

[6] *To Read or Not to Read: A Question of National Consequence* (Washington, D.C.: National Endowment for the Arts, 2007), pp. 12ff.

some fundamental ways. The task remains the same as it always was – namely, to create an awareness of a book and an author among potential readers and buyers. But, as one publicity director put it, 'The channels that are available to us, and the channels that enable that process to happen, have changed. There have been seismic changes on that front.'

From mass media to micro media

One of the most significant changes has been the decline of traditional 'mass' media, especially television and the print media like newspapers and magazines, and the growing importance of more specialized 'micro media' as key channels for the marketing and promotion of books. The traditional mass media have not become irrelevant – far from it. Television appearances, TV tie-ins, glowing reviews in major newspapers like the *New York Times* or the *Washington Post* can make a big difference to sales and can be the spark that lights a fire. But publishers can rely less and less on these traditional channels, both because it is harder to get books into them and because they are less effective than they used to be. 'It used to be, get one big hit on the *Today Show* and you're off to the races; take out some advertising in the *New York Times*, you're off to the races,' observed the marketing manager at one large house. 'Nowadays, rather than find out one big thing, our jobs are much more about finding 50 smart things to do. I often think about it like this: between us and our readership there's a brick wall and we have little hammers, and if we keep hitting that wall eventually we'll punch through it.' So the aim of the marketing manager – to stick with this analogy – is to figure out what hammers they can use, big and small, to try to punch through the wall and get multiple hits for a book. And 'depending on who you talk to in the marketing world, it takes anywhere from 6 to 12 touches in somebody's mind to make a decision to buy.'

Publishers can rely less on traditional media partly because there is less of it available to them. It is getting harder and harder to get books reviewed in the mainstream press because the amount of space devoted to book reviews has declined in many newspapers. In 2001 the *Boston Globe* merged its book review and commentary pages; in 2007 the *San Diego Union-Tribune* closed down its book review section; and in 2008 the *Los Angeles Times* killed its stand-alone Sunday Book Review section and merged it into another section in the Saturday edition of the paper, reducing the amount of space devoted to books. Even the *New York Times*, which is one of the few metropolitan newspapers in the US to have retained a stand-alone Book Review section, has shrunk the size by nearly half, from the 44 pages it averaged in the mid-1980s to the 24–28 pages it typically has today.[7] With the weekly news magazines like *Time* and *Newsweek* it is even worse. 'As recently as seven or eight years ago, they would do full previews of television, movies and books,' explained one publicity manager. 'Their coverage of books would be three to four pages in the magazine and they would write at length about several key titles. By 2006–2007, you have one page or half a page for books, postage stamp of a jacket, one sentence. Nothing memorable that sticks in the mind of the consumer/reader – it's gone. That column space, those column inches, have eroded. Newspapers and magazines, many of them allies, asset bases for our business, have become pale versions of their former selves. And we're just starting to come to terms with that.'

It is much the same with mainstream television. The *Today Show*, *Good Morning America* and the *Early Show* all used to have book producers and give a lot of space to books, but books have become less of a priority for them. 'I've had conversations with producers who say to me, "Oh, the author talking head? We're so over that. Novelists? Nobody's interested in novelists."' This publicity manager didn't give up easily. He pointed out that the NYTimes.com website lists the articles most frequently emailed by NYTimes.com readers and that, when they tallied these up at the end of the year, the most emailed story of 2006 was the ten best books of the year. 'I use this when I sit down with the morning shows and say, "You can't tell me that people aren't interested in books because clearly they are. You need to be responsive to your viewing public and if you're not going to do the author talking head, why don't you deal with summer reading?" And so they do that now – they do summer reading and they do gift books. But I gotta tell you, it's like pushing boulders uphill.'

While traditional mass media like newspapers, magazines and television have become what this publicity manager describes as 'a declining asset base' for the publishing industry, there are exceptions. One is radio, especially National Public Radio or NPR. 'NPR is a key component of outreach. Shows like *Morning Edition* and *All Things Considered*: their week-to-week listenership has gone up in a

---

[7] Steve Wasserman, 'Goodbye to All That', *Columbia Journalism Review* (Sept.–Oct. 2007).

significant way over the last 18 months. So we devote a lot of our time and energy to try and work with those shows. And it's not just the shows themselves, but NPR has a presence online. But I'm not sure the growth they've experienced at NPR offsets the loss we've experienced in the print community.' Another important exception is Oprah, and, in the British context, Richard and Judy, to which we'll return below.

With the declining significance of traditional media as channels for marketing and promoting books, publishers have increasingly focused their marketing efforts on other things. In most publishing houses there will be a meeting about a year before a book is published when marketing managers will set the marketing budget for the book and draw up a marketing campaign. The budget is typically set as a percentage of the expected revenue based on the book's P&L – for example, 6.5 per cent of total revenue. 'So at the lower end, maybe that budget is $5,000, maybe it's $3,500. At the upper end, maybe that budget is $500,000. Most books fall in the middle, if not closer to $5,000,' explained the marketing manager at one of the imprints in a large corporate house. 'And what we do is we say, "OK, we have this much money to spend, $5,000 or $500,000. What is it we need to do to reach the reader? Who are the readers? Where are they? How are we going to reach them?" That's a conversation that includes, in our company, the publisher, the editor, the publicist, a sales representative and the marketing team.' The challenge is to figure out what you can do with a given amount of money to try to reach what you think is the main audience for the book.

One element of the traditional book marketing campaign which has become less important in recent years is the multi-city author tour. It is still there and still important for certain kinds of books and certain authors, especially those who can draw a big audience, but it doesn't have the significance it once did. 'They were huge in the 1980s and 1990s,' explained the marketing manager, 'but look at it this way: every single author you put on the road, unless they're sleeping on their brother-in-law's couch, you're looking at 1,000 to 1,500 bucks per market. That's a lot of books you've got to sell in order to pull that back.' Moreover, there's a lot going on in cities these days and people don't come in the way they used to. 'We had an author – a well-known author, a huge author – and he went to an event: two people showed up. Maybe it was because the local basketball team was playing that night, we don't know.' So in general, publishers are now much more selective and strategic about putting authors on the road.

They are also much more cautious about print advertising. 'Advertising does not sell books,' stated one marketing manager bluntly. 'Our advertising budgets are about the amount of money that a major corporation would spend on the doughnuts at their photo shoot.' The proportion of the marketing budgets devoted to print advertising has declined over time at most of the large trade houses. This is a matter of some consternation for authors and agents, many of whom believe – unlike most publishers – that print advertising does sell books. It's also a source of dismay for newspapers and other print media who have lost the advertising revenue (and who sometimes cite this as a reason for axing or curtailing their book review sections).

So if marketing managers are relying less on author tours and print advertising, what are they doing to bring their books to the attention of readers? Most marketing managers will tell you that they are focusing their efforts more and more on trying to identify specific, fine-grained ways of reaching the people who comprise what they see as the readership, using an array of different channels which, in addition to traditional print media, now include a variety of new media, from email lists to websites and blogs. One marketing manager put it like this:

> Suppose we're publishing a novel about vampires – good genre fiction. Well, we're not going to get a review in the *Times* daily, we're not going to get advertising in the *Times* daily, but let's identify 200 vampire enthusiast groups – there are probably 2,000 of them – and let's find out who they are, where they live and let's market to them. Let's send them an email, one person in every group gets a free book to talk about. Let's find out what conventions they go to, they congregate once a year at this convention of vampire fans, and let's make sure that we have something at that convention to get the word out. So those types of activities are really what can help move a book along in that circle, well below the radar of the mainstream media, because the mainstream won't touch it. Or suppose we're publishing a legal thriller: let's go out and find the law professors that might respond to this and where they go on vacation; let's send them a copy of the book and have them start talking about it. Word of mouth – we try to build up word of mouth.

Building word of mouth is the key here: how can you get people talking about a book, telling their friends or colleagues or customers that the book they've just read is terrific? Word of mouth tends to have a cumulative character, in the sense that the more you can get people talking about a book, the more likely it is that they will tell others about it, who will in turn tell others and so on, leading to a kind of rising tide of positive chatter. Despite the preoccupation with the media among media scholars and commentators, good old-fashioned word of mouth remains the cornerstone of the marketing effort. But of course it's more complicated than this might suggest, because media are among the tools you use to try to build word of mouth and, indeed, some of this word of mouth takes place in the media or online – it is, to some extent, mediated word of mouth. Publishers will often target what they call, rather ungraciously, 'big mouths' – anyone they can think of who has some position of influence, whether they are review editors or feature writers or agents or opinion leaders of some kind, 'just people who talk a lot', as one publisher put it. They may send them advance reading copies well ahead of the actual publication date in order to get people reading the book, talking about it and recommending it to others – in short, generating buzz. In the case of Dan Brown's *The Da Vinci Code*, for example, the publisher sent out a large number of advance reading copies in order to stimulate interest and excitement before the book was published. 'One of the many strategies we concocted was that what's going to sell this book best is the reading experience,' explained one of the publishers who was directly involved in planning this particular campaign.

So instead of doing 3,000 advanced reading copies we actually did 10,000 reading copies, and we did them in various waves. So we sent advance reading copies to booksellers, we sent advance reading copies to what they call 'big mouths', we sent advance reading copies to competitive reps, we sent advance reading copies to reviewers, we sent advance reading copies to feature writers. And then we repeated it. We wanted to get people reading the book, because I knew that if they read the book they would talk about it. What I didn't know is how right I was. Because ultimately when this book first came out it entered the ethos, so that you couldn't go to a dinner party without having this book discussed. That's why the book became such a phenomenon: word of mouth just took it to heights that no one ever dreamed of. Dan Brown sold more copies of *The Da Vinci Code* in its first week on sale than he had sold for all his other books combined.

Generating excitement about a new book is also about timing. You have to try to find a publication window when there's not a lot happening, especially if you're trying to launch a new or less well-known author. 'If you can hit a window where there's not a lot of new known quantities out so people come into the bookstore saying "I don't see anything here that's exciting; I'm going to try this new author," then you stand a chance,' explained one sales director. 'But if all of a sudden there are five or six big-time authors that they've read before, then that new author kind of loses out. And that's a key part of the business, to find that window.' Publishers can check the competition lists that are produced by Barnes & Noble and other retailers so they know what everyone else is publishing and when they're planning to publish it, and then they can position their books in relation to that. Of course, if they are publishing a new book by a big brand-name author like John Grisham or Patricia Cornwell, they don't have to pay much attention to the competition list – 'We just pick a date that works for him and everybody else stays away from it.' But if they are trying to make a book by a new or less well-known author, they will check the competition list and aim to publish it when there is not much else of any consequence coming out. If a publication date they had originally envisaged turns out to fall within a crowded period when the book would run the risk of being eclipsed by others, they will move the date by up to several weeks. They can get the competition lists early enough to enable them to lock in on a date well in advance.

Having locked in on a publication date does not mean that all of the marketing and publicity effort is geared exclusively to this date – on the contrary, and this is one of the key respects in which marketing has changed in recent years. In the traditional book marketing model, the marketing and publicity effort was all engineered with a view to break at the time of publication, like a great wave crashing on the shore, the theory being that this would maximize the public's awareness at the very moment when the book appears physically in the bookstores. But in the new media environment of today, marketing managers and publicists will often try to build the marketing campaign over time, getting people talking about a book and generating interest and excitement well in advance of publication. There are several reasons for this.

In the first place, by building anticipation among potential readers they can generate demand at the grassroots level, thereby helping to ensure that the book gets off to a strong start when it is actually published. In the best-case scenario they might even be able to put a book by an unknown author straight on to the bestseller list, which immediately gives it a high level of visibility in the marketplace. Perhaps the best example of this phenomenon was Elizabeth

Kostova's *The Historian*: a first novel that sold in an auction for $2.1 million and that, when it was published in 2005, went straight to number one on the *New York Times* bestseller list in its first week on sale. How on earth did the publisher achieve this remarkable feat? 'It happened because of the growth of the chains and the growth of the internet,' explained one of the publishers who witnessed it at close hand. 'What the chains have learned is that with the growth of non-bookstore outlets they can make a bestseller out of an unknown writer. The non-bookstore outlets can sell James Patterson or Michael Connelly but they're much more careful about unknown writers. So if the chains find something they're excited about they'll take a big position and work on promoting it aggressively to their customers and try to make a success for themselves.' And thanks to the internet, the marketing the publisher did to its primary customers and to various intermediaries – to booksellers, librarians, critics, website bloggers and others – trickled down to readers and book buyers. In other words, buzz is more likely than it ever was to spill beyond the industry as such:

> The kind of buzz that we build within the industry now actually gets out to consumers at such a level that when a book by an unknown writer comes into bookstores it can enter the bestseller list at number one. Booksellers get behind it, feature it aggressively on their websites before publication and in the email blasts they do to their customers, saying 'coming on such and such a date'. And beyond that, the world of blogs, websites, reading groups, bookclubs – people who are hungry for information about what's cool, what's exciting – has grown and that information is now available to them. They're searching the publishers' websites, they're talking to each other, and so the excitement that we spread within the industry is spreading outside the industry as well. It used to be that a book would start at the bottom and climb as word spread across the country slowly through monthly magazines, weekly magazines, newspapers – these slow communications. Then it began happening that the bestselling authors would come out right at number one. But now it's happening for unknown writers and that's incredibly exciting. The ability for a publisher to communicate with consumers about an unknown writer at that scale is exhilarating. It's a huge change in the industry.

There is another reason why publishers have moved away from the traditional marketing model, with its emphasis on the great wave of publicity breaking on publication date, towards a greater emphasis on pre-publication publicity hits: namely, 'to drive pole position on Amazon'. As one publicity manager explained, 'What you have now is the ability to capture a sale prior to the book's availability in the physical environment that you didn't have 20 years ago.' This pre-publication publicity and pre-order phenomenon can be hugely significant for publishers, partly because it can help to put a book on to the bestseller lists as soon as it is published, since all the pre-ordered books will count as the first-day sale when the book is actually released. And hitting the bestseller lists early is important because it results in front-of-store placements in the big retail chains, if the book is not already there. 'Once you become a bestseller you tend to be more visible in other environments. There isn't one list that is important, it's the aggregate that is important, and it's important because of visibility, because of the awareness they foster on the part of the consumer – "Oh yeah, I saw that book, I heard about that book."'

Pre-orders are also important because they can help the publisher overcome initial resistance they might face from buyers in the big retail chains, who might take the view that a book presented to them by a sales rep is not as big as the publisher thinks. 'We were having trouble with Borders and Barnes & Noble with [a recent book],' the publicity manager continued. 'They didn't see it as a big book. And then when we started to work it prior to publication, getting people talking about it online, the book was a top 15 on Amazon a couple of weeks prior to publication. And Barnes & Noble and Borders both came back and upped their orders by two or three thousand copies.'

The way this publicity manager saw it is that every book is published on a linear continuum, and their job as marketers and publicists is to create a 'wave of awareness'. In the past, the aim was to make this wave break on the day of publication and wash over the public in the days and weeks immediately after publication. But now it's a slower build and there are more things happening on the way. 'Every book is different and you can't apply the same rules to every title. But as a general rule, the strategy that is being adopted now is pre-publication. It's pre-publication PR, pre-publication awareness, to help drive pole position on Amazon.'

The growth of online marketing

The shift of marketing focus from traditional mainstream media to online channels is reflected in the reallocation of marketing resources within many publishing houses. The extent of reallocation varies from house to house, depending on the nature of the list and the importance they attribute to online channels at a management level. At one of the large publishing corporations in the US, the proportion of the total marketing spend (including co-op) devoted to online marketing doubled from 3.5 per cent in 2006 to 7 per cent in 2007, and was set to grow again by a similar amount in 2008. At one of the imprints within this corporation, the shift to online was even more dramatic. Phil, the online marketing manager at this imprint, had joined the company in 2006. His background was not in book publishing; he had managed web properties for an illustrated magazine before he joined this company 18 months previously. He was valued not so much for his experience in publishing as for his knowledge of the fast-moving world of the web and his ability to use this knowledge to find new and creative ways to market books – 'It allows me to bring a different spin to traditional book publishing,' observed Phil. When he arrived in 2006, only 10 per cent of the imprint's marketing budget (excluding co-op) was devoted to online marketing, compared to 60 per cent devoted to print; 18 months later, online marketing was accounting for 65 per cent of the budget, compared to 15 per cent devoted to print (see figure 6). This is a huge shift over a very short period of time.

So how is the online marketing budget being spent? Phil broke down his main activities into three areas: online advertising, online outreach and the management of web properties. Most of the budget is taken up by online advertising, since, as Phil explained, 'We're moving more of our advertising dollars online as opposed to print.' Even with big-name authors, they will commonly advertise in the

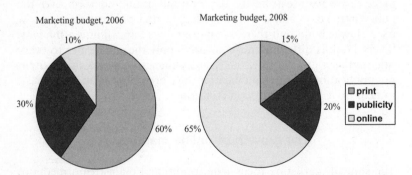

Figure 6   Breakdown of one US imprint's marketing budget, 2006 and 2008

New York Times Online rather than doing it in print. They also use Google's advertising programme a lot, since it enables them to target specific sites and demographics. 'The nice thing about the web is that we can hit the niche audience. Next week we're taking a book that's about music and we're only showing ads to people whose computers are in Austin, Texas, because it's a big music town and there's a music festival that starts there next week. So it only serves the ads if the computer is coming from a certain zip code.' Another advantage of Google advertising is that it is easily controlled, so if the ad isn't working you can turn it off and if it is working well you can turn it up. As with all advertising, part of the aim is to drive sales by getting consumers to click through to Amazon or to their own e-commerce site, but part of the aim is also to produce impressions – that is, to get the book and the author seen. 'We want the impressions just like we would with print advertising,' said Phil. 'We want people to see the book jacket; we want to brand the author. Since 15 per cent of all book sales happen online, there's a part of me that wants to drive the clicks and get people to our e-commerce site or to Amazon. But I also want the other 85 per cent to be in the bookstore and recognize the book either because they saw an ad or they saw something else that we did online.'

While advertising takes the lion's share of the online marketing budget, much of Phil's effort is focused on what he calls 'online out-reach'. 'We outreach to bloggers, and that's a big part of what we do because it just gets the conversation going.' They build up and main-tain lists of hard mailing addresses for bloggers in different areas – political bloggers, for example – and then they mail them finished copies of the book about three weeks before publication. 'And the way that we pitch bloggers is a lot different from the way publicity would pitch an editor,' explained Phil. 'In publicity they'll send the book with a press release, they'll follow up, they'll make phone calls. We drop the book in an envelope with nothing else and mail it to them and don't follow up. I have personal relationships with a lot of these bloggers, so they'll know they can email me if they have a ques-tion or if they want bonus content with the author, whether it's a Q&A or a podcast or an excerpt. But the goal is to get these books out to as many bloggers as possible.' They'll send out anywhere from 100 to 400 books to bloggers – just pop it into a bag and send it off, no cover letter, no press release or follow-up, nothing. And they won't do any of these traditional things because Phil knows that bloggers aren't, and don't want to be, traditional review editors. 'I've done the research and met with bloggers, whether it's the conventions or just when they're around, and they really want to distance themselves from traditional media. They don't want to be straight reviewers; they want to almost sort of come to it on their own, you know. So we make it available but then they can decide how they want to write about it. And from my point of view, it doesn't matter if they're going to write a review or if they're just going to mention the book – that's fine with me, because it all helps to get the conversation going. And once this stuff is online it all gets indexed, so the more times that somebody's talked about the better.'

Phil gives an example of a book they recently published about the Bush administration. The author was well known in the blogosphere, which gave him a platform online and helped when it came to identifying bloggers to whom books could be sent. Although the book was critical of the Bush administration, they sent it to conservative bloggers as well, because even if they wrote about it negatively it would help to create interest and intrigue. 'The more people who are talking about the book, the better, and the nice thing about the web is that people are constantly talking. You know, somebody might be sitting at work and they continue to go to these places and they sign up for feeds. So they're just constantly engaged.' With this particular book they sent out about 350 copies in total – 'to right-wing bloggers, left-wing bloggers, anything'. After he sent out the books, Phil used Google Alert to find places where a lot of chatter was going on, 'and that's when I'll approach the blogger myself and offer them up a Q&A or an excerpt or a book jacket or a podcast, just because then they re-post it and it goes back to the top and it just starts the conversation all over again. That's when we then hope that people are going to Amazon, going to Barnes & Noble, going into the bookstores. So it's like kind of continuing to hit with different and unique content to the point where somebody's saying "Now I have to buy this book."' In the case of this particular book, the campaign was a resounding success. 'We did a strong pre-order campaign. There was no print advertising; there was no real publicity; it was all web driven. And we drove the numbers up and it was on the top ten at Amazon before it went on sale. Then it hit the bestseller list right after it went on sale.' Having got the book onto the bestseller list the week it went on sale, the book took on a life of its own, since the bestseller list gives a book a great deal of visibility 'and that's when the conventional media starts paying attention to it'.

This kind of online campaign works particularly well for political books, since the political blogosphere has a great deal of traffic and many lively and engaged communities of bloggers and readers, but it can work well for other kinds of non-fiction and for fiction too. One of the things that Phil spends a great deal of time doing is helping authors create their own websites and blogs so that they can help to generate interest in their books – and this doesn't just apply to political books. This is part of what is involved in the management of web properties.

The basic difference between managing web properties, on the one hand, and online advertising and blog outreach, on the other, is that 'with advertising and blog outreach, it's us going out into the world and trying to be effective. When it comes to managing our web properties, that's in terms of pulling people in to us.' A big part of managing web properties is maintaining an up-to-date website, and that means creating as much new and original content as possible and changing it frequently – in Phil's case, two or three times a week, 'just because the last thing I want is somebody coming to a website, even if it's been two or three days, and thinking, "Well, this is old news." People don't want to see static content.'

In fact the issues are more complicated than this, because it's also about search engine optimization – that is, about creating a site architecture and content that is friendly for the Google crawler. Being visible in the online world is, to a large extent, a matter of being visible to the search engines, and above all to Google. But just as importantly, it's about tailoring your site and content in such a way that it's ranked high in search results – if it isn't, then your content is, for all practical purposes, invisible. The Google algorithm is a closely guarded secret, 'a whole black art/science unto itself', as one online marketing manager put it, but those who work in online marketing make it their business to understand at least some of the ways in which it works. They know, for example, that if you have a Flash object – a multimedia platform commonly used for adding animation and interactivity to web pages – you need to attach some text to it, because Google doesn't crawl into a Flash object and won't pick it up. Many YouTube videos are done in Flash but it is the text around them that makes them 'hyper-relevant' and visible to the crawlers. The Google algorithm also values the freshness of the content, so the more frequently the content is changed, the higher it will tend to rank in a Google search. Wikipedia is perfect for a search engine because the crawler sees the content and the content is constantly changing, so Wikipedia often comes out ranked at or near the top in Google searches.

Managing web properties is also about creating or encouraging communities of readers by doing newsletters, sending information out to reading groups and either starting blogs or helping authors to start blogs. Why is it so important for authors to start blogs? 'Just because it gives the author a platform to be out there and to start talking,' says Phil. In order to get their authors to start blogging, Phil and his team do all of the technical legwork. 'We set up the templates, set everything up on the back end so people can find the blog, and then let them unleash and do their thing.' Phil gives the example of an author who was writing a book for them about living with Asperger's syndrome. They set up a blog for him and got him blogging before the book was published. The author was very engaged, constantly posting new material, 'not always about the book, he's just talking in general. He would get 50 comments right away and he'd respond to them. It was a really engaging process. And it was something that picked up a lot of steam. The media was talking about it, and every time you went to a book signing people would say, "Oh, we read your blog."' They provided the author with lots of book-related content to add to his site – the book jacket, an excerpt from the book, a podcast of the author reading from the book, a short video of the author, a diary of author appearances, links to a dozen places where readers could buy the book, etc. The podcasts and videos that Phil produced or edited were also posted on Amazon, Barnes & Noble, YouTube and other sites to maximize exposure on the web. When this particular book was published it went straight on to the bestseller list and remained there for a long time – 'It kind of got a life of its own.' Even now, as they prepare to release a paperback edition, the author is constantly posting new material and engaging with others, including potential readers, through his blog – 'he continues to blog and just kind of keeps the momentum going.'

A striking illustration of how the innovative use of online media can increase visibility and drive sales is provided by Kelly Corrigan's *The Middle Place*, an uplifting memoir by a happily married mother of two who discovered one day that she had breast cancer. Initially published in January 2008 in hardcover, it was a modest success, selling 35,000 copies. The author is an articulate, charismatic woman and, after the publication of the book in hardcover, she began speaking to groups of women in various settings. She filmed herself on one of these occasions and sent the video to her publisher – a trade house owned by a large multimedia corporation – to see if they could use it. The publisher had just created a small digital marketing group, staffed by two women who had no background in book publishing ('I did that purposely,' explained a senior manager, 'because I think it's really important at this particular time in publishing to bring in people who don't carry all the baggage with them, who look at things objectively and try to figure out new and different approaches'). The digital marketers decided to edit the video so you could see the author reading and see the audience reaction, enabling viewers to get a sense of the emotional connection between them. They didn't release the video immediately but held on to it until mid-December 2008, just a few weeks before the paperback was due to be released. Then they posted the video on YouTube and sent it to a small group of women in the company with an email saying, 'Here's the final video. Would each of you please send it to a group of your women friends and encourage them, if they like it, to pass it on.' At the end of the video there was a picture of the book with a notice that it was available in paperback. 'I sent it out to a group of about 30 or 40 of my friends, basically saying, "I never send out this kind of thing but it's so effective, I really encourage you to watch it and, if you like it, share it,"' said one senior manager in the company. 'One week after we posted the video on YouTube and a few of us sent it around to our various friends, there were 250,000 views on this video. Two weeks later there were over 500,000 views and I had people sending me the video not knowing I had anything to do with it.' The video had gone viral.

The paperback of *The Middle Place* was released in January 2009 and by March it had sold 350,000 copies. As soon as the book began to take off, the traditional retail chains saw a sales opportunity and started to get behind the book. Borders decided that they would try to get this book to the top of the *New York Times* bestseller list and they put out a special instruction to all their store managers, giving it prominent in-store placement. 'So the book, which was around ten or twelve on the list for several weeks, all of a sudden shot up to four, then to three, knocked off President Obama's *The Audacity of Hope* at two and now we've got one more to go. *Three Cups of Tea* is still number one.' *The Middle Place* never managed to knock *Three Cups of Tea* off the number one slot, but it did spend 25 weeks on the *New York Times* bestseller list.

Of course, online marketing strategies don't work for every author and every book. There is no easy formula that can be applied – much depends on the type of book, the topic and the author, and the challenge for the digital marketer is to craft a strategy that works for the particular book he or she is seeking to promote, given the subject matter and the particular strengths and limitations of the author. Some kinds of books – like new fiction – are less amenable and some authors are just not interested or able to work in these environments. But increasingly one of the questions publishers are asking when they are considering a new book at proposal stage is whether the author has the ability to engage in some form of online marketing, whether it's blogging or maintaining a website or creating a video that can be posted online or marketed virally. For in the internet age, these new forms of online marketing are becoming more and more decisive in shaping the visibility of books and their fate.

The battle for eyeballs

The marketing and publicity campaign is one side of the struggle for visibility; the other side is the battle for eyeballs in the bookstores and other retail outlets. 'I will say this: fundamentally,' remarked one marketing manager at a large New York house, 'if you can win the battle in the first 50 feet of the bookstore, if you can get on that front table, if you can get on that end cap, if you can get in front of somebody's eyeballs, you have a much better chance of success than if you went back into the section, spine out, alongside every other cookbook that's ever been published.'

Part of the thinking here is that if you've mounted a good marketing and publicity campaign you will drive consumers into the bookstores, and then you want your book to be there at the front of the store so they can find it easily, pick it up and buy it. Or just as importantly, if they walk into a bookstore to browse, or perhaps to look for a specific book but not yours, they will see your book, remember that they heard something about it somewhere and add it to whatever else they might happen to be buying on that occasion – in other words, it becomes an impulse purchase. If your book is not in the front of the bookstore, displayed cover up or cover out, but merely stocked spine out in a specialist section somewhere in the store, you'll lose that impulse purchase. 'If you walk into a major retail outlet, there may be 30,000 square feet in that store, and within that 30,000 square feet there are maybe 50,000 titles, maybe more, maybe 100,000 titles,' the marketing manager continued. 'If there's something that's right in front of you as you walk in, you're much more likely to stop and look at it. A lot of consumers say, "I need a book on this specific topic; I am going into that section," and then maybe they'll find your book. But you might walk into Barnes & Noble saying, "I want to buy a great novel" and on your way go, "Oh, look at that cookbook, I would love that, or my wife would love that cookbook." You lose that if you're in section – you'll never get that impulse buy.'

So how important are impulse purchases in trade publishing? Are publishers right to be so concerned about where their books are placed and how they're displayed in the bookstores and other retail outlets? Table 11 summarizes data from Bowker's PubTrack on impulse purchases of books by outlet for 2007. PubTrack surveyed over a million consumers in the US who bought books in different outlets, from Amazon and the large retail book chains to the mass merchandisers and warehouse clubs. Consumers were asked whether they planned to buy this specific book at that specific time, planned to buy this specific book but not at that specific time, planned to buy a book but not this specific book, or didn't plan to buy a book at all. The final group – those who didn't plan to buy a book at all – are clear impulse purchases. The data show that 29 per cent of all book purchases are impulse purchases of this kind. But they also show that the proportion of impulse purchases varies greatly from outlet to outlet – it's lowest on Amazon (15 per cent) and other e-commerce sites (16 per cent) and highest at the warehouse clubs, where impulse purchases account for nearly half (45 per cent) of all book sales. Barnes & Noble, Borders and the large bookstore chains are in between (17–20 per cent).

However, what is even more striking about these data is what they show in terms of the intention to purchase a specific book. A substantial proportion of individuals who bought a book were planning to buy a book when they went into a store (or went online) but were not planning to buy *this specific book*: the fact that they ended up buying *this specific book* was itself unplanned. If we look at these two groups of individuals together – those who didn't plan to buy a book at all (the strict impulse purchasers) and those who, while planning to buy a book, were not planning to buy *this specific book* – then the proportions are startling (the final column of the table). A total of 57 per cent of all book buyers in the survey bought either on impulse or without having planned to buy this specific book. And once again, the proportion varies greatly from outlet to outlet, ranging from 31 per cent at Amazon and 51 per cent at Barnes & Noble to a staggering 73 per cent at the warehouse clubs. In other words, just over half of Barnes & Noble's customers and nearly three-quarters of those who bought books in a warehouse club did so either on impulse or without having planned to buy this specific book.

This data undoubtedly provides some support for the view that the battle for eyeballs in the front of the bookstore – and even more so the battle for space in the warehouse clubs for those kinds of books

Table 11 Impulse purchase by outlet, 2007

	Planned/Not planned less Not reported	Planned this specific book at that specific time	Planned this specific book, but not at that specific time	Planned a book at that specific time, but not specific book	Not planned, impulse purchase	% planned	% impulse	% impulse plus not specific book
Total panellists (population)	1,061,914	278,358	180,723	295,131	307,702	71%	29%	57%
Total e-commerce/internet	233,808	90,505	64,238	40,879	38,186	84%	16%	34%
Amazon.com	154,254	65,010	41,295	25,151	22,798	85%	15%	31%
Total large chain bookstores	269,935	92,496	45,288	81,164	50,987	81%	19%	49%
Total Barnes & Noble (net)	140,030	43,522	25,209	42,815	28,484	80%	20%	51%
Total Borders Group (net)	109,248	41,640	16,603	32,221	18,785	83%	17%	47%
Other/Independent bookstores	73,578	12,993	9,186	32,422	18,977	74%	26%	70%
Total mass merchandisers	74,171	12,025	12,175	24,206	25,766	65%	35%	67%
Target stores / Super Target	14,309	2,501	2,790	4,765	4,252	70%	30%	63%
Wal-Mart / Super Wal-Mart	53,593	8,934	8,709	17,068	18,882	65%	35%	67%
Total warehouse clubs	38,073	4,846	5,390	10,840	16,996	55%	45%	73%
BJ's wholesale club	4,717	1,069	797	1,264	1,586	66%	34%	60%
Costco	16,173	2,030	2,370	4,773	6,999	57%	43%	73%

Source: Bowker PubTrack.

that are stocked by them – is crucial for the commercial success of a book, and it is therefore not surprising that publishers are prepared to devote so many resources to securing front-of-store placement. 'If you don't get your books promoted [through in-store placement] it's so, so rare that you can make a book work,' said one sales director who had been in the business for many years. 'I mean you can do it, there are other things you can do, like have a great publicity campaign to get people to come in and say, "I want to buy . . . Do you have it? Where is it?" But especially on a track-record author who publishes a book every year or every two years and there's really a following for them, you've got to have that up front because if you don't and people can't spot it you're going to already be behind the eight ball.'

In the US, in-store placement is typically funded through what is called 'co-op' (or cooperative advertising). Essentially, co-op is a cost-sharing arrangement between the publisher and the retailer in which the publisher pays for part of the retailer's promotion costs. Each publisher will have its own co-op policy. Most trade publishers calculate what they are prepared to make available to a particular account as a percentage of that account's net sales in the previous year. The amount can vary from 2 to 4 per cent, depending on the publisher. So if a publisher's terms are 4 per cent of the prior year's sales, then a retailer who sold $100,000 of this publisher's books in the previous year would have $4,000 of co-op to spend in the current year. This money goes into a pool which can be used by that account to promote the publisher's books in their bookstore or on their website, in ways that are agreed on a book-by-book basis between the sales rep or account manager and the buyer. Sometimes incremental supplements are made to the pool in order to include specific titles in special bookstore promotions, like a 'buy one get one free' or 'buy one get one-half off' promotion on paperbacks.

For the large trade houses, the total amount spent on co-op has grown enormously in recent years and now represents a substantial proportion of the overall marketing spend. At one large US publishing corporation, offline co-op represented 38 per cent of the total marketing budget in 2007 – the largest single item. And online co-op, spent with Amazon and other e-tailers, was in addition to this. At another major US publishing house, co-op represented a little more than 50 per cent of their marketing spend. And this has changed dramatically in the last couple of decades. 'In the 1980s it was probably more like 30–35 per cent,' said one sales director, 'and now it's become more than 50, close to 60 per cent.'

To get a book in a front-of-store display in a major retail chain like Barnes & Noble is not entirely within the control of the publisher. What typically happens is that the sales managers for the national accounts present the new titles to the central buyers at the retail chains and let them know what their expectations are for the book – how big a book it is for them, how many copies they'd like the retailer to buy, etc. The buyers decide which titles they want to buy in what quantities based on their own assessment of the book, the sales histories of the author's previous books, the cover and various other factors, and they often tie co-op money into the buy. 'They're going to say, "Great, I love the book, what are you going to do for it?" And then you say, "Well, I don't really have that much money. I can only spend $10,000." They'll go, "OK, well I can't buy 25,000." They play like that,' explained the sales director at a large US house. There's a to-and-fro between the sales rep and the buyer to determine how many copies they're going to take and how much the publisher is going to spend to support it. The sales managers and buyers then negotiate what kind of in-store promotion would be appropriate – placement on a front-of-store table, a middle-of-store section, an endcap (a book display at the end of an aisle) or a 'stepladder' (literally a stepladder that is stacked with books and placed near the front of the store – 'The damn thing sells books like you can't believe,' said one sales director), how many stores for how many weeks, etc. The rates vary depending on the type of placement, the type of book (cloth, trade paperback, mass market), the buy size, the number of stores, the number of weeks and the time of year (it is much higher in the run-up to Christmas, for example). The most expensive table is right at the front, and the further back you go the less expensive it becomes. Typically, placement on a central front-of-store table in a major US retail chain for two weeks would cost the publisher $10,000 for all stores, perhaps half that for stores in the major markets (about a third of the number of stores), and less again for so-called A-Stores (perhaps 10–15 per cent of the number of stores). For a table in a back section you might pay $3,500. And a stepladder could cost $25,000 for a week. These placements will be linked to the quantity of the buy. As a rough rule of thumb, in-store placement works out at around a dollar a book for a new hardcover.

Given the cost of putting a book in a front-of-store display in a major retail chain, it's crucial that the book performs – crucial not just for the publisher, who is paying a premium to put the book there, but also for the retailer, who is tying up valuable real estate. It is therefore not surprising that publishers tend to monitor the sales of new books very closely in the first few days and weeks after publication. The major trade publishers get daily sales feeds from the big retail chains which enable them to see on a day-by-day basis just how quickly their top-selling books, including those with in-store promotions, are moving. Within the large publishing houses a great deal of attention is focused on the performance of new books during the first few days and weeks after publication because the sales and marketing directors know that, for many books, this is the make-or-break time.

Backing success (and letting dead fish float downstream)

At one major US house they have what they call the 'breakfast meeting' every Thursday morning. Other houses have something similar, though the specific arrangements vary from house to house. Bill, the sales director at this house, is an old hand on the retail side of the business, having started out as a sales trainee at what was then an independent house in the 1970s and worked his way up, moving houses as they were bought and merged before becoming sales director of this group. 'The purpose of the breakfast meeting', explained Bill, 'is to go through all of our big books that have just landed or are ready to land – maybe just landed in the last two weeks or ready to land in the next two weeks, in that period. We have all our sales numbers, and we compare it to the author's last book. So we've got a really great snapshot of how we're doing week to week compared to that author's last book.' Each of the imprints in the corporation is assigned a time slot for the breakfast meeting, and the imprint's publisher, together with the key editorial, marketing and publicity people, come in for their 40-minute slot to meet with the sales director and his team. They go through the imprint's new big books one by one and talk about what they can do to support them.

Some books start off well. The account managers have managed to ship out a lot of books, publicity has lined up some television appearances and the early signs are good. 'Everybody is a little nervous about having so much up front,' explains Bill; 'They wait and see and then all of a sudden the book starts moving and they jump.' He takes as an example a book they just published the previous day – let's call it *Crisis*:

> We put out 102,000 copies, which is a very nice number. First book he's written. He was on *Meet the Press* in Washington on Sunday. It

goes on sale yesterday and all of a sudden the book takes off – it's number one on Amazon right now as we speak. We got really strong daily sales at Barnes & Noble yesterday – like I think they sold 14,000 yesterday, which suggests that's going to turn out to be a great sale. And that's going to catapult it to probably number two or three on their non-fiction list. And I'm thinking if it's number one on Amazon, two or three on Barnes & Noble, two or three on Borders and the clubs took it but not that big, it will probably be number three or four on the *New York Times* list a week from today. So we start calling the accounts and say, 'Hey, I'm calling to tell you *Crisis* is starting off Gangbusters.' You know, we'll call Barnes & Noble, and they'll look it up and say, 'Oh, man, yeah, I saw it too.' Or sometimes the buyer calls us. In this case we were on top of it, and so now we've just pushed the button for more. We had 13,000 on hand at the on sale date in our warehouse. That all went, and we printed 20,000 more. That all went. We pushed the button again yesterday for another 50,000.

The ability of the large publishing houses to monitor sales through the cash registers of the major retail chains on a daily basis is crucial here, as is their ability to lean on their printers to turn around reprints in a matter of days – 'It usually takes about four to five days as long as we have jackets,' explained Bill, 'and we had jackets.'

At the same time as they're reprinting and resupplying the retail chains, they are also putting more resources into marketing and publicity. 'There's a lot more money coming in, his tour schedule is unbelievably packed and he's got a *60 Minutes* that's not even happening until late September [we were talking in July]. So for the next two months he's got something going on with this book. And so we're going to support him and add more money to the advertising budget.' 'So you divert resources to back success when you see it?' I ask. 'Absolutely, that's how we do it,' replied Bill. 'They have a budget set but that budget was probably based on about 125,000 copies. And now that we're going to be probably closer to 200,000 in a week, that budget will increase.' As soon as a book shows signs that it's going to take off, the sales, marketing and publicity operations mobilize behind it and look for ways to support it with extra advertising, trying to get more radio and TV appearances, extending the author's tour or putting together a new tour to cities where the book is doing particularly well, and so on.

The large publishing organizations are remarkably quick at responding to the first signs of success. They are not blundering dinosaurs – far from it. They may not know in advance which books are going to take off – they have their hunches but there is always a large element of uncertainty. However, the daily sales feeds from the major retail chains – together with the real-time Amazon rankings – give them a sensitive set of tools for monitoring sell-through on a daily basis during the first few critical days and weeks after publication. And the sales, marketing and publicity operations are geared and resourced in such a way that, when they see that a fire is starting to ignite, they are able to pour generous quantities of fuel on the flames. In a hits-driven business like trade publishing where there is a high level of uncertainty about when and where the hits will occur, the key is to structure the organization in a way that enables you to respond quickly and effectively to the first signs of success. As one publicity manager put it, 'When a book begins to move you throw as many resources behind it as you possibly can, because once a book breaks through the noise of our culture, once you've got that awareness of the consumer, bingo. You really have to do everything you can to keep it going, to maximize it. Ultimately it's the amplification effect: you want to keep the momentum going.'

Of course, not all new books take off like *Crisis* – in fact, most don't. So what do you do at the Thursday morning breakfast meeting when you see that a book isn't moving as you expected or hoped? 'We look at the marketing director and the publicity director and we say, "What's going on?"' explained Bill. He continued:

It's usually more the publicity at that point. The marketing takes longer to do – we don't need any more brochures; they're not going to spend any more money running an ad in the *Times* usually, because that's a waste of money in most cases, especially if the books are dead. So we need a TV hit, we need a radio hit, we need something, you know. So that's what we find out. We need a great review or something. But in my experience, if we're having troubles in the store and they're not flocking into the store, they're going to have troubles on the publicity side. And so we get to a point where we just cut bait and say, 'You know what, let's move on.'

The publicity director is urged to do what she can at this stage to help breathe life into a book that is defeating their expectations. She will call review editors to see if reviews are in the works, call producers to see if radio or TV appearances can be fixed up and generally do whatever she can to stimulate media interest. But if further appeals fall on deaf ears and sales fail to pick up, then the marketing and publicity effort will be wound up pretty quickly – 'In two to three weeks we might pull the plug,' says Bill. 'But in all honesty most of our planned expenditures are in the very beginning anyway, so if the author is on tour we're not going to tell them, "Come back home, we're not paying for your hotel." They're usually on the road for a week and a half, two weeks, something like that; we let them run that out in case for some reason something clicks. And we've already committed co-op, so that's going to stay in place. So we basically don't print any more – we definitely don't print any more. And if there are any more expenditures, like if there was maybe a small ad being planned in the *Times* that was going to cost, you know, five or ten grand, they would probably cut that.'

The publicity manager at one of the imprints in another large publishing corporation put it like this: 'If a book's not working there's not a lot you can do. And if the fish is dead you let it float downstream. I'm sorry, but just let her go, baby. Some publishers keep throwing resources at dead fish. They say, "Oh, we'll try this, we'll try that" – it's crazy, it's the craziest business I've ever seen. I mean, if it's not moving and you've done everything you can in the road leading up to publication, if you've made all the right choices, what are you going to do?'

The six-week rule

So how long does a book have out there in the marketplace to show signs of life? How many weeks before it becomes a dead fish that will be left to float downstream? 'That's the other thing that's changing tremendously in our business,' says Bill; 'the window is just becoming like a blink of an eye. A book in the past would take longer and it would sustain itself longer. Now it jumps out of the gate and then it takes off and then all of a sudden, two weeks later – I don't want to say it's dead because it doesn't take off and then go like this [he draws a steeply declining line with his finger], it takes off and then it goes like this [his finger draws a line that declines more gently] – pretty gradual but steeper than you would think. I would say the life of a book today is about six weeks. And quite frankly it's even shorter than that, but you probably have six weeks and that's it.'

In this respect, trade publishing is becoming more and more like the movie business, with its heavy emphasis on box office sales on the opening weekend. In trade publishing the window of opportunity is measured in weeks rather than weekends, but the window is definitely shrinking. Today a book has just a few weeks – typically no more than six, and in practice often less – to show whether it's going to move, and if it's not moving then it will be pulled out of promotions and the marketing spend will be wound down or cut off. It's simply too expensive to keep a book on a front-of-store table if it's not selling pretty briskly. And if the book has been sold into the price clubs, then it will need to turn over at a certain rate in order to keep its place – if it falls below this rate it will be pulled and returned to the publisher. All these pressures stemming from an increasingly chain-dominated retail marketplace have compressed the time frame during which new books are given an opportunity to succeed. If it's clear from the sales figures that the book is beginning to work then the publisher will mobilize behind it, pour more fuel on the flames, invest more time and energy and resources into making it a success or keeping its success going. But if five or six weeks go by and, despite renewed efforts by the publisher, nothing much is happening in terms of sales, then it's pretty much over. It has six weeks to take off or die.

While the six-week rule applies as a general principle, in practice sales patterns vary a good deal from one type of book to another and, indeed, from one book to another. Publishers are finely attuned to the differences. New fiction tends to match closely the six-week rule, even for successful books – the spike will be much higher for the successful books but the shape of the curve will be broadly similar. Bill runs his eyes down a printout of sales figures: 'Take this book by [PB]; he's one of our really big authors. We've sold about 280,000 copies gross of that book – we've done great with this book. But if you look at this you'll see here's week one. OK, B&N sold 9,200 copies. Then – this is typical – it drops almost in half in week two. And then it starts to gradually go down. So in the sixth week, which is right here, it sold 2,000. So from nine to two in six weeks. By week nine it's at 700 copies, and then it's down to 443 by week eleven.' And that was a very successful book – 280,000 gross is a very strong sale for a hardcover fiction title. This was a new book by a known author who has an established readership, so the sales pattern is both strong and predictable, but still short-lived.

New fiction by an unknown or little-known author will typically display the same pattern of rapid decline but the figures will be much lower overall. 'General fiction right now is one of the hardest categories to break out in,' explained one marketing manager at a large house. 'We're selling a lot fewer books,' he continued, and it's getting harder and harder to build the book and get them to break out beyond a small circle of readers. Whereas 10–20 years ago a large publisher might ship out 10,000–15,000 copies of a new novel by an unknown writer and sell 6,000–10,000 net, now they're more likely to ship 5,000–6,000 and sell perhaps 3,000–4,000 – in any case well below 10,000. And at that level of sales, questions will be asked in a large house about whether it's worth their while to continue publishing books of this kind, given the amount of time and energy they take up and given the need to meet budget targets without significantly increasing the number of titles going through the system.

So why has it become harder to break out new fiction? No doubt there are many factors that underlie this trend, but there are two that are probably of paramount importance. One is that the publishing industry – the big corporate publishing houses together with the retail chains – have become very good at building brand-name authors and increasing the sales of each new book by the big-name commercial fiction writers, and this is crowding out the market. 'It used to be you could find space for new fiction; now it's hard,' explained a sales analyst at one large New York house. 'More big authors, commercial fiction writers – James Patterson used to do two books a year; now he's doing six, plus a children's book. He's crowding out the space.' Another factor is the decline of the independent bookstores. The independents were traditionally very good at building books – books that would start small and build slowly, thanks in part to the support they would get from independent booksellers who, if they liked a book, would get behind it, make it a 'staff pick', hand-sell it and continue to display it in a window or on a table despite the fact that the book might only be ticking over modestly. 'Independents were the bastion for building books,' the sales analyst continued. 'But as independents keep getting smaller and smaller as a base, that is not really happening any more. Barnes & Noble and Borders have their discovery programmes, things like that, but they're not working at the level that independents used to do in terms of loving and building an author or building a book.'

With non-fiction the decline is generally less dramatic than it is with fiction – the sales are still strongest in the first three to four weeks, 'but then,' explained Bill, 'even after week 12, it could still be selling a third of what it sold initially, not 10 per cent.' Bill scans the spreadsheet until his eyes settle on a non-fiction title – 'OK, here's a good example of a non-fiction book that starts off slow and then starts gaining momentum. B&N sell only 355 in their first week. Then it jumped three times that. Then it jumped again. So by week four it's up to 1,250. So it's climbing and then it gets to a point and starts to slow down a little bit. So that's non-fiction. On fiction you wouldn't get that. Fiction is more predictable.'

The bunching of sales in the first few weeks has become more accentuated over time. If you were to take a general non-fiction book without front-of-store promotion and look at its sales pattern ten years ago, you would find – explained a sales analyst who makes it his business to model these things – that around 30 per cent of the sales would take place in the first four weeks. 'Now it's 42 per cent in the first four weeks,' he explained, showing me the graph on his computer screen, 'and that's without promotion.' If you add in pro-motion, the percentage will be higher because the first week sales will be higher. Ten years ago, the first week would not be the biggest week. Now it is, whether the book has front-of-store promotion or not. 'The reality is that because of all the pent-up demand for the pre-sale, your first week is your biggest week in most cases. And if the book is being promoted by front-of-store promotion in the store, it's by far your biggest week.'

Prior to publication, the sales analyst does a sales forecast for each of their big books – 'what we call the A titles' – which represent about 10 per cent of the books published by his company in any one year. For each A title he maps out how many copies they're expecting to ship into each channel and to each key retailer in each channel, and how many copies they're expecting them to sell, and then they compare this forecast to what actually happens. Each title will have its own distinctive profile, depending on what kind of book it is, who the author is and how they expect it to perform in the different retail sectors. They have generic models – literary fiction will typically display one pattern, romance fiction another, serious current affairs another, and so on. But regardless of the type of book, one overall trend is clear: 'What's happening over time every year is that it's getting steeper and steeper,' says the analyst, referring to the curve of the graph which shows sales by week following the date of publica-tion. 'What this means is that we're getting more sales concentrated in the first couple of weeks. And that is especially true for any of what you could call commercial books.'

Of course, there are always the exceptions. Most books will follow the typical patterns and match the curves of the analyst's graphs pretty closely, though the volume of sales will vary greatly from title to title. But there will always be some titles that fail to conform. For example, there are some titles that this analyst calls 'the tipping books', meaning 'books that trend up'. These you can't really model in advance, because part of what makes them a tipping book is that something happens out there – it could be a publicity break or some other trigger – that gives them a boost so they 'really sort of ignite and unexpectedly take off'. Many of the books that turn out to be bestsellers fall into this category: the publisher, the editor, the sales and marketing directors, all may have thought that the book would do pretty well, but no one really thought it would become the runaway success it turned out to be. '[Y] is a good example,' says the analyst, picking one well-known non-fiction bestseller from their list. 'It shouldn't have been that big. You know, we started out with 70 [thousand] and everyone says, "This book is going to be pretty good." But no one was sitting there saying, "We'll be at a million." We're now well over a million, closer to two.'

So what is it that makes a book take off, break out of the normal patterns and turn into an unexpected success? Of course, there is no single, simple answer to this question – if there were, some publishers would be a lot richer and more successful than they are. There are many different drivers that can transform the fate of particular books. In some cases they kick in early and propel a book straight on to the bestseller lists, which immediately gives the book high visibility in a crowded marketplace, as happened with books like *The Da Vinci Code* and *The Historian*. In other cases a book may not take off in the initial hardcover edition but may build more slowly in trade paperback, getting taken up by book clubs across the country and eventually snowballing into something big. A good example would be Kim Edwards's *The Memory Keeper's Daughter*, a book that did moderately well in the original hardback edition for a first novel but really took off as a trade paperback, selling more than 2.5 million copies in the US alone. Similarly, while Khaled Hosseini's *The Kite Runner* did well in the original hardback edition for a first novel, it was really the trade paperback edition that took off, selling more than 4 million in the US. A book that might be deemed a modest success or even a failure in the original cloth edition can break out in a subsequent trade paperback edition, thanks in part to the book clubs and an interest that may be spread largely by word of mouth.

While there are many different drivers that can 'tip' a book and help turn it into a runaway success, there is one driver that has been perhaps more significant than any other single factor today: it can be picked by Oprah, or, in the case of the UK, by Richard and Judy.

The Oprah effect

There is nothing quite like Oprah or Richard and Judy when it comes to triggering an upsurge in sales. A book that might be trundling along in relative obscurity will suddenly acquire a kind of prominence and visibility that publicists could imagine only in their wildest dreams. 'It's almost too terrifying to contemplate what our industry would look like in her absence,' said one publicity manager at a major US house, reflecting on the significance of Oprah. 'If you actually went back and looked at the numbers over the past three years and just took out the *Oprah* selections and all the books that were featured in *Oprah*, our business would probably decline by 15 per cent. She's had that much impact.'

The Oprah Book Club began in 1996 as a regular feature of *The Oprah Winfrey Show*.[8] In the first few years Oprah selected roughly a book a month to discuss on her show, usually with the author present, though the number declined from 2001 on. In 2003 she began to include some classic books in her selections, picking Steinbeck's *East of Eden* in 2003 and Tolstoy's *Anna Karenina* in 2004. The books picked by Oprah invariably experienced a huge surge in sales. Steinbeck's novel, 51 years old when it was picked by Oprah, immediately shot to the top of the *New York Times* paperback fiction bestseller list and remained there for seven weeks. Similarly, when it was announced at the end of March 2007 that Cormac McCarthy's *The Road* would be the next book in the Oprah Book Club, it went straight onto the paperback fiction bestseller list and remained there for 19 weeks.

We can see the Oprah effect very clearly if we track the sales of a book like Elie Wiesel's *Night* – a harrowing account of the Holocaust based on Weisel's own experiences as a young Jewish boy who was sent with his family to Auschwitz and Buchenwald following the German invasion of Hungary in 1944. Originally published in Paris by a small French publisher in 1958, the book was translated into English and published by Hill & Wang in 1960 – Arthur Wang paid an advance of $100 and the book sold just over 1,000 copies

---

[8] See Cecilia Konchar Farr, *Reading Oprah: How Oprah's Book Club Changed the Way America Reads* (Albany, N.Y.: State University of New York Press, 2005); Kathleen Rooney, *Reading with Oprah: The Book Club That Changed America*, 2nd edn (Fayetteville, Ark.: University of Arkansas Press, 2008).

in the first 18 months. The book went on to establish itself as an important text on the Holocaust and was read in classrooms alongside Anne Frank's diary. Sales were boosted by the release of a mass-market paperback edition by Bantam in 1982 and the award of the Nobel Peace Prize to Wiesel in 1986. By the early 2000s, Night was selling 2,000–3,000 copies a week in the US and was a solid backlist title. However, when Oprah announced on 16 January 2006 that she had chosen Night for her Book Club, sales soared. Table 12 and figure 7 chart the sales in the run-up to and the aftermath of the Oprah pick. Sales of the mass-market paperback in late 2005 and the first two weeks of 2006 fluctuated between 1,500 and 4,000 copies per week. In January 2006 Hill & Wang issued a new trade paperback edition with a new translation and a new preface by the author and with the Oprah Book Club logo on the cover. Sales in the week ending 22 January 2006 – the week Oprah announced that she had picked the book – were around 140,000 (11,845 copies of the mass-market paperback together with 127,325 copies of the new trade paperback edition, though bear in mind that the BookScan data will underrepresent the mass-market sales, since BookScan doesn't have access to sales data from Wal-Mart, Sam's Club and some other outlets where mass-market books are sold); this was a 36-fold increase on the sales in the previous week. Night jumped immediately to number one on the New York Times bestseller list for paperback non-fiction, pushing James Frey's A Million Little Pieces – another Oprah pick – into the number two slot. Wiesel's book remained number one for 24 weeks, and remained on the New York Times bestseller list for a further 56 weeks until September 2007, by which time Hill & Wang had sold more than 1.250 million copies of the trade paperback. Oprah's choice catapulted a stable backlist title into a runaway bestseller.

So what explains Oprah's unique role in the publishing industry? Why do her book selections have so much more impact than other forms of media coverage? Four reasons stand out. First and foremost, she has established a bond of trust with her viewers. They have come to trust her selections as a reliable guide, a trustworthy source of advice about which books are worth their money and, above all, their time. Faced with the bewildering array of books to choose from, a limited amount of money to spend and many competing demands on their time, many readers are looking for guidance: they are happy to turn to what they see as a trusted and disinterested source of advice to help them choose. Oprah is a trusted cultural intermediary whose selections reduce complexity in a saturated marketplace.

Table 12   The Oprah effect: US weekly paperback sales for Elie Wiesel's *Night*, October 2005–April 2006

Week ending (d/m/y)	Mass-market paperback	Trade paperback	Total paperback
2/10/2005	3,842		
9/10/2005	2,807		
16/10/2005	3,330		
23/10/2005	2,682		
30/10/2005	2,442		
6/11/2005	2,540		
13/11/2005	2,641		
20/11/2005	2,508		
27/11/2005	1,617		
4/12/2005	3,484		
11/12/2005	2,160		
18/12/2005	1,907		
25/12/2005	1,865		
1/1/2006	1,555		
8/1/2006	2,895		
15/1/2006	3,841		
22/1/2006	11,845	127,325	139,170
29/1/2006	9,881	86,688	96,569
5/2/2006	6,519	62,211	68,730
12/2/2006	4,643	44,391	49,034
19/2/2006	3,822	35,352	39,174
26/2/2006	4,171	34,015	38,186
5/3/2006	2,970	25,081	28,051
12/3/2006	3,171	23,819	26,990
19/3/2006	2,673	23,343	26,016
26/3/2006	3,018	23,636	26,654
2/4/2006	2,517	19,951	22,468
9/4/2006	2,387	17,492	19,879
23/4/2006	1,641	12,445	14,086
30/4/2006	1,967	14,997	16,964

Source: Nielsen BookScan.

Given the importance of the relationship of trust between Oprah and her viewers, it is not surprising that Oprah should have reacted so negatively to the disclosure that James Frey's *A Million Little Pieces* – which was selected by Oprah in September 2005 and quickly soared to number one on the *New York Times* bestseller list for

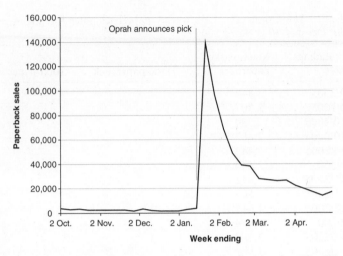

Figure 7   The Oprah effect: US weekly paperback sales for Elie Wiesel's *Night*, October 2005–April 2006
Source: Nielsen BookScan.

paperback non-fiction – contained numerous fabrications. Oprah invited Frey back on her show in January 2006 to confront the allegations and grilled him angrily. 'It's difficult for me to talk to you, because I really feel duped,' she told him. 'But more importantly, I feel that you betrayed millions of readers.' Oprah was riled because she knew very well that readers could feel disappointed and even betrayed not only by Frey but by her too, since her standing as a reliable and trustworthy guide was called into question by her selection of a book that was presented as a memoir and turned out to be laced with falsehoods. In relationships based on trust (even when these are mediated relationships), there is nothing more threatening than actions that could be perceived as betrayals.

The second feature of Oprah that makes her selections so influential is that she gets behind books, expresses strong opinions about them and emphasizes their transformative power. 'Oprah is all about opinions,' said one publicity director. 'Oprah is all about "this book changed my life, it's going to change your life too." She's always been very public about the impact that books have had on her life, how they changed her life, how they made her a better person, how they opened up worlds for her. And you'll hear booksellers say that what she did for our industry is she brought a whole new customer into the store. People who hadn't read before, people who'd never been in a bookstore before, came in looking for the way to Oprah's Book Club selection.' The way Oprah discusses books – expressing strong opinions about them and emphasizing their capacity to make you think about and even change your life – is very different from the way that other TV shows, like the *Today Show* and *Good Morning America*, tend to present books. 'They're part of news divisions,' explained the publicity director. 'They're not allowed to come in and say, "Hey, you know, I love this book."'

The third feature that makes Oprah so influential is that her selections are tied in to the growth of reading groups. Reading groups are not new but they have grown substantially in number over the last decade or so.[9] According to one estimate there are now 20 million members of book clubs in the US, a number that has doubled over the last eight years. Many of these book clubs are loose associations of individuals who get together from time to time to socialize and discuss books they have all read. Some are linked to bookstores that provide places for readers to gather, recommending books, hosting readings and other author events and even functioning as a kind of community centre in some small towns and rural communities. The books selected by Oprah are often adopted by reading groups, and Oprah actively encourages the formation of book clubs with guidelines on 'How to start a book club' posted on her website. Books that become popular among reading groups can take on a life of their own, growing in popularity as they become talked about in the loosely networked worlds of the reading groups.

A fourth feature of Oprah that gives her selections such power in the marketplace is that the brand operates as a mark of distinction that singles out a small handful of books and classifies them as members of an exclusive club. This mark of distinction is then recycled continuously in the marketplace. The books are reprinted with the official insignia of Oprah's Book Club on the cover and they benefit from special promotions in bookstores and retail chains. The more crowded the marketplace becomes and the more perplexing the range of choices faced by the consumer, the more significance this mark of distinction acquires as a means of increasing visibility and reducing complexity.

---

[9] See Jenny Hartley, *The Reading Groups Book*, 2002–3 edn (Oxford: Oxford University Press, 2002).

In the UK, the Richard and Judy Book Club shared many features in common with Oprah's Book Club. In some ways modelled on Oprah, the Richard and Judy Book Club began in 2004 and, over an eight-week period leading up to the British book awards in March, they would discuss one book each week, bringing in a celebrity or two to chat about the book and usually including a clip of some ordinary people talking about what they felt about the book. Unlike Oprah's Book Club, Richard and Judy actively solicited suggestions from publishers, who were invited to submit up to five books per imprint. Although Richard and Judy never explicitly stated the selection criteria, it was implicitly understood by publishers that they were looking for books that were neither highbrow literary works nor mass-market commercial fiction but rather – as one manager centrally involved in the Richard and Judy Book Club put it – 'that middle ground of really good, challenging books'. The Book Club was very much oriented to the kinds of books that would be of interest to reading groups, 'i.e. with lots of discussion points, lots of topics for elaborating upon within a programme and digging out and taking up the issues within the books'. Following the success of the Book Club, Richard and Judy introduced a second series of Summer Reads which ran from July until the end of August.

As with Oprah, the books selected by Richard and Judy typically experienced a huge surge in sales. One British publisher who had a book on the first Richard and Judy list recalled how astonished he was by the speed and size of the impact:

We had a book on the first list – it had just been published in paperback, and the expectation was that it would sell about 25,000 altogether, which is not bad, not great. It had sold 14,000 at the time it was picked. You know, they have celebrities talking about the book on the programme, and that was the moment you suddenly saw something very extraordinary happening: the book went straight to number one on Amazon. I think Amazon bought every copy we had left. That was the paperback. The hardback had been published a year before and there were around 300 copies left in the warehouse, and that went to number two on Amazon within the next ten minutes. And we couldn't keep it in print, we simply couldn't keep it in print, because nobody knew what this phenomenon was, so we reprinted 10,000. By the time the programme where they choose the winner went out, which is about a month and a half, two months later, it had sold 620,000. So the effect on the balance sheet was huge.

By 2008 the Richard and Judy Book Club was accounting for 26 per cent of the sales of the top 100 books in the UK.[10]

Oprah and Richard and Judy are prime examples of what I shall call 'recognition triggers'. I use the term 'recognition trigger' to refer to those drivers of sales that have three characteristics. First, they are triggers based on a form of recognition that endows the work with an *accredited visibility*. Thanks to this recognition, the work is now both *visible*, picked out from an ocean of competing titles and brought into the consciousness of consumers, and *deemed to be worthy of being read*, that is, worth not only the money that the consumer would have to pay to buy it but, just as importantly, the time they would have to spend to read it. Visible and worthy: a form of recognition that kills two birds with one stone.

The second characteristic is that the recognition is bestowed by individuals or organizations other than the agents and organizations that are directly involved in creating, producing and selling the work. Literary agents, publishers and booksellers cannot produce the kind of recognition upon which recognition triggers depend. They can produce other things, like the buzz and excitement that surround an author or a book, and these forms of laudatory talk can have real consequences, as we have seen. But recognition triggers presuppose that those individuals or organizations who bestow the recognition are, and are seen to be, independent in some way and to some extent from the parties that have a direct economic interest in the book's success. It is this *independence and perception of independence* that enables recognition triggers to grant worthiness and explains in part why they can have such dramatic effects.

The third characteristic is that, precisely because recognition is bestowed by individuals and organizations that are independent and seen to be so, it follows that publishers themselves have only a limited ability to influence the decisions that result in the bestowal of recognition, and hence a limited ability to control their effects. They certainly try to influence these decisions where they can, or to second-guess the decision-makers where they can't directly or indirectly influence them, but at the end of the day the decisions are not theirs. So recognition triggers introduce yet another element of unpredictability into a field that is already heavily laden with serendipity.

---

[10] *Sunday Times*, 15 June 2008.

While Oprah and Richard and Judy are one kind of recognition trigger that has become increasingly important in the field of trade publishing (and probably the most important today in terms of the scale of its effects), they are not the only kind. There are others, stemming from different forms of recognition – each has its own specific characteristics, its own array of agents and organizations, its own hierarchies and its own typical patterns of sales effects. Book prizes are another form of recognition that plays an important role in the field of trade publishing, especially for certain kinds of books, such as literary fiction and serious non-fiction.[11] Of course, winning prizes is important in and for itself: it adds symbolic value to every individual and organization associated with the book – to the author above all, but also to the agent and the publishing house. But winning a major prize, even appearing on the short list for a prize, can also have a direct impact on the sales of the book, as publishers and editors know only too well. 'The Booker shortlist was the one thing that could turn a sow's ear into a silk purse,' recalled one British publisher. 'Get on the Booker shortlist and you could sell another 25,000 copies just by being on the shortlist. And if you won it you could sell possibly another 200,000 copies.'

Another kind of recognition trigger is the movie adaptation. 'There's one thing that is almost as good as Oprah for a book,' said a sales analyst at a large US publishing house, 'and that is when it becomes a movie. People want to be told what to buy and a movie is an imprimatur. A book that becomes a movie has been selected by someone as worthy of being made into a movie. Even if the movie has been trashed and didn't do well, sales of the book go through the roof.' The figures bear out his view. *Angels and Demons* was the second of Dan Brown's books to be turned into a movie, although the book had actually been published three years before *The Da Vinci Code*. First published in hardcover in 2000, *Angels and Demons* had been available in a mass-market paperback edition since 2001 and as a trade paperback since 2006. It enjoyed a long spell on the *New York Times* bestseller list for paperback fiction between 2003 and 2006, remaining there for 148 weeks. By early 2008, however, sales of both the mass-market and trade paperback editions had fallen off considerably and the book had become a solid but unex-

---

[11] For an excellent account of the rise of prizes in literature and the arts, see James F. English, *The Economy of Prestige: Prizes, Awards, and the Circulation of Cultural Value* (Cambridge, Mass.: Harvard University Press, 2005).

ceptional backlist title, selling between 1,000 and 2,000 copies a week in the mass-market edition and less than 1,000 copies a week as a trade paperback. The release of the movie in May 2009 gave the book a second wind. A typical Hollywood blockbuster starring Tom Hanks, the movie got mixed reviews but did reasonably well at the box office, taking the top slot on the first weekend in the US, 15–17 May 2009, and grossing over $120 million domestically in its first month. Table 13 and figure 8 track the sales of the paperback

Table 13   The movie effect I: US weekly paperback sales for Dan Brown's *Angels and Demons*, January–July 2009

Week ending (d/m/y)	Trade paperback	Mass-market paperback	Trade paperback movie tie-in	Mass-market paperback movie tie-in	Total paperback
4/1/2009	987	3,672			4,659
11/1/2009	904	2,711			3,615
18/1/2009	887	2,418			3,305
25/1/2009	712	2,263			2,975
1/2/2009	843	2,463			3,306
8/2/2009	1,942	5,060			7,002
15/2/2009	1,937	5,306			7,243
22/2/2009	1,553	5,648			7,201
1/3/2009	1,612	5,360			6,972
8/3/2009	1481	4,628			6,109
15/3/2009	1,463	5,074			6,537
22/3/2009	1,324	4,928			6,252
29/3/2009	1,683	6,138	3,816	3,662	15,299
5/4/2009	1,274	4,252	9,814	13,086	28,426
12/4/2009	1,036	3,082	9,486	15,756	29,360
19/4/2009	1,074	3,202	9,527	14,125	27,928
26/4/2009	1,557	4,321	12,260	18,128	36,266
3/5/2009	1,741	4,559	12,477	17,927	36,704
10/5/2009	2,151	5,407	14,442	20,339	42,339
17/5/2009	2,268	6,355	17,133	24,064	49,820
24/5/2009	2,123	5,713	14,685	21,295	43,816
31/5/2009	1,595	4,514	10,912	16,526	33,547
7/6/2009	1,249	3,512	7,409	12,248	24,418
14/6/2009	955	3,032	5,075	10,223	19,285
21/6/2009	936	3,220	4,367	9,796	18,319
28/6/2009	642	2,492	3,022	7,107	13,263
5/7/2009	535	2,152	2,286	5,854	10,827
12/7/2009	496	2,038	2,043	4,785	9,362
19/7/2009	416	1,755	1,764	4,182	8,117
26/7/2009	410	1,603	1,733	3,834	7,580

Source: Nielsen BookScan.

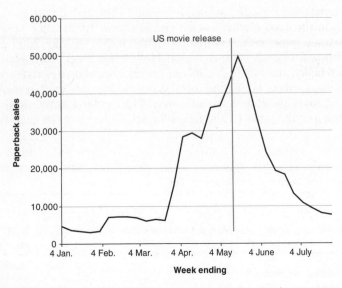

Figure 8   The movie effect I: US weekly paperback sales for Dan Brown's *Angels and Demons*, January–July 2009
Source: Nielsen BookScan.

editions of *Angels and Demons* in the period before and after the movie was released. Sales began to rise in February 2009, with interest stimulated by the advance publicity for the movie, and by the end of February *Angels and Demons* was back on the *New York Times* bestseller list for mass-market paperback fiction (again, the BookScan data will underrepresent the mass-market sales). In March 2009, Simon & Schuster brought out new movie tie-in editions of the book in both trade paperback and mass-market formats. By April sales had jumped to around 30,000 copies a week, and by the end of April *Angels and Demons* was now also on the *New York Times* bestseller list for trade paperback fiction. When the movie was released on 15 May, sales jumped to around 50,000 copies a week, and by 31 May the book was back in the number one spot on the *New York Times* bestseller list for mass-market paperback fiction. It remained on the mass-market paperback bestseller list for 20 weeks, and on the trade paperback bestseller list for nine weeks. In the six-month period leading up to and following the release of the film, *Angels and Demons* sold well over 500,000 copies in paperback –

more than five times the number of copies it sold in the whole of the previous year.

The movie effect is not restricted to thrillers and commercial fiction: even literary fiction displays a dramatic movie effect. Table 14 and figure 9 chart the sales of the paperback editions of Ian McEwan's *Atonement* in the period before and after the movie was released in the US in December 2007. *Atonement* has been available in paperback since 2003, when Anchor released a trade paperback edition. By early 2007 the book had settled into the pattern of a stable but modest backlist title, regularly selling between 1,000 and 2,000 copies a week. Once again, the movie changed all that. In November 2007 Anchor released a new trade paperback edition and in December they released a new mass-market paperback – both were movie tie-ins with pictures of the leading actor and actress, James McAvoy and Keira Knightley, on the covers. Sales began to climb in November, ahead of the movie's US release on 7 December. By Christmas the book was selling over 77,000 a week, including nearly 50,000 in the new trade edition and over 13,000 in the mass-market edition (again, these data will underrepresent the mass-market sales). By 20 January 2008 *Atonement* was number one on the *New York Times* bestseller list for trade paperback fiction, and ninth on the list for mass-market paperback fiction. It remained on the trade paperback fiction bestseller list for 26 weeks and on the mass-market bestseller list for 14 weeks. The movie was not a Hollywood blockbuster in the style of *Angels and Demons* but the sales uplift was just as marked, if not more so: more than 640,000 copies of *Atonement* were sold in the six months just before and following the release of the movie, nearly ten times more than the number of copies sold in the whole of 2006.

Although not as large and long-lasting as the uplift typically produced by an Oprah pick, the movie effect is impressive nonetheless. The Oprah effect tends to produce a huge and very sudden surge in sales that follows the announcement of the pick. Sales fall off quickly but they remain buoyant well into the future, as the book becomes integrated into the reading groups that rely on Oprah for their selection of reading material. The movie effect displays a somewhat different pattern: sales of the book begin to increase several weeks or even months before the movie is released, as publicity for the movie kicks in and booksellers increase their stock-holding of the book and begin to re-promote it. Sales increase again when the publisher releases the movie tie-in editions, typically in both trade paperback and mass-market formats. Sales then surge when the movie comes

Table 14   The movie effect II: US weekly paperback sales for Ian McEwan's *Atonement*, September 2007–March 2008

Week ending (d/m/y)	Trade paperback	Trade paperback movie tie-in	Mass-market paperback movie tie-in	Total paperback
2/9/2007	1,647			
9/9/2007	1,643			
19/9/2007	1,440			
23/9/2007	1,584			
30/9/2007	1,774			
7/10/2007	1,871			
14/10/2007	2,084			
28/10/2007	2,258			
4/11/2007	2,439			
11/11/2007	2,613	3,143		5,756
18/11/2007	2,407	4,436		6,843
25/11/2007	2,549	5,275		7,824
2/12/2007	2,462	5,817	2,161	10,440
9/12/2007	5,928	14,589	5,431	25,948
16/12/2007	10,615	30,019	9,054	49,688
23/12/2007	14,267	49,066	13,746	77,079
30/12/2007	8,700	33,678	11,179	53,557
6/1/2008	7,098	27,696	9,867	44,661
13/1/2008	6,131	21,885	9,848	37,864
20/1/2008	6,004	23,093	10,477	39,574
27/1/2008	5,492	21,395	8,681	35,568
3/2/2008	4,530	18,515	8,146	31,191
10/2/2008	4,069	14,860	7,196	26,125
17/2/2008	3,730	13,629	7,235	24,594
24/2/2008	3,601	11,505	6,605	21,711
2/3/2008	3,326	10,730	6,539	20,595
9/3/2008	2,855	8,359	5,545	16,759
16/3/2008	2,866	8,624	5,338	16,828
23/3/2008	3,284	9,630	6,239	19,153
30/3/2008	2,716	7,102	3,963	13,781

Source: Nielsen BookScan.

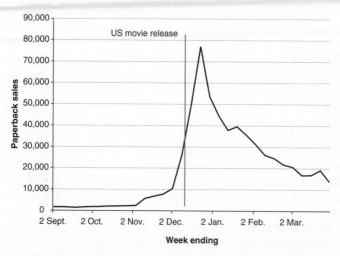

Figure 9   The movie effect II: US weekly paperback sales for Ian McEwan's *Atonement*, September 2007–March 2008
Source: Nielsen BookScan.

out, typically peaking a week or so after the movie's release, and then gradually fall off. Like the Oprah Book Club, the movie raises the book and the author to an altogether different plane of public visibility, catapulting a book from relative obscurity, or from a quiet life on the backlist, onto the paperback bestseller lists and turning the author into a name with recognition value, if he or she doesn't have it already.

While the sales uplifts produced by these various recognition triggers are hugely significant in terms of driving sales and tipping books into bestsellers, they are also quite unpredictable from the viewpoint of the publisher. Publishers can and do try to second-guess the decision-makers and tailor some of their publishing in the hope that it will be selected for the kind of book club or prize that can make a real difference to sales – this was probably easier to do with Richard and Judy than with Oprah. 'The folks in Chicago [where the Oprah Book Club is based] are very guarded about how the book club operates,' said a publicity manager in a New York house; 'You can't pitch the book – they're not receptive.' On the other hand, with Richard and Judy publishers were invited to submit books and a great deal of behind the scenes activity went into trying to influence the selection process. 'There is so much kind of lobbying and pressurizing and clever tactics used to get on Richard and Judy that actually the idea that a book has been plucked out of obscurity and ended up on Richard and Judy is a great kind of media story but actually it's not really the truth,' explained one British publisher. 'We all know people, we've all made it our business to know people. We all make sure that we are singing from the same hymn sheet, that we're all saying the same things. We agree beforehand which books we're going to enter into Richard and Judy, and these are the ones that we do the lunching and the schmoozing and all the rest of it for. You hand-pick those.' Nevertheless, while publishers, marketing managers and publicists could try to influence the Richard and Judy picks by carefully selecting the books they submitted and making sure they were all singing from the same hymn sheet when they pitched them to the club, there was still a large element of unpredictability, since the final selections were made without input from publishers. You could choose books that seemed to match closely the aims of the show and make a good pitch but, at the end of the day, the selection committee could simply pass over your books and pick someone else's, for reasons entirely outside your control.

Given the importance of the Richard and Judy Book Club for stimulating book sales in the UK, it's not surprising that many in the publishing industry watched the demise of the televised show with apprehension and dismay. In August 2008 the contract with Channel 4 – a major terrestrial broadcaster – came to an end and Richard and Judy moved to UKTV's new digital network Watch. Viewing figures on the new channel were much lower: on Channel 4 they had up to 2.5 million viewers, but on Watch they had 200,000 for the first show and 53,000 for the second; the figures fell to as low as 11,000 for subsequent shows. In May UKTV announced that the *Richard and Judy* show would end in July 2009, six months before the end of the contract, because of poor ratings. Just as British publishers had to cope with the demise of the *Richard and Judy* show, so too American publishers are now having to come to terms with life after Oprah's Book Club, which ended its 15-year run on 25 May 2011. The kind of visibility that these shows were able to give to books and authors by featuring them on mainstream television will be greatly missed by publishers, though they may find some consolation in the fact that new shows with smaller audiences either have appeared or are likely to appear on more specialized networks: Amanda Ross, the independent producer responsible for the original Richard and Judy Book Club, launched *The TV Book Club* on More 4 in January 2010, and

Oprah has said that she plans to develop a show for books and authors on OWN, the new Oprah Winfrey Network.

Rising returns

One consequence of a marketplace dominated by large retail chains where the window of opportunity for most books is small (and getting smaller) is the escalating level of returns. 'Today no one wants to own inventory,' observed one sales manager who has been in the business for 30 years, starting off as a bookseller in New York. 'When I was a bookseller you had an assortment on the shelves and your turn rates were important but it was important that you had certain sections of the store and that you were maintaining a selection for the odd browser or passer-by. Now no one wants to own inventory for more than 12 weeks; back then it was six months. So the industry has speeded up. This is a slow industry in a fast world and that's a wrenching change.'

For most large trade publishers, return rates today average around 30 per cent; that's probably around 5 per cent more than it was a decade ago. But this average figure doesn't tell you much because it conceals huge variations between different kinds of books and between different retailers. Backlist books generally have much lower return rates, generally in the low teens. So a publisher with a strong backlist will tend to have a lower average return rate. Children's books also tend to have a lower return rate. But for frontlist adult hardcovers the return rate probably averages around 45 per cent. 'And probably that would be a plus or minus 15 per cent – you know, 30 to 65 per cent is probably standard,' explained one sales analyst. 'The books that don't work get 60 per cent returns; the books that work tend to get 30. The market basically wants to ship to about 35 to 40 per cent.' That means that for every 100 new hardcovers shipped out, somewhere between 30 and 60 will come back to the publisher as returns. The publisher will build into the P&L for each new book a write-down figure for returns – typically set at 30 or 35 per cent of gross sales.

The main retail channels deal with returns in different ways. Bill talks me through some of the typical practices. Although most new books will have six weeks to prove themselves, Barnes & Noble and Borders are pretty good about holding on to books beyond the six-week window. 'Barnes & Noble and Borders will really hang on to books, in most cases for probably three to four months, unless they bought way too many. If they bought, say, 25,000 copies of this book and it turned out after a month they sold 5,000, they'll call us and say, "Listen, I can't be sitting on 20,000 of this, it's tying up a lot money. We're paying 15 bucks for this. So I'm going to send you back 12,000, OK?" That gives them 5 plus 12 . . . 17 . . . that means they have about 8,000 in the stores. That's what they'll do. So they wouldn't wipe it out completely. But if it's a novel and it's really bombed, after three, four months – clean. They'll send it all back.'

The wholesale clubs like Costco work in different ways. 'They sell a shit load of books for the right book but they have the shortest window and they have strict guidelines for dollars.' Bill elaborates:

So if they bought this book and put in, say, 20,000 copies, and Costco's got 500 stores give or take, they put it in among their 500 stores, not evenly but depending on the store. And now they're selling this book for 40 per cent off 30 bucks, OK, so they sell it for $18. They have to sell $20,000 worth of the product per week, for the whole chain. So what happens if they don't sell $20,000 is they put it in sell-down. They'll usually keep it for about three weeks and if it doesn't sell they'll send it back. So when you make a decision to put a book into a club it's a very risky decision. I mean the decision's not risky for Patsy Cornwell or John Grisham because you know exactly what they can sell on that. But if you want to put a new author in there, or a new cookbook that they'd never had before, it's risky as hell, because if it doesn't work you get a ton of it back. You get 85 per cent of it, 90 per cent of it back. And that always takes time to go through. They have to send it back to the wholesaler, the wholesaler has to pack it and send it to you. That could take two months. And so if for some reason you need stock on that for other places, you can never get it in time. By the time it comes back you don't need it and you've got all these returns. So you've got to be careful. When you get the gross sale into a club you're excited as hell and then two months later you're really unhappy if it didn't work.

The rise of the mass merchandisers and warehouse clubs and their growing involvement in the book trade have made it possible for publishers to sell books in much higher quantities – together with the rise of the retail book chains, they have brought about the hardback revolution described in chapter 1. There are now many more outlets for books – Wal-Mart alone has 3,500 locations in the US, and with Target and the price clubs the number of mass-merchandise outlets for books has grown tremendously. 'But on the other hand,' says Bill, 'the people who are running those departments aren't book people; they tend to be retail people, the lowest-paid workers who don't really care about books. And so they bring in a whole bunch of books, they do the best they can showing them and then it's over. And so you're exposed with many more returns than you were 15 to 20 years ago. So it's good and bad – you're getting many more gross sales and you're getting many more net sales, but the return rate is going up because of that.'

Unless they are damaged, returned books will generally be put back in the publisher's warehouse. Some may be used to fulfil orders from another retailer but many – in some cases all – will eventually be remaindered. A typical sequence is this: first hardcover edition released in, say, April of one year; trade or mass-market paperback released in the following April; then six months after the paperback was released the hardcover returns will be remaindered and sold for $4.95 or $5.95 on the remainder tables in Barnes & Noble and elsewhere. 'You don't want to screw up your paperback so you'll hold off,' explains Bill. But if you can remainder the book it's better than pulping everything because at least you'll get something back – 'You might get a buck and a half for that, so it helps at least to print the thing.' If the returns are high it may make sense to pulp half or more before they remainder it – 'We'll just eat it,' says Bill, because the remainder buy you get is based on how many you have. The more copies you have, the less your buy. 'So you can get a better price per unit if you don't have quite as many. And plus you don't want to have so many out there. So we'll do that on some of the biggies.'

High returns are costly for publishers. Not only is a great deal of time and money wasted in packing up and shipping books that are never sold, and then packing up and returning them to the publisher's warehouse, but printing books that are eventually pulped is wasteful and expensive, and the cost of writing off unsold stock goes directly to the publisher's bottom line, depressing still further a profit margin already under pressure. So what can publishers do about it? Short of a fundamental reform of the supply chain and of the terms on which books are sold to the trade, there are two things that publishers can do – and most of the large trade publishers are doing these things to some extent.

First, they can try to improve supply chain capabilities so that they minimize the impact of the inherent uncertainty of the market. 'Taken to the logical extreme,' explained the COO (chief operating officer) of one large trade house, 'if there were zero replenishment time when a book is sold in a retail shop, if you could print it and have it back on the shelf right away, then most of this problem would go away. Well, we can't. That being said, we've made efforts to speed up the process and reduce the time it takes to order and receive a reprint. So it used to be that, you know, five to seven days would be considered a fast reprint, and we've gotten that down to three or four days depending on certain conditions. So that buys people a couple of days and lets the publishers put off making certain decisions until they have more information. We're trying to make the distribution process faster to again shave off a couple of days.' The faster the publisher is able to reprint, the less need there is to print large quantities in the first place; they can afford to print more cautiously, hedging their bets and tying up less working capital in stock, in the knowledge that they can order and receive a reprint in a few days if necessary. And the faster the publisher is able to resupply the retailer, the less need there is for the retailer to order large quantities to begin with, since they know that if the book begins to take off and sell briskly they can resupply in time to meet ongoing demand. It is partly the fear of being out of stock and unable to resupply when demand is high that encourages retailers to overstock, and since all stock is returnable there is no penalty for doing so.

The second thing publishers can do is try to improve their information and forecasting capabilities, and use these capabilities to adjust their supply practices. The traditional practice in trade publishing is for sales and accounts managers to sell in new books, wait for the buyers to place their orders and then supply stock in the quantities ordered by the retailers. 'It's very much a push system,' said the COO, 'so we push all the inventory out there, we hope that someone will buy it, if they don't it all comes back, as opposed to much more of a pull system where we only put out what people want.' Of course, it's very difficult to figure out what people will want when you're dealing with a product like books – the uncertainty of demand is an inherent feature of trade publishing. But rather than relying largely or exclusively on retailers, whose orders are, in effect, their provisional assessments of potential demand, publishers can try to develop their own tools for assessing potential demand and use these to modify their supply practices.

Some trade publishers have created special units or departments to do just that. 'We invented a supply chain department a good three years ago,' explained Don, a sales analyst at one of the large publishing groups in New York. 'The purpose of that is to measure and understand our customer base and print wisely. The primary goal was to become more efficient, to reduce returns, and not to be left with lots of excess inventory at the end of the day.' They collect data from their customers, both retailers and wholesalers, load it into their data warehouse and use it to spin off various kinds of reports. 'So these days, compared to, say, five, ten years ago, we have a much, much better understanding of what's actually happening in the marketplace. And that in turn drives our decisions.'

What Don's team tries to do is to drill down below the level of what their primary customer, the retailer or wholesaler, thinks the demand is likely to be, so that they can form their own view of potential consumer demand and use this as a basis to evaluate the orders from retailers and wholesalers – to assess their assessments, as it were. 'In a big concept sense, it's seeing what's happening at the consumer level as opposed to our customer demand level. Because we've clearly seen that our customers are making their own decisions and those decisions are sometimes good, sometimes bad.' The traditional way that publishers have done business is to supply whatever their customers ask for – if the retailer or wholesaler wants it, the publisher supplies them. 'What we're doing differently now is we're saying, "Look guys, you don't need this," where our data supports this behavior.'

Don and his team have developed a variety of models for different kinds of books, for particular authors and for different retailers and retail channels – romance, mystery, celebrity biography, B&N, Borders, Amazon, mass merchandisers, institutional, etc. – and they use these to try to forecast the sales patterns of specific new books in different retail outlets. He takes the example of a biography of a well-known movie star they published recently. It was a big book, one of their lead titles. They put out 125,000 copies and it went straight on to the bestseller lists in week one. Their customers immediately came back and reordered, but the assessment of Don and his team was that the shelf-life of this book would be short and demand had peaked, so they decided not to reprint. They had some extra inventory which they allocated in what they felt was a fair and sensible way. 'So even though some of our customers were crying for more, we turned it off. As it turned out, the sell-through was pretty good because it followed the forecasted curve for a celebrity biography.' They knew that the window for this kind of book is typically very short and that they would be getting returns early on, so they could plan to use returns to fulfil some reorders, thereby reducing the risks that would be involved in doing a quick reprint.

Of course, this isn't going to work for all books – 'It depends on the book, on the genre and on the market obviously; you have to look at each book and you can't paint any broad generalizations.' Don accepts that there are going to be some cases where it makes good sense to use the traditional distribution model. 'There are times when you'll accept a higher return rate on a book because you're rolling the dice. You want to give it a chance. So on some books you're going to say, "OK, we'll accept it, we might have a huge success with it, it's hard to tell right now," and so you're going in with your eyes open. You have to take risks in business.' But there are other books where the distributions are small and most of the sales are going through Amazon and other online retailers or through specialist bookshops and yet some customers are ordering 200 or 300 copies and distributing them to a few stores, where they sit on shelves, spine out, and then come back with 85 per cent return rates. 'And so looking at that we might say, "OK guys, don't buy these 200 books, we'll supply them to you if you're dot.com sales," because dot.com are our niche customers and we don't want to turn that off.'

While developing models to try to predict consumer demand and second-guess the retailers can provide publishers with an effective set of tools to try to reduce returns and combat the inefficiencies of the supply chain, it also has risks of its own. You might well lose some sales by dint of the fact that books are not available in key outlets when demand is high, and might even prevent a book from taking off by precipitously shutting down the supply chain. 'The complexity here', said one COO who spends a lot of his time working on this problem, 'is that no one knows exactly how many books you have to have on hand at retail in order to sell more books. So in other words, if you put one in a store it probably gets lost and you don't sell any, unless someone happens to be looking for that specific book. If you put 30 up in the front it kind of says, you know, "Hey look at me," and there's marketing value in that. And no one knows exactly – you know, if you put in 30 you sell 20, if you put in 20 you sell 2. No one knows exactly how that math works.' Given this uncertainty, there are many voices in the publishing houses that will argue in favour of shipping out more rather than less, on the grounds that the more visible and plentiful the book is in the retail spaces, the more it is likely to sell. Moreover, all the large trade publishers are under tremendous pressure to meet ambitious sales targets, which creates an additional incentive to ship out as many books as you can – an incentive that grows stronger as the end of the financial year draws near. The demand for year on year revenue growth tends to encourage the large trade publishers to maximize shipment and fulfil their customers' orders as quickly as they can, but high returns which put downward pressure on margins is the price paid for adhering to this traditional distribution model.

Improving supply chain capabilities and the ability to forecast consumer demand are important steps forward in the struggle to deal with the problem of returns, but they are really tinkering at the edges. 'The physical side of the business is as broken and inefficient today as it was 15 years ago,' commented one COO who joined a large house in the mid-1990s and has spent much of his time since then trying to deal with this problem. 'So in spite of the fact that there's much better technology and much better information, at the end of the day we still print millions of books that never leave the warehouse because there's not demand for them and ship out millions of books that come back and get pulped, so that whole cycle just doesn't work very well.' Given the current structures and established practices of the trade publishing business, there is no easy solution to this problem. This may be a problem that calls for a more radical reform, such as moving to a policy of firm sales for higher discount, at least for a certain range of titles. There have been some attempts to experiment with reforms of this kind, though how successful and widespread they will become, in an industry that has become deeply wedded to a distribution model based on the possibility of returns, remains to be seen.

— 8 —

THE WILD WEST

Up till now we have been analysing trade publishing in a general way, drawing examples from both the US and the UK. There are good grounds for doing so: if my argument is sound, the field of English-language trade publishing has a certain 'logic' or dynamic that applies equally to Britain and the US, as the two main centres of English-language trade publishing. But while the same logic applies to both and many of the same publishing corporations are active in both countries, there are important differences in the ways that trade publishing works in the US and the UK, and it is these differences that I want to examine in this chapter.

The logic of the field

Figure 10 summarizes the logic of the field of English-language trade publishing. As we've seen in previous chapters, three key developments – the growth of the retail chains, the rise of literary agents and the consolidation of publishing houses under the umbrellas of large corporations – have shaped the evolution of trade publishing in the English-speaking world since the 1960s. These three developments have created a field which has a certain structure and dynamic or 'logic'. It has led to the polarization of the field, with four or five large corporate groups occupying dominant positions and a large number of small independent publishing operations on the margins, while relatively few independent medium-sized publishers remain active in the field. It has led to a preoccupation with 'big books' which, in the web of collective belief that permeates the field, are regarded as potential bestsellers and, as a result, are able to command

1   Growth of retail chains

2   Rise of literary agents

3   Consolidation of publishing houses

1   Polarization of the field

2   Preoccupation with big books
    (i)   Track record
    (ii) Comps
    (iii) Platform
    (iv) Web of collective belief

3   Extreme publishing

4   Shrinking windows

5   High returns

Figure 10   The logic of the field

high advances in the market for content. Since for many books no one knows at the point of acquisition whether they will actually become bestsellers, those involved in the process of acquisition have to rely on other things in order to attach a value to an asset whose value is, at that stage, strictly unknowable. Typically they rely on four things: the author's track record, comparable books, the author's platform and the web of collective belief. The budgetary process of the large corporate publishers obliges them to focus a great deal of time and energy on closing the gap between the ground-up sales forecast based on books in the pipeline, on the one hand, and the corporation's expectations for growth and profitability, on the other, leading to an annual scramble for new books, and above all big books, which can be put together quickly and published fast – in other words, 'extreme publishing'. The growth of title output in the context of declining review space and consolidated retail outlets that charge a premium for front-of-store displays has shrunk the window of opportunity for new books, giving each new book less time to be noticed and make an impact and encouraging publishers to put more effort and resources behind those books that show early signs of success while giving up on those that don't. And the growing role of the big retail chains which order large quantities of new books and require them to turn over quickly, combined with the shrinking window of opportunity for each new book that is published, has helped to produce historically high levels of returns.

To describe this dynamic as the 'logic of the field' is not to say that the field is logical – there is much about this dynamic that could be regarded as illogical, irrational and inefficient, not to mention wasteful. The logic of the field is an analytical and explanatory concept, not a normative one. Nor is it to suggest that the 'logic' exists like some cold force of nature, a rigid and impersonal structure that determines the actions of individuals and operates independently of their will – this is not the sense that I'm giving to this term. The logic of the field, as I use this term here, is simply a summary way of describing the distinctive set of processes and preoccupations laid out in figure 10, a set of processes and preoccupations that interrelate in definite ways and that, taken together, create the context within which those who work in the field of English-language trade publishing – whether publishers, agents or booksellers – do what they do. It is a set of processes and preoccupations that is specific to this field – it is quite different from the processes that characterize the field of, say, scholarly book publishing, or the field of college textbook publishing. It is also a set of processes and preoccupations that has a certain self-referential, self-reinforcing character, in the sense that the key players in the field are locked together in a system of reciprocal interdependency such that the actions of each, pursuing what they perceive as their own interests (or those of their clients), tend to elicit a certain pattern of action from other players in the field. 'It's a system that sort of feeds on itself,' reflected one agent who, having been in the business for over 50 years, was inclined to take a long-term view. 'And it's a form of evolution. Though in this particular instance there is no intelligent design.'

Of course, not every player in the field, whether it is a publisher, an agent or a bookseller, is affected by these processes and preoccupations in the same way and to the same extent. Not every trade publisher works like a large corporation, most independents don't seek to acquire gap-filling books in the way that publishers in the large corporations do, innumerable 'small' books are still published (by corporate publishers as well as independents), some books turn out to be slow burners that languish during the initial six-week window of opportunity but then build more slowly over time, perhaps even becoming a bestseller despite their slow start, and so on. Trade publishing is an extremely diverse industry and there are countless exceptions to every rule. But to understand what has happened in the world of trade publishing we need to delve beneath the surface and bring out the basic structure and dynamic of the field. Grasping the logic will not enable us to explain everything that happens in the field; the world is always messier than our theories of it, and this maxim applies with particular force to the world of trade publishing, where there are many different players interacting with one another in diverse ways to produce a huge number of unique cultural objects, each launched into a marketplace where serendipity rules. But complexity does not mean that this world is without order.

The logic of the field is a dynamic in which some players are more fully implicated than others but from which no player is wholly excluded. Its effects are felt throughout the field, regardless of who you are and where you are positioned in the field. Of course, the large corporate publishers are implicated in this dynamic more than others, since their size – both in terms of their financial resources and their output – as well as their reputation places them in the centre of the field. But even a small independent publisher on the margins of the field is not entirely unaffected by this dynamic. The small independent may not be preoccupied with big books in the way that the large corporate publishers are and will not be obliged to 'mind the gap' in the way they must, but even the small indie press will feel the effects of these pressures in certain ways – for example, by being excluded from the submission lists of the most powerful agents or treated as a B-list or C-list client, or by losing one of their authors to a large house who is able to pay more. The logic of the field is not a set of rules that every player in the field must follow. It is more like the lines of force that structure a magnetic field: a strong magnet in one part of the field will exert its effects throughout the field. If you're small piece of metal on the margins it may not affect you very much, but in no part of the field will you be entirely shielded from its effects.

Once we understand the logic of the field it is much easier to make sense of things that happen in the world of trade publishing – things that might otherwise seem puzzling, if not bizarre. Take Randy Pausch's *The Last Lecture*: now, once we understand the logic, it all makes much more sense. Why would a publisher be willing to pay $6.75 million for a short book by a man who had never written a trade book before, and to do so on the basis of nothing more than a 15-page proposal and a video of his lecture? Remember that the auction is being held in October 2007, just after the corporate publishers have completed their budgeting process and are searching intensively for big books to plug the gap for 2008. This is a book that will be written very quickly (it has to be: the prognosis is not good), so it can be published in April 2008, early enough to make a big difference to 2008 sales if it does become a bestseller. Pausch is, in effect, a first-time author, so there is no track record to spoil the imagination: liberated from the tyranny of data, the sky is the limit. There is also a very good comparable title which the agent can liken it to: *Tuesdays with Morrie*, which was a huge bestseller in the late 1990s, selling more than 12 million copies. And it just so happens that the agent handling *The Last Lecture* is the very same agent who handled *Tuesdays with Morrie*, which enables him to cite this comp with some authority and gives more credibility to the idea that *The Last Lecture* will repeat the earlier success. The author, while certainly not a celebrity, has in fact acquired a rather significant platform in the short period since he gave his lecture, since the video of the lecture was posted on YouTube where it was viewed by 6 million people. He also appeared on CBS News, *Good Morning America* and the *Oprah Winfrey Show*, which not only gave him a high degree of visibility but also endowed him with the kind of trusted recognition that only Oprah can bestow, giving further credence to the view that this is a man who could write the kind of inspirational book that would have mass appeal, reaching people who are not regular book buyers, the kind of book that would lead Oprah and others to say, 'This is a book that changed my life.' Just as importantly, there was a great deal of buzz about this book, everyone in the know, scouts included, was talking about it and the words were being backed up by money, hype translated into buzz, as several of the big houses were willing to bid in the millions, thus creating an extensive and self-reaffirming web of collective belief that this book will become a bestseller and repeatedly raising the stakes for the parties who were willing to stay in the game.

The five publishers who were still in the bidding by the time it reached $5 million were all publishers owned by large corporations, since only they could afford to take risks at this level. The fact that Hyperion was willing to stay in the game and outbid the others in the end is not surprising: they are a frontlist-driven house, backed by the Disney Corporation and hugely dependent on publishing a small number of frontlist bestsellers in order to make their budget. They had also published two very successful books by Mitch Albom and they were taking his books, both *Tuesdays with Morrie* and *The Five People You Meet in Heaven*, as their model. It was a big bet, but the senior managers at Hyperion felt very sure about it and were determined to do everything they could to get it. 'We probably even would've gone higher,' said one, reflecting on the confidence they felt at the time.

When the auction took place in October 2007, paying $6.75 million for a short book by an unknown author seemed excessive to many observers, including many publishers who had bid for the book at one stage but either pulled out or lost out. It was a high-risk strategy that could easily have backfired on Hyperion. What if the author didn't live long enough to finish the book, let alone see it published? What if the book didn't live up to the publisher's expectations, and tens of thousands of the copies shipped out eventually came back as returns? Either was quite possible – at the time of the auction, no one really knew. It was a classic big-book gamble.

As it happens, things panned out well for Hyperion. Their marketing campaign was carefully tied into the media that had made Randy Pausch a public phenomenon in the first place. Since the video of 'The Last Lecture' had been viewed by many millions online, Hyperion created a dedicated website that would reach out to and link interested parties, including the pancreatic cancer groups. They also sent a crew to film Randy Pausch and his family and they supplied Amazon, b&n.com and others with an exclusive video. They used their connections at Disney to get an hour-long special about the book on ABC News. Since so much about this book was linked to the internet and the media more generally, they self-consciously chose to design the book as an old-fashioned book, with a cover and thick, rough-edged paper that emphasized the traditional, physical nature of the book and the timelessness of its message.

Everything fell into place. The book was published in April 2008 and went straight to number one in the 'hardcover advice' section of The *New York Times* bestseller list. The major accounts took half a million copies in cloth, the following day an additional 400,000 copies went out and the day after that the numbers had swollen to 900,000. The book remained at the top of the bestseller list throughout the summer and autumn. By October 2008 it had sold through more than 3.6 million copies in hardcover and was still selling around 50,000 a week. Moreover, thanks to the buzz that was generated when this book was being auctioned and that was relayed to overseas publishers by the scouts whose job it was to report on what was hot in New York, Hyperion was able to recover a substantial part of their advance through the sale of foreign rights. They had earned back around $2 million in foreign rights even before the book was published, and by October 2008 they had sold rights in 37 languages; Korean rights alone sold for $300,000. Betting on big books by authors with no track record is a very risky business, but in the case of *The Last Lecture*, the bet paid off handsomely.

I noted earlier that cultural fields have linguistic and spatial boundaries: the logic of the field that I've analysed here applies to English-language trade publishing but not necessarily to trade publishing in France or Germany or Spain or other countries where the languages, institutions and developmental trends have been different. The structures and dynamics of trade publishing in these countries will be shaped by developments that are specific to them. Some developments will be similar – many countries have experienced consolidation both in the sphere of publishing houses and in the retail sector – while others will be different. For example, while literary agents certainly exist in continental European countries, they are nowhere near as prevalent and they don't have anything like the power that agents in New York and London have, and this in turn makes a big difference to the logic of the field.

However, my focus here is on English-language trade publishing. I've said that the logic of the field is broadly similar in the US and the UK – New York and London are the two metropolitan centres of English-language trade publishing and the field stretches across the Atlantic, embracing both countries (and, indeed, Canada, which, in terms of most forms of publishing and other creative industries, is inextricably interwoven with the US). As we've seen, most of the largest publishing corporations are both active and dominant on both sides of the Atlantic, agents are powerful players in both countries (a few have offices in both), retail chains have grown at the expense of independent booksellers in both the US and Britain, and the vast majority of books that are published in English will be either published or at least distributed on both sides of the Atlantic. The logic of the field, as summarized in figure 10, applies to Britain just as much as it applies to the US. And yet this doesn't quite capture everything. There are important differences between Britain and the US in terms of the structure and dynamic of the fields. What are these differences and how can we analyse them?

Of course, there is a big difference in terms of scale. The US market is at least five times the size of the UK market: you can sell a lot more books in the US, and this has big implications in terms of the revenues that can be generated and the expectations of authors and agents. The scale is also very different in terms of geography: the US is effectively a continent (literally so when you add Canada), and this creates a whole range of problems and opportunities in terms of sales and marketing – let alone the logistics of the supply chain – which simply don't exist, or exist on a much smaller scale, in the UK. But is there anything more than this?

The discount wars

It's just before 9:00 a.m. and my breakfast meeting with the sales director of a large New York publishing corporation is drawing to a close. We've been talking for over an hour in the private dining room at the corporate headquarters in Manhattan; I have time for one last question before she rushes off to her first proper meeting of the day. 'I know you've spent some time in the UK and you're familiar with the marketplace there,' I begin; 'What would you say the biggest difference is between the UK and the US?' She looks across the table at me with a wry smile on her face. 'Terms of trade,' she replies. 'We call it the Wild West.'

The Wild West she was referring to was of course Britain, not the US. We commonly think of the United States as the land of unbridled capitalism where the free market reigns supreme and government regulation is minimal, whereas Britain is often thought of as a more regulated society where the harsh realities of the marketplace are softened by government intervention and a more beneficent welfare state. Of course, there is some truth in this common view – the National Health Service in Britain provides a much more comprehensive health care system than the largely private, insurance-based system in the US, for example. But in the world of books it is exactly the opposite. Why? How can we explain this?

In the US the discounting practices of publishers are governed by the Robinson-Patman Act, which, as explained earlier, makes it illegal for suppliers (including publishers) to offer different discounts to retailers who occupy a similar market position. Following the legal battles between retailers and publishers in the 1990s, the American book trade has settled on a relatively open and transparent system for discounting and co-op advertising, and American publishers are acutely sensitive to the risks involved in tampering with this system. Publishers devise a discount schedule which they use with all their customers, who receive the same discounts on individual titles as other customers in the same class. Wholesalers may receive higher discounts than retailers but all wholesalers will receive the same discount because they are in the same customer class. Trade publishers will typically offer a full trade discount of, say, 46 or 48 per cent on most or all of their books. Some publishers may offer a lower discount (or 'short discount', as it is commonly called) of 32–34 per cent on books that are regarded as more specialized in character, such as professional or academic books. All retailers are offered similar terms; the large retail chains are not given higher discounts than the small independent booksellers simply by virtue of the fact that the chains are big and have more market muscle – to do so would open the publisher to legal action under the Robinson-Patman Act.

While the Robinson-Patman Act tends to level the playing field in terms of discounts, in practice there are numerous subtle ways in which the large chains can leverage their size to exact better terms from publishers. For instance, the big retail chains might be given more favourable credit terms – 90 days rather than 30 or 60 days – and this can make a real difference to a retailer's cash flow, especially in a business where much of the stock is slow-moving. Moreover, the big retail chains are able to invest much more in infrastructure than the small independents, and this can reduce the time and expense involved in processing orders. 'So, for example, when Barnes & Noble gets a box of books in from any major publisher there's a sticker on the outside that has to be scanned and it immediately reconciles with the invoice which has been electronically sent to their computer system and spews out the stickers for sticking and it's done,' explained the manager of a small independent bookseller in New York City. 'We still have to open every box and take out every book – it costs us much more in man hours to get books out than it ever would for a chain.'

But probably the most significant areas where the big retail chains benefit more than the small independent retailers are co-op advertising and in-store placement fees. Again, publishers that have co-op advertising schemes will make them available to all retailers, regardless of size, but since the volume of business that the large publishers do with the big retail chains is so much greater than it is with the small independent booksellers, it means that, in practice, the publishers are paying much larger sums to the retail chains, who will as a result have much larger co-op budgets to play with. Moreover, many small independent booksellers simply don't bother to claim co-op money, or don't realize that it's available for them to claim. 'One of the sales reps told me that the largest hit to the bottom line at the end of the year for publishers is all the money that independents did not take for co-op, because all that money was set aside under co-op rules and they didn't know how to cash it in, and so they didn't get it,' said one independent bookseller. Many large publishers will also increase their co-op budgets with particular accounts by making incremental supplements to the pool in order to take advantage of special promotions – 'You can always supplement the pool and add to it on a book-by-book basis,' explained a marketing manager at one of the large houses. These incremental supplements to the co-op pool are additional cash injections from which the big retail chains with their special promotions – buy two get one free, buy one get one-half off, and so on – tend to benefit most. Large publishers may also have special partnership programmes with the big retail chains that create a degree of flexibility in their arrangements and enable them to get more than they pay for, such as more titles in a promotion, etc.

There is another way in which a major retailer with a growing market share can try to leverage their position to increase the payments they receive from publishers under co-op advertising schemes: they can argue that their percentage should be calculated not on the previous year's sales but rather on the likely sales for the current year – a figure which, given the retailer's growing market share, is likely to be higher than the previous year, thus generating a higher co-op pool for the year. At least one major retailer has taken this line. 'They would say to a publisher, "Look, we're growing much faster than the rest of the industry and you have this co-op policy that says that we earn a pool of money based on last year's sales. Don't you see that that's unfavourable to us because of the way we're growing? Why should we be held to the same standards that other people are held to? You know, we're already in the hole as far as co-op,"' explained one sales director who found himself faced with this argument from the retailer. Given the size and strategic importance of the retailer, it wasn't easy to resist. He could stall, he could try to shift the discussion to other issues, but he knew that, in the end, he would have to give some ground – 'It's an ongoing conversation. You might have to lose some battles to win the war.'

So while in principle the Robinson-Patman Act creates a level playing field among retailers in the US, in practice there are many ways in which this playing field can be turned into rough and uneven ground that gives the large retailers certain advantages either because they are able to leverage their size and strategic importance to exact better terms and conditions or because the small independent booksellers are less efficient, less well-equipped in terms of their IT infrastructure or simply less well-organized. But all of this pales into insignificance when compared to the market conditions that exist in the UK, where the demise of the Net Book Agreement coupled with the absence of any legislation comparable to the Robinson-Patman Act has led to tremendous pressure on publishers to increase the discounts they give to the largest and most powerful retailers.

The British publishers who sought to break up the Net Book Agreement in the 1990s were clear in their minds about why they wanted to do this, and they had their own views about what a post-NBA world would look like. 'It was about taking books to the people,' recalled David, the managing director of a large publishing house in the UK who was a sales director at the time. 'It sounds very grand and it's still true now. It was about opening up books as a sexier entertainment code and that's still very much our mantra today as a publisher. So we knew full well that if we could manipulate margin, shave our margins in reality, we could help books enter areas of retail where they currently did not show – supermarkets in the main but other places as well. Busting open the high street if you like.' Behind the challenge to the NBA in the early 1990s was a straightforward economic calculation: it was assumed that the increase in the volume of sales that would be generated by discounting books would more than compensate for the cost of the price cut and the erosion of margin that would ensue. And the increase in the volume of sales would result both from the discounting itself and from the fact that, by allowing books to be discounted, publishers would be able to get books into a whole new array of retail outlets – the supermarkets above all, but also other retail outlets for which price was a key factor in their competitive offer. 'We wanted to have books where the people are rather than simply trying to persuade the people to go to where the books are.'

While the principal motive behind the assault on the NBA was economic and commercial, it was also inseparably linked to a particular cultural outlook. The publishers who opposed the NBA were in many cases critical of what they saw as the elitism and snobbery of traditional publishing. In their view, the traditional publishing business was a rather closed and self-referring world which prided itself on its own judgements of taste and quality and looked down upon books that were more popular in style and intent. By contrast, they viewed books as firmly and unashamedly part of the entertainment industries. 'Publishing is about entertainment; it's about good quality writing at a reasonable price,' continued David. 'We deliver the promise of entertainment, whatever that might be. And the great frustration we felt is that this is an industry riddled with elitism and snobbery, and it still is to a degree. There is still a battle going on. But we felt very strongly that there were more people to be tapped into on an entertainment basis and that a good book could be a book that sells a million copies, not necessarily one that sells 15,000 copies after winning the Booker. So our vision was that the business can work on a very, very commercial basis. It doesn't have to be wrapped up and tied down in a kind of literary yoke, if you like. I mean the books have to have a very high quality and it's not a case of publishing rubbish, but it doesn't need to be constrained in that way.'

Under the direction of its charismatic founder, Tim Hely Hutchinson, Headline – which by the mid-1990s had become Hodder Headline – was one of the first major houses to de-net. They did a deal with John Menzies, the Scottish stationer and tobacconist, to give them extra discount on selective hardbacks, on the understanding that they would pass the extra discount on to the consumer and add some of their own. At the time, the normal trade discount to high-street stationers like Menzies and WH Smith was 45 per cent on hardbacks and 50 per cent on paperbacks. Hodder Headline gave Menzies 55 per cent on selected hardbacks. 'They would, in theory, pass 10 per cent on, and the book would be 25 per cent off, so we'd share the discount. Menzies as a retailer would make a big song and dance about the fact that this would be cheaper than anyone else on the high street, they could do big displays and it just gave a marketing message – that was the idea,' explained David, who had been directly involved as a sales manager in the negotiations with Menzies. Other retailers and some publishers protested vehemently, and there was a period in the mid-1990s when the situation remained very unclear. 'But the whole thing then tumbled quite quickly and suddenly it was like, OK, we've embraced it, the industry de-netted, and it was a free for all.'

While the initial de-net deals were done with stationers like Menzies, the collapse of the NBA opened the doors for general retailers and supermarkets like Tesco and Asda to become involved in frontlist bookselling. 'Asda was the biggest,' continued David. 'We had fantastic deals with Asda who would buy what we called at the time "megabins", pallets of books that they would wheel onto the middle of the floor to sell them. I think the first one I did was Stephen King. The Stephen King novel came out and there were 300,000 copies in cardboard boxes. They just wheel them into the foyer, £3.99 – I think the cover price was £5.99, £2 off, £3.99 – and they alone would sell 300,000.' Books were attractive for the supermarkets because they were seen as aspirational and educational: 'It's a non-food product that's seen as good. We were natural bedfellows because the supermarkets trade a lot on being family friendly and what they like about books is that they give them a facade of respectability.' At the same time, for the publisher the traffic through the supermarkets was of a different order of magnitude from what they'd been accustomed to: 'We knew that the big four supermarkets were getting near to 50 million people a week through their stores. That's something that Smith's couldn't do in a year.' Not only was there a lot of traffic through the supermarkets, it was repeat traffic. 'And repeat means: "Here's the latest John Grisham, we know you love John Grisham, so here's the new one." And, "You were here last week, you finished that book, here's another like it."'

As we saw earlier, the collapse of the NBA was followed by a dramatic shift in the market shares of the different retail channels for trade publishers in the UK, and the shift was particularly marked for those publishers whose list was skewed towards commercial fiction and non-fiction – that is, towards the kinds of books that could be sold in large numbers through the supermarkets and other non-traditional outlets. Prior to 1994, the high-street chains like WH Smith and the bookselling chains like Waterstone's dominated the retail sector in the UK – 'Together they would've had around 90 per cent of the market,' David explained. But by 2007, 'chain bookshops, and within that they count Smith's, Waterstone's, Borders, Sussex Stationers and other bits and bobs', he continued, shuffling through a small pile of printouts which he retrieved from a corner of his desk, 'is now approximately 30 per cent of the market for adult consumer books.' He proceeded to fill out the picture:

So 30 per cent in overall terms, of which Waterstone's have 12 per cent, Smith's have 10 per cent and the rest falls down below it. Independents still maintain a 10 per cent share, which is interesting. Supermarkets will be 17 per cent, of which Tesco's has nearly 9 per cent share on its own, and Asda has around 6 per cent. And then it tumbles down, Sainsbury's and all the rest. So as a sector, the supermarkets have 17 per cent against what you would call our traditional channels which are still 30 per cent, but that would've been 90:10, not even that, in the early 1990s. And the other crucial change is online. Amazon have 8 per cent of the market and online in total is 11 per cent, and that's all new, I mean it's nicked from elsewhere, within the last five years.

Not only do the supermarkets and online retailers now represent large retail channels for books, they are also the channels that are growing, unlike the traditional channels which are either static or declining, that is, losing market share to the new non-traditional channels. The growth of the supermarkets has slowed down somewhat – the rapid expansion of their market share in the early 2000s was partly a matter of catching up. The channel is now more mature and it is unlikely to continue to grow at the same rate but it is growing nonetheless, which is more than one can say about the traditional retail channels.

The expansion of the non-traditional retail channels is seen by many trade publishers in the UK as an opportunity. If this is where the market is growing, then it makes good sense, many publishers say, to supply more product into this channel. 'We understand what's going on in the mass market and we're not above making sure that we are feeding it,' commented the managing director of one large UK publishing house. This is particularly true for commercial fiction and for those areas of commercial non-fiction like celebrity publishing and the so-called 'misery memoir'. This managing director explained how they had set up a new commercial fiction imprint that was aimed explicitly at acquiring, developing and supplying books to the supermarkets. 'We've got to seize back the agenda with retailers, seize back the agenda with talent, and say, "We understand the market, we understand the consumers. If you come and join our team, it will be the best team to be on." That is my strategic imperative at the moment.'

But the publishers have paid a price for the growing role of supermarkets and other non-traditional outlets in their retail mix, and there is one aspect of this price that stands out above all: they have been subjected to pressure for higher and higher discounts. The 'discount drift', as Jane, a publisher at a large UK house, described it, began around 1997, 'when we were getting squeezed by the supermarket sector'. Publishers started giving discounts of 57.5 per cent – a huge increase on the discounts of 45 per cent for hardcovers and 50 per cent for paperbacks that were standard in the early 1990s. The situation was complicated by the fact that the supermarkets were being supplied by wholesalers who were taking a slice of the pie. 'So the industry thought, OK, we give them more, they have to have a slice and we don't have to do anything, we don't have to go and put books on shelves and we don't have to send reps in – fine, cost of service is small, in we go.' But gradually the discounts drifted up still further – 'We drifted up to 60, and then for some deals we drifted over 60 to 62.5. We were starting to get worried,' explained Jane.

When the wholesaler servicing Tesco went bankrupt in the early 2000s, the large publishers seized the opportunity to try to regain the initiative. 'So we said, "This is our moment to draw the line in the sand."' Some managed to claw back a couple of percentage points in the transition from the old wholesaler to the new one. 'Where things might have been drifting above 60 we really clawed it back to 60 being the top.' Jane concedes, however, that this line has been hard to hold. 'We had a moment when we drew back. Now I couldn't put my hand on my heart and say that all of us now have not drifted from that. Because it becomes a bigger and bigger part of our customer base; we are all trying to gain advantage in the supermarkets. The big thing about the supermarkets is that the space is smaller and more finite than everywhere else, so you need to get a slice of that and you need to get a bigger slice.' So would they ever go above 60 per cent now? 'Yes.' Would they occasionally go as high as 65 per cent? 'Yes.' Would they go to 70? 'No.'

So why are British publishers willing to give such high discounts to the supermarkets? Why don't they just walk away from these high-discount deals which squeeze their own profitability? Sometimes they do. 'Oh yes, we walk away all the time,' said one sales director at a large UK house, with a certain chutzpah. 'It's quite important. If we have a run of saying yes, then we will sometimes say no just to say no, because it's important. It's like slapping a child, you know. We do it with each other. It's almost ritualistic.' But Jane's view probably reflects a more realistic assessment of the publisher's position in the post-NBA world. 'Mostly we try and make it work,' she explains. 'Because you need them?' I ask. 'Yes, yes,' she replies. 'So they're in a very strong position?' 'Yes, of course they are. Good God, yes.'

To the outside observer, this might all seem very puzzling. After all, supermarkets still represent only 17 per cent of the market – a sizeable share, to be sure, but still significantly less than the 30 per cent represented by the retail book chains. And Tesco's share is still less than Waterstone's. So why are publishers seemingly so submissive in their dealings with the supermarkets?

It's not easy to get to the bottom of this. 'It's quite a sort of complex economics,' said the CEO of one large UK publishing house. 'Let's take a hypothetical book,' she tries to explain.

A hypothetical channel comes to you and says, 'I quite like this book and I'm prepared to stock it, but this is what you're going to have to pay me for it.' If you say no, that's fine, they don't stock it. The next call you get is from the author, you know, when they're basically saying, 'Where is my book? You promised that I would get X.' And you say, 'Well I'm terribly sorry but we didn't give this particular channel the discount.' Does that work? No. You then get the agent on the phone saying, 'This is outrageous, you know, I should have gone to the publisher up the road who would have given it away,' and so on. So although the agent community says, 'The publishers are weak, they keep giving stuff away, why can't they stand up to so and so,' that's all fine until it's your author on the phone, quite rightly saying, 'I have worked for two years to produce this and you've got some little bloody dispute with that particular channel and it's ruined my life,' and the awful thing is, it has ruined their life. Hence the problem.

So the problem, it seems, is that the agents and authors won't allow the publishers to walk away from high-discount deals with the supermarkets. They would be outraged. They would feel that the publisher, out of narrow self-interest, had refused to deal with a major channel, and therefore had prevented the book from doing as well as it could have done and put the author's career at risk. In other words, the publishers are being forced into these high-discount deals by the agents and authors – or so this CEO seems to be saying.

Is that a plausible explanation? I put it to an agent who has been in the game for a long time. 'That's a good one,' he says, in a tone of amused disbelief. 'That's simply not the case.' He concedes that if a publisher decided not to agree terms with a major retailer like Waterstone's so that a particular author's book was not stocked by them, then that would be a source of great concern and 'there would have to be a conversation between the agent and the author about it.' But he pours scorn on the idea that what drives publishers to do high-discount deals with supermarkets is the fear of backlash from agents and authors. 'A few years ago Hodder Headline tried standing up to Tesco on James Patterson. They did not agree terms on one of James Patterson's many books and that book was not stocked by Tesco – and Patterson personally was consulted about this decision and endorsed it – but that's the last time they did it. The next book that came along Hodder Headline made a deal with Tesco once again. They'd learned from that experience. They couldn't lose the hundred/ hundred and fifty thousand copy sale to Tesco that they had lost last time around. So there we are,' he says. Point made.

The CEO was not necessarily wrong, but she was, at best, telling only part of the story. Some publishers are reluctant to admit that their own interests are served by doing deals that put their margins under tremendous pressure. To understand why this is so, you have to see that the role of supermarkets in the sales of the bestselling titles is disproportionate to their overall market share. While supermarkets represent 17 per cent of total adult trade sales in the UK overall, for the more commercial books their share can be 30–40 per cent or even more. And this means that the supermarkets have become a crucial gatekeeper in determining which books end up on the UK bestseller lists – not the only gatekeeper, of course, and there are plenty of books that make it onto the bestseller lists even though the supermarkets' share is small. It depends on the book. For paperback fiction the supermarkets are crucial – it's difficult to get into the top ten without the supermarkets. They're also increasingly important for paperback non-fiction and for hardcovers, though in these cases the situation is more complex. 'With non-fiction hardcover you can certainly get into the bestseller lists for six months of the year without the supermarkets,' explains Jane. 'They are the key in fiction paperback, and in non-fiction paperback probably – hence the rise of misery. But in hardcover they are not always the only answer, though they are obviously very important. Tesco's proudest achievement last year was to have 40 per cent of the Alan Bennett sale – that's quite a lot.'

Publishers need the supermarkets because they need to get their books into the bestseller lists, and while the supermarkets may only have 17 per cent of the overall market share, their market share for the bestselling titles is far greater than this, and hence their power to put books on the bestseller lists is far greater than that of other retail channels. This is the hidden truth that explains why publishers find it so difficult to walk away from supermarket deals even though the discount terms are punishing. It also goes some way to explaining why the UK bestseller lists have such a different character than the US bestseller lists, although a full explanation of this difference would no doubt have to take account of other things. 'The whole industry is buggered by this,' explains Jane.

We need to get into the bestseller list because we pay such high tickets – I'm talking now in the commercial fiction and non-fiction area. We pay huge tickets for most of those properties you see in the bestseller list, and you're driven to pay that because you're up against everybody else. And therefore, as a result of that high ticket, you have to sell lots of copies, you have to show to this incredibly rapacious industry and to all the authors that you're making them as successful as possible.

So if you don't make them number one, then (a) you've paid the high ticket and you're losing and (b) they'll move off to someone else. So therefore you obviously have to be in the supermarkets to do that. So we've got this ghastly scenario, a sort of negative vicious circle.

Dancing with the devil

There are some who suggest that, by doing these high-discount deals with the supermarkets, publishers are pursuing their short-term interests in a way that will damage the industry in the long term. They are, as one bookseller put it, 'dancing with the devil'. Why might one say this? Two reasons.

In the first place, the supermarkets are selling books at very low prices. Famously, Asda sold the final volume of the Harry Potter series for just £5, far below the publisher's recommended retail price of £17.99. The prices at Asda and other supermarkets were so low that some independent booksellers found themselves in the somewhat absurd position of buying their stock from supermarkets, since they could get it cheaper from them than they could through the normal book supply chain. Tesco and Asda sell many of their paperback books at a standard price of £3.86, and some sell for £3.49 or less. Because these books are selling at low prices in places where they will be seen by a substantial proportion of the population, the supermarkets' pricing policies are changing the public's perception of the value of books. 'If you asked the public four years ago how much a paperback costs, they'd probably say £5.99, £6.99,' the bookseller continued. 'Now they're more likely to say, "I don't know, £4." That's a massive value change.' And it's a change that can affect people's purchasing decisions. 'At Christmas people will say, "Well, I didn't come in and buy the hardback of 'X', *Planet Earth* or whatever the book of Christmas is, because it's half price everywhere so everyone would know I hadn't paid full whack for it and therefore it was deemed to be a cheap present, and you go, "What?! That's crazy."'

The second reason why publishers might be damaging their own long-term interests by doing high-discount deals with the supermarkets is that, while the supermarkets can shift a lot of copies of the books they stock, they will only ever stock a very limited range of titles, and they will stock them only so long as they are selling at high rates of turnover. Publishers need specialist booksellers and a healthy retail sector in order to break out new titles, to make available the full range of their output and to stock books that are selling more slowly: booksellers, both the high-street chains and the independents, are their shop windows. But by supplying the supermarkets with the bestselling titles at high discounts, publishers are – or so one might argue – making life more difficult for the very booksellers on whom their own long-term vitality as an industry depends. 'It doesn't take a lot for the levers to move only a little bit, in terms of margin, rent, rates, utilities costs, to suddenly drive you from being a £10 million profit-maker to bust,' the bookseller explained, 'and I don't think the publishers necessarily understand that.'

I put these points to Jane, who has no sympathy for this line of argument – 'No, I completely disagree,' she replies tersely. In Jane's view, the supermarkets and Amazon are the two retail channels who know what they're doing and she's happy to support them, whereas the specialist retail bookshops 'wouldn't know how to entice a reader if they tried'. Their complaints about being given disadvantageous terms relative to the supermarkets are, she says, self-serving and misleading. 'Looking at discount in isolation is the most ridiculous thing,' she says. 'What you have to look at with all your customers is cost to serve. The discount is only part of this. There's also the marketing money, the servicing from here – i.e. the sales time, the servicing through our distribution centre, the cost of returns, the whole thing. The most expensive cost of serve without question is Waterstone's, the second most expensive is Smith's and the third is the supermarkets.' Waterstone's is hugely expensive for publishers to serve because 'you're dealing with a completely dysfunctional distribution system', explains Jane, where 'they want you to deliver two books to every branch and then they want to send them back when they don't sell, and they don't sell because they're not getting the customers in.' On top of that, the high-street booksellers charge marketing money for front of store placement. Compared with the high-street book chains, 'the supermarkets are the most straightforward you can imagine, because you go direct from the printer, you drop big wadges and they reorder big wadges, we have one person going to see them and as yet they don't charge marketing money.'

So Jane dismisses out of hand the suggestion that the high-street bookselling chains are being given disadvantageous terms. 'The discount argument is absolutely ridiculous and pathetic. We support Waterstone's way beyond their usefulness to us, way beyond, for some emotional nonsense. Of course, we don't want our books only to be available in Tesco's, I'm not saying that at all. I'm saying that there are different ways of engaging consumers for a wider range of books than Waterstone's are offering. So every time they come and ask us for more discount, we say, "Just give us your vision of how you're going to engage the readers and we'll support it."'

Jane's views are forcefully expressed – 'This is fairly radical stuff,' she warns me in advance – and they reflect her own background in the more commercial side of trade publishing, which has the most to gain from the expansion of the market brought about by the growing involvement of supermarkets in the book trade. But hers is by no means a lone voice. Many publishers express dismay at the state of Waterstone's and at what they see as their unimaginative retailing strategies, and they regard the supermarkets as a valuable part of the retail mix which has helped to bring books to a wider range of consumers who wouldn't normally go into a specialized bookstore. At the same time they know that they need a flourishing retail sector and that the supermarkets alone could never provide outlets for the range of books they publish. What is less clear is whether the high-street bookselling chains, facing pressure from the high-discounting supermarkets on the one hand and Amazon and other online retailers on the other, are in a position to sustain their businesses in the medium to long term without something akin to the kind of level playing field that exists in the US and elsewhere.

The margin squeeze

One consequence of the different market conditions that exist in the US and the UK is that, while publishers in both countries face downward pressure on their margins, they do so for structurally different reasons (see figure 11). In the US, the downward pressure on margins stems primarily from escalating advances. Publishers in the US experience pressure on the retail side too, as the most powerful retail organizations seek to increase their share of the pie by negotiating better terms, claiming more co-op money and so on, but the existence

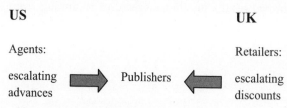

Figure 11   The squeeze on publishers' margins

of the Robinson-Patman Act greatly reduces the scope for retailers to negotiate special terms, since additional discount given to one retailer would, by law, have to be given to all retailers in the same class. The result is that discounts in the US tend to remain relatively stable and have fluctuated very little over time.

In the UK, by contrast, the downward pressure on publishers' margins stems primarily from the escalating discounts that have followed the demise of the Net Book Agreement. In the absence of anything comparable to the Robinson-Patman Act, the most powerful retailers are able to use their market muscle to extract higher discounts from publishers, and are able to play publishers off against one another for access to the limited number of high-visibility, high-velocity retail spaces they make available for books. The overall impact has been an upward drift in the average discount that publishers offer to the retail sector: roughly 10 per cent of margin has been transferred from publishers to retailers in a period of less than ten years. The pressure for more discount – and higher marketing spend in the case of the high-street bookselling chains – is always there. Publishers resist, they threaten to 'draw a line in the sand' and occasionally they walk away from high-discount deals. But only rarely do they have a book like Harry Potter which is such a must-have, non-substitutable item that they can take a hard line and still get their books into the high-velocity space of the supermarkets.

So while the logic of the field applies equally to trade publishers in the US and the UK, the way that this logic works itself out is different because it is shaped by the distinctive commercial and regulatory environments that exist in each country. Trade publishers are situated in the space between agents on the one side and retailers on the other, and pressure from both sides tends to put downward pressure on their margins. In the US this pressure stems primarily from escalating advances, reflecting the power of the agents who handle the rights for the most sought-after content, while in the UK it stems primarily from escalating discounts, reflecting the power of the large retail chains in a post-NBA world. In short, the same logic applied in different contexts results in similar pressures stemming from different sources.

9

THE DIGITAL REVOLUTION

The transformation of the field of trade publishing was a process driven above all by social and economic factors, by actors and organizations pursuing their aims, responding to changing circumstances and taking advantage of new opportunities in the competitive field of Anglo-American trade publishing. But interlaced with this transformation and contributing to it was a technological revolution that first began to make itself felt in the book publishing industry in the mid-1980s and became a source of increasing speculation and concern from the early 1990s on. By then the digital revolution had already convulsed the music industry and seemed set to cause similar disruption in other sectors of the creative industries. The rapid growth of the internet from the mid-1990s on served only to heighten speculation. By the late 1990s many publishers were pouring millions of dollars into electronic publishing projects of various kinds and venture capitalists were launching new companies aimed at digitizing book content and making it available in a variety of formats. 'The digital future' became the theme of countless conferences, the subject of innumerable articles and a key topic of conversation in the boardrooms of the publishing houses themselves. Bower and Christensen's 1995 article on 'Disruptive Technologies'[1] had warned bluntly of the dangers faced by leading companies if they resisted new technologies on the grounds that mainstream customers didn't want them and projected profit margins weren't big enough: by failing to act they would run the risk of leaving the field to smaller companies who

---

[1] Joseph L. Bower and Clayton M. Christensen, 'Disruptive Technologies: Catching the Wave', *Harvard Business Review* (Jan.–Feb. 1995), pp. 43–53.

would be able to create a market by experimenting with new products and put themselves in pole position if and when the new products eventually took off. The message was not lost on corporate chiefs. The large publishing houses were scrambling to be at the forefront of a technological revolution that seemed to many to be inevitable.

The conviction that the publishing industry was on the edge of fundamental change was strengthened by the reports of management consultancy firms in the late 1990s and early 2000s, many of which were predicting that ebooks would quickly become a substantial and growing part of the market. Among the most frequently cited was a report published in 2000 by PricewaterhouseCoopers which forecast an explosion of consumer spending on electronic books, estimating that by 2004 consumer spending on ebooks would reach $5.4 billion and would comprise 17 per cent of the market. A study by Arthur Andersen, commissioned by the Association of American Publishers and published in the same year, predicted that the ebook market would be anywhere from $2.3 billion to $3.4 billion by 2005 and would represent up to 10 per cent of the consumer book market. Expectations were also raised by the startling success of one of Stephen King's early experiments with electronic publishing. In March 2000 he published his 66-page novella *Riding the Bullet* electronically, available only as a digital file that could be downloaded for $2.50: there was an overwhelming response, resulting in around 400,000 downloads in the first 24 hours and 600,000 in the first two weeks.

The downs and ups of ebooks

Notwithstanding Stephen King's good fortune, the predictions made by PricewaterhouseCoopers and others turned out to be overly optimistic, at least in terms of the timescale. Those publishers who were actively experimenting with ebooks invariably found that the levels of uptake in the early 2000s were much lower than the consultants and many others had been projecting. Sales of individual ebooks numbered in the tens, in some cases the hundreds, but were nowhere near the hundreds of thousands, let alone millions, of copies that many had expected. Moreover, the bursting of the dot.com bubble in the late 1990s brought a new mood of scepticism about the internet economy and its capacity to transform traditional business models. From 2001 on, a period of retrenchment set in, and both publishing firms and private investors began to curtail their investments and lower their expectations. Many of the new electronic publishing divisions and ebook programmes – some of which had been launched with much fanfare and at considerable expense only a year or two earlier – were either closed down or radically scaled back. The ebook revolution had stalled and no one knew when it would get underway, or if indeed it ever would.

The mood of uncertainty continued through 2006 and 2007, and the question of ebooks and their role in trade publishing remained a hotly contested issue. Actual sales of ebooks for all the major trade publishers remained very low, both in terms of units and in terms of revenue, and they were showing no signs of significant growth. Based on figures I received from trade houses at the time, I estimate that ebook sales represented around 0.1 per cent of their overall sales in 2006. By the end of 2007 the share had risen to perhaps 0.5 per cent – still an insignificant number, 'statistically irrelevant', as a senior manager at one of the large houses put it. Against the background of persistently sluggish sales, opinions were sharply divided about how the ebook revolution, if indeed it was a revolution, was likely to pan out. On one side were the digital advocates who, unfazed by the disappointments of the previous decade, remained firmly convinced that the ebook revolution would happen eventually. On the other side were the digital sceptics who remained attached to the traditional print-on-paper book, valued its materiality and meaningfulness as an object and doubted whether – in the world of trade publishing at any rate – it would ever be replaced in any substantial way by electronic files read on screens. And somewhere in between were the digital agnostics – those who didn't profess to know one way or the other how the future would unfold and were happy or resigned to adopt a wait-and-see approach, continuing to do what they did pretty much as they always had while the technological revolution took its own course. The differences between these positions were differences in disposition and inclination as much as anything, since there was no factual evidence at that time to settle the matter one way or the other.

The digital advocates could offer half a dozen reasons why ebooks had not yet made much headway: the reading devices were not good enough, the publishers had not made enough of their content available, the prices were too high, etc. But as the technology improves and the prices come down, we will see, they confidently predicted, a dramatic increase in ebook sales. The early proponents of the ebook revolution were right when they said the future was digital; they were just wrong about the timescale. Digital advocates are fond

of repeating the technophile's maxim that people tend to overestimate the impact of technological change in the short term and
underestimate it in the long term. Just wait, they say. A new generation of 'digital natives' is growing up with computers and iPods and
mobile phones and by the time they start reading they will feel perfectly comfortable reading books on screen (if they read books at
all). They will not have the same attachment to the print-on-paper
book as their parents and grandparents did. The publishing industry
is still waiting for its iPod moment but when it comes, everything will
change very quickly. Just look at what happened in the music industry: for the digital advocates, the music industry is the future of
publishing foretold.[2]

In the eyes of the digital sceptic, the arguments of the ebook champions were full of holes. They just don't seem to appreciate, said the
sceptics, that the print-on-paper book has certain qualities that are
valued by readers and that the ebook can never capture or reproduce.
The book is an aesthetically pleasing form, a work of art in its own
right with a stylish cover and attractive design which is gratifying to
hold, to open and to own. It is also exceptionally user friendly:
nothing is easier than turning the pages of a book and reading clear
text on white paper. The eyes are not strained and you can move back
and forth with ease. It never runs out of batteries, it never freezes up
and it doesn't break if you drop it. A book, moreover, is a social
object: it can be shared with others, borrowed and returned, added
to a collection, displayed on a shelf, cherished as something valued
by its owner and taken as a sign of who they are and what matters
to them, a token of their identity. None of this, say the digital sceptics,
is offered by an ebook. The ebook is pure content and, as such, it
can never reproduce the materiality of the book. In the print-on-paper

---

[2] The line of thinking developed by the digital advocates tends to be well represented
in the press, since journalists and other commentators love to write about technologies
that seem capable of ushering in radical change. There are also countless websites
and blogs speculating about it, think tanks dedicated to it (see, for example, the
Institute for the Future of the Book, at www.futureofthebook.org) and even a minor
subgenre of literature – for the most part published, as it happens, as old-fashioned
print-on-paper books, an irony not lost on some of the authors – that heralds the
imminent demise of the book and either mourns or celebrates its passing, from Sven
Birkerts' elegant lament in *The Gutenberg Elegies: The Fate of Reading in an Electronic Age* (London: Faber & Faber, 1994) to Jeff Gomez's brash, no-doubts, no-
regrets manifesto, *Print is Dead: Books in Our Digital Age* (New York: Macmillan,
2008).

book the content and the form are inseparable, and it is this unique combination, say the sceptics, that is precisely what is valued by readers.

While digital advocates are inclined to see what happened in the music industry as the writing on the wall for the publishing industry, the digital sceptic can give you a handful of reasons why music is a poor analogy for the book. Most consumers want to listen to short, two- or three-minute songs rather than whole albums, and most albums are simply collections of songs, including many songs that listeners would prefer to skip anyway – not true with the book. The quality of the listening experience with digital music is generally higher than it is with traditional analogue forms of musical reproduction – not true with reading on screen or with any digital reading device, where the quality of the reading experience, even with e-ink technology, is worse. There are real advantages to being able to carry a compact musical library around with you so that you can listen to whatever song or album happens to suit your mood whenever you want, and this simply wasn't possible in the days of the old vinyl LP, or even the days of the cassette tape – once again, the analogy with the book is poor, since the book is eminently portable, and most people, unless they happen to be busy executives who spend a lot of time on airplanes or people who take inordinately long holidays, have no need to carry a virtual library around with them. For most people most of the time, one book will do.

One senior figure at a large technology firm who works closely with trade publishers, and who has been heavily involved with ebooks and other forms of electronic content delivery for many years, summed up the sceptic's case in 2009 with elegance and force:

The utility of having a print book in digital format for trade publishing is probably one on a scale from one to five, because all you're doing is replicating the narrative experience of page turning and linear reading in a digital form. Are you improving the experience for most users? Probably not – you're probably actually degrading the experience for most users in terms of the resolution, the convenience and everything else. Sure, you can carry 80 books around on this $400 reader, but the number of people I know who require 80 books to be carried around at one time is very small. For narrative, immersive reading, digital readers are a complete waste of everyone's time. It will never be a big business on the trade side, in my opinion. And if I'm wrong in 20 years, then I'm wrong, but I don't think I will be. This is not the music business – these aren't two- or three-minute songs.

It's not the newspaper business – they don't have a shelf life of a day or an hour. It's not the magazine business – narrative content you can get through on a subway ride. None of that is the book business on the trade side. That's why I think print will continue to have a life for the great majority of sales on the trade side of the business.

Faced with these sharply opposing views and the absence of clear-cut evidence to help one decide between them, many people in the industry were happy to take a back seat and wait to see what happened. They may have had their own personal inclinations and leant mildly in one direction or the other, but when asked about the future they were content to remain agnostic. They admitted that they really didn't know what the future held in store; they may have felt some unease, trepidation even, about a future where so much seemed uncertain, but they were happy to leave others – better placed and better informed, they hoped – to grapple with the issues. Some senior managers on the verge of retirement expressed a mild sense of relief that they would not have to deal with the challenges that would face their successors – 'I'll be watching from the sidelines,' said one CEO who was soon to retire. This was an industry that found itself in the midst of a technological storm, keenly aware that change was taking place all around it but unsure about what its implications were likely to be for its own ways of doing business and its future.

By the autumn of 2009 the decade of confused anticipation was over: when the change began, it happened more quickly and decisively than most commentators had expected. The sales of ebooks had risen sharply, so much so that the digital advocates could feel – now with some empirical backing – that their optimism had been warranted, while the sceptics were quietly eating their words and the digital agnostics were struggling to adjust to an unfamiliar world. What had changed? One word: Kindle. In fact, the change had begun earlier, almost imperceptibly, with the launch of the Sony ebook reader in the US in 2006. This was followed by a small but significant upturn in the sales of ebooks in late 2006 and 2007. When we spoke in early 2008, the manager of the digital division of one major US trade house said that their ebook sales in 2007 had grown by more than 50 per cent over the previous year, and that the increase was based primarily on sales for the Sony reader. However, it was the launch of the Amazon Kindle on 19 November 2007 that really changed the situation. Like the Sony reader, the Kindle used e-ink technology rather than backlit screens, which simulates traditional ink on paper and minimizes battery use; it also used wireless connectivity, free for the user, to enable readers to download ebooks and other content directly from Amazon, making it very easy to buy ebooks. The release of the Kindle was immediately followed by a surge in ebook sales: the same trade house that had seen ebook sales grow by 50 per cent in 2007 now saw its ebook sales leap by 400 per cent in 2008. This was a sudden and dramatic change. Although ebook sales still represented a very small proportion of overall revenues for most New York trade publishers at the end of 2008 – probably just under 1 per cent – the numbers were much higher than they'd ever been and they were growing fast.

The upward surge in ebook sales both continued and accelerated throughout 2009 and 2010. In the view of the manager of the digital division mentioned above, the introduction of the Kindle represented a kind of watershed, 'a tipping point', as he put it. 'In 2006 the question, "Who wants to read a book like this?" was a very open question. I think that question has now been answered.' He foresaw a snowball effect where there would be more and more devices coming into play in the ebook market and more retailers wanting to sell ebooks, and in fact this is exactly what happened. In November 2009 Barnes & Noble launched the Nook, with e-ink technology and free access via a wireless connection to the Barnes & Noble store, followed a year later by the Nook Color equipped with a 7-inch full-colour LCD screen. In April 2010 Apple launched the first version of its slick, stylish iPad, selling 3 million devices in the first 80 days; by the time the iPad 2 was launched in March 2011, more than 15 million iPads had been sold worldwide. Unlike the Kindle or the Nook, the iPad was a true multipurpose device with a full colour screen which could be used to do most of the things one can do with a laptop or desktop computer; reading books is but one of its many functions. The iPad was soon followed by a plethora of other tablet devices launched by manufacturers seeking to mimic the features of the iPad while undercutting it on price.

The appearance of a new generation of devices that were much more stylish and user friendly than the ebook readers of the early 2000s, coupled with the aggressive promotion of ebooks by major booksellers with large and established clienteles, was the critical convergence of factors that underpinned the dramatic upsurge in ebook sales from 2008 on. The remarkable pattern of growth can be seen from the data collected by the Association of American Publishers and the International Digital Publishing Forum. Together they have gathered data on ebook sales in the US from 12 to 15 trade publishers from 2002 to the present – the results, presented as

Table 15   US trade wholesale ebook sales, 2002–2011

Quarters	Revenues	Quarters	Revenues
Q1 02	$1,556,499	Q4 06	$7,000,000
Q2 02	$1,258,989	Q1 07	$7,500,000
Q3 02	$1,329,548	Q2 07	$8,100,000
Q4 02	$1,649,144	Q3 07	$8,000,000
Q1 03	$1,794,544	Q4 07	$8,200,000
Q2 03	$1,842,502	Q1 08	$11,200,000
Q3 03	$1,789,455	Q2 08	$11,600,000
Q4 03	$1,917,384	Q3 08	$13,900,000
Q1 04	$1,794,130	Q4 08	$16,800,000
Q2 04	$1,887,900	Q1 09	$25,800,000
Q3 04	$2,460,343	Q2 09	$37,600,000
Q4 04	$3,477,130	Q3 09	$46,500,000
Q1 05	$3,161,049	Q4 09	$55,900,000
Q2 05	$3,182,499	Q1 10	$91,000,000
Q3 05	$2,310,291	Q2 10	$88,700,000
Q4 05	$2,175,131	Q3 10	$119,700,000
Q1 06	$4,100,000	Q4 10	$136,800,000
Q2 06	$4,000,000	Q1 11	$229,200,000
Q3 06	$4,900,000	Q2 11	$226,400,000

The data in this table represent trade ebook sales via wholesale channels in the US only. The table represents data submitted by 12–15 trade publishers, which include the big six trade publishers; it does not include library, educational or professional electronic sales. The definition used for reporting electronic sales is 'All books delivered electronically over the internet or to hand-held reading devices.' The AAP and IDPF began collecting data together in Q1 2006. Data for Q4 2010 and Q1 and Q2 2011 are supplied by the AAP.

Source: Association of American Publishers and International Digital Publishing Forum.

quarterly totals up to the second quarter of 2011, are shown in table 15 and figure 12.

The data show that ebook sales were very low and largely static up to the end of 2005, generally hovering around $2 million. They doubled in the first and second quarters of 2006, and by mid-2007 they had quadrupled. Revenues for 2007 as a whole were up 60 per cent on the previous year. The growth in 2008 and 2009 was even more dramatic. Sales doubled between the fourth quarter of 2007 and the fourth quarter of 2008, and revenues for 2008 as a whole were up by nearly 70 per cent on the previous year (less than the 400

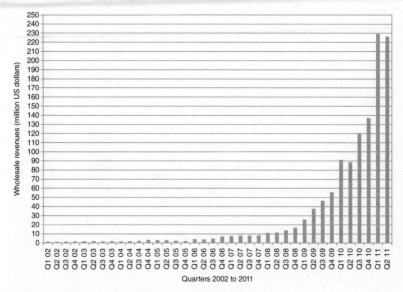

Figure 12   US trade wholesale ebook sales, 2002–2011

per cent reported by the publisher above but impressive nonetheless). The rapid growth continued through 2009 and 2010, with sales reaching nearly $230 million by the first quarter of 2011 and over $450 million in the first half of 2011 – two and a half times the sales recorded in the first half of the previous year and 20 times the sales recorded in the first half of 2008. This is fierce growth.

For the large trade publishers in the US, the surge in ebook sales has meant that a growing proportion of their revenues is being accounted for by ebooks rather than traditional print books, whether hardcover or paperback. Although the precise figures vary from house to house, the overall pattern of growth of ebook sales as a percentage of overall revenue looks roughly like figure 13. For most large US trade publishers, ebooks accounted for around 0.1 per cent of overall revenue in 2006 and 0.5 per cent in 2007; in 2008 this grew to around 1 per cent; in 2009 this was up to about 3 per cent; by 2010 it had risen to around 8 per cent and in 2011 the figure is likely to be between 18 and 22 per cent (possibly even higher for some houses). The surge was particularly dramatic in the period around Christmas 2010. 'The week before Christmas it was 12 per cent of our business, the week after Christmas it was 26 per cent,'

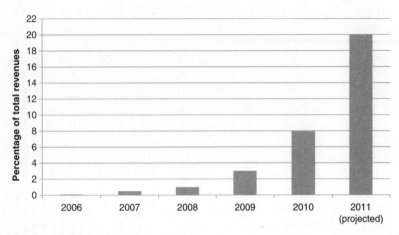

Figure 13   Ebook sales as a percentage of total revenues of major US trade publishers

explained the CEO of one large trade house. It had more than doubled in one day – no doubt thanks to the fact that many people had received reading devices as Christmas gifts and wanted to load them up with books.

The steep rise in the overall proportion of revenues accounted for by ebook sales is striking and significant in itself, but it masks important variations in terms of different categories of books – and, indeed, in terms of different authors and different books. While many commentators had expected the ebook revolution to be driven by businessmen who wanted to carry business books with them and read while travelling, in fact the biggest shift for mainstream trade publishers has not been business books: it has been in the area of commercial fiction, especially genre fiction like romance, science fiction, mystery and thriller. 'It became clear early on that these categories were just perfect for the ebook format,' explained Sally, the head of the digital publishing group in one of the large corporations. 'These are categories where people consume a lot of books and they are always waiting for the next one.' For fiction as a whole, ebooks were accounting for around 40 per cent of overall sales in this corporation by mid-2011, but in some categories of genre fiction and for some authors the percentages were even higher – 60 per cent for some categories like romance, some authors as high as 80 per cent. The big bestsellers by brand-name authors have also seen a big shift to ebook sales but the percentages tend to be lower. Sally put this down to their increased visibility in the marketplace: 'The bestsellers have tremendous ebook sales but still overall more print percentage because they get more shelf space, more visibility. I do expect the bestsellers always to have more p-ratio just because of exposure in the marketplace. The books that don't get the huge shelf space exposure have the higher e-percentages, especially in those categories where people just consume a lot.'

While the shifts are strongest in commercial fiction and especially genre fiction, there has been a strong shift in literary fiction too. Jonathan Franzen's *Freedom* – one of the literary highlights of 2010 – sold around 750,000 copies in hardcover and 250,000 ebooks in the US during its first year, so ebooks comprised around 25 per cent of its frontlist sale. While literary fiction lags behind commercial fiction and genre fiction in terms of the shift to digital, the percentages are still high – and much higher in 2011 than they were only a year earlier.

Non-fiction has also seen a significant shift to digital but it generally lags behind fiction, both commercial and literary. 'While some people expected to see very rapid adoption in business books, we haven't seen that,' explained Sally. 'The consumption patterns are different. These books aren't being read voraciously on the go, they're being used more like reference works where it's more convenient to have them on your shelf. So they're lagging behind but they're trending up.' As with fiction, the non-fiction books that have seen the biggest shift to digital are those with a simple narrative structure that you read from beginning to end, especially at the more commercial end of the market – celebrity biography, popular narrative history, big ideas books, etc. Sally put the ebook percentage for narrative non-fiction in her company at around 20 per cent in mid-2011. Anything more complicated – books that use colour, like art books or children's books, or books that are used more like a reference work that the reader wants to read slowly over time and dip in and out of – has lagged far behind.

So how are these trends likely to evolve in the coming years? Like all of the large publishing houses, Sally's company is constantly trying to figure it out, modelling and remodelling the possible scenarios on the basis of the latest sales figures and the breakdowns between print and digital for different categories of books. 'We just went through this exercise last week,' explained Sally, 'looking at the major categories and what we think will happen. Fiction will be high – I think we put in something like 75 per cent', with even higher percentages for genre fiction. Print will remain an important format in fiction but it will become the junior partner in the print–digital split – at least in the view of Sally and her fellow modellers. 'I think there will always be physical formats but of fewer titles. The physical book format is here to stay for quite a while, just because of the demographic,' she continued, though with an emphasis on 'quite' that suggested she wasn't entirely sure in her own mind how long this would last. 'I think there are always going to be some people who prefer the physical book.' But Sally and her colleagues are already envisaging a time in the not too distant future when they will be publishing some books in ebook formats only, with no print edition.

Of course, Sally and her colleagues may be wrong about all this: this is an industry in a state of flux, the numbers changing from month to month, and no one – not even the industry insiders – can predict with any confidence how things are likely to evolve in the coming years. What the proportions are likely to be in one or two years' time, let alone five or ten years' time, is anyone's guess. Will ebooks become 30 per cent, 50 per cent, even 90 per cent of publishers' total sales in the next few years? The truth is, no one knows. Most people have an opinion but no one knows a thing. 'I wish I could give you wisdom,' said one CEO in 2011, speaking with unusual frankness, 'but I have no idea. The consumer will act to define this – it won't be defined by Amazon or Barnes & Noble or Apple or us. Maybe only 26 per cent of people in America will want to read on devices and maybe we never go up another percentage point. On the other hand, maybe 100 per cent in the next three years switch over to reading devices. We just don't know. Anyone who tells you anything else is telling you a complete load of shit.' By its very nature this is an unpredictable trend, dependent on a host of incalculable factors from as yet unknown innovations to the habits and tastes of readers, and there is no way that anyone can know for sure whether the trend will continue to arch upwards or will level off or even decline at some point. Trying to predict the pattern of ebook sales over the next two to three years is like trying to predict the weather in six months' time.

Regardless of what the exact figures turn out to be, there can be no doubt that we are witnessing major changes that could have profound consequences for the industry as a whole. It is simply too early to say what these consequences will be, but already many are beginning to wonder if the traditional revenue models of trade publishing – which have relied on market segmentation and the temporal phasing or 'windowing' of editions that are differentially priced – can be sustained in the face of the ebook surge. If an ebook is available at the same time as the trade hardcover is published and at a significantly lower price, then what consequences will this have not only on the sales of the hardcover, but also on the sales of any subsequent paperback editions? Will this make it harder to publish in trade hardcover in the first instance, cannibalizing the sales of the hardcover to the point where it ceases to be economic, at least for some books and some authors? Will it undermine the sales of a subsequent trade paperback edition, which, apart from appearing a year later than the ebook, might be a dollar or two more expensive? Will it kill off the mass market paperback, the sales of which had already been declining for some while? And what consequences will these changes have, if indeed they occur, for the revenue streams and profitability of the publishing houses themselves? No one knows the answers to these questions but many in the industry are wondering anxiously about them. They are watching, experimenting, carefully scrutinizing the figures day by day and month by month as if they were tea leaves, searching for clues about their future.

It is also too early to say whether the dramatic developments in the US market are the harbinger of things to come elsewhere or will turn out to be another instance of American exceptionalism. Outside of North America, the UK market is probably the most developed in terms of ebook sales, but it still lags well behind the US. The sales manager at one of the large UK trade publishers reported that ebooks represented around 2 per cent of their business in 2010, which is about a quarter of the equivalent US figure. He expected this to rise to about 8 per cent by the end of 2011 and to continue to grow after that, but always lagging behind the US. In other markets and other languages, where reading devices are less prevalent and more expensive, where the infrastructure for the purchase of ebooks – free wireless connectivity to a trusted and well-stocked ebook store – is less developed and where attitudes towards books may be different, one might expect to see a slower and less decisive shift. Whether this is a temporary lag or a sign that there will be different patterns in different languages and countries is unclear – again, there are many opinions but no one knows.

Whatever happens in the coming years, the developments since 2008 have made it perfectly clear to everyone that the publishing industry will not remain untouched by the technological revolution that is sweeping through other sectors of the creative industries. It may not be affected in the same way as the music industry or the newspaper industry, but affected it will be. The surge in ebook sales has made this palpable, but in fact the digital revolution in the publishing industry has been underway for many years. Ebooks are part of a deeper transformation that dates back to the 1980s and that goes to the very heart of the publishing business – what I call 'the hidden revolution'.[3] This is not so much a *revolution in the product* but rather a *revolution in the process*. Regardless of what the final product looks like, the process by which it is produced is completely different. Thanks to the hidden revolution, the book had become a digital file by the end of the early 2000s. It was ready to be delivered in whatever format the market demanded, whether this was the traditional print-on-paper book or an ebook to be read on some as-yet uninvented reading device.

The hidden revolution

So what is the hidden revolution in publishing? In order to make sense of this, we need to see that the digital revolution has affected the publishing business in many different ways – we can distinguish four different levels: (1) operating systems; (2) content management and the digital workflow; (3) sales and marketing; and (4) content delivery.

1 Operating systems The most immediate respect in which digitization has affected the publishing industry is in terms of operating systems and information flows. Like many sectors of industry today, the management systems in all major publishing houses are now thoroughly computerized and management information is compiled and circulated in digital forms. Since the mid-1980s most publishing firms have been engaged in a continuous process of investing in the computerization and digitization of their offices and operating systems. They have built or installed back-office publishing systems which store bibliographical and other data on each title and can be accessed by anyone in the organization who can log onto the network. Financial data, sales data, production details and other information are held in dedicated IT systems, and a high proportion of the communication within and between organizations now takes place electronically. Email has become the communication medium of choice. Documents – including proposals and manuscripts – are commonly circulated as electronic files rather than printed texts, a development that has facilitated multiple submissions and auctions.

---

[3] See Thompson, *Books in the Digital Age*, ch. 15, on which some of the following analysis is based.

The development of IT systems has undoubtedly generated efficiencies and has enabled some costs to be eliminated or reduced, but the level of investment required to build and maintain state-of-the-art IT infrastructures is very substantial indeed. While this factor alone has not driven consolidation in the publishing industry, it is not irrelevant to it, because this is one area where small houses can be disadvantaged and large corporations can achieve significant economies of scale.

It is not just the working practices and information flows within firms that have changed: the digital revolution has also led to the digitization of the supply chain. The systems for managing stock and transferring it between different organizations within the supply chain have been computerized. More and more bookstores introduced electronic point of sale (EPOS) facilities to track the sales of individual titles and manage stock flows, and the ordering of stock from wholesalers and publishers was increasingly handled through dedicated electronic ordering services like PubNet, TeleOrdering and First Edition. The use of increasingly automated EDI (Electronic Data Interchange) systems has become a pervasive feature of the supply chain. The development of sophisticated computerized systems for stock management and control has also become an important source of competitive advantage for the large retail chains and for the large wholesalers, like Ingram and Baker & Taylor in the US and Bertrams and Gardners in the UK. By expanding their inventories and developing computer-based information systems that enable them to fulfil orders in one or two days, the large wholesalers can provide a highly efficient, one-stop service to bookstores, who can reorder stock on a daily basis in the light of their computerized point-of-sales data.

2 *Content management and the digital workflow* The computerization of operating systems is not of course unique to the publishing industry – most sectors of industry have experienced similar transformations during the last two decades. But digitization has the potential to transform the publishing industry much more profoundly than this, precisely because the publishing industry – like many sectors of the creative industries – is concerned fundamentally with symbolic content that can be codified in digital form. Hence the whole process of creating, managing, developing and transforming this content is a process that can in principle be handled in a digital form – from the moment when an author composes a text by typing on the keys of a computer to the final creation of a file in a format that can be used by a printer. A central part of the history of the publishing business

since the early 1980s has been the progressive application of the digital revolution to the various stages of the production process, leading to the gradual rise of what we could call 'the digital workflow'. From the viewpoint of the production process, the book itself has been reconstituted as a digital file – that is, a database. To the production manager, that's all it is: a file of information that has been manipulated, coded and tagged in certain ways. The reconstitution of the book as a digital file is a crucial part of the hidden revolution.

This process did not take place effortlessly – on the contrary, it was a long, arduous transformation, still continuing today, in which many of the traditional practices of the publishing industry were eclipsed by new ways of doing things. It didn't simplify things but in practice made them more complex, partly because new procedures had to be invented and partly because the digital world, with its plethora of file types and formats, programming languages, hardwares, softwares and constant upgrades, is in many ways more complicated than the old analogue world of print. Typesetting was one of the first areas to be affected. The old linotype machines, which were the standard means of typesetting in the 1970s and before, were replaced in the 1980s by big IBM mainframe typesetting machines and then, in the 1990s, by desktop publishing. Typesetting costs plummeted: in the 1970s it typically cost $10 a page to get a book typeset from manuscript, whereas by 2000 it was costing between $4 and $5 a page despite the decrease in the value of the dollar produced by two decades of inflation. But for those who lived through the changes, this was a difficult and confusing time. The job of the typesetter was being redefined and lines of responsibility were being blurred. Many of the tasks formerly carried out by typesetters were being thrown back on production staff who were, at the same time, trying to use and adapt to new technologies that were in constant flux.

By the mid-1990s, many of the technical aspects of book production, including typesetting and page design, had been transformed by the application of digital technologies, but there were two areas of the workflow where progress was more erratic: editing and printing. When an editor receives a manuscript from an author, he or she will read the text and comment on it, often suggesting revisions that may range from small stylistic alterations to major structural changes. This process of editorial revision may happen more than once, as the editor works with the author to try to improve the text. Once the manuscript has been accepted by the editor, it will go through another process of editing, commonly known as copy-editing, in which a specialized copy-editor, often working freelance for the publisher, will line-edit the text, correct grammatical or stylistic errors, query anything that is unclear, eliminate repetition, make sure that the bibliography and any other technical aspects are in order and mark up the text for the typesetter. Both the editor and the copy-editor have traditionally worked with a typescript or printed manuscript. There are advantages in working with a printed text – it's easier to find your way around, to move back and forth between pages and keep track of the changes you've made. Many editors and copy-editors would find it difficult to work on screen, especially if a text needs a lot of structural or developmental editing.

There are other problems in trying to work with the electronic files supplied by authors. Often the electronic files contain numerous detailed errors and inconsistencies – for example, not differentiating between the letter O and zero 0, between hyphens and en-dashes, and so on. Errors of this kind have to be picked up and corrected. If the copy-editor (or assistant editor) also has to transfer corrections made on paper to the electronic file sent by the author, the costs involved in doing this begin to outweigh any advantages there might be in working with the author's disk. 'I can send the manuscript with mark-up to a compositor in Asia who could double-key it to 99 per cent accuracy *and* add the tags for page layout for half the price it would cost me to hunt and peck the corrections in Word. So do I pay someone $30 an hour to hunt and peck corrections or do I have it re-keyed, double-keyed with additional functionality, for half the price? Well, throw the disk out and have it re-keyed,' explained one production manager at a large trade house. So although the author's keystrokes are in principle the point at which the digital workflow could begin, in practice, at least in trade publishing, the digital workflow usually begins when the copy-edited manuscript is re-keyed by the compositor. In some fields of publishing – in some university presses, for example – procedures have been introduced to clean up authors' files ('initial prep', as some production managers call it) and copy-editors have been encouraged to edit onscreen using the tracking and comment features of Word, but these are not standard practices throughout the industry. Many trade publishers continue to pencil edit on paper and then have the manuscript re-keyed by the compositor, who supplies the publisher with a clean electronic file incorporating the tags for page layout.

The second area where progress has been more erratic is printing. Until the late 1990s, most publishers used traditional offset printing for all of their books. Offset has many advantages: print quality is high, illustrations can be reproduced to a high standard and there are significant economies of scale – the more you print, the lower the unit cost. But there are disadvantages too: most notably, there are significant set-up costs, so it is uneconomic to print small quantities. It was difficult to print fewer than 500 copies, since the unit costs were too high to be practicable. So backlist titles that were selling a few hundred copies or less per year were commonly put out of print by many publishers, and the large trade houses often drew the line much higher. It simply wasn't economic for them to keep these books in print, taking up space in the warehouse and reprinting in small quantities if and when the stock ran out.

The advent of digital printing changed all that. The basic technology for digital printing has been around since the late 1970s, but it was not until the 1990s that the technology was developed in ways that would enable it to become a serious alternative to the traditional offset presses. With the appearance of Xerox's DocuTech printer and similar machines from other manufacturers in the early 1990s, the quality, speed and cost per page of digital printers were beginning to reach levels at which they could compete with offset printing on short print runs. The quality was not as high and the reproduction of halftones remained distinctly inferior, but with improvements in technology the quality was getting better and better. By the end of the decade, the reproduction quality for straight text was, to the untrained eye, indistinguishable from offset printing, although there was still a discernable difference in the quality of halftones.

As the technology improved, a number of players entered the field in the late 1990s and early 2000s offering a range of digital printing services to publishers. Of particular significance in this context were two services: short-run digital printing (SRDP) and print on demand (POD). SRDP is simply the use of digital printers to produce small quantities of books – anything from 10 or 20 copies to 300 or 400 copies. It works with the same distribution model as books printed by traditional means: the publisher orders books to be printed, the books are shipped to the publisher's warehouse where they are held in stock and copies are then distributed through the normal channels in the normal way. The only difference is that the books are printed digitally and the quantities are smaller than they would be if the books were printed by traditional offset. Since the unit cost for digital printing is basically static, there is a point – currently around 400 copies for a normal book – at which the unit costs switch over: below that point it will be cheaper to print digitally, and above that point it will be cheaper to print using a traditional offset press. Thanks to

SRDP, publishers now had the full range of print quantities available to them. They could continue to reprint books, and keep them in print and in stock in perpetuity, simply by switching over from offset to digital printing.

SRDP is just a different method of printing, but POD is more than that: it is a fulfilment system that uses digital printing to fulfil a specific order. True POD is the printing of a text in response to the demand of a particular end user. As one of the senior managers involved in setting up Lightning Source – one of the pioneers of POD and still a leader in the field – put it, 'It used to be print book, sell book. We say no, no. Sell book, print book.' So, for example, if an individual customer places an order for a book, whether through a traditional bookseller or through an online retailer like Amazon, then the order can be transmitted to the POD supplier, who will print the book, ship it out and, depending on the service offered and which party collects the money, either pay or invoice the publisher. The POD supplier holds a file of the book on its server but does not hold any stock of the book, since the book is printed to meet the demand. Physical stock is replaced by a 'virtual warehouse'.

By the early 2000s, many publishers in the English-speaking world were using some version of digital printing for their slower-moving backlist titles, whether SRDP or true POD. Those in the fields of academic and professional publishing were among the first to take advantage of these new technologies: many of their books were specialized works that sold in small quantities at high prices, and were therefore well suited to digital printing. Many trade publishers were accustomed to dealing in the larger print quantities for which offset printing is ideal, but they eventually came to realize – in some cases with the help of the long-tail thesis first put forward by Chris Anderson in 2004[4] – that there was value locked up in some older backlist titles that could be captured by using digital print technology. Publishers – academic, professional and trade – began to mine their backlists, looking for older titles for which they still held the copyright, scanning them, turning them into PDFs and re-releasing them as digitally printed books. Books that had been left to die many years before were suddenly brought back to life. It is one of the ironies of the digital revolution that, so far from ushering in the death of the book, one of its most important consequences has been to give the

---

[4] See Chris Anderson, *The Long Tail: Why the Future of Business is Selling Less of More* (New York: Hyperion, 2006).

printed book a new lease of life, allowing it to live well beyond the age at which it would have died in the pre-digital world and, indeed, rendering it potentially immortal.

3 *Sales and marketing*   The digital revolution has also had, and continues to have, a profound impact in the areas of sales and marketing. The dramatic rise of Amazon is only the most obvious respect in which the retail environment of book publishing has been transformed by the internet. The significance of Amazon is not to be measured only in terms of its market share as a retailer (itself substantial, and still growing). It also stems from the fact that Amazon and other online booksellers use a retail model that is fundamentally different from that of the traditional bricks-and-mortar bookstore. In the Amazon model, the availability of books to the consumer is no longer tied to the physical availability of the book in the bookstore (or even in the retailer's warehouse); availability is virtual, not physical, and hence it is not dependent on the prior decision of a buyer to stock the book in the store. Of course, the Amazon model does not entirely eliminate the gatekeeper role of the buyer, since Amazon does hold stock of some books in its warehouses and whether it does or does not hold stock has a big impact on fulfilment times. Nor does it eliminate the role of marketing money in determining the visibility of particular titles, since Amazon has its own forms of co-op advertising and paid-for marketing campaigns. Nevertheless, the Amazon model does introduce something new into the retail space: a consumer offer in which the visibility, availability and sales of a book are less dependent – not wholly independent, but certainly less dependent – on the decisions and interactions of intermediaries in the bookselling chain, in particular on the decisions of sales reps and others in the publishing houses about which books to prioritize when they call on buyers, and on the decisions of buyers about which books to stock and in what quantities, as well as an array of related decisions about how and where to display the books, how much co-op money to put behind them and so on. The weakening of this link is precisely why Amazon has become a mechanism used by buyers and other managers in bricks-and-mortar bookstores to check on the soundness or otherwise of their initial purchasing and stocking decisions.

The digital revolution has also done something else equally important and in some ways more far-reaching in terms of the way the publishing business works: it has, as we've seen, turned sales figures into publicly available forms of knowledge. The gathering of accurate sales figures and sales histories, based on point-of-sale data and made available (at a price) to all players in the field, has changed the rules of the game. It is no longer possible to hide, to pretend, to make out that an author's previous books have been a tremendous success when, in fact, they have not, as anyone can now check the sales figures (within certain limits). Hype still has a crucial role to play in the publishing game, but hype based on inflated figures is largely a thing of the past. The digital revolution has created a kind of transparency in terms of sales figures that simply wasn't there before. It has also given rise to a kind of tyranny of numbers whose consequences may be less benign (a point to which we shall return).

Just as the digital revolution is transforming the sales environment, so too it is having a profound impact on marketing and the multiple ways in which publishers seek to generate awareness of their books among readers and consumers. The e-marketing revolution in publishing is only just beginning. Many initiatives are already underway and many more are in the pipeline or at various stages of conceptualization and development. In an earlier chapter we saw how some of the large trade publishers are shifting more and more of their marketing resources away from traditional print media and into online marketing activities of various kinds: this trend is set to continue and to take ever more elaborate and varied forms. Increasingly publishers will use the online environment to build direct connections with consumers and to facilitate online interactions between writers and readers – this is happening already, as we saw in chapter 7, and there is every reason to believe that it will continue. For every major trade publisher today, expanding their e-marketing activities and trying to understand how best to use the online environment to reach out to their readers and grow their readership are among their most urgent priorities.

Another aspect of marketing and promotion which has become very important for publishers is what could be called 'digital sampling'. Of course, it has always been possible to browse books before buying them. The traditional way of doing this was to go into a bookstore and page through the book, perhaps sitting in a corner somewhere and reading a few pages, before deciding whether to buy it. But the online environment makes it possible to dissociate browsing from the turning of printed pages in a bricks-and-mortar bookstore. Publishers can now allow readers to browse a book online – they can see the table of contents, read the blurb on the cover, dip into the text and perhaps even read a chapter or two. Both Amazon and Google provide publishers with programmes of this kind – Amazon's 'Search Inside the Book' and Google's 'Book Search'. These programmes are viewed by most publishers as an online shop window, an additional marketing tool that will enable readers to discover their books, find out more about them and encourage them to buy. If you are browsing a book online you are only a click away from buying it: a panel on the screen makes it easy for viewers to buy the book from Amazon and other bookstores or directly from the publisher.

The key issue with digital sampling is where you draw the line between sampling and consumption. You want to allow the reader to have enough exposure to the text to enable them to get a clear sense of the content and, hopefully, decide to buy the book, but you don't want them to be able to read so much of the text that the decision to purchase becomes redundant. Where do you draw the line? Different publishers draw the line in different places – some say 5 per cent of the book, some say 10 per cent, some say 20 per cent, some say you can read two pages forward and two pages back and then you hit a wall and the rest of the text is blanked out. Both Amazon's Search Inside the Book and Google's Book Search use restricted access models of this kind that are agreed contractually with the publisher. Other publishers prefer to vary the sampling model depending on the type of book – for example, in a work of non-fiction or a reference work, episodic sampling may be the best model, whereas in a work of fiction it might be better simply to allow the consumer to read the first chapter or two and nothing else. 'So for fiction I tend to be even more expansive in allowing for a continuous read of the beginning of the book because I think that's how you get the best flavour of whatever you're potentially buying,' explained a senior manager at one of the large trade houses. 'With non-fiction and especially reference-oriented non-fiction you have to be a little more careful because people may only want individual pages at individual times. You've got to make sure that the models of sampling fit with the content of the book so that you're delivering enough sampling for someone to know that they want it but not so much that they get everything they wanted without actually having to pay for it.'

4   Content delivery   So even before one broaches the issue of content delivery, it is clear that the digital revolution has had, and is continuing to have, a profound impact on the book publishing industry. Anyone who suggests otherwise is simply ill-informed or misinformed. But there is no doubt that it is the fourth level – that of content delivery – where the potential impact of the digital revolution is most profound. There is one basic characteristic of the book that makes this fourth level possible: the content of the book is separable from the form. This is a characteristic that the book shares in common with other products of the media and creative industries – films, music, newspapers, etc. – and is the reason why the impact of the digital revolution in these industries is potentially so much more disruptive than it is in, say, the refrigerator business. In essence, the digitization of content dissociates content and form. It captures content in a way that separates the content from the particular form in which it is, or typically has been, realized; it also captures content in a way that is sufficiently flexible to enable it to be realized, at least in principle, in a multiplicity of other forms. The physical book – the print and paper and binding and glue, the material object of a certain shape and size and weight – is a particular vehicle or form in which this content has been customarily realized for some 500 years, but it is not the only form in which it has been realized in the past, nor is it the only form in which it could be realized in the future. The digitization of content simply highlights a characteristic that was always part of the book but was obscured by the elegant union of content and form in a particular physical object. It brings out, more clearly than was previously the case, that the real value of the book lies in the content that is embedded in the physical form of the book, rather than in the physical form as such – hence the oft-repeated slogan associated with the digital revolution, 'content is king'.

It is not difficult to see that if book content is delivered to end users in an electronic form rather than in the form of the physical book, it transforms the supply chain and turns the traditional financial model of book publishing on its head. It is no longer necessary to lock up resources in physical books (with the attendant costs of paper, printing and binding), store them in warehouses, ship them to bookstores and wholesalers, accept them as returns if they are not sold and ultimately write them down and pulp them if they turn out to be surplus to requirements. In a world where content was delivered entirely electronically, publishers could bypass most if not all of the intermediaries in the traditional book supply chain and supply content either directly to the end user through their own website or via online intermediaries like Amazon. The costs associated with producing, storing and shipping physical books would be eliminated and the problem of returns would vanish in a click. It's a seductive vision. It's hardly surprising that ebooks have had, and continue to have, many champions, including many who work in the publishing industry. So why did it take so long for this vision to gain real traction in the marketplace? Why did the ebook revolution, which sounds so sensible when described from a purely operational point of view, make such slow and erratic progress in the first decade of the twenty-first century?

Among those who work in the ebook business, four reasons are commonly put forward – we alluded to some of these earlier but let's now examine them in more detail. First and perhaps most importantly, there was the problem of *hardware*: the early reading devices were expensive, clunky and awkward to use. The screens were small and the resolutions were poor, and many people were reluctant to spend several hundred dollars on dedicated reading devices which might turn out to have a short life. Amazon's Kindle – with its sleek appearance, its use of e-ink technology to mimic the effect of print on paper and the ability to download books directly via a wireless network without having to use a computer or go online – clearly marked a quantum leap forward in terms of technical design and ease of use, and the new generation of tablet computers, led by the iPad, has integrated the reading of books into the array of activities supported by a stylish, multipurpose device. The initial prices of dedicated reading devices may have put off some potential users – the Kindle was priced at $399 when it was first released in November 2007; but the prices came down quickly and it wasn't long before the devices began to look very affordable (the third generation of the Kindle, launched in 2010, was being sold for $139). With the launch of Barnes & Noble's Nook in 2009, the availability of the Sony ebook reader, the Kobo and other reading devices and the flooding of the marketplace with iPads and other tablet computers, the hardware problem was no longer the issue it had been in the early 2000s.

Second, there is the problem of *formats*: the early days of ebooks were characterized by a bewildering array of proprietary formats which were not interchangeable across different reading devices. This was confusing and off-putting for consumers, who were disinclined to invest in devices that could be rapidly eclipsed by technological change. The problem is comparable to that faced by other technologies in the early stages of development, like the format war between Betamax and VHS in the early development of the VCR, or the format war between Sony's Blu-ray and Toshiba's HD-DVD in the development of high definition DVD. This remains a problem in the ebook marketplace, as the most popular reading devices use proprietary file formats that are specific to the device. There have been attempts to create a standardized format for ebooks – first the Open eBook standard, followed by the ePub format that was launched by the International Digital Publishing Forum in 2007; but the ePub format is not supported by all devices (most notably, not as of yet by the Kindle).

Third, there is the problem of *rights*: there was considerable confusion about who owns the rights to exploit the content of a particular book in an electronic format. Is it the publisher? The author? And what should be paid to whom? Most older contracts between authors and publishers were drawn up at a time when the idea of exploiting content electronically was not even imagined, so there is no provision in the contract to indicate who controls the rights and how revenue is to be distributed. Can publishers assume that they control the electronic rights for earlier books they have published, even though the contract does not explicitly grant them these rights? Or do these rights remain with authors and their agents – and if so, are they free to assign the rights to someone else or even publish the works themselves in a digital format? The issues are rendered even more complex by the problem of embedded rights – that is, the copyright on material that is embedded in the text, such as quotations or illustrations. The publisher may have cleared permission to use this material for the print edition of the book, but can it be assumed that this permission can be transferred to an electronic edition? Or does the publisher have to go back to all of the original rights holders, assuming they can be tracked down, and clear the rights again for the ebook? No one really knew the answers to these questions as they simply hadn't arisen before, and many publishers were inclined to wait and see what norms might emerge before moving ahead on their own and risking copyright infringement.

Finally, there is the question of *price*: on the whole, publishers and retailers chose to price ebooks at levels that were roughly comparable to the price of print books, or at most 20 per cent below the price of the prevailing print edition. This was partly experimental, and partly an acknowledgement of the fact that, while there were some savings involved in delivering book content in electronic formats, these savings were not as great as many people assumed – all the acquisition, editorial and development costs were still there, the books still had to be designed and typeset, royalties still had to be paid (and probably at higher levels), there were still the marketing costs and the publisher's overheads, and then there were the additional costs involved in building and maintaining the IT infrastructure to support ebooks. The costs associated with the production of the physical book – print, paper and binding – are in fact a relatively small proportion of publishers' costs (though there are of course additional costs associated with warehousing and shipment, as well as the cost of returns). However, this does not go down especially well with consumers, for whom the perceived value of an ebook is significantly lower than that of a print book simply because it lacks the physical traits of the printed book. So pegging ebook prices at the same level (or slightly below) the prices of physical books deterred many consumers from making the transition – or at least this is the view of some.

For many who work in the industry, these four factors go a long way to explaining why ebooks failed to take off as quickly as many had expected; they also explain why, once a variety of high-quality devices were available and prices had come down, the surge in ebook sales was both sudden and strong. There is, however, an important element missing from this account – namely, the crucial role of the trusted intermediary in the supply chain. The fact that, from November 2007 on, ebooks were being actively promoted by Amazon was enormously significant, since millions of readers had grown accustomed to buying their books from Amazon, had given them their credit card details and had come to trust them as a reliable retailer of books. This was just enough to lower the threshold of anxiety that had disinclined so many readers in the past from switching over to ebooks – how do I know that this device will be any good, that it will be worth all the money, that I'll be able to get the books I want and won't have to worry about complicated things like formats and compatibility, that the reading experience will be agreeable and that the device and all the books I've bought won't be superseded by something else in six months time? Now, with Amazon providing its own devices, with prices falling and more and more ebooks being made available by one of the most trusted retailers of books in the business, the time for many readers to experiment had come.

It is therefore not surprising that Amazon was able very quickly to establish a dominant position in the emerging market for ebooks. Their aggressive pricing policy undoubtedly helped (more on this below) but their reputation among readers as a trusted retailer of books was probably also a vital factor. This also helps to explain why Barnes & Noble quickly moved into second place when it launched the Nook – contrary to the expectations of many in the industry, who thought the iPad would steal the show. Like Amazon, Barnes & Noble is a trusted retailer of books with a large and well-established clientele, and it was able to leverage its reputation among readers when it launched its reading device. It was also able to showcase and hand-sell its device in the front of stores across the country, which would have greatly helped its campaign too. Although estimates of market share in the rapidly changing ebook marketplace are notoriously unreliable, it seems likely that Amazon had around 90 per cent of the ebook market in the US at the beginning of 2010, but that this had fallen to 55–60 per cent by the middle of 2011. Barnes & Noble experienced strong growth through 2010 and probably had around 20–25 per cent of the ebook market by the middle of 2011 – 'definitely the strongest number two', as one industry insider put it. Apple was in third place with around 10–12 per cent of the market and the remaining 8–10 per cent was shared between Sony, Kobo and other smaller players.

Up till now we've been analysing the reasons for the erratic progress of ebooks but we have done so in a rather undifferentiated way. We haven't considered why some forms of content might lend themselves to being made available electronically more readily than others, and why some might be embraced more quickly by users. In the following two sections I shall try to shed some light on these issues by distinguishing more carefully between different forms of content and examining the ways in which new technologies can enable content providers to add real value to it. This will enable us to see that the impact of new technologies on the modes of content delivery is likely to vary from one field of publishing to another depending on a variety of factors, including the nature of the content, how people use it, who is paying for it and how much they are paying, the kind of value that can be added by delivering it electronically and the extent to which this added value is appreciated or valued by users. The idea that there will be an inevitable one-way migration from print to online dissemination is too simple. It may be a compelling idea for those who are inclined to believe that technology is the pacemaker of social change, but the world is often much more complicated than the technological determinist would like us to think.[5]

Technologies and added value

There are at least nine respects in which new technologies can enable content providers to add real value to their content: (1) ease of access; (2) updatability; (3) scale; (4) searchability; (5) portability;

---

[5] The following analysis draws on the framework developed in Thompson, *Books in the Digital Age*, pp. 318–29.

(6) flexibility; (7) affordability; (8) intertextuality; and (9) multimedia. These features are not unique to the online environment (they also apply in varying ways to other forms of electronic storage) and using new technologies to add value to content is not something that applies only to publishers: publishers are just one class of content providers among many others, and the types of content they provide may be less amenable to the value-adding features of new technologies than other types of content (such as recorded music). But here I'll examine these value-adding features in relation to the forms of content handled by publishers and with a particular focus on the delivery of content online or via wireless connectivity.

1 *Ease of access*   One of the great advantages of delivering content electronically is ease of access. In traditional systems of content provision, access to content is generally governed by certain spatial and temporal constraints – libraries and bookstores, for instance, are located in specific places and are open for certain hours of the day. But content delivered electronically is no longer governed by these constraints: in principle it is available 24/7 to anyone who has a suitable connection and the right of access. There is no need to go to a library to track down a book or a journal article if the content can be accessed from one's office or home. The personal computer or handheld device, located in a place that is convenient for the user or carried with them, becomes the gateway to a potentially vast body of content which can be accessed easily, quickly and at any time of the day or night. Moreover, unlike the traditional printed text, an electronic text available online can in principle be accessed by many users simultaneously (even if, in practice, access may be restricted to one user at a time).

2 *Updatability*   Another feature of content delivered electronically is that it can be updated quickly, frequently and relatively cheaply. In the case of content delivered in the form of the traditional printed text, making changes or corrections is a laborious process. Changes can be made to the text at any point up to the typesetting stage, but once the text is typeset it is costly to alter. Printed texts cannot be changed: once they are printed the content is fixed. But content delivered electronically is not fixed in a printed text, and hence it can be altered and updated relatively easily and cheaply. This is a particularly important feature in cases where the content is dealing with material that is in a state of continuous flux, such as financial data. But there are many other contexts where the capacity to update content quickly, frequently and cheaply is an important trait and can add real value.

3 *Scale*   Undoubtedly one of the most important features of online content delivery is scale: the capacity to provide access to large quantities of material. The internet economy is an economy of scale – it offers the possibility of providing access to collections of material that are extensive and comprehensive, of providing a range of choice and depth which is simply not possible in most physical collections. It is this scalability of the internet economy which has driven the online aggregation business. Numerous intermediaries have emerged with the aim of aggregating large quantities of content and selling this on to libraries and other institutions. Part of what is attractive to libraries is the ability to gain access to large quantities of content at relatively low costs, or at costs that are significantly lower than they would have to pay if they were to acquire the same content in a piecemeal fashion. Part of what is attractive to end users is the knowledge that they can find what they are looking for at a single site – a one-stop shop. By providing scale, that is, access to very large quantities of data or content, the content providers (or intermediaries) can add real value. In the internet economy, the whole is more than the sum of its parts, precisely because the comprehensiveness of a collection is valued for its own sake. However, it is important to stress that it is not quantity alone which is valued, but rather quantity which is perceived as relevant to what the user wants and needs – that is, *pertinent scale*. Intermediaries that set about aggregating large quantities of content while paying little attention to what end users actually wanted soon found that quantity alone does not suffice. What end users generally want is pertinent scale, not scale for the sake of it.

4 *Searchability*   A fourth feature of content delivered electronically is enhanced search capacity. The traditional printed text offers its own means for searching content – the table of contents provides a guide to the content of a book, and the index is effectively a search mechanism for the printed text. But the capacity to search a digitized corpus of material using a search engine based on keywords or names is infinitely quicker and more powerful than the traditional search mechanisms employed in printed texts, and the search capacity can be extended to much larger quantities of content. Search capacity can be provided both within a corpus and across corpora, thus providing the end user with a powerful means of searching for and accessing relevant content. This way of adding value is complementary to, and in some ways required by, the provision of scale. For the end user, there is not much value in having scale, even pertinent scale, unless you have an effective means of locating the content that inter-

ests you. The greater the scale, the more valuable – indeed essential – it is to have an effective means of searching the database.

5 *Portability*   Despite scale, content stored and transmitted electronically also offers the possibility of increased portability for the end user. In a digitized format, content is not tied to any particular medium of delivery, like the print-on-paper book. It is versatile, transferable, liberated from a specific material substratum and capable of being stored on any number of devices, provided it has not been locked into a particular device and the format is not proprietary. Moreover, the compression that can be achieved in a digital format enables a large amount of content to be held on a very small device. The traditional printed book is also a very portable object – that is part of its appeal. But the volume of content that can be made easily portable in a digital format is far greater than anything that could be achieved in the medium of print. Large amounts of content downloaded online or via a wireless network can be stored on a computer or some other much smaller device, such as an iPod or cellphone or dedicated reading device, and carried easily from one place to another, without the weight and sheer inconvenience that would be involved in carrying large numbers of books.

6 *Flexibility*   Content delivered electronically offers the possibility of greater flexibility for the end user depending on the functionality that has been built in by the content provider or device manufacturer. In the case of music, for example, the listener can skip over tracks on an album or create their own playlists by selecting their preferred songs. Most ebook reading devices allow users to vary the size of the typeface – a valued feature for many older readers with failing eyesight – and to look up words in a built-in dictionary, among other things. On the other hand, there are forms of flexibility that could be added to digital content but which may not be for reasons that are economic and/or legal rather than technical, such as the ability to share the content with others. And there are other forms of flexibility, like the ability to flick back and forth between pages, that may be lost or diminished in the transition from traditional physical products to content delivered electronically.

7 *Affordability*   Delivering content digitally also enables it to be delivered more cheaply. Savings can be made by eliminating the manufacture of physical products like the print-on-paper book – although, as noted earlier, these costs are much lower as a proportion of overall costs than most people assume. Further savings can be made by eliminating many of the stages and players in the traditional

supply chains for physical products – the physical warehouses, the packaging, the transport costs and the cost of returns. Taken together, these amount to real savings for content providers, and there is an expectation on the part of consumers that at least some of these savings will be passed on to them – a kind of 'digital dividend'. Exactly what this amounts to will vary greatly from one form of content to another and even one supplier to another, but there can be no doubt that cost reduction and lower prices are major factors driving the shift to digital content delivery.

8 *Intertextuality*   Another feature of the online environment is that it is able to give a dynamic character to what we could describe as the referential function of texts. In the traditional medium of the printed text, the capacity to refer to other material is realized through conventional literary devices such as references, footnotes and bibliographies: these are mechanisms for referring the reader on to other texts upon which the author has drawn or which the author regards as important, interesting and/or worthwhile. In the online environment, the referential function of the text can be made much more dynamic by using hot links to enable the reader to move to other pages and other sites. These links can be of various kinds – links to other pages, to other texts, to other sites and resources of various kinds, to bibliographies, biographies and online bookstores. Through the use of hypertext links, the content provider can enable the end user to access referred-to texts quickly and easily, without having to locate the text physically. And whereas references in printed texts can be updated only when there is a new edition of the work, hot links can be updated incrementally and at any time.

9 *Multimedia*   The delivery of content electronically also enables the content provider to use a variety of media and to supplement text with content delivered in other forms, including visual images, streaming video and sound. There are contexts in which this can enable content providers to add real value – for example, where it enables them to use colour illustrations that would be too costly to reproduce on the printed page, or to use streaming video to reproduce a speech or to illustrate a complex process. Of course, there are costs associated with the provision of multimedia content – it may be costly to produce and permission fees may be high. It may also be difficult to use, in the sense that the files may be large and slow to download. But it does at least offer the possibility of adding a kind of value to content which would not be possible in traditional print formats.

Technologies and fields of publishing

If we want to understand why the digital revolution has affected different sectors of the publishing industry in different ways in terms of content delivery, then a careful analysis of the kinds of value that can be added to content in an online environment is a good place to begin but it is not enough. We also have to see that different publishing fields operate in different ways, that different types of content lend themselves to online delivery more readily than others and that end users will have their own views about whether the value added by new technologies is, in any particular case, *valuable to them* – or at least sufficiently valuable to them to induce them to access content in this way and pay for it, if indeed the content is being delivered in such a way that the content provider is expecting the end user to pay for it. In other words, technologies always exist in specific social contexts and their usefulness or otherwise is shaped by a variety of contextual factors. Added value, like beauty, is in the eye of the beholder. It is a contested social phenomenon. What end users regard as valuable, and how valuable they regard it, may not be the same as what content providers regard as valuable, and how these different valuations play out will vary from field to field and from one form of content to another.

Consider some examples. The field of scientific and scholarly journal publishing experienced a rapid and decisive shift from print to online delivery in the late 1990s and early 2000s. This dramatic transformation was driven forward by the large scientific journal publishers like Elsevier and Springer, who invested heavily in the development of online platforms and in creating fully fledged digital workflows for journal production, but it was also actively encouraged and supported by librarians in the research libraries that comprised the primary market for journals. There are several reasons why the transition to online delivery was so rapid and decisive in the field of scientific and scholarly journal publishing:

- The market for scientific and scholarly journals was an institutional market: these journals were not bought by individuals paying out of their own pocket but by institutional gatekeepers – librarians – who had access to annual budgets that had to be spent on content acquisition.
- The subscription model for journals already existed and it was easy to adapt this model to a site licence for journals deliv-

ered online. Librarians were familiar with the business model and were keen to be able to provide an additional service to their users.

- The move into an online environment provided new opportunities for the aggregation of content and for generating the kind of pertinent scale that can add value, and this feature was valued by both librarians and end users. Journal publishers with large numbers of journals could offer special deals to libraries and library consortia to gain access to the whole corpus (e.g. Elsevier's ScienceDirect or Thomson's Web of Science), and third-party aggregators (e.g. Gale) could offer packages of content assembled from a variety of different publishers.

- The nature of journal content also lent itself to online dissemination. Journal articles are generally very short – as short as two to three pages, but usually no more than 20 pages – and hence they can be either read on screen or printed out with ease. Particular journal issues are for the most part arbitrary collections of articles which bear no intrinsic connection to one another (with the exception of themed issues), and hence the end user is likely to read only a specific article rather than a series of articles. Since users are generally looking for specific articles on specific topics, the capacity to search for relevant material across a large corpus of material is a valued feature. Moreover, scientists and academics are accustomed to working on their computers, and having journals available online, so that they can access them anytime from their desktops and offices without having to visit a physical library, is a feature that is highly valued by them.

These and other factors go a long way to explaining why scientific and scholarly journal publishing was one of the first areas to move rapidly and decisively into an online environment. This is a form of publishing that exists within a specific institutional space (publishing organizations selling content on a subscription basis to libraries with acquisitions budgets), where the nature of the content (short articles on discrete topics, easily read on screen or printed out) is amenable to online dissemination and where there are clear gains to be achieved in terms of added value (including scale, searchability and ease of access), gains that are valued both by the institutional intermediaries paying for the content and by the end users. But even in the sphere of scientific and scholarly journal publishing, the migration to online dissemination has not – or at least not yet – been total. While librarians are keen to offer their users the ability to access journals online, many remain concerned about the 'archiving problem' – that is, how they can ensure perpetual access to journal content for which they have already paid. What happens if at some future date they cancel the subscription, or if at some future date the journal folds or the publisher goes out of business? How then will they be able to ensure access to back issues unless those issues are sitting physically on their shelves? If the electronic content is to be held in escrow by a third party, who will bear the costs of doing so and manage the collection? Until librarians are convinced that the archiving problem has been satisfactorily solved, many will continue to insist on receiving hard copies of each issue as well as access online and the economies that could be achieved by moving entirely into an online environment – both in terms of production costs and in terms of shelf space – will not be realized.

Another field of publishing where there has been a clear and irreversible shift to online dissemination is reference publishing. Large reference works, like comprehensive encyclopaedias and dictionaries, have migrated to online environments as their primary medium of content delivery, even if they continue to be made available in print as well and to offer a range of smaller, print-based spin-off products. Again, there are several reasons why this happened:

- Large multivolume encyclopaedias like *Encyclopaedia Britannica* faced intense competition in the early 1990s from electronic encyclopaedias like Microsoft's *Encarta*, which were compiled on CD-ROM and given away as promotional extras with the sale of new computers. The proliferation of free encyclopaedias, even if they were less comprehensive and inferior in quality, undermined the market for the large, expensive, multivolume work. Sales of *Britannica* and other traditional encyclopaedias collapsed in the 1990s. If they wanted to survive, they had to reinvent themselves as branded resources that were primarily electronic, and ultimately web-based, in character. They could continue to produce a range of print-based products but their primary mode of content delivery would have to become electronic.

- Encyclopaedias, dictionaries and other reference works lend themselves to online dissemination for several reasons. They are accumulations of discrete pieces of knowledge – 'bitty' forms of content. Users do not generally read a reference work from cover to cover but rather consult it in order to answer a specific question or gain a specific piece of knowledge; the capacity to search quickly for a specific piece of information is therefore a highly valued feature. Similarly, cross-referencing to related material is valued by users.

- Scale is also vital for many reference works: the more comprehensive they are, the more useful they are likely to be for the user. Of course, this is not always the case: sometimes a concise reference work, like a dictionary, a travel guide or a book of recipes, may be quite adequate for the purpose at hand. But there are many purposes for which the scale and comprehensiveness of the reference work will be regarded by users as a positive asset. In the medium of print, large, comprehensive reference works of this kind are very costly to produce and very costly to buy. They are also clumsy and unwieldy and can take up a great deal of space. Making them available as online databases overcomes these disadvantages precisely because the online economy is an economy of scale.

- Reference works need to be regularly updated. It is very costly to do this in the print medium, but a reference work can be continuously updated and expanded, relatively easily and cheaply, in an online environment. This feature has, of course, been incorporated into the very raison d'être of Wikipedia, which actively encourages users to become content creators and contribute to the continuous process of updating, amending and expanding the content that comprises the online encyclopaedia.

- For some reference works like encyclopaedias, the use of multimedia, including colour illustrations, sound and streaming video, can also add a kind of value that is appreciated by end users.

For these and other reasons, the online environment provided a natural home for some large reference works: given the nature of the content and the way it was typically used, the kind of value that could be added in the online environment was the kind of value that was appreciated by many users. The problem for content providers was twofold: how to develop a business model that would enable them to charge for their content, and how to position themselves in this new environment in a way that would enable them to ward off the threat posed by much cheaper alternatives (or even free alternatives, as in the case of Wikipedia and other online resources).

For large reference works like the *Oxford English Dictionary* or multivolume encyclopaedias (especially those of a more specialist kind, like the *International Encyclopedia of the Social and Behavioral Sciences*), suitable business models were readily at hand: since their primary market for the complete set was mainly an institutional market, that is, libraries, schools, universities and other institutions of this kind, they could replace the one-off transaction fee for the complete set in print either by a one-off transaction fee for the work made available on CD-ROM or DVD, or by a site licence to an online resource for which the institution would pay an annual subscription fee based on the size of the institution and the number of users. Since the main market for these works was institutional, the fee – whether transaction or subscription – could be set at a high level, as the institutions were already accustomed to paying substantial fees for these works.

What was much less clear was how content providers could charge for reference content that was traditionally packaged in much smaller formats, like small dictionaries or one-volume encyclopaedias on more specialized topics. Many of these smaller works were sold to individual consumers on a transactional basis – one book, one sale, end of transaction. It was not at all clear that they would want to buy this content in electronic formats. For many purposes, having a reference work available in a concise printed format is more convenient than using a reading device or checking online, even if the electronic resource is much more comprehensive – it's much easier, for example, to open a cookbook to a favourite recipe and lay it on the kitchen counter than it would be to look up a recipe online and print it out. Nor was it clear that institutions would want to purchase this content in an electronic format, precisely because it lacks the one thing that is of particular value to institutions – scale. Smaller reference works have therefore continued to survive and, indeed, flourish in traditional printed formats while their larger brethren migrated online.

So there are good reasons why the field of scientific and scholarly journal publishing and the field of reference publishing have experienced a migration – partial in some cases, but clear and irreversible nonetheless – from print to online content delivery. However, in other publishing fields the situation is much less clear. In the field of scholarly book publishing, for example, there has been a great deal of experimentation with electronic content delivery since the late 1990s. This is partly because the field of scholarly book publishing had been experiencing serious difficulties for many years, stemming largely from the steep decline in the sales of scholarly monographs, and there were many who believed or hoped that the digital revolution would provide a solution to the problems of scholarly monograph publishing. Many different initiatives were launched, some funded by philanthropic organizations with an interest in scholarly communication, such as the Mellon Foundation, some funded by third parties and venture capital seeking to develop commercially viable businesses, and some funded by publishers themselves. I have examined a variety of these initiatives elsewhere and will not repeat the analysis here.[6] Suffice it to say that, despite the hopes of many in the scholarly publishing community, there is no *obvious* electronic solution to the problems of scholarly monograph publishing. Just as the digital revolution was not the origin of the problems faced by scholarly book publishers, so too it is unlikely to be their salvation. The reasons for this are not technical, but primarily economic and cultural. Academic publishers and others have made scholarly books available online, either as individual ebooks or as part of a database that is offered to customers on a transactional or subscription basis, but the take-up of these offerings has been modest to date and the amount of revenue publishers have been able to generate has been small. Up till now, academic publishers have benefited much more from what I've called the hidden revolution – especially the ability to print small quantities using digital technologies, to reduce print runs and to keep books in print long beyond their natural life cycle in the pre-digital age – than they have from making scholarly book content available online.

It also seems clear that, to the extent that there is a market for scholarly book content delivered online, it is more likely to be an institutional rather than an individual market, at least for the near future. The electronic initiatives that have been most successful to date in the field of scholarly book publishing are those which have clearly targeted the institutional market – above all, the research libraries. Whether scholarly books are sold to libraries on a title by title basis (as with NetLibrary, dawsonera and various library suppliers) or sold as part of a scholarly corpus of books on a subscription basis (as with publisher-based initiatives like Oxford Scholarship Online or with third-party ventures like the Humanities E-Book project), it is libraries that provide the most robust market for scholarly books in electronic formats. The reasons are not difficult to see: librarians have budgets to spend on content acquisition; they are accustomed to acquiring digital products and predisposed to do so,

---

[6] See Thompson, *Books in the Digital Age*, ch. 13.

especially if they think this will reduce pressure on shelf space and provide extra functionality for library users (such as access from their desktops); and the business models, whether transactional or subscription based, are familiar, well tested and easy to administer. There is every reason to believe that in the coming years we will see a slow but steady increase in the sale of scholarly book content into research libraries in electronic formats. However, this is not to say that it will necessarily be at the expense of printed books, which will continue to be purchased by many libraries, either instead of or in addition to electronic versions, and will in all likelihood remain for some while to come the preferred medium for individuals who wish to purchase scholarly books for their own use.

If this analysis is correct, then what we're likely to see in the field of scholarly book publishing is not a wholesale migration from print to electronic dissemination but rather the development of *mixed models of revenue generation*. The kind of migration that has occurred in scientific and scholarly journal publishing may not be a good model for what will happen in the field of scholarly book publishing. A scholarly book is a different kind of object from a scientific journal and it is used in different ways. It is fine to browse a book online or to search a text to find what you need, but if you want to read all or most of a scholarly book, and be able to move back and forth in the book and study it carefully, most readers prefer to have a printed version. Hence it seems likely that, at least for the foreseeable future, the making of scholarly book content available online will take place *alongside* the continued publication of books in printed formats. Academic publishers may gradually move away from the traditional model of revenue generation, which depended almost exclusively on the sale of printed books, to more mixed models that still depend largely, perhaps even overwhelmingly, on print sales while also seeking, at the same time, to diversify revenue streams – for example, by generating a proportion of their revenue from the sale of site licences, from the sale of ebooks and/or from the licensing of content. But for the foreseeable future scholarly book publishers are going to continue to rely heavily on revenue from print sales. The income they generate from electronic sales will, in all likelihood, be incremental additions, and quite modest ones at that.

If scholarly book publishing presents a mixed picture, so too does trade publishing, although in this case the channels to market for content delivered electronically are rather different. Whereas scholarly book content delivered electronically has found a market primarily among institutions rather than individuals, the ebooks published by trade publishers are being bought primarily by individuals equipped with reading devices. The individuals who buy ebooks value above all their affordability, readability (easy on the eye, adjustable font size), ease of access (can be bought easily and quickly) and portability – in the surveys carried out by the Book Industry Study Group in 2010 and 2011, these are the features that tended to be regarded as most important by customers.[7] The BISG surveys also showed that the kinds of books consumers most preferred to read as ebooks tended to be straight narrative fiction (genre, commercial and literary fiction), which mirrors the experiences of trade publishers who have seen the most dramatic increases in these categories. The kinds of non-fiction that were most popular in ebook format were those with strong narrative elements, like biography and autobiography; other kinds of non-fiction, including professional and academic books, lagged well behind.[8]

While it is clear that a growing number of readers are happy to read books on reading devices, especially when the books take the form of straight narrative text, what is not clear at this stage is exactly how far the shift to digital will go in the different categories of books, each of which has its own distinctive characteristics. Readers of genre fiction and commercial fiction may value above all the ability to get new books quickly and cheaply, so that they can read them as soon as they are available; storing the book on their shelves as a keepsake may be of little value to them. On the other hand, for a new novel by a great writer or a serious work of non-fiction, there will probably always be some readers who will prefer to have the physical book. Price, ease of access and portability may not be the most important considerations for them; other things may matter more. They might simply prefer to read the text on the printed page, which is gentle on the eyes and enables them to move back and forth with ease. They might value the ability to share the text with others, lend it to others or borrow it from them, or perhaps give it as a gift. They might value the object itself as a cultural form, a material object, attractively designed and produced, durable and displayable, in which you invest

---

[7] *Consumer Attitudes toward E-Book Reading,* Report 2 of 3 (New York: Book Industry Study Group, March 2010), p. 13; *Consumer Attitudes toward E-Book Reading,* vol. 2, Report 2 of 4 (New York: Book Industry Study Group, April 2011), p. 14.
[8] *Consumer Attitudes toward E-Book Reading,* Report 2 of 3, p. 12.

a good deal of time and effort, from which you derive pleasure and satisfaction and which, having read and enjoyed it, you might wish to own, to keep on a bookshelf, to return to at some later date and dip into, consult or reread. Indeed, it's even possible that the shift to digital in certain categories of books (what one publisher described as 'disposable books' – read them, delete them, get the next) could be accompanied by a revaluation of printed books in other categories, with some readers placing greater value on printed books, especially beautifully produced hardcover editions, for those books and authors they love and treasure – who knows. Moreover, while it is relatively easy to make straight narrative text available electronically, it is far more complicated and costly to produce other types of books in electronic formats, especially heavily illustrated books like cookbooks, art books and children's books, and it's not clear at this stage whether consumers would in any case wish to buy these books in these formats. Nor is it clear whether they would wish to buy books where a great deal of multimedia content had been added – it is simply too early to say.

So how should publishers prepare themselves for a world which is changing fast but where there is still so much uncertainty about which formats will prove popular for different kinds of content and which will endure? Fortunately for publishers, they don't actually need to know which forms of content delivery will prove most popular for which types of content. While the world around them is swirling with speculation and change, they can afford to remain agnostic on the question of content delivery. For they are in the position of a water company who owns and controls the water supply but doesn't own the pipes that deliver the water to consumers. If some consumers decide that they would prefer to receive their water through a different kind of pipe, then the water company needs to be in a position to supply it for that pipe. They don't necessarily need to build the new pipe themselves – they can let others do it and take the risks. But they do need to make sure that their water can be pumped through the new pipe and that those who own and control the pipe don't have a stranglehold on the supply chain. And that means that what they need to do in the first instance is to build a digital archive.

Building the digital archive

Steve is the head of a division called Media Asset Development at one of the large trade houses in New York. He joined the company in 1995, after having worked on the digital end of the music industry for several years. He arrived at a time when the debate about digitization in the publishing industry was just beginning to be taken seriously by senior managers. Most book production was still being done in the traditional way, and then a small number of books were picked out to be produced 'digitally'. 'So there was publishing and then there was digital publishing, there was production and there was digital production. The fight since I arrived has been to get the company to stop thinking that way altogether. There is no production without files, there is no mechanism by which you can go to press anymore without it being digital. So let's stop saying "digital production" and start calling the production area "the production area".' There were people in the company who thought (and some still do) that you could hire someone in the production department who didn't understand file management – 'Huge mistake,' says Steve. 'I think we're getting that clear in the company, that if you don't understand file management, you can't be in production; it just doesn't make sense anymore. It's like saying "I understand horses and I want to work in a car manufacturer." It's like the time has passed.'

The company also came to realize that they needed to take ownership of their files in a way they had never done before. It happened around 1998–9. What triggered it was the decision to start making some of the older backlist titles available as print on demand. 'As a company we decided that print on demand is going to be something we definitely have to guarantee. No book is ever going to go out of print again. Print on demand requires a file, right, so this is the first time we had an actual requirement. Ebooks were sort of a nice toy, but a requirement came up with print on demand. This is a stake in the ground: the company is saying, "We need files." But the problem was that the files were not easy to get. The files were with the printers and compositors,' explained Steve. 'All of our printers and compositors said, "We have your files, we're storing them for you, we can give them back to you for 200 bucks or some price." We did an analysis of our title list and we figured there was somewhere around 15,000–20,000 books we wanted, so we said, "Great, give them back." The reply from our printers and compositors was, basically, "You know, we can't actually do this because we're not sure which is the last version. We've got them stripped on tapes and we've got 5,000 tapes and we'd probably have to run them all to figure out the versioning." And out of the 15,000 we asked for, 300 were available.' It quickly became clear that the printers and compositors weren't really archiving the publisher's files. They were backing up their work in progress but they weren't archiving, and there's a big difference between backing up and archiving. 'Archiving really means the book is ready to go for print at its most recent iteration in a complete file set today. Backing up is just, "Well, if we go down, can we restore?" They don't ever keep our most recent version, they just back up their work in progress. So there's no archive.'

At that point it was clear that the publisher had to create its own archive and its own archiving procedures. 'We were very clear that owning the process is what we had to do. That was a huge eye-opener – that no one else out there cares about our files but us, nobody's going to take care of them, nobody's going to version them, nobody's going to do any quality control.'

Once the company had decided that it needed to create its own digital archive, it then had to establish the archiving procedures and populate the archive with the company's digital assets. This was much more complicated than it might at first seem. First, there was the sheer quantity – with a large house like this which includes many imprints with their own long publishing histories, there were as many as 40,000–50,000 titles still in print. Then there are the different purposes for which the digital content could be used. 'Are we talking about print on demand and ebooks? Because those can be different animals. Are you talking about capturing them just to capture them, or do you really want to capture things that have immediate value? Do you want a return on investment on what you capture instantly or is it long-term investment? You start having to have those conversations. But the place we should have started, and it's the philosophy that we try to implement here, is that a book is not a book. Books are categories. Books are types. Books are different styles of things. So you can't just say, "Go capture 20,000 books."' Steve elaborates:

If you keep thinking of books as generic objects, you're thinking about them the way that they are in paper. In paper they're all the same – it's a book, you're delivering tree. So if your delivering mechanism is delivering tree, you're done. If it's delivering digital goods, they are differentiated in multiple facets. So when you start the backlist discussion, you start saying, 'What is your target? What's the specification? What are you thinking about and for what kind of book?' It gets much more complicated. The thing people always hoped was that the digital world would get simpler and it's actually a whole lot more complicated because your end result isn't the same. The end result is a database, the end result is a PDF, it's an image-based PDF, it's an XML file, it's an ad-based, Google-search-engine toolset – we're going to have many more properties digitally than we possibly could have physically. We have seven physical properties now: large print, mass market, hardcover, paperback and you have some weird digest editions and stuff like that. Online we have ad-based, widget-based, ebook-based, subscription-based, chunked content – there are hundreds of formats and types and styles. So it's a much bigger world digitally than in print. So when you say, 'Oh, let's go capture all the backlist,' it's like wait a minute, do you want us to capture cookbooks? Do you want us to capture things that are out of stock today? Do you want us to capture out of print? Do you want us to capture only the 10,000 top sellers? So we had those discussions. What we came around to was the 10,000 top-selling books of all time from that year back – let's get those and decide how to make them available. That was the backlist adventure.

Each of these 10,000 top-selling books was sent out to be scanned and turned into an XML file using OCR (Optical Character Recognition) software. It was more expensive than simply producing a PDF – it cost around $200 to turn an average-sized book into an XML file, whereas you can produce a PDF with a simple scan for around $50. PDF is fine for print on demand but it is less adaptable, cannot be used for ebook outputs and is a much larger file, and hence more expensive to store.

To the 10,000 backlist titles, they added the 4,000 or so new titles that were being produced every year, so that by 2008 they had a digital archive containing some 40,000 titles. In addition to populating the archive, they needed to develop procedures for handling the content. These involved three distinct processes – 'digital asset management', 'digital transformation' and 'digital distribution'. Steve pulled out a blank sheet of paper and drew a sketch (see figure 14). On the left-hand side of figure 14 are the different production departments of the company that are producing new books and delivering them as digital files to the Digital Asset Management (DAM) system, which is the company archive. What happens in the production departments depends on their workflow processes and the degree of sophistication they want to build into the files – if they want to do XML tagging, for example, it happens there. When the files are complete they are dumped into the DAM, the archive, which stores different kinds of files – Quark files, InDesign files, PDF files, XML files, etc. – for each book. The files for each book are stored under one ISBN, usually the hardcover ISBN, so you have four or five different

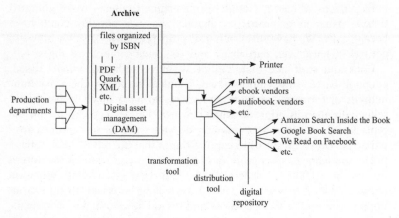

Figure 14   The digital archive

files for exactly the same book. This immediately creates a level of complexity that has to be carefully managed. So, for example, if you want to make a correction on a particular page of a particular book, you have to make sure you have procedures in place to ensure that the correction is made before the book is reprinted, whichever edition is being reprinted. 'Maintaining that print file correctly is the key,' explains Steve. 'If the archive has one thing that it has to do without fail, it's have the right version of the file for print, at all times. That's the golden rule that can't be broken.'

This may sound simple enough but it's easy to screw it up. For example, suppose one of the imprints has a book that's selling well and they need to reprint quickly, but they find that they've got a typeface corruption on page 90. The printer says he can probably fix it so they tell him to go ahead and fix it because they need the books as soon as possible. 'They get a call back saying they fixed it, that's great, we're rolling and you say, "Thank God." But that file is no longer in sync with my digital files. Did we ask for the corrected file back? No. Are we just waiting to have the same problem happen again when we do a reprint? A production error trumps everything else, period. If something's down or broken or in press and is wrong, it's got to be fixed, instantly; there's no question about it. The problem is the recovery of the file – we need the file back. It just tends to be forgotten.' So now the file at the printers is out of sync with the file in the digital archive and the publisher doesn't know how the file has been changed to correct the error. The problem could recur the next time the book is reprinted. The integrity of the files in the archive has been compromised by the need to solve the production problem and get the book reprinted quickly.

Getting people in the various publishing divisions to think differently about these issues is not easy because they are not rewarded for helping to maintain the integrity of a database; they're rewarded for selling books, and making sure that a book which is selling well is reprinted promptly and available to meet current demand is a vital part of this. But the problem is that, in focusing on their short-term problem and not thinking about the long term, they're only storing up problems for others further down the line. When the mass-market people pick up the book in a year or 18 months' time, they're picking up your problem. To avoid that, a determined effort has to be made to 'incentivize care', as Steve puts it – that is, to get people throughout the organization to see that maintaining the integrity of files is in the interests of everyone. 'The goal of publishing isn't to trip and stumble out the door and manage to toss the book in the printers and be done and say, "Thank God." The goal is to maintain appropriate and up-to-date content for the lifespan of that work.'

Apart from managing the asset store and ensuring that the most recent, corrected or updated files are being held in the system, you also have to be able to deliver content in appropriate formats to various external clients. Quark files are sent directly to the printer from the digital archive, but other files may need to be converted to other formats before they can be used by clients and vendors. So, for example, if an ebook is stored in ePub format, it may need to be converted to an ebook vendor's proprietary format, if an audio file is stored in the WAV format, it may need to be converted to an AIFF file for a particular audiobook vendor, and so on. In these cases, a transformation tool will convert the file before it's passed on to a distribution tool that sends it out to the appropriate client or vendor. Of course, it would be much easier if all these clients and vendors used the same file formats but they don't, so the transformation and distribution tools have to be geared to providing each client and vendor with files in the particular formats they require.

In addition to supplying files to vendors, some publishers will also store files in certain formats in a digital repository that is accessible by others, with rules governing what can be accessed by whom and under what conditions. In some cases the repository is hosted on the publisher's own server; in other cases it is outsourced to a third party, like LibreDigital. The purpose of the repository is to provide the publisher with a digital face to the outside world, to enable some of its content to be seen in the online world and, indeed, actively to project some of its content into this world, while at the same time retaining control over it. So, for example, the content held in the repository can be made available to Amazon and Google for their book search programmes through a dynamic web call (more on this below).

Building all these systems is complicated and expensive, and company's like Steve's had to do it when they were seeing very little if any return in terms of revenue. They were building their digital archives when the overwhelming share of their revenue was still being generated by the sale of the various print editions – hardcover, trade paperback, mass market, etc. 'I'd say it's somewhere around 97, 95 per cent,' says Steve, clutching for some rough percentages (this was 2008). 'Ebooks do make some money, audio does make some money, licensed deals do make some. So there's a bunch of little money ways in there but the vast, vast majority comes from the print file.'

In fact, of these alternative sources of non-print revenue (and leaving aside rights income, which is another issue altogether), audio was the main revenue generator during the time when the investment in the digital archive was being made. The sales of audiobooks represent a small proportion of the overall revenues of the major trade houses – probably around 5 per cent; but they were still generating far more revenue than ebooks in the period up to 2008–9. The general rule of thumb in the audiobook business is that if you have a big book that is suitable for audio, you can generate audio sales of up to 10 per cent of the hardcover print sale. So if you sell 100,000 hardcovers, you can sell up to 10,000 audios, but never more than that. And of course there are many books that are not suitable for audio and are never turned into audiobooks – given the 10 per cent rule, the audio division of a large trade house normally doesn't even consider a book unless there is a clear expectation that it will sell a minimum of 50,000 hardcovers. And then they have to consider whether it's going to work in audio – 'You know, cookbooks don't work in audio except in rare cases; diet books don't work in audio,' explained the manager of one audio division. 'And there are particular categories that can work extremely well in audio – memoirs, for example, books that have a personality-driven narrator. The commercial fiction, plot-driven fiction also works very well in audio. Literary fiction, intricate, more character-driven fiction, does not work as well in audio because your mind just can't track, the narrative has sort of gone on and you're about to try and figure out what that sentence meant.'

These principles haven't changed much since audiobooks first began to appear in the 1980s, but the way audiobooks are delivered to consumers has evolved from one format to another – 'Much of the story of audio has been about this transition, the march through the different formats.' The early audiobooks were sold as tape cassettes, but the cassette was phased out and replaced by CDs, which is now the dominant medium for the sale of audiobooks. The transition from tape to CD was a transition from analogue to digital, but the digital product was still being delivered in a physical form – the CD, often a set of five or six depending on the length of the recording, commonly sold as a boxed set. However, digital downloads are now accounting for a growing share of the market. In 2005, CDs accounted for around 90 per cent of the revenue from audio sales for the audio division of one large trade house, and digital downloads accounted for around 10 per cent; by 2007, the proportions were 85 per cent CD, 15 per cent digital download. 'I think there's going to be a point that we're probably approaching where things start to accelerate in terms of CDs dropping off and downloads accelerating and that has to do with just the penetration of the iPod,' explained the manager. However, given the importance of the iPod as an audio device, the extent to which the digital download market expands, and the rate at which it expands, are likely to depend on which retailers can sell the download that is iPod-compatible. 'Up till now, you've had only Audible and Apple who are able to sell iPod-compatible download files with DRM [digital rights management] protection,' she continues. 'And so as powerful a retailer as iTunes is, I think that there's probably been some kind of suppression of the growth of digital downloads because of only having those two retailers sell. If you went to a situation tomorrow where every retailer who sells CDs was also selling digital downloads, I think the growth rate would probably be much faster.'

Steve, for his part, was well aware that audio was the main revenue generator among the non-traditional, non-print products sold by the company and that the revenue generated by ebooks remained insignificant, but he was convinced that ebooks would grow. In his view, the print-on-paper book is just a tool like any other, a piece of technology which has some strengths and some weaknesses – 'It's a good tool, it doesn't require batteries, it's easy to use, you know, it's all that stuff. But as soon as we have a better tool, I think books are just gone. They're expensive, heavy, can't search them, there's all these things against them.' He has limited sympathy for the idea that a book might be more than that for many readers – a cultural object that might have aesthetic and emotional value for them, something they might value as they value a work of art. Sure, there are some books for which this may be true, but they're a minority – '20 per cent maybe.' Books will not cease to be printed, in Steve's view, any more than the invention of the television killed the radio or the invention of the DVD killed television. But the 'triage' will be different:

> Books aren't the same thing every time. Triage them better. Would you rather be handed the phone book or Google? Well, so don't print the phone book anymore, that's not a work of art, right? Who cares about the phone book? Most of the paperbacks you buy in the airport, wouldn't you rather just walk over to the kiosk and have it beam them into something you can take on the plane and read if it was cheaper and easier and faster? But then you say, 'Well, I want a coffee table book,' well, that's always going to exist, you're not going to replace that with digital. There are books that are objects of art and that are going to endure history and go down through the ages and you definitely want to print those. But crappy romance novels? You really want to kill a tree for them?

Of course, Steve could be wrong (though with the benefit of hindsight, his comments, made in 2008, seem remarkably prescient). But the beauty of Steve's position is that he doesn't have to be right. He just has to be ready. 'Publishers should focus on making sure they get content that sells. They don't really care how it sells, they just want to sell it. The fact that print is the medium they sell it in and they've got to make their numbers this year, that's not my responsibility. My responsibility is to make sure that we're positioned so that when something changes, it's seamless here. So when they say, "We're finding that 10 per cent of our market is now electronic," that's an opportunity, not a problem. So I would like us to be agnostic to whatever succeeds. Do I care whether or not people buy the book on a particular medium? They shouldn't care either, whether it's audio, ebook, electronic, subscription – if we sell it, that's all that we really care about.' Provided that the digital archive is built and functioning well, and provided that the company's content is stored in appropriate digital formats and properly maintained, then the publisher is in a position to respond to changes in the market. They are able and ready to deliver the content down a different pipeline – if, in fact, consumers demonstrate through their purchasing decisions that they prefer to use a different pipe.

So are there dangers in this situation for a trade publisher? What do Steve and other managers in his and similar companies worry about? They worry about many things but there are two that preoccupy them most: piracy and price.

The threat of piracy

There is nothing new about the unauthorized reproduction of books and parts of books: it has long been a feature of the world of print, exacerbated by the photocopying machine but by no means invented by it. However, with the conversion of the book into a digital file, the risks of unauthorized reproduction and circulation of book content are raised to an entirely new level. Once content is in a digital form and provided it is unsecured, it is quick, easy and cheap to produce multiple copies and to share it with others – a PDF can easily be sent to any number of recipients, or made available online for others to view or download. And all of this could be done without permission or remuneration, infringing a publisher's copyright and depriving them and the author of revenue. One need look no further than the music industry to see the havoc that can be wreaked in a creative industry by rampant file sharing facilitated by peer-to-peer distribution systems like Napster. Publishers knew they couldn't ignore the dangers. So how are they trying to deal with this threat? Essentially in three ways: security, policing and proactively supplying the market.

Security is a matter of taking care to retain control over one's digital assets and protect them against unauthorized reproduction. These issues, generally referred to as digital rights management or DRM, are an important topic of discussion and policy within most publishing companies today. Each company must form a view about what digital content it is going to make available to whom and in what form. 'What is our philosophy of distribution? Are we distributing generic files or encrypted files? Are they trusted partners or not? Are we distributing letters to go in their encrypted envelopes or are we securing the letters before we distribute them? These are another set of questions that we as a publisher need to answer,' says Steve. At his company, they've decided to distribute unencrypted files to their principal retail customers like Amazon and let them create the lock and the keys – the DRM envelope, as it were – which will be added to the file before it is sold on to a customer as an ebook. They're willing to do this because they have a clear contractual agreement with their customers that stipulates the conditions under which they can sell their ebooks, just as they have a clear agreement about the conditions under which they can sell or return their physical books: 'We're contracted with them and we assume that they won't abuse this relationship. It's the same in a way as if we send you a block of 10,000 books: we trust that you will sell them, report the sales and then return only the ones that haven't sold.' The auditing of ebook sales raises fresh issues, however, simply because you don't have the same physical calculus as you have in the world of physical books, where copies shipped out less copies returned = copies sold. This reaffirms the need to be extra vigilant when choosing your retail customers.

However, when it comes to digital sampling, Steve's company takes a more cautious view. They want to participate in Amazon's Search Inside the Book and Google Book Search but they're wary of handing over their digital content to third parties and allowing them to hold it on their servers – especially very powerful third parties like Amazon and Google. Partly it's a matter of trust, or rather the lack of it: while publishers know that their own fate has become inextricably interwoven with powerful web-based companies like Amazon and Google, they also know that their interests don't entirely coincide and they worry about ceding control of their most important asset – their content – to them. 'Many publishers in this building just like elsewhere are still not totally comfortable about giving their files to Amazon and Google,' explained one of Steve's colleagues. 'Partly it's because we're unsure what they'll do with it' – they may be cooperative now, but as they became larger and more powerful they might simply disregard the concerns and requests of publishers. There were also quality issues and more straightforward practical reasons. The publisher would not be controlling quality if it handed books over to Amazon and Google to scan, and it could not vary the rules that governed the amount of text that users could view. If the publisher held on to its content then it could devise its own access rules, stipulating exactly how much of each book can be viewed and how it can be viewed – whether 10 per cent, 20 per cent, one chapter, first chapter only, etc. It could also take down or replace an old version of a book quickly, rather than waiting the eight weeks that Amazon takes to remove a book from its programme. So Steve's company chose to build its own repository to hold digital files that could be accessed by third parties via a dynamic web call. For the consumer, the Search Inside the Book experience looks exactly the same as any other Amazon search-inside experience – you don't leave the Amazon environment. But when Amazon calls up the sample pages, it calls them up from the publisher's server rather than from Amazon's server. This enables the publisher to keep control of its own content and decide exactly what to make available and how, while at the same time benefiting from online browsing schemes like Amazon's Search Inside the Book.

While introducing measures to safeguard their content, many publishers and agents constantly monitor the internet and search for unauthorized content, and they are willing to take action against those who are deemed to be infringing their copyright. 'Harry Potter is rigorously controlled,' explained an agent who worked at the agency that managed J. K. Rowling's rights. 'We have agencies who spend all their time on the internet, surfing the internet, constantly looking out for illegal content.' And when they find it? 'Then you do your best to track down the perpetrator and either warn them off or slap a lawsuit on them.' Other agencies and publishers do similar things. Most of the large publishers either have people in-house working on this or employ outside firms, looking for pirated material online, serving notices on sites to take down unauthorized content and taking them to court if they fail to comply, all the time seeking to make it harder and harder for sites to make pirated material available while recognizing that it will be a constant struggle. 'We can wrap the stuff all we want', observed a senior manager in one of the large houses, 'but anybody can buy a book, take it home, put it through their scanner and post it on the internet – it's pretty fucking easy. You can do it in an hour and a half. Who are we kidding with our iron-clad DRM?' Security and policing are important but at the end of the day the crucial thing is to create an environment in which consumers can acquire the content, and are inclined to do so, through legitimate channels and at reasonable prices, a point to which we shall return.

Publishers as well as authors' associations have also been willing to take collective action against what they see as the illegal infringement of copyright – the most significant example being the class action launched against Google in 2005. The source of concern for publishers, agents, authors' associations and others in the publishing world was the Google Library Project. This was one part of an ambitious project developed by Google that was aimed at strengthening its position in the search engine wars – that is, in the struggle for market share between Google and its main rivals, Yahoo and MSM.

In the early 2000s Google took the view that one way it could increase its market share vis-à-vis its competitors was to look for ways to ensure that more high-quality content turned up in search results. Rather than relying only on information retrieved from the web by its crawlers, they wanted to add more high-quality content to their database so that searches would have a richer body of material to draw on. Scanning books and adding them to the database was one way to do this. Google therefore launched two programmes, the Partner Program and the Library Project, in order to add book content to their database. The Partner Program involved persuading publishers to give Google permission to scan their books; in response to a search query, a user would get a link to relevant text in the book and would be able to view a limited number of pages. The benefit to the publisher was that the book would be called to the attention of the user, who would be able to browse a few pages in Book Search and click on a link to Amazon, to the publisher's website or to another retailer to buy the book – it was, in effect, a free form of online marketing. Since the publisher had a contract with Google that regulated the conditions under which the text could be viewed and enabled the publisher to remove any title at any time, this programme was not a source of concern for most publishers.

The Library Project was another matter entirely. Google also entered into agreements with several libraries – Harvard, Stanford, the Bodleian at Oxford, the University of Michigan and New York Public Library – to scan their materials and add them to their database.[9] In response to search requests, users would be able to browse the full text of public domain materials but only a few sentences of text – what Google calls a 'snippet' – in books still under copyright. Each library would receive in return a digital copy of the scanned books in its collection. Google took the view that displaying snippets was within fair use legislation. It also announced that it would enable copyright holders to opt out of the Library Project by providing Google with a list of titles that they wished to exclude. For many copyright holders, however, Google's opt-out was turning the basic principle of copyright on its head. Rather than requiring a user to seek and be granted permission to use copyrighted material, Google

---

[9] For a more detailed account of the issues at stake, see Jonathan Band, 'The Google Library Project: The Copyright Debate' (American Library Association, Office for Information Technology Policy, Jan. 2006), at www.policybandwidth.com/doc/googlepaper.pdf.

was requiring the copyright holder to inform Google if it didn't want its copyrighted material to be used.

On 20 September 2005 the Authors Guild and several authors launched a class action against Google for copyright infringement, and a month later five publishers – McGraw-Hill, Pearson, Penguin, Simon & Schuster and John Wiley & Sons – filed a suit against Google. After many months of negotiations, the plaintiffs and Google announced a settlement on 28 October 2008.[10] In essence, the settlement proposed to create a mechanism – the Books Rights Registry or BRR – for Google to pay rights-holders for the right to display books. Google would make an upfront payment of at least $45 million to the BRR for distribution to rights-holders whose books had been scanned. Google would also be able to generate revenue by selling the ability to see full text and print out books, at prices that can be set by the rights-holder (failing which Google would set the price using a pricing algorithm); any revenues generated in this way would be split 37:63 between Google and the BRR, which would distribute its share among the rights-holders. The settlement distinguished between three categories of books – in-copyright and commercially available (meaning roughly in print or available through print on demand), in-copyright and not commercially available, and public domain – and it established default rules for what Google could do with the two categories of in-copyright books. Google estimates that the majority of published works fall into the category of in-copyright and not commercially available – as much as 70 per cent, compared to 20 per cent in the public domain and 10 per cent in copyright and commercially available. Since the rights-holders could remove specific books from Google's database, vary the default rules or opt out altogether, the category that would probably be most affected by the settlement is that of 'orphan works' – that is, works that are in copyright but are not claimed by any rights-holder.

The proposed settlement has been the subject of a great deal of criticism, both from within the US and from abroad, and it has had a rough ride in the US justice system. In September 2009 the US Department of Justice raised objections to the settlement, prompting the parties to withdraw the original agreement and submit a revised

---

[10] The full text of the settlement can be found at www.googlebooksettlement.com/agreement.html. For a helpful summary see Jonathan Band, 'A Guide for the Perplexed: Libraries and the Google Library Project Settlement' (American Library Association and Association of Research Libraries, 13 Nov. 2008), at www.arl.org/bm~doc/google-settlement-13nov08.pdf.

version, which they did on 13 November 2009. The revisions dealt primarily with the mechanisms for handling orphan works and with the restriction of the settlement to books published in the US, UK, Australia or Canada. The latter restriction was intended to meet objections from the French and German governments, which argued that the settlement did not abide by copyright laws in their countries; since a large proportion of the books in the libraries partnering with Google are not in English (perhaps as much as 50 per cent), this represented a significant reduction in the scope of the settlement.[11] The revised settlement was subject to approval by the US District Court for the Southern District of New York, and on 22 March 2011 US Circuit Judge Denny Chin announced that he was rejecting the settlement on the grounds that it 'is not fair, adequate or reasonable'. By placing the onus on copyright owners to come forward to protect their rights, the settlement was, argued Chin, inconsistent with the basic principles of copyright law – and in this respect he was affirming what many publishers had always thought. Chin also contended that the settlement would give Google 'a de facto monopoly over unclaimed works', rewarding it for engaging in the unauthorized copying of books and giving it a significant advantage over any potential competitor. While Chin's judgment was undoubtedly a serious blow to those who had worked out the settlement, he did leave the door ajar, noting that some of the objections could be met if the settlement were converted from an opt-out to an opt-in agreement. In Chin's view, the status of orphan works should be dealt with separately, by Congressional legislation rather than by an agreement among private, self-interested parties.[12]

How the parties proceed from this point on is unclear. They could revise the settlement in a way that seeks to meet the objections raised by Judge Chin or they could abandon the settlement, continue the litigation and allow the matter to be settled in the courts – it's too early to say. But whatever the eventual outcome, the dispute illustrates all too well the way in which publishers and others in the publishing industry have found themselves caught up in develop-

---

[11] For a more detailed account of the main changes in the amended settlement agreement, see Jonathan Band, 'A Guide for the Perplexed Part III: The Amended Settlement Agreement' (American Library Association and Association of Research Libraries, 23 Nov. 2009), at www.arl.org/bm~doc/guide_for_the_perplexed_part3. pdf.

[12] The full judgment can be found at: 'The Authors Guild et al. against Google Inc.: Opinion', at www.nysd.uscourts.gov/cases/show.php?db=special&id=115.

ments that are not of their own making, where the pace of change is being set by players much larger than themselves who are fighting different battles and pursuing different goals. No one in the industry has a very clear sense of where all this is heading and where it will end, nor could they be expected to – there are simply too many imponderables. There are many in the industry who would be happy to see some version of the settlement approved: they see it as a victory of sorts and they are undoubtedly right to do so, since it formally recognizes the rights of copyright holders, obliges Google to provide financial compensation for those whose books have already been scanned and places clear restrictions on what Google can do with in-copyright material. It also establishes some standards in what was otherwise completely uncharted territory, so that neither Google nor any other player can start digitizing libraries and think they can do as they wish with the content. On the other hand, there are some who fear, not unreasonably, that any settlement of this kind would put Google in an even more powerful position in the new information economy, making it effectively unassailable as the largest repository of digitized book content, a monopoly in all but name, and who argue that the cultural heritage represented by the vast numbers of books previously published – both public domain and orphan works – is simply too important to be left in the hands of a private corporation whose future direction and priorities will be decided by shareholders rather than by the public interest.[13]

The third way that publishers can respond to the threat of piracy and the infringement – actual or alleged – of copyright is to be proactive about supplying the market with content in suitable electronic formats. Many publishers take the view that nothing would do more to stimulate the illegal trade in electronic files than an inability or unwillingness of the copyright holders to meet a genuine demand for content when a reading device appears that is widely adopted by users. 'We just want to make sure, when that happens, that the industry is there to support the right kind of sell through to that device so that we don't end up with a piracy-dominated industry, as opposed to a legitimately sold industry,' explained one senior executive in a

---

[13] Robert Darnton has been the most vocal and thoughtful critic of the Google settlement and has developed a forceful argument along these lines. See Robert Darnton, 'Google and the Future of Books', *New York Review of Books*, vol. 56, no. 2 (12 Feb. 2009), reprinted in Darnton's *The Case for Books: Past, Present, and Future* (New York: Public Affairs, 2009), pp. 3–20; and Robert Darnton, 'Six Reasons Google Books Failed', *New York Review of Books* (28 Mar. 2011).

large trade house. Hence the amount of time, effort and cost that is being invested by most large houses in ensuring that their content is in appropriate digital formats and their digital archives are in good order. Like Prohibition, the non-availability of desirable content through legitimate channels is likely only to stimulate the illegal trade in contraband goods.

While issues of piracy and copyright infringement are of real concern to those involved in digital content distribution, there is another issue that is a source of growing anxiety among trade publishers. I was interviewing the senior executive just quoted in November 2007, on the very day that Amazon launched the Kindle in the US, and he, like everyone else in the publishing industry, was taken completely by surprise when Amazon announced that they were going to sell *New York Times* bestsellers and new releases for $9.99 on Kindle. 'Do you know where they got that price?' he asked me, in a tone suggesting he was still reeling from the shock. 'Didn't get it from us. As a matter of fact, they're losing money on most of the books they sell. What are they thinking?'

The spectre of price deflation

In the period up to 2008 all of the major trade houses had their own policies on ebook prices – policies that, in some cases, fluctuated rather confusingly over the months and years. In the early days of ebooks, many took the view that the list prices of ebooks should be less than the list prices of the physical books, since there are some real savings to be achieved by distributing content digitally rather than as a bound and printed book (though less than most people think, as we noted earlier). To reflect this, some publishers decided to price their ebooks at 20 per cent less than the price of the hardcover or paperback price, whichever edition is current; so a new book selling at, say, $24.99 in hardcover would be sold at $19.99 as an ebook. Others decided to sell their ebooks at a set price – say $16.99 – regardless of the price of the print version. While some price reduction for ebooks was common practice among trade houses, there were some that decided not to reduce the price at all and to sell ebooks at the same price as the prevailing print edition, on the grounds that the savings were minimal and the primary value of the book was its content, not the particular medium in which it was delivered to the consumer.

Whatever pricing policy they adopted for their ebooks, publishers would give their normal discount to their retail customers – say 48 per cent off the publisher's list price – and the retailer would be free to discount off the publisher's list price, just as they do with printed books. So even though Penguin were selling its ebooks at the same price as its printed books, Sony was selling them at 20 per cent off – in this case the discount was Sony's, not the publisher's. Most publishers expected Amazon to adopt a similar strategy, discounting off the publisher's ebook list price. What they didn't expect at all was for Amazon to announce a fixed price of $9.99 for all *New York Times* bestsellers and new releases.

The figures simply didn't add up. If a new hardcover was selling for a list price of $25 and the publisher was setting the ebook price at 20 per cent off, then the ebook list price would be $20. With a discount of 48 per cent to the retailer, the cost to Amazon would be $10.40. For Amazon to sell these ebooks at $9.99 means that they were losing 41 cents on each copy they sold, let alone making any margin to cover their costs. And if the new hardcover was selling for more than this – say it was Alan Greenspan's *The Age of Turbulence* selling at a list price of $35 – and if the publisher was not offering a discounted price for the ebook (as was the case with Penguin, who published Greenspan), then Amazon's loss on every copy they sold of the Kindle edition would be in the region of $8.20. It didn't make sense.

Of course, from Amazon's point of view there was a rationale. It wanted to make a statement: buy the Kindle (selling at $399 when it was launched) and all *New York Times* bestsellers and new releases will cost you only $9.99 – much less than the $25 or $26 you would have to pay, possibly discounted to $17 or $18, if you were to buy the hardcover edition. It was setting the price of a new book at just below the symbolic threshold of $10. Like Apple and iTunes, it was using book content as a lever to drive the sales of its hardware. It would make its money from the sale of the hardware; it would devalue content to $9.99 and, at least for the time being, subsidize any losses incurred, in the hope that this would enable it to sell enough hardware devices to establish a dominant position in the market.

So why were publishers troubled by this? Two reasons. First, it devalues the book and creates the impression in the minds of consumers that a new book is 'worth' $9.99. But this is an illusion, created by the fact that a particular, powerful player in the field has decided, for reasons largely unconnected to costs, to fix the price at a low and symbolically significant level. 'The danger with digital goods', explained one manager in a large trade house, 'is the danger that happened in the music industry. Why are songs 99 cents? Because Apple said so. Can the music industry make money at 99 cents? No. But now what does everyone think that a song should be worth? 99 cents. If books come down to $9.99, that's not realistic for us. It would kill us. We can't make any money on that price level.'

Of course, the low price was being subsidized by Amazon, which was willing to accept losses in the short term in order to establish its market position. 'But the worry', continued this manager, 'is that they're going to get people in the mindset that this is what the value is and then they're going to come back to us and say, "Everybody wants this and these other publishers are doing it and we don't want you to sell it to us for $10 anymore, we want you to sell it to us for $5." ' So the second reason to be concerned is that if Amazon succeeds in establishing a dominant position in the ebook marketplace, it will use its muscle to put pressure on publishers to reduce their ebook prices and/or increase their discounts, so that it can continue to sell frontlist bestsellers and new releases for $9.99 without making a loss.

The more powerful Amazon's position is in the ebook marketplace, the greater the danger to the publisher. 'There will be a monopoly, just like Apple with the iPod is a closed loop. Amazon is going to be a closed loop with the Kindle and they're going to say, "In this closed loop world, this is the pricing." ' Since only Amazon can sell content onto the Kindle, the consumer has to buy Kindle ebook content through Amazon. Amazon will have the same kind of monopoly on content onto the Kindle for books that Apple has in terms of DRM-protected audio onto the iPod for music. 'If that's the case,' said another manager in the same publishing house, 'what does it do to your negotiations with that retailer?'

So they then want to force you, the publisher, to offer your content to them at cheaper and cheaper and cheaper prices, so eventually they say, 'Look, we've grown a market here, we've taken it on the chin for a number of years because we have made no money on the content that we're selling, whereas we've been paying you, the publisher, the money you asked for. But now there's a big market there and we can't afford to do this anymore. So if you want to keep selling content onto the Kindle, now you need to give us a 75 per cent discount or you need to reduce your prices to $5.' And, you know, where do you go from there?

Of course, if the publisher agreed to increase the discount to 75 per cent, then it would have to give the same discount to anyone in the same sales channel and in the same ebook format – the Robinson-Patman Act would require this. 'But if there's nobody else really in the game, then it doesn't matter.'

So how does a publisher respond to this threat that is looming on the digital horizon? In the view of many publishers, the great danger is that Amazon's aggressive pricing strategy will create the impression in the minds of consumers that most of the value of a new book priced at $25 is accounted for by the paper and the print, that is, by the physical container, and that the value of the content is only worth $9.99, just as Apple created the impression that a song is worth only 99 cents. The more widespread this impression becomes, the greater the risk that this devaluation will lead to a haemorrhaging of value in the publishing industry – a draining of value out of the industry that would be greater than the savings that could be achieved by moving into a world of electronic content delivery. So the key issue for publishers is to get clear in their own minds about what the value of their content is and then do what they can to stand by their convictions when negotiating with powerful players in the ebook marketplace. One publisher put it like this:

As the publisher we have to say with clear conviction that the value of the book is the content in it and that value is $15, $20, whatever we determine it is – and by the way the value may be different for different books depending on who the author is, what the length is, what the topic is. We have to have the courage of our conviction and maintain the pricing level that we want, and then enter the negotiations with the retailer saying, 'Here is the discount we're going to offer you.' In the digital world, maybe the discount shouldn't be 50 per cent – there's no inventory, you don't have to run a distribution centre, you don't have to maintain a physical bookstore. Maybe we only need to give you a 25 per cent discount and then we kick in extra money for marketing. But we control the purse strings. So I think that it's very important right from the outset to be very firm in terms of our resolve to keep the content as valued as we need it to be. Amazon is in a period right now where they need publishers' cooperation in terms of enrolling titles in their program, and so it's not as though we don't have any cards to play.

Like most publishers, she wants to see Amazon succeed with the Kindle but she doesn't want them to be *too* successful. Publishers want to see a diversified ebook marketplace with other hardware suppliers and retailers flourishing alongside Amazon. They want to see Barnes & Noble and Sony succeed as well as Amazon, and they would like to see Apple and Google, among others, become significant players. 'If Amazon has 35 per cent of the physical sales channel and 90 per cent of the digital channel then we're all screwed,' said one CEO. The closed loop is the publisher's nightmare scenario – and all the more so if the player who controls this loop also happens to be the dominant player on the physical side of the book retail business.

Given the sensitivity of the issues surrounding price, most trade publishers have proceeded with caution when it comes to supplying content for the ebook market. They are perfectly happy to sell their books in electronic rather than traditional printed formats and to see ebooks grow, but only if this is done under conditions that will not, as one senior executive put it, 'undercut the very lifeblood of the industry'. He continued:

I don't think the authors or the publishers are in any mad rush to generate what would ultimately be a cannibalistic, or at least partially cannibalistic, phenomenon of having the material bought digitally rather than in physical form. We're happy for it to be bought digitally as long as it doesn't create a kind of cataclysmic decline in the industry's revenue. And so there's no reason to rush and underprice things to create such a decline. We'll be happy for this to develop in its own appropriate way so long as – and this is a big caveat – another industry doesn't grow up underneath. It's wholly illegal to furnish the same product to people who actually like some sort of experience but don't want to pay for it. So what we're trying to do is develop an electronic ebook industry that delivers appropriate values from attractive reading platforms at a price that seems, both to the consumer and to the author, to be an appropriate price for the value that's being delivered. I don't think we can forget that this is a very cheap form of entertainment relative to any other form of entertainment, for what it is. When you compare it to movies or games or newspapers or anything else, you look at hours of enjoyment let's say or edification or anything else that's delivered per dollar, this is a very competitive industry with the pricing today. You don't need to go to a tenth of today's pricing to deliver that kind of value, nor do I think we can say that by going to prices that are a tenth of what we have today, we will see the volume increase by tenfold. That's an impossibility, because with the demands on people's time they just won't have ten times as much time to read as they have today and they won't read ten times more just because something is cheaper.

So from this publisher's point of view, the key challenge is twofold: first, to try to keep prices of electronic content at levels that reflect their assessment of the real value of that content, that maintain the health of the industry and enable publishers to continue to reward authors, while at the same time not setting the prices so high that people feel they're being scammed; and second, to ensure that, when there are devices out there that people actually want to use, the content is readily available for those devices in appropriate digital formats so that people won't be tempted to share files illegally, as they did with music. So providing content at prices that are appropriate for the value delivered and making sure that the industry can support whatever devices turn out to become reading devices of choice for consumers: 'This is the fundamental issue for publishers to navigate over time.'

There is no need to try to speed things up – 'You're only cutting off your nose to spite your face and you'll probably be unsuccessful because consumers will come when they come.' But you don't want to slow it down either, since 'artificially slowing it down by not providing the product or having pricing that's way off the map is equally deleterious to your interests because people will find another way of getting the contents.' Provided the publisher has created a digital workflow that outputs digital files, provided they have created a robust digital archive and populated it with content in suitable digital formats, and provided they can maintain their pricing and discount structures in a way that will enable them to get the same economic benefit out of the sale of a digital edition or a print edition, then the publisher can remain indifferent about whether ebook sales become 10 per cent or 20 per cent or 50 per cent of their revenue; they can remain indifferent about whether ebook sales cannibalize print sales (as they undoubtedly would to some extent); they can remain indifferent too about the speed with which the migration to ebooks happens in those categories where it does. In other words, under these conditions the publisher can remain agnostic on the question of whether the future is digital: their house is in order and they are prepared for any number of possible future scenarios. But whether, as ebook sales grow, these conditions would actually hold – whether, in particular, publishers could hold the line on prices and discounts in the face of determined pressure from powerful retailers like Amazon – is, of course, another matter.

It was March 2009 and a year had passed since I listened to senior executives in the big trade houses in New York stressing the need for publishers to have the courage of their convictions and stand by the value of their content, maintaining prices at the levels they believe their content is worth. I was interviewing the CEO of a large US trade house and I'd barely had a chance to sit down when he started to tell me what was foremost on his mind:

> The biggest thing that's happened since the Kindle came out has been Amazon's decision to price these books at no higher than $9.99 and then my cowardly peers in the business going along with dramatically reducing the cost of an ebook, even at a time when the author advances hadn't gone down and there isn't a publisher anywhere that can disregard the revenue generated from the hardcover sales of the book. The major publishers went up and down with their prices; they were all over the place with not a lot of discernable rhyme or reason. Amazon didn't put any pressure on anybody. They had announced this price and they were sort of dancing around the issue of whether they were going to keep this or whether it was an introductory price. And the other publishers decided they were going to set a value to their ebooks that was dramatically lower, in most cases it was at least $10 lower, than the hardcover.

He was angry. He was upset. He was annoyed with his colleagues in other trade houses. Publishers speak fine words about having the courage of their convictions and holding the line on price but as soon as they're faced with a major retailer taking an aggressive position in the market they collapse. 'It drives me crazy. It's like all the things publishers have screamed about for years and years and years, that archaic distribution model we have all inherited, are finally going away and they say, you know what, let's take $5 or $6 and just throw it away. I can't understand it.'

The confusion over pricing continued throughout 2009. Publishers experimented with different ways of pricing and publishing ebooks – some were releasing ebooks at the same time and the same list price as the hardcover edition and letting Amazon discount as they wished, others were windowing ebooks, that is, delaying the release of the ebook for five or six months to try to protect hardcover sales, and some were doing both. At the same time, there was growing concern among publishers about the potentially deleterious consequences of Amazon's pricing strategy. Their concerns were amplified by the price war that broke out between Amazon, Wal-Mart and Target in October

2009, which saw prices on some new hardcover bestsellers falling to under $10.

The situation came to a head in early 2010. The new ingredient in the mix that proved to be a catalyst for change was Apple. In late 2009 Apple began talking with the big trade publishers about acquiring content for iBooks – an ebook store that it was developing for the iPad, which it was planning to launch in April 2010. It quickly emerged that Apple would prefer to use an agency model – the same model it used for music – rather than the wholesale or discount model that was traditional in the physical book trade. In the agency model, the publisher sets the price and the retailers act as the publisher's agents, taking a commission – in this case 30 per cent – on sales. In January 2010 John Sargent, CEO of Macmillan, the group of US companies owned by Holtzbrinck, flew out to Seattle to propose new terms of trade to Amazon that would be based on the agency model. Amazon rejected the proposal and retaliated by removing the buy buttons from all of Macmillan's books, both print and Kindle editions, on the Amazon site – exactly the kind of aggressive action by Amazon that many publishers had long feared. Over a weekend at the end of January 2010 many in the publishing industry were riveted to their computer screens, watching in astonishment as one of the first great conflicts of the new digital age unfolded before them. After several days of tense stand-off, Amazon backed down. It reluctantly agreed to accept the agency model, which meant that Macmillan would control the price of its ebooks and its frontlist titles could no longer be priced at $9.99. Amazon's reputation took a serious battering. 'It was appalling what they did,' commented the CEO of one large house who watched the events unfolding from the sidelines, 'and they were humiliated very quickly into switching the books back on. They had been winning the PR battle quite successfully with a number of agents until that point, and then when the agents saw the belly of the beast it was not something they liked. It was strategically a very poor move on their part.' It was, by contrast, a bold move by Macmillan in the new price wars that were emerging around ebooks, and it soon became clear that other major trade publishers would be following suit. By the summer of 2010 Hachette, HarperCollins, Simon & Schuster and Penguin had all moved over to the agency model. Of the big six only Random House held out, but in March 2011 it too moved over to the agency model.

While the adoption of the agency model by the big six trade publishers may have averted a major deterioration of prices, it's too early to say whether this is anything more than temporary. There are critics who view the agency model as a case of price-fixing and argue that it is a breach of competition rules, and it is being probed by antitrust investigators in the US, the UK and Europe. In June 2010 Texas Attorney General Greg Abbott launched a preliminary investigation, and in August a similar investigation was announced by Connecticut Attorney General Richard Blumenthal; these investigations mirror similar inquiries into Apple's business practices that are being conducted by the Federal Trade Commission and the Department of Justice. In the UK, the Office of Fair Trading began an investigation of ebook pricing in January 2011, and in March the European Commission launched morning raids on several publishing houses suspected of fixing the prices of ebooks. Amazon may have lost its battle with Macmillan and the other big trade houses in early 2010 but there are many in the business who are under no illusions about Amazon's willingness to renew the struggle. 'There's a perception in the world that there was a seismic shift in the industry: the content guys said "fuck you" and they came out ok,' reflected one CEO who had been through the switch-over from the wholesale to the agency model but suspected that the battle was far from over. 'Round one. It's like a 30-round fight that's going to go on for 10 years. I have no way of knowing that the agency model will continue to work. It could all start again.'

There is much more at stake in this debate than what might seem to the outside observer to be a fine point about comparative pricing. For one of the greatest threats facing the creative industries today is, as one perceptive retailer put it, 'the increasing commoditization of content by non-content players, which is driving down the value of intellectual property'. On the positive side, the delivery of content in digital formats could, at least in principle, enable the creative industries to eliminate or reduce some of the long-standing inefficiencies associated with traditional supply chains. But at the same time, it carries the risk – by no means hypothetical, as the music industry shows – that content becomes cannon fodder for large and powerful technology companies and retailers that use content to drive the sales of their devices and services and increase their market share, thereby devaluing intellectual property and sucking value out of the content creation process. Some would undoubtedly benefit from this; others would lose. But however this plays out in terms of the reconfiguration of the creative industries, a major devaluing of intellectual property, and a constant driving down of the price of content, is unlikely to lead to an overall increase in the quality of content over time.

10

TROUBLE IN THE TRADE

Up to now I've concentrated on analysing the structure and dynamic of the field of trade publishing and examining the consequences of the digital revolution, and I've generally refrained from expressing views of a more normative or evaluative kind. I now want to change tack and offer a more critical reflection on the field of trade publishing. Are there aspects of trade publishing that are particularly troubling or worrying? Which aspects of the way this field has developed over the last 30–40 years are, or should be, a source of concern? And concern for whom – why should anyone be concerned? Does it matter what happens in the book publishing industry today, and if so, why?

Short-termism

Publishing was traditionally a long-term business. Good publishing was about acquiring books that sold well over a long time period. Any publisher would be happy to have a book that sold exceptionally well in its first year, but the books that were of particular value were those that sold well year after year, acquiring a long and healthy life on the backlist. As trade publishing became more vertically integrated, the backlist became increasingly important as a source of profitability and stability for trade publishers. Hardcover houses were no longer selling off the paperback rights: they began to build their own backlists by launching paperback imprints or acquiring paperback houses into which they could feed their books. Some hardcover houses that had sold off paperback rights began to revert them, so that they could build their own backlist by reissuing in paperback books they had originally published in hardcover some years (even decades) before. Paperback houses, in turn, began to secure their sources of supply by launching their own hardcover imprints or acquiring hardcover houses to supply their paperback lines. As the large corporations began to colonize the field of trade publishing from the 1960s on, many sought to acquire houses with long-established backlists, precisely because they knew that backlist publishing was the most profitable and least risky form of publishing.

However, developments in the field of trade publishing during the 1980s and 1990s began to erode the traditional emphasis on backlist publishing. Three developments were particularly important. First was the hardback revolution: as the retail chains rolled out their superstores and retailers began discounting aggressively, and as the large publishing corporations began to apply mass-marketing techniques to the publication of hardcovers, the volume of sales that could be achieved on the initial hardcover edition grew exponentially. The financial formula that had underpinned the industry in the 1950s and 1960s was being turned on its head: increasingly it was the frontlist hardcover, not the backlist paperback, that was the engine of growth for the industry. By the early 2000s, paperback sales, especially in the mass-market format, had begun to fall off, undercut by the decline in the price differential between hardcover and paperback editions and the widespread availability of attractively produced, heavily discounted hardcovers.

The second development was the increasing role of large corporations in the field of trade publishing and their hunger for growth. All companies need to grow, but large, publicly quoted corporations need to grow more than others. They need to keep the stock market and their shareholders happy, and achieving regular growth and good levels of profitability is the only way to do it. The large corporations that bought up publishing houses in the first wave of consolidation in the 1960s and 1970s undoubtedly had inflated expectations of the levels of growth and profitability that were achievable in trade publishing; most bailed out when they realized that their financial goals were not going to be met and that other benefits they had hoped to reap from their acquisitions, such as creative synergies with other sectors of their media businesses, were not materializing. The corporations that became dominant in the field during the second wave of consolidation were, at least in some cases, corporations that had larger stakes in the publishing industry, were more committed to it and were more realistic about the levels of growth and profitability that could be achieved in trade publishing. They did, nonetheless, expect to see growth and good levels of profitability – double-digit if at all possible, with 10 per cent top-line growth and profits of 10–15 per cent or more as a typical target. This was an ambitious and difficult goal to achieve in an industry like trade publishing, which is characterized by a high level of serendipity, and in markets that were mature and largely static, growing by little more than the rate of inflation.

During the 1980s and 1990s it was still possible for the trade houses owned by large corporations to achieve significant growth, but they did this largely by acquiring other companies and merging them into their publishing operations. This strategy of growth by acquisition delivered benefits at several levels: it contributed immediately to the top-line growth of the company; it offered the opportunity to improve the bottom line by rationalizing back-office operations and stripping out redundancy; it increased the scale of the company as a whole, thereby increasing its market share and strengthening its leverage in its negotiations with other key players in the field; and it could add editorial diversity and prestige, raising the profile of the house and making it a more attractive destination for authors and agents. But it also served to conceal the underlying fact that achieving 10 per cent growth in a flat market would be difficult, if not impossible, to realize through organic growth alone. 'The corporations buy things for way more than they're worth to hide the fact that there is no growth,' commented one senior publisher who had worked for several large corporations and watched their behaviour at close quarters. They often end up having to write off some of the investment. Moreover, as the opportunities to grow through acquisition diminish over time, simply because there are fewer and fewer publishing houses left to acquire, the growth conundrum that lies at the heart of every publishing corporation becomes more and more apparent. They are forced to place more emphasis on high-risk bets on big books, in the hope that some of these will become bestsellers and make an exceptional contribution to growth, while at the same time looking constantly for cost-saving measures that might enable them to preserve or grow the bottom line if the top line remains relatively stagnant.

It is this pressure, rooted in the growth conundrum faced by every large corporation in the field of trade publishing, that leads inexorably to the short-termism of the publishing industry today. Within the large corporations that occupy the centre of the field, it is more and more difficult to publish for the long term, to adopt acquisition strategies that are aimed at building a backlist over time, precisely because the overriding imperative is to meet your budget targets for the current year and to fill the gap that is opened up every year, without fail, between the sales you're likely to achieve with your current through-put and the sales you're expected to achieve by your corporate bosses. 'It's an unrelenting pressure, and then you start at zero all over again,' as one former CEO put it. So a great deal of effort is invested – by middle management above all, but by editors too – in trying to find big books that will make an immediate financial impact. Extreme publishing is, by its very nature, short-termist: it is publishing quickly in order to produce an immediate effect. This does not prevent the large publishing corporations from taking chances with new authors or even taking on some books that they know or strongly believe to be small – many continue to do so for a variety of reasons, as we've seen. Extreme publishing can and does go hand in hand with the development of a varied portfolio of books. But the relentless budget pressure unavoidably produces a gradual shift of priorities within the large corporations, forcing publishers and editors to devote more and more of their energy and resources to big books which could make an immediate impact and to pay less and less attention to books that might build more slowly over time.

Does short-termism necessarily lead to bad publishing? Not necessarily. The CEO of Olympic (discussed in chapter 6) was quite right to say that sometimes books published quickly turn out to be better and more successful books because they are closer to market when they are bought. Nevertheless, it is also undoubtedly the case that a short-termist mentality leads to plenty of bad publishing. You don't have to be a cultural snob to see that a good number of the books that are put together in great haste – often ghostwritten 'autobiographies' of celebrities or heavily illustrated gossip along the lines of Paris Hilton's *Confessions of an Heiress* – and published quickly in the hope that they will help to fill a budget gap are not books that add much to the cultural well-being (or even, for that matter, the entertainment) of the human race. Many also fail in straightforward financial terms, as increasingly desperate publishers find themselves competing with other publishers who are in the same boat and paying over the odds for books whose principal raison d'être is to plug a hole. They may ship out large quantities in order to register the sales before the end of the financial year, only to find themselves inundated with high returns several months later. And the stress experienced by those who have to manage this process is palpable. As one former CEO of a large corporation put it, 'The agony and the ecstasy of the book publisher starts out with high returns in the first part of the year, disappointing sales and postponed publication dates and then sheer absolute terror as he or she contemplates the financial results based on what is actually known at that point.'

The problem is not just that the financial demands of the large corporations accentuate the emphasis on big books for which matters of quality are secondary to their immediate financial impact: it is also that the model itself is unsustainable in the long run. So long as the large corporations are able to acquire other companies and integrate them into their publishing operations, they will be able to conceal the extent to which their ability to meet their growth targets has depended on the growth and the economies of scale they've been able to achieve through mergers and acquisitions; when they are no longer able to acquire, the limitations of the model will be experienced with increasing severity. The gains achieved through acquisitions can be drawn out over several years and, combined with the occasional bestseller, they can cover over very effectively the tensions inherent in the growth conundrum. But they can't cover them over forever. Your luck will run out eventually, and when you can't fall back on further economies of scale achieved through mergers and acquisitions, you'll have to start cutting into bone. 'When you run out of spectacular bestsellers and you have no more cost savings that you can squeeze without changing the nature of the business and the company that you are, then, in a flat market, you bump up against a limit at some point,' explained the former CEO. That may be a point at which one CEO or senior manager is pushed out and replaced by another, who may, with some structural reorganization, be able to reduce overheads and squeeze more savings out of the company, thereby improving the bottom line. But the reprieve is likely to be temporary. The problem has not been solved, it's only been postponed. In all likelihood it will resurface again in a few years time because it is rooted in a contradiction that lies at the heart of the corporate publishing house – namely, the expectation of substantial growth in a market that is largely flat.

So what is the solution? Is there one? There are some senior figures in the large publishing houses who believe that CEOs should simply tell their corporate bosses that their growth targets are unrealistic. They should explain that when things are going well they can grow the top line by 2–3 per cent and they can grow the bottom line by 4 per cent but to expect anything more in a flat market is just not realistic. Would their explanations land on deaf ears? Maybe. It depends on which corporation it is, whether it's public or private and what other pressures they might be facing at a particular point in time. 'I wouldn't say they were deaf to it,' said the former CEO. 'But if you have a portfolio of businesses that are all facing the same issue, what are you going to do? You increase the pressure – this is the classic response of corporate headquarters. You increase the pressure and see who responds better. Those who respond better get fed a little bit more in terms of reinvestment and those who don't get starved and sold.' There are plenty of those working in the large publishing houses who feel this might be a better option at the end of the day. 'You're better off saying, "Hey, you know what? Sell me then, get rid of us,"' said one senior publisher. Corporate ownership has its advantages, but when it forces publishing houses to engage in activities that are concerned primarily with meeting short-term, unrealistic growth targets rather than contributing to the long-term flourishing of the publishing house and its programme, then the price to be paid for these advantages may be too high.

The short-termism of the industry is not due solely to the financial pressure produced by the unrealistic growth targets of the large corporations; it stems from other sources too, including the financial pressure produced by the large retail chains whose stock-turn requirements are much higher than those of the traditional independent bookstores and from the escalation of advances orchestrated by agents who, despite their avowals of loyalty to their clients, are locked into the same system of contestation and reward, a system that has produced a revolution of rising expectations from which no player in the field, even the small or medium-sized independent press, has been entirely shielded. For those authors who, through a mixture of talent, good connections and good luck, have enjoyed the rewards of this system, there is much to praise: advances are higher than they've ever been, books are available in more retail outlets and in more towns and cities than they ever were and, with some good marketing and a large and powerful sales force behind your book, sales can reach unprecedented levels. But these are the lucky few. For the vast majority of writers or aspiring writers, this system seems like an alien beast that behaves in unpredictable and erratic ways, sometimes reaching out to them with a warm smile and a handful of cash, inviting them to join the party and holding out the prospect of a future of riches and fame, and then suddenly, without much warning or explanation, pulling back, refusing to respond or perhaps cutting off communication completely. This is a system geared towards maximizing returns within reasonably short time frames; it is not designed to cultivate literary careers over a lifetime. Thoughtful publishers who came into the business before these features became so pronounced worry about the implications of this revolution of rising expectations for the future of literary culture: 'What keeps me awake at night is worrying about how we are going to find the next generation of authors that we can build over time to create careers. We've been lucky in that we were able to build the careers of 10 or 12 really good writers that we're still publishing now and that's marvellous, but it's the future that you have to be concerned about.'

Damaged careers

The writer's world is not the same as the world of publishers, agents and booksellers. These two worlds bump up against one another, and they need and depend on one another, but the area of overlap is small and is generally limited to ritualized interactions that occur along the boundaries. Many writers – there are exceptions, of course – know very little about the world of publishing and the structures of the field upon which their careers as writers depend: for them it is another world, located somewhere else and largely mysterious in the way it works, an object of wonder, dismay or simply incomprehension depending on the writer's experiences of it. Although publishing is seemingly about authors as much as it is about books, in fact most authors are very much on the margins of the field if not entirely external to it. Their contact with the publishing world is mediated largely through their agent (or agents if, like many authors, they have had more than one), and typically they rely heavily on their agent's knowledge and advice in order to navigate this world. The writer's world is, above all, the world of writers. Those whom many writers think of as their friends and colleagues tend to be other writers – these are the people and the networks that matter to them. Of course, it matters to them what their agents think, it matters what their editors think, it matters what their readers think, but for many writers, what matters more than anything else is what other writers think. 'I'm engaging in a conversation with other writers,' explained one young writer in Brooklyn. 'As much as writing a book is an offering to a reader it is a contribution to a conversation going on among writers, and I want to feel as if I'm conversant with those writers, the writers that I admire, the writers that are speaking most intelligently and seductively at the table. I want to contribute in ways that are meaningful and inspiring to them.'

It is in order to contribute to this conversation with other writers – or, indeed, with readers – that many writers find themselves bumping up against the world of publishing: they need this world and its players in order to do what they want to do, which is, for the most part, to write. Most writers, aspiring or otherwise, are not writing full-time: writing may be their calling, their passion, but it is rarely – except in a very small proportion of cases – their principal means of livelihood. But if they want to build a career as a writer, they know they will need the help of those whose job it is to buy and sell the written word. This doesn't mean that they come to see what they're doing as writing *for* agents or editors – in most cases they don't ('I didn't write my first book for them and I'm determined never to write a book for them in the future, so they have to be on the other side of the river,' said the young Brooklyn writer); it's simply that they realize early on in their career that they need agents and editors in order to pursue their own ends. It's a relationship of mutual dependency rather than a seamless convergence of interests.

Each writer has his or her own story of how they encountered the publishing world and what happened to them as they sought to pursue their vocation as a writer. Some of these are happy stories – young, aspiring writers who are snatched out of obscurity from a MFA (Master of Fine Arts) or MA programme by a visiting agent who miraculously secures a two-book deal with a major trade house involving staggering amounts of money ('It was just totally, totally unreal – so much more money than I had ever even contemplated that anyone would possibly ever give me in my lifetime that it was like on another planet'); or writers who had the good fortune to find an agent early on who advised them well and helped place their books with able editors with whom they have had long and cordial relationships, enabling them to pursue, with relatively little trauma, their ambition to write (and even, in a relatively small number of cases, to live from their writing). But for every happy story of this kind there are countless stories of frustration, disappointment and despair, as writers find themselves tossed about in the world of publishing as if they were a small boat on a stormy sea with no idea of where they were heading and unsure whether they would ever reach land.

Let's briefly follow the story of one. Joanne came to writing later in life – she had a successful career as a university professor before deciding, in her mid-forties, to give up her career as an academic and devote herself to writing crime fiction. She had written a novel in her spare time, found that she had a knack for it and decided she wanted to do more. Friends had advised her that she needed an agent and gave her various contacts. She sent her book to three, all of whom responded positively and said they wanted to represent her, and she chose to work with one. She knew virtually nothing about the world of publishing. She expected her agent to sell her book ('I didn't realize there was anything else') and she had no idea at all about which publisher would be a good home for it. She needed an agent to get her book published and she was happy to leave everything to her. As it turned out, her agent was well connected and in a matter of days she had lined up a good deal with a major trade house in New York. Joanne was having dinner in a restaurant when her agent phoned. '"Look," she said, "he's offered a certain amount of money," which sounded like an amazing amount of money to me, "but I want him to offer twice as much. So I'm going to turn it down on your behalf. Is that OK?" And I thought, phew, what do I know? So I said, "Alright, do it, you know – I don't know anything about it." I was exhilarated, excited and amazed.' The publisher duly doubled the advance, the book was sold in New York and the agent used this deal to help secure a good deal with a major house in London. When her agent asked her if there was any particular clause she wanted in the contract, she thought for a second and said, 'Yes, I'd like a clause saying I don't have to go on tremendously long book tours.' A complete neophyte, Joanne's greatest worry was that she was going to be exhausted by all the attention she would receive when she became a published author. Little did she know.

Joanne had seen her first book as a one-off, but her editors on both sides of the Atlantic urged her to treat it as the first in a series. '"Crime is a slow build," they said. "The way to get noticed is to have a series so that people can lock onto your central characters. So could you do another one in the same series?" And I said, "Sure."' But beyond that, no one ever advised her about how to continue the series, how to build the central character or even how often to come out with a new book – nothing, not a word, either from her editors or from her agent. She was left to her own devices. The first book was published in hardcover, followed by a mass market paperback, then the second, then the third. Feedback was minimal ('The sales are fine but, you know, we hope they'll get bigger') but things seemed to be going smoothly. After all, what did Joanne know? Her agent seemed happy, her editors seemed content and Joanne was doing what she wanted to do. But then, around 2001, just as Joanne was finishing her fifth book, things started to fall apart. This is how she tells the story:

A younger author got taken on [by my publisher in London] and I got to know her. Something happened and I realized that she had a relatively large marketing budget. And so I said to my editor, 'What's my marketing budget?' and my editor went kind of blank and I said, 'What is it?' and she said, 'Well, maybe you'd better talk to the head of marketing.' So I called him and he said, 'Your marketing budget is nil.' They had made a policy decision to put all their marketing budget on their top four or five bestsellers and withdraw, utterly, the budget from everyone else. It wasn't exactly nil because they still sent out review copies and things like that, but apart from that ring-fenced stuff, there was nothing. So I was really shocked and alarmed.

Joanne spoke to her agent and told her she was really unhappy about this. Was there anything she could do? But her agent was 'really sort of fatalistic about it – "Well, you know, that's the way things are going."' Joanne pressed – 'But can't you do anything? Can't you intervene in some way?' 'Well, mmm,' her agent replied. So Joanne continued to express her dissatisfaction to her editor and eventually the head of marketing took her out for lunch. He was new to the company, he liked Joanne and for some reason he decided to take it upon himself to offer her some friendly advice:

'You've done five books with us,' he said, 'they're good books and they're all getting better and we're really glad to have them here. But you won't get anywhere until you have a different editor. Your editor is too detached; you need somebody like [X] who's more at the centre of things.' And he told me something I didn't know – that my editor didn't even represent my books in the marketing meetings. [X] represented them and [X] might not have read them, and [X] had her own authors. That's the first time I realized that I didn't have an editor at [the publishing house] who was going to get behind my books and push them. And then he said, 'You need a new agent too. Your agent is good at getting good prices for books but we never see her here, never see her.' He had been in the job 18 months at that point and he said within his first month there he had about 20 agents who converged on him. He said they do it subtly, you know, they just kind of show up at his office door one day and say, 'Hi, welcome to the new job, how are you doing?' Just chat and stuff. And he said, 'I've been here 18 months and I've never exchanged any communication with your agent whatsoever.' It matters, he said, because the agents have to be pushing all the time in order for your book to get marketing money. And that's when I realized that the younger woman who had some marketing money when I didn't, one of the people who made me twig that I was on the slide here, had a very aggressive agent who was in there all the time.

Suddenly it all fell into place, but it was late. Ten years had gone by, five books had been written, opportunities had been missed that would never return. The head of marketing, new to the business and speaking out of turn, had told Joanne something about a writer's career that nobody, neither her editor nor her agent, had had the wits or the nerve to tell her before. 'I just wished I'd had that information ten years earlier.'

Joanne went to see her agent and became more pushy. '"Look," I said, "I really need you in there fighting for me, it's really important." And she said, "I'm an old-fashioned agent, I don't do that." So I felt kind of abandoned, like my agent wasn't there for me and the publishers weren't doing stuff they should do for my books.' Joanne decided that she couldn't stay with her agent. She realized that she needed to raise her game; she needed an agent who would get more involved in her career, could give her advice and champion her at the publishing houses. So she made appointments to see a number of other agents who had been recommended by writer friends. She decided to go with a top agent who was well known in the business – 'very, very grand' – on the grounds that her reputation would give her the kind of clout in the publishing houses that her previous agent had lacked.

By this stage Joanne had finished the sixth novel. Her new agent had read it, was enthusiastic about it, had given her some helpful feedback and sent it to Joanne's publisher. Her editor wrote back immediately and said she thought it was wonderful, but then things went quiet. Eventually her agent contacted the editor and the editor said that, while she loved the book, 'the marketing people weren't keen and weren't going to take it. That was really quite surprising – shocking actually. But my agent said, "Don't worry, don't be downhearted, it's a great book and they weren't backing you strongly enough anyway. We'll find a better home for it."' Joanne continued:

Then I heard nothing from her for 13 months, which was really weird. I left it for quite a while because I knew Christmas was coming up and it takes a long time to get things done at that time of year. So I didn't make too much of a fuss for a while. And then I started bombarding her with letters and emails and phone calls to the reception and she just blanked me; it was the most extraordinary thing. All in all, it was 13 months that she didn't get in touch with me, she didn't tell me what had happened to the book, nothing. Finally I had to go to the Society of Authors because I felt I couldn't go to another agent until I knew which editors she'd already sent it to and what their response had been and she wouldn't answer me. So I went to the lawyers at the Society of Authors and said, 'Look, I'm having this real problem with my agent,' and they sent her a letter. A month went by and she still didn't respond. So I went back to the Society of Authors again and said, 'What more can you do?' They were going to do something very fierce and then finally I got a three sentence note from the agent saying, 'Dear Joanne, I sent your book to . . .' and she named about six houses. 'They all liked it but times are difficult. If you want to talk to me about this, do pop by.' That's it. No apology. I felt just completely *blaaah*, just completely *blaaah*. It was awful.

By now Joanne's career was in serious trouble. She had published five books that had all been well received, had even won prizes, but none had broken out in the way that would convince her publishers that they were the kind of books they should get behind and push. Her sixth book had been published by a large house in New York but had been turned down by the publisher of her previous five books in London, and then her editor in New York phoned to say he was leaving the publishing house. Now she had no agent, she had no editor and she was in her early sixties – a middle-aged literary orphan. I ask her how she now feels about her career. 'I'm finding it hard to think about it at all, actually. I guess I'm in denial. I feel very alone and I'm sort of paralysed by what's happened. I'm writing my seventh book very, very slowly. It's a good book, a terrific book, I have a lot of faith in it, but I haven't shown it to any agents because I know that agents are turning people away like mad and I don't want a rejection by an agent now.' She has been a writer for nearly 20 years and she has literally no idea who will publish her next book, or indeed whether it will be published at all.

Looking back, Joanne now sees that she was terribly naive. 'I had very unrealistic ideas about what it means to be an author. I expected that, if you write a good book, your publisher will make it a success, they'll back it by things like advertising, they'll put posters in the subway and send you on a ten-city tour, whereas in reality your book goes out there, you have a little party if you're lucky and then a few people say, "I enjoyed your book," and that's that.' For most of her writing career, she had no idea at all about what those who could make or break her career were expecting from her. She got very little advice, either from her agents or from her editors, and the only person who gave her any real insight into the workings of the publishing industry was a marketing manager who was new to the business and wanted to help her out. But now it's probably too late. She realizes now that this is an industry that expects things to happen quickly, that is hungry for something new and that has little patience for what it regards as a settled mid-list author. 'If there's a plateau, that's not good enough. So the fact that there might be 5,000 or 8,000 people out there who are always going to buy your book is neither here nor there. Those people can go jump as far as the publishers are concerned. After five books, if you've not really gone up, you're out.' I ask her if she has any idea what it means to 'go up', what kind of sales her books would have to achieve for her to be in favour. 'No, no one ever told me that. I have no idea what it is.' 'So you're totally in the dark on that?' 'Yes, totally.'

Joanne is disappointed but not bitter. The way she was treated by some of her agents and editors was inexcusably shabby and she would be entitled to feel aggrieved, but she accepts part of the blame for her predicament. She feels that she was too naive about the industry when she began. If she knew then what she knows now she wouldn't have counted on her agents and editors to provide her with sensible advice and wouldn't have interpreted their encouragement as a sign of commitment or long-term support. She would have taken it upon herself to try to find out what she needed to do to try to make her career a success and she would have been much more assertive, telling her agent what she wanted her to do and spending more time chatting with people at the publishing houses, from her editors to the publicity staff, just to get them on her side. She would have talked herself up constantly, something she would have found difficult personally but which she now believes is essential 'because publishers are terribly uncertain about what's good and what's not, about what's going to be successful and what's not, and they need to hear positive things'. Above all, she would have aimed to be much more ambitious at the very outset. She wouldn't have taken the view that she could work slowly and steadily and try to build a career as a writer by writing better and better books but would have given herself ten years at most to make it big, 'because if you haven't done it by then, people will be looking to drop you'. She doesn't blame the editors. She realizes that they're subject to very similar pressures; 'They make it quickly or they don't make it and a lot of the time they're as much in the dark about what's going on as authors are.' But she does regret the fact that the big publishers have become so impatient, so preoccupied with sales figures that they're willing to cut loose authors in whom they've invested quite a lot simply because their books, however good they might be, are not displaying the upward sales curve they want to see. 'I regret the loss of a previous publishing ethic in which editors committed themselves to authors whom they thought had potential and stuck with those authors and saw themselves as developing a body of literary works rather than just churning out bestsellers. What I feel, in a funny sort of way, is a kind of nostalgia for something I never knew.'

The one solace is that Joanne has lots of friends who are writers and she spends a lot of time with them – indeed, like many writers, she makes her living not by writing but by teaching would-be writers on a part-time basis. She has become part of a community of writers that has its own forms of social life and support, from informal networks of friends to meetings and writers' conventions. It's a community bound together by a shared interest in writing and by forms of friendship and loyalty that are deeper and more important for many writers than their relationships with agents and editors ('Your peers who are writers become your friends and they won't drop you when you're not published'). The community of writers is a world apart; it intersects with the publishing world but that intersection is fraught with tension that stems from the fact that the interests of writers don't always coincide with the interests of agents and editors, a point nicely conveyed by a joke, recounted by Joanne, that was told by a well-known writer in an after-dinner speech at a writers' convention:

'Here we are,' said the writer who was giving the speech, 'a gathering again of the publishing industry, of the writing industry, the book industry. Isn't it wonderful? I can see you all out there,' he said, looking out at the people sitting at their tables in the banqueting hall. 'I can see the writers trying to look *reasonably* smart, as if they're not on the breadline, which of course they are. And there we have the publishers – dressed down of course, because they don't want anyone to know how well they're doing. And the agents,' he said, with a slight pause as he cast his eyes over the room again, 'well, we don't see that much of the agents, just the occasional fin slicing through the water.'

Of course, Joanne's story is unique, as is the story of every individual, but the trajectory of her career is not. In fact, it is all too common. Many writers find that this is not an industry that is particularly responsive to their needs and that seeks to cultivate their writing career over time; they find, instead, that it is an industry willing to take them on when they are fresh and unknown, maybe even willing to lavish upon them advances far in excess of anything they ever imagined, but quick to cast them aside if, after several books (maybe even fewer), sales don't rise to high enough levels – though what exactly those levels are remains, to most writers, a mystery, like some carefully guarded secret of the trade. Many find themselves struggling to break out of what becomes, in practice, a vicious downward cycle: disappointing sales figures mean that publishers offer less in terms of advance and provide little or no support in terms of marketing spend, and also mean that the bookselling chains order less stock and make the book less visible in the bookstores, all of which makes it more likely that sales for the next book will be even more disappointing. And so the downward spiral continues until someone makes a move to try to break it – the publisher declines the next book, or the agent decides that this writer's career is going nowhere, or the writer decides that he or she needs a different agent or publisher or both.

It is hardly surprising that many writers come to feel that they have become prisoners of their 'track'. 'Absolutely,' said one Brooklyn-based writer when I asked her if she felt trapped by her sales history. 'In fact, I've been wanting to send out a Christmas card with the ghost of Christmas past who's dragging his chains behind him, with the caption, "I wear the sales figures I forged in life." That's how I feel about my track.' Like many writers, her career had gone up and down over the years. She'd published 14 books with major imprints, had had steady sales and one or two modest successes but nothing spectacular; she had lived in hope of the breakout book that never came. Now in her early sixties, her agent had failed to sell her last book. 'My agent sent it out to 22 publishers and there were four or five who said they really loved it and wanted to publish it and they just looked at my sales figures and said no.' It's hard for her not to be despondent at this point in her career. 'I began as a writer respected by writers, by publishers, and now I've become no better than my last sales figures. So, you know, it's tough. I feel trapped. I think that's what most of my writing friends feel as well. Just trapped by these numbers.'

So what does a writer do when their career has reached this point? What options are left? Of course, they could change publishers, give up on the large houses and move to the margins of the field where they might find a small publisher who is less preoccupied with sales figures and willing to take them on. Many do exactly that. The small indie presses have many writers who are refugees from the large corporate houses, happy to have found a publisher who, they feel, takes their writing seriously and is willing to stand by them and publish their work even if the sales are modest. But some writers find that they're discouraged by their agents from making a move of this kind, on the grounds that it would look like a step backwards, 'like your career is going in reverse or something', as one writer put it. And indeed, whether discouraged or not by their agent, some writers feel that a move in this direction would be a public admission of failure.

There is another move they can make, more radical and perhaps more difficult at a personal and emotional level: they can change their name. It is not uncommon for agents to recommend this course of action, as we saw in chapter 2, but it is also increasingly common for writers to decide on their own that changing their name is the best option open to them at a certain stage of their career. 'It's like you're playing chess,' explained one New York writer in his early fifties, 'and you're not in checkmate yet but you're close and you don't have many pieces on the board. It's the only move left to me.' This writer did change his name but he didn't find it easy – 'I hate doing it because I'm proud. I would much rather have my name on my book because I wrote it, but I'm left in a very difficult position.' He'd published ten books, some with major New York houses, and won several top awards for his fiction, but he'd been dropped by his publisher, 'kicked to the kerb' as he put it, and now he felt trapped by his numbers. 'You're better off in this industry being a completely unknown person. It's better to have no history than a mixed history. It's insane, it makes no sense, but that's publishing.' In an industry that he'd experienced as systematically bruising and disempowering – 'everything in publishing is disempowering for a writer' – this was the one way left for him to try to recover some fragments of agency and self-esteem.

Are these complaints about the industry nothing more than sour grapes? The angry words of writers who were simply not good enough to make the grade? Perhaps. The publishing industry is a business of selection and some writers are, inevitably, going to be disappointed. But from the viewpoint of many writers, the problem is not selection per se. They have no problem with selection. The problem is that in an industry preoccupied with growth and the bottom line, the criterion of selection that now seems to matter more than any other is sales. 'It's not the quality, it's not the content, it's like, "Yeah, she's a great writer but look at those numbers."' They have a point. There are many agents and editors who feel genuinely committed to their writers and who value good writing, but in the tough world of trade publishing, numbers speak louder than words. Quality is often debatable but the numbers never lie. Some readers love *The Da Vinci Code*, others loathe it, but there is no publisher who would not love to have those sales figures on their balance sheet.

Of course, there's some room to be flexible even within the large corporations, as we've seen. There are imprints in some corporations that are given more leeway in financial terms, on the grounds that the symbolic value they contribute is important for the profile of the publishing house. But even these imprints are not immune to financial pressure. They too must make their numbers. So however much an editor might like a writer's work, however many prizes the writer may have won and good reviews they may have had, there is always the possibility that the writer will be dropped if their books display a disappointing sales pattern. Today more than ever, a writer's career is always hanging in the balance, rising and falling with the sales of their most recent books and always at risk of being curtailed by a disappointing track. Careers cut short and writers cut loose are among the prices to be paid for the logic of the field. They are the human costs of an industry where numbers rule in the end and where short-term growth and bottom-line profitability have come to assume more and more importance in the practical calculations of the major houses.

The emphasis on sales and profitability is not experienced in the same way and to the same degree in all sectors of the field. The pressure is greatest in those houses and imprints that are part of the large corporations, precisely because these are the organizations that are most affected by the imperative of growth and the budgetary requirements that follow from it. The small and medium-sized independents are not subjected to the same kind of pressure and can afford to take a more long-term view, and there are undoubtedly many writers who have benefited from their more magnanimous approach. But given the preponderance of the large corporations in the field of trade publishing, the fact that small and medium-sized independents often act differently does not alter the fundamental short-termism of the industry as a whole.

Diversity in question

Short-termism may be regrettable; it may be tough on those writers who have fallen out of favour with the large publishing houses and stressful for those publishers and editors who are under constant pressure to meet budget targets; it may also lead to some poor publishing. But is there any reason to think that the developments characterizing the field of trade publishing have resulted in, or are likely to result in, an impoverished culture of the book? Have the processes of consolidation and the dynamics of the field led to a decline in diversity of output, a growing homogenization of content and an overall dumbing down in the quality of the books produced? There are many who believe or fear that this may be so. Their argument generally goes like this. Thanks to the consolidation of the industry, the large corporate publishers and the big retail chains now control a large and growing share of the book market. These publishers and retailers are driven above all by the pursuit of profit and growth, and the number of copies they can sell, rather than the quality of the books they are publishing or selling, necessarily becomes their over-riding concern. The question of quality falls by the wayside as the corporate juggernauts pursue their relentless quest for profit and growth. Old-school editors who believed that publishing books was about making good literature available to the public, or contributing to the public debate by putting serious ideas and scholarly works into the public domain, are either pushed out or forced to swallow their principles and reorient their activities towards the new sales-based norms. The publishing output of the large houses becomes more homogeneous, more commercial and more closely tied to celebrity and entertainment, while good literature and serious non-fiction is increasingly marginalized, if not abandoned altogether. In the brave new world of corporate publishing and retail chains, quality literature and serious non-fiction have no place – like the independent publishing houses and booksellers upon which they once depended, they have been swept aside by the social and economic changes that have transformed the field of trade publishing since the 1960s. The result, say some critics, is a serious deterioration of contemporary culture, so much so that we are now in danger of losing some of the attributes that are essential for a vibrant, creative culture and an informed democracy.[1]

There is undoubtedly some substance to this line of argument. Within the large corporations, there are strong pressures to focus effort, attention and resources on big books, and to pay less attention to, or refrain from publishing at all, books that might be regarded as small or mid-list. There are limits to the extent to which editors can follow their hunches and experiment with new books that don't bear the obvious signs of success – though, as we've seen, these limits are always negotiable, vary considerably from one imprint and one house to another and often depend on a variety of personal and contextual features. The preoccupation with sales tends to produce a degree of homogenization within the field, since editors, publishers and agents are constantly scrutinizing sales figures and bestseller lists to see what is doing well and are quick to jump on the bandwagon of the latest success – many people in the industry bemoan what they call 'me-too publishing'. More generally, the preoccupation with big books and the reliance on the judgements of others – the web of collective belief – tends to produce a certain homogeneity in the field, since it's difficult not to be caught up in the excitement of the moment and not to be swayed by what so many of your trusted colleagues appear to believe.

But while there are limits to experimentation in the large corporations and pressures towards homogenization in the field, the issues are more complicated than the line of argument sketched above would suggest. In the first place, this argument rests on a much too simplified view of what goes on inside the world of corporate publishing. As we've seen, this is, in practice, a plurality of worlds, and different publishing corporations operate in different ways. Some operate with a highly federal model and give a great deal of autonomy to their constituent houses, imprints or divisions to develop their publishing programmes – provided, of course, that they meet certain

---

[1] André Schiffrin offers a forceful, if somewhat extreme, version of this argument: 'Books today have become mere adjuncts to the world of the mass media, offering light entertainment and reassurances that all is for the best in this, the best of all possible worlds. The resulting control on the spread of ideas is stricter than anyone would have thought possible in a free society. The need for public debate and open discussion, inherent in the democratic ideal, conflicts with the ever-stricter demand for total profit' (*The Business of Books*, p. 152).

financial conditions. Within most publishing corporations there are some houses or imprints that have established reputations for publishing works of quality, both literary fiction and serious non-fiction, and it is acknowledged, even by the most number-crunching of senior corporate managers, that publishing works of quality is and should remain an important part of what a publishing company does. It may not make a big contribution to the profit and growth of the corporation but it contributes something else that, however important economic considerations have become, has not been eliminated from the field: symbolic capital. Winning prizes still does matter, even to large publishing corporations – perhaps especially to large publishing corporations, since it is one way of showing that, despite everything, they still are real publishers. Does this mean that those publishers and editors in the large corporations who care about quality literature and serious non-fiction are not under pressure? No, it does not. Does it mean that they will always be protected, like a safe haven shielding its boats from the storm, and that their future is secure? No, it does not. But it does mean that the suggestion that there is a straightforward trade-off between quality and sales, and that the drive for growth and profit in the large corporations will necessarily eliminate all quality publishing from their programmes, is much too simple and doesn't do justice to the complex reality of life inside the worlds of corporate publishing.

There is another obvious objection to the line of argument sketched above: whatever might be happening inside the publishing corporations, they are not the totality of the field, and with many tens of thousands of new titles being published every year, it would be difficult to argue that there is a lack of diversity, or even a decline of diversity, in the field as a whole. With more than 300,000 new titles being published every year in the US and over 150,000 in the UK and with the numbers tending to increase year on year, it is not at all obvious that the culture of the book is being strangled by the financial ambitions of the large corporations. Admittedly not all of these are trade books – many are professional or scholarly books, and many may be published with very small print runs. But however you look at it, this does not appear to be a culture that is suffering from a worrying constriction in the number and range of titles produced. On the contrary, the field is characterized by a huge volume and diversity of output, and the consolidation of the large publishing houses has gone hand in hand with the proliferation of small publishing operations and a veritable explosion in the number of titles published each year.

So does this completely scuttle the line of argument sketched above? Surely, the riposte goes, the sheer number and range of books being published today is ample testimony to the vibrancy of the culture of the book and demonstrates – more clearly than any reflection on the literary merits or otherwise of particular authors or titles ever could – that the corporatization of the publishing business poses no real threat to literary culture. So is that the end of the matter? The line of argument sketched above now firmly and finally defeated? Not necessarily. In order to understand why, we need to distinguish more clearly between two kinds of diversity: *diversity of output*, on the one hand, and *diversity in the marketplace*, on the other. It is true that there is an enormous range of titles being published today, not only by the large corporations but also by the medium-sized publishers and the innumerable small presses and other players that live on the margins of the field. The diversity of output is probably as great as it's ever been, if not greater, and it would not be easy to argue that fewer works of quality, whether fiction or non-fiction, are finding their way into print than was the case 30 or 40 or 50 years ago. You can try to make this argument but you will struggle, because for every example you produce of how difficult it is today for a publisher to take chances with a new and untested voice you can find a dozen examples of where chances of just this kind are being taken.

However, the key issue in the field of trade publishing today is not so much diversity of output, it is diversity in the *marketplace*. In other words, the real source of concern is not the diversity or otherwise of the books that are *published*, but rather the diversity or otherwise of the books that are *noticed, purchased and read*. The field may be characterized by an extremely diverse output, but if only a very limited number and range of titles are picked out and noticed – that is, made visible in a crowded marketplace – then we have a different kind of problem about diversity. Publishing organizations of various kinds may be producing a diverse range of books but this diversity is not necessarily reflected in the space of the visible. And given the focus of some retail chains – especially the mass merchandisers and the supermarkets but the specialist bookselling chains too – on best-sellers, brand-name authors and fast-moving titles, there is a tendency for success to breed success and for the most successful titles to crowd out others.

Consider some figures. Table 16 and figure 15 show the number of paperback fiction titles that sold in certain quantity bands in the UK in the calendar years between 2002 and 2006. We can see that the number of titles selling between 10,000 and 49,999 copies per

Table 16   UK paperback fiction sales bands, 2002–2006

	2002	2003	2004	2005	2006
>200k	16	25	31	29	31
100k–199k	39	53	52	57	52
50k–99k	69	70	80	70	67
10k–49k	446	455	438	396	305
Total	**570**	**603**	**601**	**552**	**455**

Total consumer market sales within each given year. Sales are for A format (110 × 178 mm) and B format (130 × 198 mm) paperback fiction only.
Source: Nielsen BookScan.

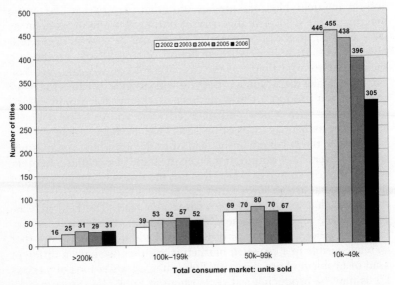

Figure 15   UK paperback fiction sales bands, 2002–2006
Source: Nielsen BookScan (A and B format pb fiction only; TCM sales within each given year).

year fell from 446 in 2002 to 305 in 2006 – a decline of 32 per cent. The number of titles selling between 50,000 and 99,999 copies per year remained fairly constant – a small number of titles, between 67 and 80. However, the number of titles selling between 100,000 and 199,999 copies increased from 39 to 52 – an increase of 33 per cent.

More dramatically still, the number of titles selling more than 200,000 copies doubled, from 16 to 31. Taking the last two bands together, the number of titles selling more than 100,000 copies per year increased from 55 in 2002 to 83 in 2006 – an increase of just over 50 per cent. What this suggests is that a small number of titles are doing better than ever, whereas the number of titles that are doing moderately well – that is, selling in the modest but still just about acceptable range of 10,000–50,000 copies in paperback – is declining significantly. The top two bands of strong-selling titles are swelling in terms of the numbers of titles included in them, but the increase here – a total of 28 more titles – is small in comparison to the decline in the number of titles lost from the lower band (141 fewer titles selling between 10,000 and 50,000 copies in 2006 compared to 2002). In other words, the market is concentrating on a small number of titles that sell well, indeed better than ever, whereas the number of titles that sell in modest but acceptable quantities is declining. This is not exactly a winner-takes-all market, but it is a *winner-takes-more* market.

Quite understandably, what happens in a winner-takes-more market is that the key players focus their attention more and more on the winners. The big agencies want to represent them, the large publishers want to publish them and the major retailers want to stock and display them, because these are the authors and the books where serious money can be made. Hence a relatively small number of authors and books tend to become the focus of attention in the field and to dominate the retail space – they appear on the front tables and dump bins of the retail chains, on the shelves and pallets of the mass merchandisers and wholesale clubs and in the limited number of slots available in the supermarkets. These tend disproportionately to be the books published by the large corporate publishers – partly because the large publishers can afford to spend more to pay for front-of-store displays but also because they are more able to pay the high advances that the winners can command in the market for content. The result is that in the major retail spaces where books are most visible to readers and consumers, the winners tend to crowd out other books. Not entirely, of course; there will always be exceptions – those small books that come from nowhere and become surprise bestsellers, confounding everyone's expectations. But this should not blind us to the fact that, despite the enormous volume and diversity in output, the marketplace for books is increasingly one in which the winners take more and everything else faces a harder and harder struggle to get noticed, bought and read. Diversity in output is not complemented by a diverse marketplace, but rather by a marketplace in which a small fraction of titles, and most commonly those backed by the resources of the large corporations, tend to dominate the spaces of the visible.[2]

Part of what it means for something to be published is for it to be publicly available – that is, available for members of the public to see and read and know about. But being available is one thing; actually being seen and read and known about is quite another. And a book or text can influence public debate or become a significant cultural entity only if it is seen and read and known about. Simply being available is not enough – it is a necessary but not a sufficient condition. Hence the forces that shape the spaces of the visible are of crucial importance both for the flourishing of cultural life and for the vitality of what one might call the public sphere.[3] Of course, the bricks-and-mortar retail stores and chains in which books are displayed and sold are only part of the complex array of venues and sites that make up the spaces of the visible, but in the culture of the book they remain a crucial part. The more that this space is colonized by large corporations who can use their financial strength to gain advantage in the struggle for visibility, the more likely it is that the cultural and public conversation of which books are part will be skewed by corporate power. More books than ever may be available, but few people will see them or read them or even know they exist. The rich diversity of output cannot make up for a marketplace that

---

[2] The fact that the highly visible display spaces tend to be populated disproportionately by books published by the large corporate publishers may not be immediately apparent to the casual observer, partly because of the large number of imprints operating under the auspices of each corporate house. However, the skewing of the spaces of the visible in favour of the large corporate groups becomes apparent as soon as one takes account of the corporate affiliations. On a typical day in 2009 in one of the Barnes & Noble stores in New York, the front table of new non-fiction books had a total of 68 books on display, 41 of which were published by imprints of the five largest corporate groups. The front table of new fiction books had a total of 66 books on display, 44 of which were published by imprints of the five largest corporate groups. Hence, on this particular day, 60 per cent of the new non-fiction books and 67 per cent of the new fiction books on display on the front two tables were published by the five largest corporate groups. Compare this with the fact that these five groups accounted for 46 per cent of the US trade market in 2007–8, and of course they account for only a small fraction of total title output.

[3] See Jürgen Habermas, *The Structural Transformation of the Public Sphere: An Inquiry into a Category of Bourgeois Society*, tr. Thomas Burger with Frederick Lawrence (Cambridge: Polity, 1989); Thompson, *The Media and Modernity*.

is systematically skewed in favour of the largest and most powerful players.

While diversity of output is not the same as diversity in the marketplace, they are of course connected, and there is a danger, not altogether fanciful, that diminishing diversity in the marketplace could eventually lead to diminishing diversity in output. If publishers find it harder and harder to get certain kinds of books or certain authors noticed, they could find themselves under growing pressure to stop publishing them. True, these books and authors could migrate elsewhere and get published by smaller houses, but that cannot be guaranteed. A marketplace becoming more constricted, with more power concentrated in the hands of fewer and fewer buyers whose decisions become ever more consequential for the fate of individual titles and authors, may eventually take its toll on the productive output of the industry. Diminishing diversity in the marketplace could force some publishers out of business and accelerate processes of consolidation, leaving fewer alternatives for authors who might be seen as marginal by the large houses.

That is why it is so important to maintain a diverse marketplace – it is vital for diversity and creativity in the industry as a whole. The decline of the independent booksellers represented a serious loss to this diversity: the more buyers there are in the marketplace, exercising their own individual judgement about which books to stock and display in their stores, the more diverse the marketplace is and the better for the industry. The demise of Borders, and the difficulties currently faced by specialized bookselling chains like Waterstone's in the UK and Barnes & Noble in the US, represent another serious threat to diversity. Although the specialized bookselling chains use central buyers, they are nevertheless committed to books as a cultural form (unlike mass merchandisers, for example, for whom books are just one more product line). They are willing – to varying degrees depending on the retailer – to take chances with new books and new authors and to hold a wide range of stock and backlist titles. They are vital shop windows for publishers. Their spaces may be skewed by powerful interests, but at least they are spaces and without them the opportunities to make books visible would be greatly diminished. Publishers would be wise to see that it is in their own interests to do what they can to ensure that these retailers are able to survive in a world where the financial pressures on bricks-and-mortar bookstores are likely to intensify, and that they are not disadvantaged by terms that give significant advantages to non-book retailers who stock a small range of titles and concentrate on winners – a point that is of particular significance in the UK, where the abandonment of the Net Book Agreement without the kind of legal protection provided by the Robinson-Patman Act in the US has created a marketplace that is heavily skewed in favour of the largest and most powerful players. Level playing fields in marketplaces are good not just for smaller retailers who have less clout in their negotiations with suppliers: at the end of the day, they are good for suppliers too.

CONCLUSION:
FACING AN UNCERTAIN FUTURE

The economic recession triggered off by the financial crisis in 2008 hit the publishing industry hard, especially in the United States. Beginning in August 2008 and accelerating through September and October, most trade publishers in the US experienced a sharp downturn in sales. In the period from July to December 2008, new hardcover sales were down by 15–20 per cent for most publishers – 'It was worse than 9/11,' as one veteran publisher put it. Even the big bestselling authors were down – Grisham, Patterson, Crichton, etc. More worrying still, core backlist sales were dropping off at a rate much higher than would normally be the case, so publishers couldn't rely on their backlist sales to cushion the impact of a frontlist in decline. And if that wasn't bad enough, the major retail chains began returning more stock than usual and buying new books more cautiously, enough for three or four weeks rather than ten or twelve weeks as they had once done, partly in order to build up their cash reserves and reduce their liabilities in case the recession turned out to be prolonged. With lower sales and higher returns, trade publishers were not just earning less; they were also facing higher write-offs for unearned advances and higher provisions for returns. And if any retailers or wholesalers went out of business along the way – as indeed some did, including Borders – they would face further substantial write-offs for bad debts that could obliterate any profit that remained. Similar trends, less dramatic, were evident in the UK.

Faced with a sharp fall-off in sales during the second half of 2008 and in the run-up to Christmas, which is usually one of the strongest seasons for trade publishers, most large publishing houses sought to do what any large corporation would: save the bottom line. If your top line is in free fall and there is not much you can do in the short term to arrest or reverse this, then the only way you can save the bottom line is to cut costs. 'In four months my agenda flipped 180 degrees,' said the CEO of one large corporation. 'Before the recession hit, my agenda was 80–90 per cent growth-oriented and 10–20 per cent focused on efficiencies. Now it is focused 80–90 per cent on efficiencies.' In a market that is no longer largely static but actually declining (suddenly and sharply), the primary concern of senior managers in the large corporations becomes one of taking costs out of the organization wherever they can, so that they are still able to show a profit, or at least to minimize the loss, despite the fall-off in sales. The axe fell harshly. Some large publishers cut out whole divisions and parcelled up their imprints among other divisions. Many jobs were shed – 3 December 2008 became known in New York publishing circles as 'Black Wednesday', as several large publishers, including Random House and Simon & Schuster, announced numerous resignations and lay-offs. Those staff remaining in post feared for their future as senior managers made it clear that, going forward, all jobs could not be guaranteed; many were anxious, demoralized and working harder than ever, as they found themselves taking on work previously done by others. For senior management the aim was simple: you cut costs until you reach a point where you risk cutting into bone, and at that point you stop and reassess. You've resized the organization, established a new baseline, and from there you can – possibly, hopefully – return to the growth agenda.

As the economic recession continued through 2009 and into 2010 and 2011, publishers found themselves having to cope simultaneously with a technological revolution that was suddenly beginning to have a major impact on their businesses. Ebooks were no longer a topic of idle speculation, the pet idea of the Head of the Digital Division who was ritually ushered in to annual meetings to talk about the digital future, like some Cassandra of the publishing world who was benignly tolerated by senior management and viewed with amused disbelief by many in the lower ranks. Suddenly ebooks were real – and, moreover, they were the only thing in trade publishing that actually seemed to be growing while everything else appeared to be either static or in precipitous decline. Now publishers had to deal not just with a major recession that was depressing their revenues but also with a technological revolution that was threatening to disrupt their businesses in new and unpredictable ways.

Are the difficulties experienced by many trade publishers in the period since 2008–9 just a temporary blip, a brief period of structural readjustment from which the publishing industry will emerge stronger and fitter than before, ready to continue on the path of ever greater output and growth? Or is this something of a watershed – a moment in the long history of the book when the path of gradual evolution tips over into something else, when the key players in the field find that their customary ways of doing things no longer work and they no longer have the wherewithal to meet the new challenges they face? The truth is that no one knows – this is an industry facing an uncertain future. There are arguments – signs would perhaps be a better word – that could incline you in either direction.

First, the temporary blip scenario: sure, the big houses have made their economies, reorganized divisions, shed posts, frozen salaries, consolidated office space, slashed marketing budgets and cut travel and entertainment accounts, all with a view to preserving profitability when top-line revenues are falling. But at the same time they are positioning themselves for a future where they are hoping to pick up the growth agenda once again and are counting on the same tried and tested formulas to deliver the financial results they need. They are not paying less for the big books they think could be bestsellers – if anything, they are paying more, placing higher and higher bets on the books that could turn out to be the winners in a winner-takes-more market while paying less for everything else (or simply declining to buy). They are not abandoning extreme publishing but, if anything, are looking harder for the instant books they can crash out quickly in the hope that they will produce a much-needed injection of cash. In a recessionary market where top-line revenues are in decline, the large corporate publishers want big books more than ever in order to cover their fixed overheads and provide what they think will be a reliable revenue stream. They are not resigning themselves to a permanently declining top line but are buying some time while they search for new ways to meet the financial expectations of their corporate masters for whom growth remains as important as ever. 'The thinking has not changed,' commented one CEO, 'they want us to grow margin and they want us to grow the top line as well. I think it's baked into the DNA of large corporations.' No signs here of a fundamental change of attitude or approach on the part of the large corporate players, a belief that the old ways of doing things are fundamentally flawed and in need of a radical overhaul. This is more like business as usual, with the tendencies inherent in the logic of the field merely exacerbated by the recession, to the benefit of those who already benefit most from it and to the detriment of everyone else. Of course, their bets may turn out to be misplaced. The sales of their hoped-for bestsellers may not fully rebound and eventually everyone in the game of trade publishing – authors and agents included – may have to adjust their expectations downward. The revolution of rising expectations that has characterized the industry over the last couple of decades may gradually morph into a gentle downward spiral. The key players who are locked together in the field of trade publishing – the large publishers, the retail chains and the agents – may turn out to be unwitting accomplices in their own undoing, and the raising of the stakes at the very moment when revenues are falling may turn out to be the opening step in a slow but unswerving *danse macabre*.

But there are also signs that something more radical is happening in this industry. There are many industry insiders who have long had doubts about the wisdom of some of the practices that have come to define the field – the competitive auctions that ratchet up the advances to levels far in excess of what most books are likely to earn, the shipping out of large numbers of books followed by the almost inevitable wave of returns, the high premiums paid by publishers and (in the UK) the high discounts given to get their books stocked and displayed in the major retail outlets, the relentless drive for levels of growth that are unsustainable in the long run – but so long as the major players could continue to play the game and satisfy the expectations of their corporate masters and key clients then the rules were unlikely to change. There was too much at stake, and the need to meet short-term financial goals would always override any doubts harboured by particular individuals in senior positions of power. However, when it becomes much harder to play the game in the old way, even for those players whose dominant position in the field gives them all the advantages, then the doubts are more likely to surface. Signs of dissatisfaction become more apparent, talk of broken models becomes more prevalent, and new experiments that seek to modify some aspects of the game – low or no advances, profit shares with authors, non-returnable sales, etc. – begin to proliferate, initiated in some cases by major players and in other cases by iconoclastic start-ups on the margins of the field. Economic turbulence gives rise to renewed questioning of the rules of the game and to new ventures that could, in some ways and to some extent, change the rules.

However, at the particular conjuncture where the publishing industry finds itself today, it is not just a matter of coping with an economic downturn that has made life more difficult for the players in the field: it is also a matter of dealing with and adapting to a technological revolution whose consequences are potentially far-reaching. The technological upheaval that has swept through other creative industries in recent years is now beginning to have a serious impact on the book publishing industry too. The dramatic surge in ebook sales, and the rapid shift from print to digital in certain categories of books, is forcing all the key players in the field to reconsider their positions. Practices that have become settled conventions in the field are suddenly opened up to scrutiny, players who have interacted amicably for years suddenly find themselves locking horns in new conflicts where the rules are no longer clear, and even the new norms that seem to be crystallizing into industry standards – like the 25 per cent royalty rate for ebooks – are but a temporary truce reflecting the current balance of power. The field of power remains but the game is changing. New players are entering the field, old and new players are jockeying for position and the rules are being redefined. Regardless of how important ebooks become in terms of the share of overall revenue they eventually represent, there can be no doubt that the traditional ways of producing, supplying and consuming books, and the symbolic and information environment of which the book has always been part, are, at the beginning of the twenty-first century, undergoing massive and far-reaching change.

No one knows how this change, combined with the economic turbulence of recent years, will play itself out in the field of trade publishing. We are living through a revolution of sorts, and one of the few things you can say for certain about a revolution is that when you're in the middle of one, you have no idea where and when it will end. Some short-term trends are easy enough to see: Amazon will continue to grow as a retail channel while specialist booksellers (including the bookselling chains) will find themselves squeezed further and further, leading to more bookstore closures and downsizing on the part of the chains. Publishers with weak balance sheets and companies that are highly leveraged will face growing financial difficulties, the pressures on medium-sized publishers will intensify and some of the large corporations will probably decide that the time has come to divest themselves of their trade publishing interests, which were always a very small part of their overall business anyway, leading to further consolidation in the hands of a small number of large corporations that remain committed to trade publishing and continue to see it as a worthwhile part of their portfolio. The decline of physical retail space will make it harder for publishers to get their books noticed, as there will be less space available for books to be displayed and for readers to discover them by browsing in bookstores, thus placing a higher premium on the physical display spaces that remain while at the same time forcing publishers to devote more and more of their marketing effort and spend to the online environment, where they will hope to find new ways of bringing their books to the attention of readers and generating interest despite the avalanche of information that already threatens to overwhelm most users. The shift from print to digital will continue, though the speed and extent of the shift will vary from one category to another, and income from non-traditional sales, both ebooks and other forms of electronic content, will become an increasingly significant part of publishers' revenues, though exactly how significant is, at this point in time, unknown – maybe 20 per cent, maybe 30, maybe 50, maybe more, no one knows. As more sales shift to digital and the sales of physical books decline, the large publishing houses will face growing downward pressure on their top-line revenue, calling into question their continued ability to generate growth year-on-year and refocusing their attention more and more on the reduction or removal of costs in order to maintain or improve profitability. At the same time, the infrastructure supporting the traditional book supply chain – warehouses, sales forces, etc. – will come under growing pressure, forcing publishers to look for new ways to keep the physical supply chain going while at the same time trying to shift the organization to a new way of doing business. Small publishing operations will proliferate as the costs and complexities associated with the book supply chain evaporate and threats of disintermediation will abound, as both traditional and new players avail themselves of new technologies and the opportunities opened up by them to try to eat the lunch of their erstwhile collaborators. Beyond these short-term trends the picture is much less clear. Many people have their hunches, but in a world where there are so many variables and where unanticipated developments could occur at any time, one person's hunch is pretty much as good as another's.

Whatever happens, it seems to me likely that the book, both in its traditional printed form and in the new electronic formats that turn out to be attractive to and desired by readers, will continue to play an important role as a means of expression and communication in our cultural and public life for the foreseeable future. Books have been, and remain for many, a privileged form of communication, one in which the genius of the written word can be inscribed in an object that is at once a medium of expression, a means of communication and a work of art. People will always want stories, and they will always want fresh ways to think about the world and about themselves. For the telling of extended stories, whether fiction or non-fiction, for the in-depth understanding of the world or the sustained interrogation of our ways of thinking and acting, the book has proven to be a most satisfying and resilient cultural form, and it is not likely to disappear soon. We should not be surprised, however, if the basic structures and dynamics that have come to characterize the world of trade publishing today – the logic of the field – were, in the rapidly changing symbolic and information environment of the early twenty-first century, to be shaken up in new and unexpected ways. For books and the publishing industry do not exist in isolation: they are, and always have been, part and parcel of a broader symbolic and information environment – in short, a culture – where they have for half a millennium played an important, even vital, role as forms in which content can be embedded, packaged and communicated to others. How books will be produced and delivered, who will do what and how they will do it, what roles the traditional players will play (if any) and where books will fit in the new symbolic and information environments that will emerge in the years to come – these are questions to which there are, at present, no clear answers.

— Appendix 1 —

SELECTED IMPRINTS OF THE MAIN PUBLISHING CORPORATIONS

Imprints are listed here alphabetically, although in practice most imprints are organized into publishing divisions or groups. The lists are not exhaustive.

RANDOM HOUSE

United States

Alfred A. Knopf	Ivy
Anchor	Kids@Random
Ballantine	Main Street Books
Bantam	Nan A. Talese
Broadway	One World
Clarkson Potter	Pantheon
Crown	Random House
Delacorte	Schocken
Dell	Shave Areheart Books
Del Rey	Spectra
Dial	Spiegel & Grau
Doubleday	Strivers Row Books
Everyman's Library	The Modern Library
Fawcett	Three Rivers Press
Fodor's Travel	Villiard
Golden Books	Vintage
Harmony	Wellspring

United Kingdom

Arrow
Bantam
BBC Books
Black Lace
Black Swan
Bodley Head
Century
Chatto & Windus
Corgi
Doubleday
Ebury
Everyman

Harvill Secker
Hutchinson
Jonathan Cape
Mainstream
Pimlico
Rider
Transworld
Vermilion
Vintage
Virgin Books
William Heinemann
Yellow Jersey

PENGUIN

United States

Ace
Alpha
Avery
Berkley
Current
Dial Books
Dutton
Firebird
Frederick Warne
Gotham
G. P. Putnam's Sons
Grosset & Dunlap
HP Books
Hudson Street Press
Jeremy P. Tarcher
Jove

New American Library
Penguin
Penguin Press
Perigee
Philomel
Plume
Portfolio
Price Stern Sloan
Puffin
Putnam
Riverhead
Sentinel
Speak
Tarcher
Viking

United Kingdom

Allen Lane
Dorling Kindersley
Fig Tree
Hamish Hamilton
Ladybird
Michael Joseph

Penguin
Puffin
Rough Guides
Viking
Warne

HACHETTE

United States

5 Spot
Back Bay Books
Bulfinch
Business Plus
Center Street
FaithWords
Forever
Grand Central Publishing
Little, Brown & Company

Mulholland Books
Orbit
Reagan Arthur Books
Springboard Press
Twelve
Vision
Wellness Central
Yen Press

United Kingdom

Abacus
Atom
Bounty
Business Plus
Cassell
Franklin Watts
Gaia Books
Godsfield
Gollancz
Hamlyn
Headline
Hodder & Stoughton
Hodder Children's
John Murray
Little Black Dress
Little, Brown

Orion
Miller's
Mitchell Beazley
Octopus
Orbit
Orchard
Philip's
Phoenix
Piatkus
Sceptre
Sphere
Spruce
Virago
Wayland
Weidenfeld & Nicolson

HARPERCOLLINS

United States

Amistad
Avon
Caedmon
Collins

Ecco
Eos
Greenwillow Books
Harper

Harper Perennial
HarperCollins
HarperCollins Children's Books
HarperEntertainment
HarperLuxe
HarperOne
HarperTeen
HarperTrophy

Joanna Cotler Books
Julie Andrews Collection
Katherine Tegen Books
Laura Geringer Books
Rayo
William Morrow
Zondervan

United Kingdom

Avon
Blue Door
Collins
Fourth Estate
HarperPress
Harper Thorsons/Element

HarperCollins Children's Books
HarperEntertainment
HarperFiction
HarperSport
The Friday Project
Voyager

SIMON & SCHUSTER

United States

Atria Books
Fireside
Free Press
Gallery Books
Howard Books

Pocket Books
Scribner
Simon & Schuster
Threshold
Touchstone

HOLTZBRINCK

United States

Faber and Faber, Inc.
Farrar, Straus & Giroux
Forge Books
Griffin Books
Henry Holt
Hill & Wang
Macmillan
Metropolitan Books
Minotaur
North Point Press

Owl Books
Picador
Roaring Brook Press
Sarah Crichton Books
St Martin's Press
Thomas Dunne Books
Times Books
Tor Books
Truman Talley Books

United Kingdom

Boxtree

Campbell Books

Macmillan

Macmillan Children's Books

Macmillan New Writing

Mantle

Palgrave

Pan

Picador

Rodale

Sidgwick & Jackson

Think Books

Tor

Young Picador

— Appendix 2 —

NOTE ON RESEARCH METHODS

This book is based on research that was carried out between 2005 and 2009, primarily in London and New York. Having previously studied the worlds of scholarly book publishing (including the university presses) and higher education publishing (including the college textbook publishers), my aim in this research was to study the world of trade publishing – that is, the world of general interest books that are aimed at a wider public and sold through high-street bookstores, general retailers and other outlets. I planned to focus primarily on mainline adult fiction and non-fiction; I was not proposing to examine in detail the more specialized domains of trade publishing such as children's books, illustrated art books, diet, health and self-help books, or more specialized genres like romance and science fiction. I also planned to restrict my focus to English-language trade publishing, and more specifically to the trade publishing business in Britain and the US. The inclusion of both Britain and the US was essential in my view, since most of the large trade publishers operate as international organizations and have a major presence in both of these countries, and since Britain and the US are both the principal sources of content for trade publishers operating in the English language and their two most important markets. Focusing on just one of these countries would be partial at best and would fail to do justice to the internationalized, and increasingly globalized, character of English-language publishing.

The main research method I used was the semi-structured in-depth interview. The great advantage of this method for the kind of research I was setting out to do is that it enables you to get inside organizations and get a feel for how they work, allows you to explore issues in depth and helps you to see the world from the viewpoint of particular individuals located at particular positions within the field. I always assured my interviewees that they and their organizations would remain anonymous, and that anything they said that was confidential would remain so. This was vital, in my view, since we were often discussing sensitive issues about strategy, organizational politics and performance, and since it is difficult to talk about a business like publishing without using particular examples and individuals to illustrate your points. I wanted interviewees to feel free to discuss these issues openly, without having to worry about whether their views would be reported verbatim and attributed to them in print or whether their organizations would be named. Assurances about anonymity and confidentiality were an essential part of building trust in a relationship where the richness and quality of the communication is directly dependent on the extent to which the interviewee trusts the interviewer and believes that what they are doing is worthwhile. All interviews were recorded and transcribed – although, my assurances about anonymity and confidentiality notwithstanding, there was the odd occasion when I was asked to turn off the recorder while a particularly sensitive issue was discussed.

Interviewing is an underestimated art. It's not so much a method as a skill or craft that you learn by doing – you get better and better but, in my experience, you never feel like you've mastered the art. Partly this is because your questions as an interviewer get better as you understand more about how an industry and the organizations within it work; rereading my first interviews, I am always struck by how naive some of my questions now seem, how many opportunities I missed and how many tantalizing comments I failed to follow up. Partly it's also because every interview situation is different and you can't anticipate what will happen in the course of the interview, what kind of rapport you will establish with the interviewee or even how long it will last. Sometimes you go into an interview expecting to have an hour only to find that an emergency has cropped up and your time has been cut in half. Then there are other occasions when a scheduled hour turns into an hour and a half or even two, and when the interview turns into a flowing conversation with no real time constraint. As an interviewer you have to have the flexibility and sharpness of mind to respond to these varying circumstances, to seize unexpected opportunities when they arise and make the most of whatever time you're able to get.

I always went into interviews with a structured set of topics and questions, tailored to the individual and organization concerned, but I never treated this plan as fixed: I allowed the conversation to flow in different directions depending on the interests and experiences of the interviewee and his or her judgement about what was important and what was not. Sometimes things came up in an interview that I had not thought about in advance, perhaps didn't even know existed; part of the skill of a good interviewer is to be able to see the importance of these unanticipated revelations, to put aside your preconceptions and, on the spur of the moment, find a way to follow up these fresh openings. An interview is a living, flowing conversation, and, as in any conversation, timing is crucial: something unexpected is said, you have a chance to follow it up if you can find the right words quickly, and then the opportunity is gone. If you miss it, it may never come again – this might be your only hour with this particular person. Of course, you might be able to send them an email afterwards – 'Could I just ask you one more question about something you said?' – but it's never the same: in all likelihood you won't get a reply, and if you do, it will almost certainly lack the kind of spontaneous frankness and insightful detail of an answer given to a direct question asked face-to-face in the full flow of a conversation. I often found myself coming out of an interview thinking, 'If only I had asked that question then...'

I was lucky: I had many second chances to ask questions I had failed to ask the first time around and to follow up points that had come up in the course of an interview, as I was able to interview many individuals twice or even three times over the course of several months or, in some cases, several years. This turned out to be invaluable as a way of deepening my understanding of the business of trade publishing and how it was changing. Sometimes second interviews are much more revealing than first interviews, partly because the relationship and a degree of trust have already been established and partly because the basic ground has already been covered: now you can focus on particular issues and explore them in much greater depth. But they can also be more revealing because your own understanding of the business and the field has improved since the first interview, so your questions are more precise and to the point.

While interviewing can be a wonderful way of gaining insight into how organizations work, it also has its limitations. However generous your interviewees may be (and some of mine were extraordinarily generous), their time is limited and other commitments are always pressing in; you can learn a lot in an hour or two but much, necessarily, will remain unsaid. More importantly, some interviewees are more open than others; some will lean back in their chair, throw their feet up on the table and tell you frankly and unselfconsciously how things work and how they do what they do, while others will sit behind their desk and try to fill the time with anodyne descriptions of general trends or bland statements of company policy, occasionally glancing nervously at the microphone. Whenever I found myself faced with organization speak (it happened, though less frequently than one might think), I tried, as gently as I could, to cut through it: I wanted to know what really mattered to the individual I was interviewing, how they really did what they did and what they really thought about it. But however many times you come back to a question and ask it again in a slightly different way, sometimes you can never be entirely sure that what you're hearing is what this person really thinks, or merely what they want you to think they think. This is why it helps to spread your net widely and not to rely too much on the words of any one individual. Usually you can tell – if you're a reasonably competent person skilled in the ordinary arts of conversation – when someone is speaking honestly and openly and when they're having you on. But you can never be entirely sure.

My interviews were focused above all on the three key players in the field of trade publishing: publishers, agents and booksellers. I selected the publishing houses carefully. Working with the large corporate publishers was essential, since they had become such dominant players and occupied what could be thought of as the centre of the field. But I also wanted to talk with people working at medium-sized and small houses – some so small that they were literally a one-man one-woman operation run from a computer and a telephone in their apartment in their spare time – to see how their perspectives and working practices differed and to understand the difficulties they faced. I wanted to understand the similarities and differences between Britain and the US, so I made sure that I worked with publishers in both countries. At the large and medium-sized houses I interviewed CEOs, CFOs, COOs and other senior managers, including sales and marketing managers and, where they existed, the managers responsible for developing digital strategy and new business initiatives. I interviewed many publishers, editors and other staff at different levels of the organization, from the heads of imprints and divisions and senior editors who had worked for the company for many years to junior editors and editorial assistants who had been with the organization for only a year or two (and, in some cases, less). As new entrants to the field, junior editors and younger staff are still learning the ropes and they lack the standing, the authority, the security and, in some cases, the conviction of their more senior colleagues, all of which means that they tend to have a different and, in some respects, fresh perspective – outsiders within; some things that their senior colleagues take for granted are still puzzling to them, and listening to them describe the practices and procedures to which they were trying, sometimes struggling, to adapt helped to throw these practices and procedures into sharp relief. I also interviewed a number of former CEOs, publishers and senior managers who had retired from the business for various reasons; in some cases I was able to interview them both when they were in post and after they had left. These post-retirement interviews were often tremendously insightful: the fact that these individuals were retired tended to give them a certain distance from the organizations that had once employed them and enabled them to speak with a kind of candour that would have been difficult while they were still in post.

I interviewed a wide range of agents, including well-known and well-established agents who were the founders of, or partners at, large and powerful agencies; agents who had recently split off from established agencies and set up their own agencies, or who had given up their careers as publishers or editors and 'gone over to the other side'; and a number of younger agents who were working for agencies and struggling to build their own careers. On the retail side, I interviewed people working for some of the large bookselling chains as well as a variety of independent booksellers; I also interviewed some of the book buyers at supermarkets in the UK.

To set up interviews, I drew on existing contacts where I had them – having previously carried out research on academic publishing, I already had many contacts in the world of trade publishing. I also asked interviewees for their advice on other people who, in their view, would be worth interviewing, and I was able in this way to generate a constantly expanding network of contacts and potential interviewees. Access was easier than one might have imagined. Publishing is an industry of the word and those who work in this industry – publishers, editors, agents and others – like to talk. The only area where I experienced any significant difficulties in terms of access was on the retail side of the business. Not among independent booksellers – they were only too willing to talk, feeling, as many do, like a profession under siege. But the big retail chains were a different story. Getting access to the people at the top was not so hard – they were surprisingly generous with their time; but trying to get access to the middle management, and to key players like buyers, was, in some cases, like trying to find a back door into Fort Knox. One way or another, I managed to speak to enough buyers or former buyers to feel that I had some grasp of the way they worked and the problems they faced, though this is one area where I would have liked to have been able to do more.

Apart from interviewing people who worked for publishers, agencies and book retailers, I also interviewed a variety of other people who were connected in some way to the world of trade publishing, including book review editors working at key review media like the *New York Times Book Review*, fiction editors working at key literary magazines like the *New Yorker*, producers working for the book clubs of television programmes like the *Richard and Judy* show, freelance designers working for both large and small publishers, scouts working on a retainer for foreign publishing houses, managers working for technology companies that have a stake in the publishing field and, of course, writers – including writers writing under their own names, writers writing under pseudonyms and 'ghostwriters'. While I was not setting out to study the world (or worlds) of writers, it was always part of my plan to carry out interviews with a number of writers; in the end I did more than I had originally planned, partly because the interviews themselves were so interesting and partly because they offered a very different and crucially important perspective on a field to which writers both belong and don't belong, like some distant cousin who is tolerated but not really welcome at the family gathering. A proper study of the worlds of writers would be a wonderful project in its own right, but this was not the project on which I was embarked here.

Altogether I did around 280 interviews, amounting to around 500 hours of recording. Most interviews were around an hour and a half in length (the standard time period I asked for when setting up the interview), but many lasted two hours and some went on for considerably longer. Once the interviews had been transcribed, I read them, noted common themes, filed them away and returned to them later, rereading some interviews many times over the months and years. Since I had done all the interviews myself, I was already familiar with the contents, but the details fade with time; rereading them and noting common topics and themes was a helpful aide-memoire when it came to developing the main lines of argument and analysis.

In addition to conducting interviews, I sat in on acquisitions meetings at some of the large trade houses, which gave me a sense of how decisions were taken and business was handled in a large organization. Many publishers were also happy to share sales figures and other internal documents with me. I visited Nielsen BookScan, Bowker and the Book Industry Study Group, and all of these organizations gave me generous access to their data and research reports. I kept detailed field notes throughout the time that I was doing research; these notes, filling a dozen notebooks, were a way of highlighting for myself certain themes that were emerging from the research and beginning the process of trying to make sense of the world in which I was immersed.

Making sense of a world like trade publishing is no easy task: like many spheres of social life, this is a messy and confusing world, full of arcane practices and eccentric individuals but above all just very diverse and complex. There are many different publishing houses, each with its own history and distinctive organizational features, there are hundreds of agents and agencies and thousands of booksellers; these and other players are constantly interacting with one another in elaborate and shifting ways, and this complex field of interaction is itself conditioned by a range of factors – social, legal, economic, technological – that often arise outside the field and extend well beyond it. Trying to make sense of all this is like being faced with a large pile of pieces from a jigsaw puzzle, not knowing what the puzzle is a picture of or even whether the pieces in front of you make up a picture at all. My assumption was that, if you fiddled around with the pieces for long enough and looked at them from different angles, you would eventually be able to see how they fit together, you would be able to discern some order in the chaos, some structure in the flux. Or, to recall a different metaphor used in the Introduction, if you listened attentively to people speaking a language you didn't understand, you would eventually be able to grasp the rules of grammar that make their language intelligible and enable them to communicate with one another. My task as the analyst was to find this order and bring it to the fore, to grasp these rules and make them explicit – or, to put it more technically, to reconstruct the logic of the field. Reconstructing this logic is a way of trying to identify the forces and processes that are most important in shaping the structure and development of the field; it is a way of separating the essential from the inessential, the things that matter most from the things that matter less. It is not saying that other things are unimportant or have no place in a full account of the world of trade publishing; it is simply saying that they are less important if you want to understand what makes this world tick.

Of course, I may have got it wrong. It could be that the factors I've picked out and linked together in what I call the logic of the field are less important than I think, or that I've overlooked something that is crucial if you want to understand how the world of trade publishing has evolved over the last 40–50 years – if so, then, as with any serious attempt to make sense of the social world, my reconstruction is open to revision and my argument open to criticism. But the basic assumption underlying my approach is that, despite the enormous complexity of this world and the arcane, even baffling character of some of its practices, it is a world that can be understood.

'To be understood' does not mean that we have to settle for something less than a rigorous, social scientific account of this world, as if 'understanding' were the feeble sibling in the family of the social sciences. To understand that which is puzzling, to clarify that which is obscure, to render intelligible that which seems at first to defy our comprehension – these are perfectly legitimate goals of social scientific inquiry. Only those wedded to an archaic and narrow-minded conception of the social sciences would think otherwise. But to put it like this does not do full justice to the notion of the logic of the field. For reconstructing this logic is not just a way of understanding a world that might strike one as puzzling and obscure: it also helps us to see why the players in the field act as they do – why, for example, some players situated at some positions in the field are willing and able to pay so much for a particular book by a particular author while other players situated at other positions are not, or why some organizations owned by large corporations are willing and eager to acquire other publishers while other organizations are not, and so on. In other words, the logic of the field has some explanatory value: it helps us not just to understand a world but also to explain why the actors and organizations that inhabit this world act as they do. This may not be explanation in the sense of trying to formulate a general law that demonstrates a regular relationship between cause and effect, but there are more ways of thinking about explanation, tailored more sensitively to the kind of place that the social world is, than this simplified model of explanation as law-like regularity would suggest.

The logic of the field provides the backbone for my account of the world of trade publishing – without it, we might have a collection of good stories but it would be spineless, it would lack structure and argument and it would give the reader no sense of the dynamic processes that bind the key players together in relations of competition and mutual dependency. But at the same time I've tried to flesh out this account by weaving into the analysis the views and stories of particular individuals. These are always individuals situated at particular points in the field or on the margins of the field, often belonging to organizations that are themselves situated at particular positions. As explained earlier, I've given pseudonyms to most of these individuals and invented names for their organizations to preserve their anonymity; in the small number of cases where I've attributed the views expressed in interviews to actual individuals, I've done so with their permission. I've quoted them pretty much verbatim, though I've taken the liberty of tidying up the grammar now and again and of removing some of the idiosyncrasies of the spoken word when I felt they would hinder rather than help the reader. Of course, deciding which individuals from among the many I interviewed should be given a voice in this way was not easy, not simply because there were so many who spoke with great force and eloquence about the world of which they are part and to which they have devoted most if not all of their professional lives, but also because any selection is necessarily going to be partial – a particular set of views from a particular set of places expressing a particular set of experiences. But when these voices are placed within the context of the structure and dynamic of the field, their partiality can be relativized. They can be seen for what they are: not disembodied voices claiming some special privilege to speak authoritatively about this world, but rather voices speaking from particular positions within the field, drawing on all the knowledge and expertise they have gained to speak about this world as they see it, to explain how they do what they do and to describe their experiences of it. The viewpoint of any individual player in the field is just that: a view from a point. Its singularity is not a partiality that distorts our understanding of this world but rather a complementary moment that enriches it – it is the particular within the general, the concrete within the abstract. Weaving the views and stories of individuals into the analysis brings the logic of the field down to earth and gives the reader a glimpse – or, more precisely, a series of glimpses – of what it is to inhabit this world, to live in its different neighbourhoods and to speak the language that all of its inhabitants have, in their own idiomatic ways, learned to speak.

As with any attempt to understand the world of others, I place a great deal of weight on what those whose world I have sought to understand make of my attempt to understand it. When I finished a draft text I sent it to a number of individuals who work in the field of trade publishing in Britain and the US and invited them to comment on it. This was extremely valuable as a check on my own understanding of their world and as a way of ensuring that the details of my account were accurate; it also gave me a chance to test my account of the logic of the field against the experiences and intuitions of key players. I did not take the view that the validity of my account required any and every member of the field to accept it as a fair and accurate account of their world – that would be far too stringent a requirement. But I did and do believe that if this account were entirely unrecognizable to those whose world it is, then I would have failed in my task to make sense of it. That they should recognize in my account the outlines of a world they know from within, that they should see it as a fair and accurate representation of their world (albeit not the only possible representation), was, in my view, an important test of the validity of my account, even if it was not the only one. They didn't have to agree with every detail of my account or share my critical assessment, but I would expect them at least to recognize in this account the contours of their world. For it is, after all, the language they speak whose rules we are seeking to understand.

BIBLIOGRAPHY

Anderson, Chris. *The Long Tail: Why the Future of Business is Selling Less of More*. New York: Hyperion, 2006.

Austin, J. L. *How To Do Things With Words*, 2nd edn, ed. J. O. Urmson and Marina Sbisà. Oxford: Oxford University Press, 1976.

Bagdikian, Ben H. *The New Media Monopoly*. Boston: Beacon Press, 2004.

Band, Jonathan. 'The Google Library Project: The Copyright Debate', American Library Association, Office for Information Technology Policy (Jan. 2006). At www.policybandwidth.com/doc/googlepaper.pdf, accessed Dec. 2009.

Band, Jonathan. 'A Guide for the Perplexed: Libraries and the Google Library Project Settlement', American Library Association and Association of Research Libraries (13 Nov. 2008). At www.arl.org/bm~doc/google-settlement-13nov08.pdf, accessed Dec. 2009.

Band, Jonathan. 'A Guide for the Perplexed Part II: The Amended Google–Michigan Agreement', American Library Association and Association of Research Libraries (12 June 2009). At wo.ala.org/gbs/wp-content/uploads/2009/06/google-michigan-amended.pdf, accessed Dec. 2009.

Band, Jonathan. 'A Guide for the Perplexed Part III: The Amended Settlement Agreement', American Library Association and Association of Research Libraries (23 Nov. 2009). At www.arl.org/bm~doc/guide_for_the_perplexed_part3_final.pdf, accessed Dec. 2009.

Berg, A. Scott. *Max Perkins: Editor of Genius*. New York: Riverhead Books, 1978.

Birkerts, Sven. *The Gutenberg Elegies: The Fate of Reading in an Electronic Age*. London: Faber & Faber, 1994.

Bourdieu, Pierre. *The Field of Cultural Production: Essays on Art and Literature*, ed. Randal Johnson. Cambridge: Polity, 1993.

Bourdieu, Pierre. *Language and Symbolic Power*, ed. John B. Thompson. Cambridge: Polity, 1991.

Bourdieu, Pierre. *The Rules of Art: Genesis and Structure of the Literary Field*, tr. Susan Emanuel. Cambridge: Polity, 1996.

Bourdieu, Pierre. 'Some Properties of Fields', in his *Sociology in Question*, tr. Richard Nice, pp. 72–7. London: Sage, 1993.

Bower, Joseph L. and Christensen, Clayton M. 'Disruptive Technologies: Catching the Wave', *Harvard Business Review* (Jan.–Feb. 1995), pp. 43–53.

Bradley, Sue (ed.). *The British Book Trade: An Oral History*. London: British Library, 2008.

Brown, Albert Curtis. '"The Commercialization of Literature" and the Literary Agent', *Fortnightly Review*, vol. 80 (1 Aug. 1906).

Caves, Richard E. *Creative Industries: Contracts between Art and Commerce*. Cambridge, Mass.: Harvard University Press, 2000.

Cerf, Bennett. *At Random*. New York: Random House, 1977.

Coser, Lewis A., Kadushin, Charles and Powell, Walter W. *Books: The Culture and Commerce of Publishing*. New York: Basic Books, 1982.

Crystal, David. *English as a Global Language*. Cambridge: Cambridge University Press, 1997.

Dardis, Tom. *Firebrand: The Life of Horace Liveright*. New York: Random House, 1995.

Darnton, Robert. *The Case for Books: Past, Present, and Future*. New York: Public Affairs, 2009.

Darnton, Robert. 'Google and the Future of Books', *New York Review of Books*, vol. 56, no. 2 (12 Feb. 2009).

Darnton, Robert. 'Six Reasons Google Books Failed', *New York Review of Books* (28 Mar. 2011).

de Bellaigue, Eric. *British Book Publishing as a Business since the 1960s: Selected Essays*. London: British Library, 2004.

de Bellaigue, Eric. '"Trust me. I'm an agent": The Ever-Changing Balance between Author, Agent and Publisher', *Logos*, vol. 19, no. 3 (2008), pp. 109–19.

English, James F. *The Economy of Prestige: Prizes, Awards, and the Circulation of Cultural Value*. Cambridge, Mass.: Harvard University Press, 2005.

Epstein, Jason. *Book Business: Publishing Past Present and Future*. New York: W. W. Norton, 2001.

Farr, Cecilia Konchar. *Reading Oprah: How Oprah's Book Club Changed the Way America Reads*. Albany, N.Y.: State University of New York Press, 2005.

Feather, John. *A History of British Publishing*, 2nd edn. London: Routledge, 2006.

Fishman, Charles. *The Wal-Mart Effect: How an Out-of-Town Superstore Became a Superpower*. London: Penguin, 2006.

Gasson, Christopher. *Who Owns Whom in British Book Publishing*. London: Bookseller, 2002.

Gillies, Mary Ann. *The Professional Literary Agent in Britain, 1880–1920*. Toronto: University of Toronto Press, 2007.

Gomez, Jeff. *Print is Dead: Books in Our Digital Age*. New York: Macmillan, 2008.

Greco, Albert N., Rodriguez, Clara E. and Wharton, Robert M. *The Culture and Commerce of Publishing in the 21st Century*. Stanford, Calif.: Stanford University Press, 2007.

Habermas, Jürgen. *The Structural Transformation of the Public Sphere: An Inquiry into a Category of Bourgeois Society*, tr. Thomas Burger with Frederick Lawrence. Cambridge: Polity, 1989.

Hall, Max. *Harvard University Press: A History*. Cambridge, Mass.: Harvard University Press, 1986.

Hartley, Jenny. *The Reading Groups Book*, 2002–3 edn. Oxford: Oxford University Press, 2002.

Hepburn, James. *The Author's Empty Purse and the Rise of the Literary Agent*. London: Oxford University Press, 1968.

Herman, Edward S. and McChesney, Robert W. *The Global Media: The New Missionaries of Corporate Capitalism*. London: Cassell, 1997.

Horvath, Stephen. 'The Rise of the Book Chain Superstore', *Logos*, vol. 7, no. 1 (1996), pp. 39–45.

Korda, Michael. *Another Life: A Memoir of Other People*. New York: Random House, 1999.

Kovač, Miha. *Never Mind the Web: Here Comes the Book*. Oxford: Chandos, 2008.

Lane, Michael and Booth, Jeremy. *Books and Publishers: Commerce against Culture in Postwar Britain*. Lexington, Mass.: D. C. Heath, 1980.

Lewis, Jeremy. *Penguin Special: The Life and Times of Allen Lane*. London: Viking, 2005.

Maher, Terry. *Against My Better Judgement: Adventures in the City and in the Book Trade*. London: Sinclair-Stevenson, 1994.

McChesney, Robert W. *Rich Media, Poor Democracy: Communication Politics in Dubious Times*. New York: New Press, 1999.

Miller, Laura J. *Reluctant Capitalists: Bookselling and the Culture of Consumption*. Chicago: University of Chicago Press, 2006.

Nord, David Paul, Rubin, Joan Shelley and Schudson, Michael. *A History of the Book in America*, vol. 5: *The Enduring Book: Print Culture in Postwar America*. Chapel Hill, N.C.: University of North Carolina Press, 2009.

Oda, Stephanie and Sanislo, Glenn. *The Subtext 2007–2008 Perspective on Book Publishing: Numbers, Issues and Trends*. Darien, Conn.: Open Book, 2007.

Publishing in the Knowledge Economy: Competitiveness Analysis of the UK Publishing Media Sector. London: Department of Trade and Industry and UK Publishing Media, 2002. At www.publishingmedia.org.uk/download/02dti_competitive_analysis.pdf, accessed Dec. 2009.

Publishing Market Watch: Final Report, submitted to the European Commission, 27 Jan. 2005. At ec.europa.eu/information_society/media_taskforce/doc/pmw_20050127.pdf, accessed Dec. 2009.

Reading At Risk: A Survey of Literary Reading in America. Washington, D.C.: National Endowment for the Arts, 2004.

Rooney, Kathleen. *Reading with Oprah: The Book Club That Changed America*, 2nd edn. Fayetteville, Ark.: University of Arkansas Press, 2008.

Schiffrin, André. *The Business of Books: How International Conglomerates Took Over Publishing and Changed the Way We Read*. London: Verso, 2000.

Schiffrin, André. *Words and Money*. London: Verso, 2010.

Shatzkin, Leonard. *In Cold Type: Overcoming the Book Crisis*. Boston: Houghton Mifflin, 1982.

Smith, Anthony. *The Age of Behemoths: The Globalization of Mass Media Firms*. New York: Priority Press, 1991.

Spector, Robert. *Amazon.com: Get Big Fast*. London: Random House, 2000.

Stevenson, Iain. *Book Makers: British Publishing in the Twentieth Century*. London: British Library, 2010.

Striphas, Ted. *The Late Age of Print: Everyday Book Culture from Consumerism to Control*. New York: Columbia University Press, 2009.

Sutherland, John. *Bestsellers: A Very Short Introduction*. Oxford: Oxford University Press, 2007.

Taleb, Nassim Nicholas. *The Black Swan: The Impact of the Highly Improbable*. New York: Random House, 2007.

Tebbel, John. *Between Covers: The Rise and Transformation of American Book Publishing*. New York: Oxford University Press, 1987.

Tebbel, John. *A History of Book Publishing in the United States*, vol. 3: *The Golden Age between the Two Wars, 1920–1940*. New York: R. R. Bowker, 1978.

Tebbel, John. *A History of Book Publishing in the United States*, vol. 4: *The Great Change, 1940–1980*. New York: R. R. Bowker, 1981.

Thompson, John B. *Books in the Digital Age: The Transformation of Academic and Higher Education Publishing in Britain and the United States*. Cambridge: Polity, 2005.

Thompson, John B. *The Media and Modernity: A Social Theory of the Media*. Cambridge: Polity, 1995.

To Read or Not to Read: A Question of National Consequence. Washington, D.C.: National Endowment for the Arts, 2007.

Under the Radar. New York: Book Industry Study Group, 2005.

Used-Book Sales: A Study of the Behavior, Structure, Size, and Growth of the US Used-Book Market. New York: Book Industry Study Group, 2006.

Wasserman, Steve. 'Goodbye to All That', *Columbia Journalism Review* (Sept.–Oct. 2007).

Whiteside, Thomas. *The Blockbuster Complex: Conglomerates, Show Business, and Book Publishing*. Middletown, Conn.: Wesleyan University Press, 1980.

Wischenbart, Rüdiger. *Diversity Report 2008: An Overview and Analysis of Translation Statistics across Europe* (21 Nov. 2008). Available at www.wischenbart.com/diversity/report/Diversity%20Report_prel-final_02.pdf, accessed Dec. 2009.

Wischenbart, Rüdiger. 'The Many, Many Books – For Whom?' (11 Sept. 2005). At www.wischenbart.com/de/essays__interviews_rw/wischenbart_publishing-diversity_oxford-2005.pdf, accessed Dec. 2009.

INDEX

Page numbers in *italics* refer to tables; *a* denotes appendix.

'A' lists *see* big books
access, digital technology 340
add-ons 228
advances
   brand-name authors 216–18
   large corporations 139, 151, 152
   medium-sized publishers 178
   Randy Pausch: *The Last Lecture*
     1–3, 295–6, 297–8
   role of agents 68–9, 93–5,
     97–8
   small independent publishers
     108, 159, 165
   university presses 185
agency model 375–6
agents
   'A' lists 188
   author–publisher interaction
     16–17
   career issues
     apprenticeships/mentoring
      78–80
     building a client list 77–85
     payment 80
     poaching/losing authors 67–8,
      81–2, 84–5
   and editors 73–6, 89–91, 206–8,
     210–11

and medium-sized publishers 178
origins of 59–63
proliferation of 71–7
roles 85–100
   author career management
     97–100, 383–94
   contract negotiation 95
   pitching 88–93
   rights management 62, 65–6,
     69–70, 95–6
   selling/advances 68–9, 93–5,
     97–8
   social networking 87–8,
     89–90
   submission process 86–7
and small independent publishers
     159–60, 165, 172
super-agents 63–71
track record 92–3, 206–7
UK 59–61, 62
US 61, 62
Albom, Mitch: *Tuesdays with
    Morrie* 296
Amazon 41–6, 48–9, 58, 407
   backlist sales 222
   BookScan 200
   digital rights management
     (DRM) 361–2, 370

Kindle (ebook reader) 318–19, 336, 368, 369–70, 371–2, 374, 375–6
  marketing and sales 332, 338–9
  pre-publication publicity 250–1
  Search inside the Book 333–4, 362–3
  UK 43, 55–6, 58, 310
American Booksellers Association (ABA) 31–2, 33–4
Andersen, Chris 314, 331
Angels and Demons (Brown) 278–9, 279
antitrust legislation 106–7, 109
  ebooks 375–6
  Net Book Agreement (NBA), UK 51–3, 56, 301–4, 312, 401–2
  Robinson-Patman Act (1936), US 33–4, 299–302, 311–12, 371, 401–2
Apple
  iBooks 375
  iPad 319, 338, 339, 375
  iPod 316, 342, 359, 370
apprenticeships/mentoring of agents 78–80
archives *see* digital archives
Asda 46, 56, 303, 304, 309
Association of American Publishers 314, 319–20
Association of Author Representatives 71
Atonement (McEwan) 281–3
auctions 93, 209–11
audiobooks 358–9
author–agent–publisher interaction 16–17
authors
  brand-name 190, 212–19
  career management 97–100, 383–94
  community of 390–1
  multi-city tours 246
  new 142–3, 201, 214–15

'orphaned' 88
  platform 87–8, 204–5
  renaming 98, 392
  symbolic capital 9
  track record 198, 199, 201–2
  see also advances; losing/ poaching authors

B. Dalton Booksellers 27, 29, 34
backlist titles 220–2, 331–2, 377–8
Barnes & Noble 27–30, 32, 33–4, 34–5, 41, 48
  b&n.com 41–2, 43, 44
  BookScan 200
  Nook (ebook reader) 319, 336, 338–9
  out-of-copyright classics 221
  returns 285–6
  small independent publishers 158
  Sterling 118, 221
Bertelsmann 109, 113, 116, 121
bestseller lists 251
  New York Times, US 186, 198, 249–50, 257, 271, 272, 278, 280, 297, 368, 369
  UK 57, 308
bestsellers
  ebooks 322–3, 368, 369
  small independent publishers 164–5
  vs big books 193–4, 211–12
  vs quality books 140–1, 160–2
Bezos, Jeff 41
big books 188–9, 381, 395
  brand-name authors 190, 212–19
  growth conundrum 189–95
  marketing and sales 269–70
  valuing the valueless 195–212
  virtues of backlist 220–2
  see also extreme publishing
'big mouths' 248
'black swan industry' 191–2, 193
bloggers/blogosphere 160, 253–5, 254–6
Bloomsbury 125, 175, 181

Bodley Head (CBC) 121
book clubs 270
book fairs 96
Book Industry Study Group (BISG)
    153–5, 351
book prizes 278
Book Rights Registry (BRR) 365
BookScan 198–201, 218
Borders 27, 28–9, 30, 32, 33–4,
    34–5, 41, 48
    Books Etc., UK 55, 57
    BookScan 200
    Borders.com 42
    returns 285–6
Bourdieu, Pierre 3–4
Bower, J.L. and Christensen, C.M.
    313–14
brand-name authors 190, 212–19
Brown, Curtis (Curtis Brown) 61,
    76, 77
Brown, Dan
    Angels and Demons 278–80,
    279
    Da Vinci Code 38, 200–1, 248,
    393
budgets *see* finance/budgets
buzz 96, 194, 195, 250

Cape, Jonathan 121
capital
    of agents 77
    of publishing fields 5–10
careers
    of authors 97–100, 383–94
    see also agents, career issues
'carriage trade' 26
cash flow 107–8, 162–3, 173–4
Cassells 61, 122
CD-ROMs/CDs 346, 348, 359
Cedar Press 134–6
celebrity books 204, 226, 289,
    380
centralized and federalized models
    of corporations 126–30
Century Hutchinson 121–2
Cerf, Bennett 103, 105–6, 107

Chatto, Bodley Head and Jonathan
    Cape (CBC) 121
Cheetham, Anthony 121–2
'co-op' (cooperative advertising/
    in-store placement) 34, 45,
    261–3, 300–1
commercial bestsellers *see* bestseller
    lists; bestsellers
commission-only agents 80
community of authors 390–1
competition law *see* antitrust
    legislation
competitive market of publishing
    field 10–11
'comps' (comparable books) 202–3
Consortium 155–6, 168, 179, 180
content acquisition 16–18, 19,
    159–60
content censorship 141–2
content development 20
content management and delivery,
    digital technology 327–32,
    334–9
contract negotiation 95
copy-editing, digital technology
    328–9
copyright infringement, digital
    technology 337, 361–8
Corrigan, Kelly: *The Middle Place*
    256–7
Costco 47, 48, 286
cover design 39
Curtis Brown 61, 76, 77

Da Vinci Code (Brown) 38, 200–1,
    248, 393
Daunt, James 58
department stores 26, 27
    see also named department stores
digital archives, building 352–61
Digital Asset Management (DAM)
    system 355–6
digital revolution
    building a digital archive 352–61
    content management and delivery
    327–32, 334–9

copyright infringement 337, 361–8
operating systems 326–7
sales and marketing 332–4
digital rights management (DRM) 361–3, 370
'digital sampling' 333–4
digital technologies 406–9
and added value 339–44
copyright infringement 337, 361–8
entry costs of small independent publishers 155
and fields of publishing 344–52
hidden revolution 326–39
infrastructure of large corporations 152
online marketing 247–8, 251–8
'teaching machines' 105, 106, 107
see also ebook readers; ebooks
Dillons 52, 53, 54–5
'discount drift' 305–6
discounts 148–9, 299–309
hardback vs paperback, decreased price differential 40
and long-term interests of publishers 309–11
online 42–3, 45–6
and price deflation, digital technologies 368–76
role of mass merchandisers 46–51
transparency of 34
see also antitrust legislation
Doubleday 40, 113, 201
DVDs 348

ebook readers 318–19, 336
Kindle 318–19, 336, 368, 369–70, 371–2, 374, 375–6
Nook 319, 336, 338–9
Sony 318, 336, 369

ebooks 314–26
price 337–9, 368–76
sales and revenue 315, 318–25, 407, 408
vs print-on-paper books 315–18, 323–4, 334–5, 351–2, 359–61
economic capital 5–6, 9–10
economies of scale
large corporations 147–52
online content delivery 341
economy of favours, small independent publishers 156–8
editors 6–7
and agents 73–6, 89–91, 206–8, 210–11
copy-editing, digital technologies 328–9
large corporations 137–9, 140, 148
financial issues (Star) 131–3, 139
myths 143–5
organizational changes (Cedar Press) 134–6
track records 205, 206
see also judgement/tastes of editors/publishers
elitism 302–3
English language
Anglo-American trade publishing 12–14
European media conglomerates 109, 112–13
rights 62, 69–70, 95
EPOS (electionic point of sale) systems 198, 199
BookScan 198–201, 218
Epstein, Jason 35, 40
European media conglomerates 109, 112–13
see also named media conglomerates
external readers 208–9

extreme publishing
  gap-filling 223–9, 230–3, 236–7
  public *vs* private corporations
    233–6
  short-termism 380
  small and medium-sized
    independents 236–7
  unknowns 229–30, 231

Faber 162, 175
  'Alliance' 180–2
federalized and centralized models
  of corporations 126–30
field, concept of 3–5
film rights/screenplay adaptations
  62, 66, 235, 278–83
finance/budgets
  cash flow 107–8, 162–3, 173–4
  economies of scale 148–9
  investment and risk-taking
    functions of publishers 20
  management responsibility
    139–40
  marketing 246
    'co-op'/cooperative advertising
      (in-store placement) 261–3
    online 252–3
  P&L (profit & loss) 131–2, 133,
    138–9, 197, 235, 246, 285
  see also advances; discounts;
    extreme publishing; sales
financial crisis and recession
  403–6
first-time authors 142–3, 201,
  214–15
flexibility, digital technologies 342
forecasting capabilities 288–90,
  289, 291
foreign language rights 62, 66,
  69–70, 95, 96
Frankfurt, Harry: *On Bullshit* 186
Franzen, Jonathan: *Freedom* 323
Frazier, Charles 178
Freedom (Franzen) 323
freelancers' rates, large *vs* small
  publishers 157–8

French media conglomerates 109
  Vivendi 116
  see also Hachette
Frey, James: *A Million Little Pieces*
  273–4
front-of-store displays 238–9, 258,
  262–3

Galaxy 230–3
gap-filling 223–9, 230–3, 236–7
German media conglomerates
  109
  Bertelsmann 109, 113, 116, 121
  see also Holtzbrinck
Google
  Book Search 333–4, 362
  copyright infringement case
    (Library Project) 363–7
  marketing and sales 253, 254,
    255
  Partner Program 364
Grann, Phyllis 214
Grove Atlantic 175, 178
growth conundrum, publishing
  corporations 110–11,
  189–95, 378–82
growth phase, publishing
  corporations 108–13

Hachette 109, 115, 118, 121, 122,
  123–4
  centralized–federal spectrum 129
  imprints 123, 412*a*
Hamish Hamilton 119, 120
Hamlyn, Paul 122
Harcourt 116, 118, 175
hardback and paperback market
  36–41, 111, 178, 184, 221,
  270, 271–2, 287, 377–8
hardback revolution 37–41, 221,
  286–7, 378
HarperCollins 52–3, 113, 114,
  116, 118, 120, 125
  censorship 141–2
  centralized–federal spectrum 129
  imprints 114, 125, 412–13*a*

Harry Potter series 118, 125, 181, 309, 312, 363
Harvard University Press 183
Heanage, James 54
Heinemann, William 60, 122
Hill & Wang 271–2
The Historian (Kostova) 249–50
HMV Media Group 54–5, 58
Hodder Headline 52, 123, 303, 307
Holtzbrinck 109, 115–16, 118, 125
  centralized–federal spectrum 129
  imprints 125, 413*a*
Houghton Mifflin 116, 118, 175
human capital 6–7
Hutchinson, Tim Hely 52, 123, 303
Hyperion 222, 296–8

imprints 410–14*a*
  see also under named corporations
impulse purchases 258–61
independent bookstores 26, 27
  decline of 31–3, 401
  legal challenges to chains 33–4
  and small independent publishers 158
independent publishers *see* small independent publishers
information technology (IT) *see entries beginning* digital
intellectual capital 6, 7–8
International Digital Publishing Forum (IDPF) 319–20
international rights 69–70
intertextuality, digital technologies 343
iPad (Apple) 319, 338, 339, 375
iPod (Apple) 316, 342, 359, 370
ISBN 154–5, 355–6

Janklow, Morton 63, 64–5, 71
John Murray 123
Jonathan Cape (CBC) 121

journals
  literary 81
  scientific and scholarly 344–6
judgement of agents 75–6
judgement/tastes of editors/publishers 102–3, 136
  big books 195–8, 202–5, 208–9, 211
  small independent publishers 127–8, 160–1

Kindle (ebook reader) 318–19, 336, 368, 369–70, 371–2, 374, 375–6
King, Stephen 314
Klopfer, Donald 105–6
Knopf 106, 178
Kostova, Elizabeth: *The Historian* 249–50

Lane, Allen 36, 119–20
large corporations *see* publishing corporations
The Last Lecture (Pausch) 1–3, 295–6, 297–8
Library Project, Google, copyright infringement case 363–7
literary agents *see* agents
literary journals 81
Little, Brown (Grand Central Publishing) 112, 115, 121
Liveright, Horace 103
logic of the (publishing) field 11–12, 14, 292–9, 312
losing/poaching authors
  agents 67–8, 81–2, 84–5
  brand-name 214–15, 218–20
  medium-sized publishers 176–9
  small independent publishers 165–7
  university presses 185, 186–7

McEwan, Ian: *Atonement* 281–3
MacMillan 51, 115–16, 125, 375
magazines 81
Maher, Terry 52

mall stores/superstores, US 27–37
Mamut, Alexander 58
management and coordination
        functions of publishers 20–1
manuscripts, preparation for
        submission 86–7
margin squeeze 311–12
market share
    UK publishers 123–5
    UK retailers 57–8
    US publishers 116–18
    US retailers 48–51
marketing and sales 17–18, 21
    backing success 263–6
    battle for eyeballs 258–63
    digital technologies 332–4
    diversity 397–400
    economies of scale 148
    front-of-store displays 238–9,
        258, 262–3
    hardback and paperback 36–41,
        111, 178, 184, 221, 270,
        271–2, 287, 377–8
    mass media/micro media 244–51
    returns/unsold stock 285–91
    six-week rule 266–70
    statistics and struggle for
        visibility 239–44
    television 245–6, 271–85
    see also Amazon; online marketing
MCA 214
media attention
    mass/micro 244–51
    small independent publishers
        163–4, 172
    television marketing 245–6,
        271–85
media conglomerates 109–11,
    112–13
    see also named media
        conglomerates
medium-sized publishers 115–16
    difficulties of 174–9
    and gap-filling publishing 236–7
    and small companies, clubbing
        together 179–82

mentoring/apprenticeships of agents
        78–80
Menzies 303
mergers and acquisitions 103, 104,
        105–13, 127, 148
Michael Joseph 119, 120
'mid-list' titles 184
middle managers 140, 380
The Middle Place (Corrigan) 256–7
A Million Little Pieces (Frey)
        273–4
Mosaic 234–6
multimedia, digital technologies
        343
multiple submissions 93, 209
Murdoch, Rupert 109, 114

National Endowment of the Arts
        (NEA) Reading at Risk
        survey 241–2
Neilsen, Arthur/Neilson Company
        198–9
Net Book Agreement (NBA), UK
        51–3, 56, 301–4, 312,
        401–2
new authors 142–3, 201, 214–15
New York Times bestseller list 186,
        198, 249–50, 257, 271, 272,
        278, 280, 297, 368, 369
News Corp 109, 114
news magazines 245
newspaper reviews 244–5
niche audiences 247–8, 253
Night (Wiesel) 271–2, 273
Nixon, Richard (book) 63–4
Nook (ebook reader) 319, 336,
        338–9
North California Booksellers
        Association, legal case 33–4
not-for-profit organizations 156
    university presses 182–7

Octopus Publishing Group 122
Olympic 223–9, 380
On Bullshit (Frankfurt) 186
one-on-one submissions 93

online marketing 247–8, 251–8
  see also Amazon
operating systems, digital
      technologies 326–7
Oprah Book Club, US 271–5, 276,
      278, 281–3, 284
Orion 121–2
'orphaned' authors 88
Ottakar's 54, 57
out-of-copyright classics 221
outsourcing 17, 18, 20
  initial selection to agents 75–6
  small independent publishers
      155–6
    freelancers' rates 157–8
    third-party sales and
      distribution 167–9, 173

P&L (profit & loss) sheets 131–2,
      133, 138–9, 197, 235, 246,
      285
paperbacks
  fiction sales, UK 397–400
  and hardback market 36–41,
      111, 118, 184, 221, 270,
      271–2, 287, 377–8
  rights 36, 38, 111, 178, 377–8
Patterson, James 218, 250, 268,
      307
Paul Hamlyn Books 122
Pausch, Randy: The Last Lecture
      1–3, 295–6, 297–8
PDFs (portable document files)
      331, 354–5, 361
Pearl, Frank 179, 180
Pearson 109, 113–14, 120
Pearson Longman 120
Penguin 113–14, 116, 118,
      119–20, 125
  backlist 221, 222
  centralized–federal spectrum 129
  ebooks 369
  imprints 114, 125, 411a
Perseus Books Group 169, 179–80
piracy see copyright infringement,
      digital technologies

pitching 88–93
platform 87–8, 204–5
plurality of publishing fields 4
poaching see losing/poaching
      authors
POD (print on demand) 331
portability, digital technologies 342
portable document files (PDFs)
      331, 354–5, 361
pre-publication publicity 250–1
Price Clubs 46–7
Price, Sol and Robert 46–7
PriceWaterhouseCoopers 314
Princeton University Press 186
print advertising 247
print on demand (POD) 331
print runs and reprints 149–50
print-on-paper books vs ebooks
      315–18, 323–4, 334–5,
      351–2, 359–61
printing technologies 59, 329–32
private vs public corporations
      233–6
profit & loss (P&L) sheets 131–2,
      133, 138–9, 197, 235, 246,
      285
proposals, preparation for
      submission 86–7
publication date 248–9
publisher-owners 102, 103, 104,
      158–9, 160–2, 236–7
Publishers Group West (PGW) 169,
      179, 180
publishers, key functions of
      18–22
Publishersmarketplace.com 71–2
publishing chain 14–22
publishing corporations 101–5,
      410–14a
  and author career 383–94
  benefits of scale 147–52
  centralized and federalized
      models 126–30
  diversity issue 394–402
  European media conglomerates
      vs US 112–13

publishing corporations (cont.)
  financial crisis and recession
      403–6
  five myths about 140–6
  growth conundrum 110–11,
      189–95, 378–82
  growth phase 108–13
  micro-environments 130–40
  'synergy' phase 105–8
  UK 119–26, 411*a*, 413*a*
  US 113–18, 410*a*, 411*a*, 413*a*
  see also big books; extreme
      publishing
publishing fields 3–14
  logic of 11–12, 14, 292–9, 312
publishing houses, hierarchy of
      90–1
publishing schedule 228
PubTrack 259, *260*
Putnam 214–15
Putnam Berkeley 120

quality
  authors and agents 67–8
  and diversity 394–402
  and extreme publishing 228–9
  key functions of publishers 20
  vs bestsellers 140–1, 160–2

Random House 103, 105–7, 113,
      116, 118, 123–5
  backlist 221, 222
  CBC 121
  centralized–federal spectrum 129
  headquarters 130
  imprints 113, 123–5, 410–11*a*
  and medium-sized publishers 178
Rashid, Ahmed: *Taliban* 186
rationalization, mergers and
      acquisitions 127, 148
RCA 107, 113, 119
reader loyalty 213
reading, decline of 241–2
reading groups 275
'recognition triggers' 277–83
Reed Consumer Books 52

Reed Elsevier 116, 122
reference publishing, electronic
      346–8
relational character of publishing
      fields 4–5
renaming authors 98, 392
research methods 415–24*a*
resources *see* capital
Restrictive Practices Court, UK
      52–3
retail chains
  and agents 62
  and backlist titles 221
  'co-op' (cooperative advertising/
      in-store placement) 300–1
  hardback revolution 37–41, 221,
      286–7, 378
  and large corporations 150–1,
      400–2
  UK 51–8, 303–4, 305–11
  and university presses 184–5
  US 26, 27–37, 46–51, 285–6
returns/unsold stock 285–91
Reynolds, Paul Revere 61
Richard and Judy Book Club, UK
      276–7, 278, 283–4
rights
  Book Rights Registry (BRR) 365
  digital rights management
      (DRM) 361–3, 370
  digital technologies 337
  English language 62, 69–70, 95
  film/screen adaptations 62, 66,
      235, 278–83
  foreign language 62, 66, 69–70,
      95, 96
  out-of-copyright classics 221
  paperback 36, 38, 111, 178,
      377–8
  and role of agents 62, 65–6,
      69–70, 95–6
risk-taking 20, 75–6, 152
Robinson-Patman Act (1936), US
      33–4, 299–302, 311–12,
      371, 401–2
Rosenthal, Arthur 183

Safire, Bill 63, 64
salaries of agents 80
sales
    Book Industry Study Group
        (BISG) 153–5, 351
    and distribution, small
        independent publishers
        167–9, 173
    ebooks and ebook readers 315,
        318–25, 407, 408
    paperback fiction, UK 397–400
    records (EPOS/BookScan)
        198–201, 218
    reps 39, 190–1
    see also marketing and sales;
        retail chains
Sam's (Wholesale) Club 46, 47, 48,
    200
Sargeant, John 375
scholarly and scientific journal
    publishing 344–6
scholarly/academic book publishing
    digital technologies 348–51
    university presses 182–7
screenplay adaptations/film rights
    62, 66, 235, 278–83
searchability, digital technologies
    341–2
self-publishers 154
selling cycles
    cash flow 107–8
    gap-filling 223–9, 230–3,
        236–7
    title prioritization 189–91
selling/advances, role of agents
    68–9, 93–5
short-run digital printing (SRDP)
    330–1
short-termism 377–83, 408
Simon & Schuster 112, 114–15,
    118, 120, 125–6
    backlist 222
    centralized–federal spectrum 129
    imprints 413a
six-week rule 266–70
'small books' 192–3

small independent publishers
    advances 108, 159, 165
    and agents 159–60, 165, 172
    and authors 165–7, 392, 393–4
    bestsellers 164–5
    countercultural stance 161–2
    economy of favours 156–8
    freelancers' rates 157–8
    and gap-filling publishing
        236–7
    and growth of publishing
        corporations 102–3, 104
        UK 1119–26
    and growth of publishng
        corporations 108–9
    and independent bookshops 158
    media attention 163–4, 172
    and medium-sized companies,
        clubbing together 179–82
    outsourcing 155–6
    social networks 160, 166–7
    third-party sales and distribution
        167–9, 173
    virtues and vulnerabilities
        152–74
    working capital 158–9, 162–3,
        173–4
social capital/networks 6, 7
    agents 87–8, 89–90
    authors 390–1
    small independent publishers
        160, 166–7
Sony
    ebook reader 318, 336, 369
    and Penguin 369
Sparrow Press 170–3
SRDP (short-run digital printing)
    330–1
Star 130–4, 139
Sterling 118, 221
stock turnover 34–6, 49–50
submissions
    multiple 93, 209
    one-on-one 93
    process 86–7
super-agents 63–71

supermarkets, UK 56–7, 57–8,
303–4, 305–11
superstores/mall stores, US 27–37
supply chain 14–15
capabilities 287–9, 290, 291
symbolic capital 6, 8–10
'synergy' phase, publishing
corporations 105–8

Taliban (Rashid) 186
tastes of editors/publishers see
judgement/tastes of editors/
publishers
technology
printing 59, 329–32
see also entries beginning digital
television marketing 245–6,
271–85
Tesco 56, 193, 303, 304, 306, 307,
309
Thomas Nelson 118, 119, 174
Thomson Organization 119
Thomson, Roy 119
Tilling 122
Time Warner 115, 118, 121, 123
timing of publication 248–9
tipping books 269–70
title output statistics 239–40, 241
title prioritization 189–91
'Total Consumer Market' (TCM),
BookScan UK 200
track records
of agents 92–3, 206–7
of authors 198, 199, 201–2
see also brand-name authors
of editors 205, 206
translations 13
foreign language rights 62, 66,
69–70, 95, 96
Tuesdays with Morrie (Albom) 296
typesetting, digital technology 328

United Kingdom (UK)
agents 59–61, 61
Amazon 43, 55–6, 58, 310, 311
bestseller lists 57, 308

Books Etc. 55, 57
dominant publishing groups
119–26
ebook sales and revenue 325
margin squeeze 311–12
market share
publishers 123–5
retailers 57–8
marketing
retail chains 51–8, 303–4,
305–11
Richard and Judy Book Club
276–7, 278, 283–4
and sales 301–11
media conglomerates 109
Net Book Agreement (NBA)
51–3, 56, 301–4, 312,
401–2
paperback fiction sales 397–400
publishing corporations 119–26,
412a, 414a
Restrictive Practices Court 52–3
title output statistics 240, 241
'Total Consumer Market' (TCM),
BookScan 200
United States (US)
agents 61
ebook sales and revenue 319–25
margin sqeeze 311–12
market share
publishers 116–18
retailers 48–51
marketing
Oprah Book Club 271–5, 276,
278, 281–3, 284
retail chains 26, 27–37,
46–51, 285–6
and sales 298–9, 299–302
New York Times bestseller list
186, 198, 249–50, 257, 271,
272, 278, 280, 297, 368,
369
publishing corporations 113–18,
410a, 412–13a
vs European media
conglomerates 112–13

Robinson-Patman Act (1936)
33–4, 299–302, 311–12,
371, 401–2
title output statistics 239–40,
241
see also Amazon
university presses 182–7
unknowns, extreme publishing
229–30, 231
unsold stock/returns 285–91
updatability, digital technology
340
used-book market 44–5

value chain 15–17
'vertical integration' of publishing
38, 111
Viking Press 120
Vivendi 116

Wal-Mart 46–7, 48, 49, 286–7
BookScan 200

Walden Book Company/
Waldenbooks stores 27, 28,
29, 30, 34
Waterstone, Tim 53, 54, 55
Waterstone's 53–5, 57, 58, 304,
310–11
Watt, A. P. 59–60
web of collective belief 76, 194–5,
205–8, 209
Weidenfeld & Nicolson 121–2
WH Smith 53, 54, 57, 123, 304
wholesale clubs 46–8, 286
Wiesel, Elie: *Night* 271–2, 273
Wikipedia 255
winner-takes-more market 399–400
Winton, Charlie 169
word of mouth marketing 247–8
Workman 222
Wylie, Andrew 63, 66–71, 211

Yale University Press 186
YouTube 255, 256, 257